ANNUAL SURVEY OF AFRICAN LAW

VOLUME VI-1972

Editors

N. N. RUBIN, BA, LLB
Advocate of the Supreme Court of South Africa
and the High Court of Swaziland
Lecturer in African Law, School of Oriental and African Studies,
Institute of Advanced Legal Studies, University of London
and
E. COTRAN, LLB, LLM, LLD, Dip IL
Of Lincoln's Inn, Barrister of Law
Lecturer in African Law, School of Oriental
and African Studies, University of London

Annual Survey of African Law

VOLUME VI-1972

Edited by
N. N. Rubin and E. Cotran

REX COLLINGS : LONDON : 1975

First published in 1975 in Great Britain by
REX COLLINGS LIMITED
69 Marylebone High Street, London, W1

ISBN 0860 36 003 2

First published in the United States 1975
by Rowman and Littlefield, Totowa, NJ

US-ISBN-0-87471-790-6

Printed in Great Britain by
Biddles Ltd Guildford Surrey

CONTENTS

PART II: L'AFRIQUE FRANCOPHONE
(FRANCOPHONIC AFRICAN COUNTRIES)

PART III: OTHER AFRICAN COUNTRIES

TABLE OF CASES

Q

R

S

Y

Z

TABLE OF STATUTES
AND OTHER LAWS

PART I

Commonwealth African Countries

CHAPTER ONE

GHANA

Gordon Woodman

CONSTITUTIONAL AND ADMINISTRATIVE LAW

On 13 January the armed forces assumed power, suspended the 1969 Second republican Constitution, and established the national Redemption Council (NRC) as the supreme governing body. This event determined most of the more important legal developments during this year.

The new constitutional arrangements are set out in the National Redemption Council (Establishment) Proclamation, 1972. S. 1 establishes the NRC, consisting of the persons specified in the First Schedule. These were nine members of the armed forces (increased to 11 a few days later),[1] and the police officer who had been appointed Inspector-General of police a few hours after the coup. S. 2 suspends the 1969 Constitution, abolishes the office of President of Ghana, removes from office the prime Minister, Leader of the Opposition, and all ministers and ministerial secretaries, dissolves the National Assembly and all political parties, and prohibits the formation, operation and membership of political parties. It then provides in s. 3 for the exercise of legislative power and the continuance of existing laws:

'3. (1) Until such time as a new Constitution is promulgated by the people of Ghana, the Council shall have power for such purposes as they may think fit to make and issue Decrees which shall have the force of law in Ghana.

(2) Subject to any Decree made under the immediately preceding subsection, any enactment or rule of law in force in Ghana immediately before the 13th day of January, 1972 shall continue in force and any such enactment or rule of law may by Decree of the Council be revoked, repealed, amended (whether by addition, omission, substitution or otherwise) or suspended.

(3) Where any enactment or rule of law in force immediately before the 13th day of January 1972 is in conflict with any provision of a Decree made by the Council the said provision shall prevail over the enactment and to the extent to which the enactment conflicts with the provision of the Decree, that enactment shall be deemed to be amended by the Decree.

(4) Any Decree made by the Council may be amended or revoked or suspended by another Decree of the Council.

(5) The exercise of the power of the Council to make a Decree, if not signified by the whole Council, may be signified under the hand of the Chairman or such other member of the Council as may be authorized in that behalf by the Council.

(6) Every Decree made by the Council shall, as soon as practicable after it is made, be published in the *Gazette*.

(7) A Decree made by the Council shall, unless otherwise provided in that Decree, come into force on the date of publication of that Decree in the *Gazette* . . .'

The Proclamation provides for the continuance in existence of the courts, with the judges who were holding office immediately before the coup, of the public service, and of the judicial service and public service commissions.[2] The armed forces continue in existence as previously constituted, with a Commander-in-Chief appointed by the NRC.[3] The Attorney-General, to be appointed by the NRC, is to be entitled to attend all meetings of the Council.[4]

The other important section of the Proclamation vested the executive power of the State in an Executive Council, to be appointed by the NRC, and comprising the members of the NRC and such other persons as the NRC might think fit. The NRC might assign responsibility for any subject or department of state to a member of the Executive Council, who would than be styled a 'Commissioner'.[5] In the meantime the NRC was to be the Government of Ghana.[6] In fact only officers of the armed forces were appointed commissioners, except for two: the Attorney-General and Commissioner for Justice, and the Commissioner for Internal Affairs (who was the police member of the NRC). This provision of the Proclamation was re-written three months later by the Affairs of State Decree, 1972,[7] s. 9, to read:

'24 (1) The executive power of the State shall vest in the Chairman of the National Redemption Council and shall be exercised in accordance with this Proclamation and any other law for the time being in force.

(2) The National Redemption Council may appoint an Executive Council comprising such persons as the Council thinks fit.

(3) The Chairman of the National Redemption Council shall be the Chairman of the Executive Council.

(4) In the exercise of the executive power the Chairman shall whenever practicable, act in accordance with the advice of the Executive Council.

(5) A member of the Executive Council shall hold office at the pleasure of the National Redemption Council, and subject to such terms and conditions as the National Redemption Council may direct.

(6) Subject to the provisions of this section, the Executive Council shall be charged with the general direction and administration of the Government of Ghana.

(7) The National Redemption Council may from time to time assign responsibility for any subject or department of State to any member of the Executive Council and where responsibility is so assigned the said member shall, subject to the provisions of this section, discharge such responsibility subject to any general policy laid down in relation thereto by the National Redemption Council:

Provided that no exercise of such responsibility shall be questioned in any court on the ground that it contravenes any general policy so laid down.

(8) Members of the Executive Council to whom responsibility has been assigned in respect of any subject or department of State shall be styled 'Commissioners'.

(9) Without prejudice to the provisions of this section, the Executive Council shall have power to recommend to the National Redemption Council for consideration such measures (whether legislative or otherwise) as the Executive Council may consider necessary or expedient in the public interest . . .'

This amending decree also made provision for members of the Executive Council to resign or be replaced during incapacity, for the remuneration of members, for the Executive Council to regulate its own procedure, and for the publication of appointments and assignments of responsibility.

The Affairs of State Decree, 1972, makes other amendments to the Proclamation. These tend to increase the nominal status of the Chairman of the NRC. It is possible that this was done merely for convenience, since the decree recites in the preamble:

'Whereas article 36 of the Constitution provided *inter alia* that the President shall be Head of State and Commander-in-Chief of the Armed Forces of Ghana;

And whereas articles 57, 58 and 59 of the Constitution provided for the conduct of Ghana's international relations, the appointment of diplomatic representatives of Ghana abroad, the reception of envoys accredited to Ghana and the execution of treaties on behalf of Ghana;

And whereas upon the suspension of the said Constitution it has become necessary to make new provision for the afore-mentioned matters . . .'

The decree provides that the Chairman of the NRC is to be Head of State and Commander-in-Chief of the armed forces.[8] Whereas under the Proclamation the membership of the NRC could be altered only by decree, it is now provided that the Chairman is to be responsible for the appointment and removal of members upon the advice of at least two-thirds of the members, while he can be removed by a unanimous decision of all members.[9] Provision is made in this decree for the delegation of executive powers,[10] the transfer of executive functions,[11] and for proof in court of the due exercise of powers.[12] Later in the year the Chairman was given further powers, concurrently with the NRC, to assign responsibilities to Commissioners, and to replace members temporarily unable to act.[13]

Returning now to the immediate consequences of the coup, the legislation of January was directed mainly to the initial problems in the establishment of a new regime. The Preventive Custody Decree, 1972,[14] conferred powers of detention without trial on the NRC, and provided for the imediate detention of 265 prominent members of the Progress Party, the former government party. Another decree provided for the forfeiture of assets of the Progress Party and supporting organizations.[15] This was later extended to the other political parties.[16] Presumably this was felt necessary since they also had had no right to exist since the Proclamation, despite the mitigating factor of their impotence before the coup. The Oaths Act, 1960,[17] was replaced by the Oaths Decree, 1972.[18] Citizens of Ghana were prohibited from leaving the country without exit permits; this restriction was initially to last for only one year, and was in fact repealed in May.[19] The assets and bank accounts of various persons were frozen and placed under the control of a custodian of assets.[20] The persons initially affected were the Progress Party and individuals and organizations who had been its prominent supporters. Later the measure was extended to others, in some cases on grounds of political involvement, and in some as a means of facilitating investigations of alleged corruption.[21] The holding of firearms and ammunition was controlled.[22] An indemnity was granted in respect of acts in connection with the coup.[23]

After January the legislation in this area had less an emergency character, although much was directed towards aspects of the overthrown regime deemed in need of investigation or change. The Progress Party now being considered an enemy of the state, the defunct Convention People's Party of Nkrumah was considered no longer in need of special treatment. The NRC therefore repealed the Criminal Code (Amendment) (No. 2) Act, 1971,[24] which had been enacted by the Progress Party government to prevent any revival of support for the CPP.[25] The Trades Union Congress, dissolved by that government, was revived.[26] Next it was considered that the Progress Party had, through its nominees on the controlling bodies, exercised deleterious control over the statutory corporations, the universities and the Centre for Civic Education. New appointments were made to the first two classes of bodies, while the Centre for Civic Education was dissolved.[27] The process of investigation got under way with the establishment of Assets Committees to investigate, in respect of persons designated by the NRC, the existence, nature, extent and method of acquisition and disposal of their assets, and in particular the legality of acquisition of assets.[28] Each assets committee was to consist of a judge of a superior court, an accountant, and a member of the armed forces. It was to have the power to subpoena witnesses. Interested persons might be represented by counsel. The same decree forfeited the assets of certain leaders of the Progress Party, subject to a power of the NRC to restore any assets for the avoidance of hardship. A commission of inquiry was established to investigate that ever-popular source of governmental misconduct, the award of import licences, government loans, and construction contracts, during the period of the Progress Party government.[29]

As these measures showed, the problem of corruption concerned the NRC from the start. Indeed, the Proclamation made provision for continuing the office of Auditor-General and for his functions.[30] The Commission of Inquiry into Bribery and Corruption established by the previous regime was continued in existence,[31] and, when a question later arose as to its powers of entry and seizure, a decree was enacted to strengthen it.[32] When it was found that cocoa buying agents had been failing to pay farmers for cocoa purchased, a decree was enacted to compel speedy payment, with the sanctions of forfeiture of assets and long imprisonment for non-compliance. To prevent legal delays the NRC conferred on itself the power to give directions to give full effect to the decree 'notwithstanding any law to the contrary', and 'for determining any matter about which any doubt exists'.[33]

Some of the foregoing enhanced the powers of the state against the subject. They were further enhanced by the reintroduction of the Attorney-General's fiat as a condition of certain suits against the state and its agencies. The requirement is not, however, general. The fiat is required firstly for actions on various contracts and debts entered into before the coup, and usually involving foreign parties or payment in foreign currency;[34] and secondly for claims to execution or attachment in suits against statutory corporations.[35] Further, a prohibition was imposed on actions in respect of statements of the government and government-controlled press, made in the four months following the coup.[36]

There was throughout the year concern with security and public order. The measures against supporters of the former regime have been noted. In addition an early decree established a National Security Council, headed by the Chairman of the NRC, with exclusive authority for the collection of information, consideration of policy and supervisory control in national security matters.[37] The Public Order Decree, 1972,[38] confers powers on the Commissioner responsible for internal affairs to prohibit the possession or carrying of firearms or ammunition, the holding of public meetings or processions, or the celebration of any custom, and to impose curfews. However, the power is limited. It is to be exercised only 'as may reasonably be required in the interests of defence, public safety, public order, public morality, public health or the running of essential services, or to protect the rights and freedoms of other persons'. Police permission is required for meetings, processions and the celebration of traditional customs in public places, but it is provided that the police officer to whom application is made 'shall consider [it] fairly and impartially', and shall issue a permit 'unless he is satisfied on reasonable grounds that it is likely to cause a breach of the peace or to be prejudicial to national security'. Reasonable restrictions may be prescribed. Reasons for any refusal must be given in writing. An Act of 1970 was activated to confer on members of the armed forces not below the rank of sergeant the powers of police officers for the prevention and detection of crime and the apprehension of offenders.[39] Concern with security was increased in the middle of the year by reports of a plot to overthrow the NRC, resulting in a Sedition Decree and trials by military tribunals. This development will be described under later headings.

The institution of chieftaincy was not greatly affected, the relatively prominent position restored to it in the years following the fall of the Nkrumah regime being retained. The Proclamation expressly retained in force the Chieftaincy Act, 1971,[40] and continued in existence the Houses of Chiefs, Traditional Authorities and committees thereof.[41] The NRC also retained the existing provisions for stool lands.[42] During the year the Electoral Commissioner made rules for the election by chiefs of members of the National House of Chiefs,[43] and the Chairman of the NRC regulations for the functioning of Traditional Councils.[44]

Finally, a number of developments from June onwards were directed towards longer-term constitutional arrangements. After several months' experience of government, the NRC set up a Special Action Unit 'to follow up decisions of the National Redemption Council and the Executive Council and to ascertain to what extent they are being executed'. The Unit was to have a wing called the Expediting Committee to receive and investigate complaints from members of the public against public officers, and from subordinate members of the public service alleging victimization, and 'to make frequent and unadvertised visits to public offices where members of the public are entitled to call for service' to ensure that the responsible public officers did not waste the time of persons resorting to them for services.[45] With a view to improving the effectiveness of the border guards, they were incorporated into the army.[46] The Local Administration Act, 1971,[47] which provided elaborately for a new system of local government, was brought into force. Some amendments were, however, made. Primarily these were to allow management committees to continue to function in place of elected members of District and Local Councils, there should be members appointed by the NRC.[48] The problem, noted in previous *Annual Surveys*, of past nationality legislation was attacked. It was enacted that the Ghana Nationality Act, 1971,[49] was to be the sole determining whether a person born before its commencement was a citizen, with the sole exception that it should not deprive a person of citizenship if he had been declared a citizen by a court after the commencement of the Act. However, special provision was made to empower the Commissioner for Internal Affairs to naturalize certain persons who had lost their nationality as a result of the Ghana Nationality (Amendment) Decree, 1969.[50]

JUDICIAL AND LEGAL SYSTEM

The National Redemption Council (Establishment) Proclamation continued the existing judicial and legal system without any immediate change. We have seen already that certain assets committees and a commission of inquiry were set up soon afterwards.

The security emergency of mid-year produced a most important development. The Subversion Decree, 1972,[51] established a new offence of subversion, to be discussed below, with minimum sentences of death in some cases and 15 years' imprisonment in all others. It made the following provisions for the trial of the offences.

'4. (1) Subject to subsection (2) of this section, any person who commits an offence under this Decree shall be tried by a Military Tribunal as provided in this section.

(2) Where any person does any act which constitutes an offence under this Decree as well as under any other enactment the Attorney-General may direct in writing that he shall be proceeded against and tried under the other enactment and such direction shall have effect accordingly.

(3) The Commander-in-Chief of the Ghana Armed Forces or such other authority as may be authorized by him may convene a Military Tribunal under this section.

(4) Any authority who convenes a Military Tribunal may, subject to the provisions of this section, appoint as members of the Tribunal officers of the Armed Forces of Ghana.

(5) A Military Tribunal appointed under this section shall consist of a President who shall be an officer of the Armed Forces not below the rank of Lieutenant-Colonel in the Ghana Army or its equivalent in the Ghana Navy or the Ghana Air Force and not less than[52] four other members all of whom shall be officers of the Armed Forces not below the rank of Major in the Ghana Army or its equivalent in the Ghana Navy or Ghana Air Force.

(6) A decision of a majority of the members of a Tribunal appointed under this section shall be deemed to be the decision of the Tribunal.

(7) The decision of a Military Tribunal appointed under this section shall be final and no appeal shall lie from such a decision.'

The minimum size of the tribunal was later reduced to a President and two other members.[53] The first trial under these provisions started a few weeks after their enactment.

The other important change in the judicial system was the abolition of the Supreme Court.[54] This was explained in a government statement on the grounds that (a) the main function of the court had been to interpret the 1969 Constitution, which was no longer in force, and (b) the court had heard few appeals during its existence. Justices of the court who had held judicial office immediately before their appointment to the court were to revert to those offices. The superior courts therefore reverted to a two-tier system of High Court and Court of Appeal. However, provision was made for a full bench of the Court of Appeal to review and determine decisions of the Court of Appeal on questions of law and where there had been a miscarriage of justice. Thus there was a reversion to the system which had existed before the Supreme Court was set up under the 1969 Constitution. Ironically, before the abolition of the Supreme Court a judgement in the Court of Appeal, speaking of that system, had said:

> 'It could not be overlooked that the full bench had powers of review which are denied to the ordinary bench . . . The effect of the exercise of those powers is the same as if it were an appellate court over and above the ordinary bench . . . *De jure*, the ordinary bench and the full bench may be two divisions of the same court; *de facto*, the latter exercises powers of review amounting to such powers as an appellate court would have over a court inferior to it . . .
> "A rose by any other name, smells as sweet." '[55]

Another change quite widely discussed was the extension of liability to jury service to women.[56]

Considering the sources of law, we find that the new regime showed the common propensity of military regimes for a rapid rate of legislation. In this year the Proclamation and 139 decrees were passed, compared with 37 Acts in 1971. However, the ease with which decrees could be enacted meant that some were scarcely more than typographical corrections of others,[57] and some dealt with relatively minor matters which might ordinarily have been within the sphere of subordinate legislation.[58] Fortunately the new form of principal legislation did not lead to the total abandonment of the explanatory memorandum. Several important measures of law reform were enacted with these, which may assist in their interpretation.[59] While the number of Ghanaian statutes increased alarmingly, the number of applicable English statutes declined. In 1971 the English 'statutes of general application' had been reduced to an authoritative list in the Courts Act, 1971.[60] That list was reduced in this year by the deletion from it of 14 items, leaving only 25.[61]

There were a few developments in judicial practice regarding the sources of law. The Court of Appeal re-asserted the primacy of judicial decisions, where available, as authorities on customary law. In *Fiaklu* v. *Adjiani*[62] the plaintiff sought to contend that by custom the proper authority to grant land in Kokomlemle (Accra) was the Korle priest. The court held that, while this was quite possibly the ancient custom, judicial decisions had established that the concurrence of the Ga and Gbese stools was essential, and that this was the law. Indeed, Sowah, J.A., went so far as to say:[63]

> 'Whatever be the content of a custom, if it becomes an issue in litigation and the courts are invited to pronounce thereon, any declaration made by the courts supersedes the custom however ancient and becomes law obligatory upon those who come within its confines. To the extent therefore that a declaration is

inconsistent with a part of the content of a custom, that part in my view is abrogated.'

In *Hausa* v. *Hausa*[64] Bentsi-Enchill, J.S.C., emphasized the creative role of the courts in the exercise of this authority. Speaking of the requisites of the customary-law will, he said:[65] 'For as long as our legislature abstains from regulating this area of our traditional law, it is evident that the burden lies on the courts to regulate it as best they can.' He noted the danger of making the requisites too rigorous, and then suggested that guidance might be obtained from: a declaration of customary law with statutory authority by the Akim Abuakwa State Council; a proposal for variation of custom adopted by the Asanteman Council, which did not become legally binding; The Wills Act, 1971,[66] regulating common-law wills, and copied from England; and Islamic law. It may be noted that the case in question did not involve Akim Abuakwa customary law, Ashanti customary law, common law, or Islamic law. Thus Bentsi-Enchill, J.S.C., was clearly using these instances by way of example in an avowedly creative act. Apaloo, J.S.C., argued similarly.[67]

In determining the content of the common law of Ghana also there was at least one instance of increasing catholicity. In *Mechanical Lloyd* v. *Croft*[68] a preliminary ruling was sought on whether the plaintiffs could seek injunctions to restrain breaches of statutes. The plaintiffs and defendants were competitors in business. The plaintiffs alleged that the defendants were in breach of the Exchange Control Act, 1961, and the Ghanaian Business Promotion Act, 1970.[69] Hayfron-Benjamin, J., summed up the problem thus:[70]

'The objectives of these statutes vary, for example, the Ghanaian Business Promotion Act, 1970, is meant to ensure that a sector of the economy is reserved to Ghanaian entrepreneurs; other statutes such as the Exchange Control Act, 1961, are meant to regulate the flow of foreign currency and others are meant to ensure that competition in trade is fair. All are however designed to secure and protect the national interest. Most of these statutes provide penal sanctions for their breach. The question is whether quite apart from these penal sanctions a person can claim relief from any one alleged to be in breach of the statutes.'

In the present case the plaintiffs did not claim damages, and did not allege interference with their business, but rather claimed an injunction. The court continued:[71]

'Where the statutes are regulatory of trade or business generally, the English practice has been to rely on the criminal law to punish breaches. A trade competitor has generally been denied the right to sue to restrain another tradesman from acting in breach of a statute. This attitude must be due to the efficiency of the British police, and the promptness with which breaches of statutes are detected and suppressed. In America where police in early days were not very efficient, greater latitude is shown to claims by business competitors to enforce statutes designed to protect or regulate trade and industry. The Ghana police however honest they may be, have not got the necessary machinery and resources to ensure prompt and decisive suppression of breaches of intricate legislation like the Exchange Control Act, 1961, and other statutes designed to protect the public interest in trade, industry and commerce.'

The court would 'seek guidance and inspiration from the American experience'. Case-law and an article in the *Harvard Law Review* were then cited to show that plaintiffs were there granted standing to sue competitors who obtained trading advantages by breaches of statutes. This was so even when the statutes did not evidence concern for the competitive position of the plaintiffs' class, and no public nuisance was involved. The court continued that the novelty of the claim was no reason to reject it (citing in this instance English authorities). However, since no allegation of damage or its likelihood had been made in the pleadings, no reasonable cause of action was disclosed.

The Court of Appeal again had occasion to consider the system of precedent and the statutory provisions thereon. In *In re Agyepong*[72] the court was invited to hold itself bound by *Nimoh* v. *Acheampong,*[73] a decision of the Court of Appeal in 1959. In support of this contention counsel cited a decision of 1970 in which the Court of Appeal had held itself bound by the 1964 decision of the then Supreme Court. The court in the present case held that 'with the promulgation of the 1960 Constitution, the Supreme Court, a completely new institution became the final Court of Appeal. Appeals to the Privy Council were stopped and the Court of Appeal which fathered *Nimoh* v. *Acheampong* was abolished. The Supreme Court was not made a successor of any of the previous courts'. This was confirmed by the 1960 Constitution, article 42(4), which provided that the Supreme Court should 'in principle' be bound by its own decisions, but not be otherwise bound to follow the decisions of any court on questions of law. Moreover, after the suspension of the 1960 Constitution the Courts Decree, 1966,[74] abolished the existing courts and established a new Court of Appeal, which was not a successor to the 1960 Supreme Court. The 1966 Court of Appeal was governed by a provision worded in the same way as article 42(4) of the 1960 Constitution. Therefore 'decisions given by the Supreme Court between 1 July 1960 and October 1966, were constitutionally denied any binding efficacy after the coming into operation of the Courts Decree, 1966.' The 1964 decision thus ceased to have binding effect.[75] The next development was the enactment on 22 August, 1969, of the new Constitution, in which article 125(2) provided that the Court of Appeal was to be bound by 'the decisions binding on the Court of Appeal as it existed immediately before the coming into force of this Constitution'. Therefore 'the only decisions binding on the present Court of Appeal before the suspension of the 1969 Constitution, are those given between October 1966 and 22 August 1969 and those given since that date by the present Court of Appeal itself.' The court did not consider whether the suspension of the 1969 Constitution might have changed this. Neither did it consider an equally intriguing question: was it not bound by the 1970 decision to the effect that the post-1966 Court of Appeal was bound by the pre-1966 decisions of the Supreme Court? The decision reached confirms that the rather frequent revisions of the courts system have had the side-effect of periodically freeing the highest court from being bound even 'in principle' by any decisions at all.

In contrast, one decision emphasizes that the High Court ought to respect decisions of the Court of Appeal. In *Sogbaka* v. *Tamakloe*[76] one party relied in part on a decision of the Court of Appeal in 1969. The other pointed out that this had been criticized by the High Court in 1971. In the present case the court disapproved of the criticism, saying:[77]

> 'I have always found it difficult to appreciate the reasoning which acclaims a decision as binding and authoritative and yet subjects it to criticism. The principle of *stare decisis* as I understand it, prohibits such public ventilation of dissent sometimes dragged to lengths of decrial . . . If this rule is not strictly enforced the authority of a precedent may be whittled away by gradual and piece-meal judicial nibbling. The judge's duty to allay doubts with positive decisions would then have turned to the creation and multiplication of doubts.'

The powers and duties of legal practitioners towards their clients were discussed in three reported cases. One held that the phrase 'if the parties can come to an agreement among themselves' in the Supreme [High] Court (Civil Procedure) Rules, 1954 (LN 140A) included agreements between counsel. Counsel normally had unlimited power to do what was best for his client until his authority was withdrawn, and the court would accept counsel's statement from the bar as to the extent of his authority in any particular case.[78] Another case held that a practitioner was not accountable to his clients for paying money due to them to their agent if he had no reasonable cause to suspect that the agent was fraudulent. This was a case where a registered insurance claims agent had assisted the plaintiffs in making a successful insurance claim, had received the compensation from the practitioner whom he engaged on the plaintiffs' behalf, and failed to pass any part of it to the plaintiffs. The plaintiffs sued the practitioner and the agent for the compensation money, but succeeded only against the latter.[79] Thirdly, in a case brought by solicitors against a former client for their fees, the defendant contended that the bill should be referred to a taxing officer for taxation. The Legal Profession Act, 1960,[80] s. 31, provided that no such reference might be made after 12 months from the date when the bill was served except under special circumstances. The court held that the proviso gave it an absolute discretion, which it would exercise in the defendant's favour as the bill appeared as if it might contain over-charges. Moreover, the court had an inherent jurisdiction, in exercising disciplinary control over its officers, to order taxation of a bill at any time, and the Legal Profession Act had not impliedly curtailed this jurisdiction.[81] This was one of three cases in which the courts had to resort to their inherent jurisdiction to do justice when the enacted law seemed insufficient; this may be a growing trend.[82]

The Council for Law Reporting Decree, 1972,[83] replaced the Council for Law Reporting Act, 1971,[84] without any significant changes.

ECONOMIC CONTROL

The NRC adopted a policy of detailed regulation of the economy through licensing and other controls. This entailed a number of decrees, often supported by relatively stringent criminal provisions. Some of the latter will be referred to under the heading of Criminal and Penal Law.

A new Price Control Decree, 1972,[85] was enacted to consolidate and develop the existing enactments, which had been passed between 1962 and 1966. Similarly the Diamonds Decree, 1972,[86] consolidated the law controlling the finding, sale and export of diamonds, and the Customs and Excise Decree, 1972,[87] consolidated the law on that subject. In a new measure a Prices and Incomes Board was established to formulate an incomes and prices policy, and collect data on trends of incomes and prices. It was given authority to set binding guidelines for collective agreements on incomes, and to make other regulations for effectuating the principles and provisions of the decree.[88] Other enactments were more specific. For example, the construction of new petrol stations was prohibited.[89] An early decree retained in force the provisions of the 1969 Constitution controlling stool lands.[90]

There was further evidence this year of a determination to secure Ghanaian control of the import sectors of the economy. The NRC retained in force restrictions on the land-holding rights of persons who were not citizens of Ghana.[91] As noted, the Attorney-General's fiat was made necessary for actions against the state on contracts entered into before the coup and involving payment abroad, foreign parties or foreign currency.[92] The Insurance (Amendment) Decree, 1972,[93] provided that every insurance business carried on in Ghana was to be owned by Ghanaians to the extent of at least 40%, and, if a company, was to be incorporated in Ghana. All government insurance business was to be with the State Insurance Corporation. The decree also set up a government-owned Reinsurance Organization, to which was to be ceded 20% of every insurance policy.

In December two more dramatic steps were taken towards Ghanaian control of the economy. The Mining Operations (Government Participation) Decree, 1972,[94] stated in the preamble:

'Whereas it is in the interest of national development and of the well-being of the people of Ghana and it is in furtherance of the general economic policy of the National Redemption Council of promoting self-reliance that the State assume a controlling interest in the ownership of the productive facilities employed in the development of the natural resources of Ghana, while at the same time encouraging private participation in such development whether Ghanaian or foreign . . .'

It then vested the assets of the two remaining foreign-owned mining concerns in two companies established by the decree. In these new companies the government was to hold 55% of the equity capital and the former owners 45%. The majority of the board of directors including the chairman of each was to be appointed by the government. The technical management of the new companies was to be the responsibility of the former owners, upon such terms and conditions as might be agreed with the government. Compensation was to be paid for the 55% of the assets of which each foreign company had been divested. The value of the assets was to be calculated on the basis of their net written down value for income tax purposes in the books of the foreign companies. Shortly afterwards similar measures were taken in respect of three foreign timber companies, the decree providing that it might be extended to others. The compensation provision here was different. The timber companies were to be paid over a period of not less than five years at an interest rate not exceeding 2½ per cent per annum. Payment was to be in Ghanaian currency, but the government would employ its good offices to transfer as soon as practicable sums due to non-citizens.[95]

Finally, one measure dealt more peremptorily with a group of companies incorporated in Ghana but controlled by aliens. The Loyalty Group of Companies (Forfeiture) Decree, 1972,[96] recited that this group had 'entered into illegal and fraudulent transactions' which had 'caused damage to the economy of Ghana', and vested their assets in the state without compensation.

CRIMINAL AND PENAL LAW

The principal statutory developments here reflect the new regime's concern with two areas of government: national security, and the economy.

The initial steps to protect national security, which involved amendments to the criminal law, have been mentioned under the heading of Constitutional and Administrative Law. In mid-year the discovery of an alleged subversive plot led to the enactment of the Subversion Decree, 1972.[97] This provided:

'1. Notwithstanding any law to the contrary, a person shall be guilty of the offence of subversion who—
(a) prepares or endeavours to overthrow the Government by unlawful means; or
(b) prepares or endeavours to procure by force any alteration of the law or the policies of the Government; or
(c) prepares or endeavours to carry out by force any enterprise which usurps the executive power of the State in any matter of both a public and a general nature; or
(d) incites or assists or procures any person to invade Ghana with armed force or unlawfully to subject any part of Ghana to attack by land, sea or air or assists in the preparation of any such invasion or attack; or
(e) without lawful authority (the proof of which shall be on him) imports into Ghana any explosive, firearm or ammunition; or
(f) kills or attempts to kill or conspires with any other person to kill any member of the National Redemption Council or the Executive Council or a Regional Commissioner or any other citizen of Ghana with a view to securing the overthrow of the Government or with intent to coerce any other citizen of Ghana into opposing the National Redemption Council or otherwise into withdrawing or withholding his support from the National Redemption Council; or
(g) commits the offence of robbery; or
(h) smuggles or attempts to smuggle any timber, diamonds or gold out of Ghana;[98] or
(i) steals any cocoa, diamond, gold, underground telephone cable, or any telephone wire attached to or connected with a telephone or telegraph pole, or any motor vehicle;[99] or
(j) wilfully damages any public property by act of violence; or
(k) organizes or incites any other person to go on a general strike likely to cause suffering to the general public; or
(l) steals any funds intended for the purchase of cocoa; or
(m) smuggles or attempts to smuggle any cocoa out of Ghana;[100] or
(n) hoards any goods, contrary to the Price Control Decree, 1972 (NRCD 17); or
(o) unlawfully deals in any foreign currency notes in a manner likely to damage the economy of Ghana; or
(p) steals any public funds; or
(q) offers a bribe to obtain any import licence, or takes a bribe to allocate any import licence; or

(r) being a member of the Armed Forces, the Police Service or a public officer, demands or takes any bribe; or

(s) impersonates any member of the National Redemption Council or the Executive Council or a Regional Commissioner or falsely and dishonestly represents to any person that he is acting in accordance with instructions, orders or a request of the National Redemption Council or Executive Council or any member thereof or a Regional Commissioner; or

(t) does any act with intent to sabotage the economy of Ghana.

2. A person guilty of subversion shall upon conviction be liable—

(a) to suffer death by shooting by firing squad in the case of a person guilty of any of the acts described in paragraphs (a) to (j) of section 1 of this Decree, and

(b) to a term of imprisonment not less than fifteen years and not more than thirty years in any other case.

3. A person who knows of the commission of any act of subversion but does not forthwith report it to a member of the National Redemption Council or Executive Council or to any police officer not below the rank of Sergeant or to a member of the Armed Forces not below the rank of Sergeant in the Ghana Army or its equivalent in the Ghana Navy or Air Force shall be guilty of an offence and liable on conviction to imprisonment for a term not less than fifteen years and not more than thirty years.'

As already seen, offences under the decree were triable by military tribunal. It is hardly necessary to remark on the curious and extensive collection of acts listed in s. 1, or on the vagueness of the last class.

Criminal legislation in respect of the economy was extensive, because of the NRC's move towards a command economy, and perhaps partly also because of an increased confidence in the possibility of changing behaviour by criminal sanctions. The early introduction of new price control measures included the creation of criminal offences for infringements.[101] The Price Control Decree also created the offence of smuggling out of Ghana certain goods with controlled prices, and the maximum penalty for this was increased a month later.[102] Hoarding of goods, also made an offence by the Price Control Decree, was subsequently made a class of subversion. The Foreign Exchange Decree, 1972,[103] was directed exclusively to setting the penalties for misstatements made for the purpose of obtaining transfers of foreign exchange from Ghana. Minimum penalties were set, increased by an amendment two months later.[104] Another decree imposed the death penalty for the unlawful export of gold or diamonds,[105] before it was made a class of subversion carrying the same penalty. Finally the Petroleum Products Decree, 1972,[106] consists largely of criminal provisions designed to prevent the adulteration or smuggling of or speculation in petroleum products.

A notable aspect of the new penal provisions is the frequent occurrence of the minimum sentence. The most severe instances have already been seen in the Subversion Decree, but in some cases this incorporated provisions enacted earlier in the year. Thus in the first month of its existence the NRC had passed a decree requiring a sentence of death or life imprisonment for robbery,[107] and two months later concern over the stealing of telephone wires resulted in a decree providing for a minimum sentence of five years' imprisonment for this offence.[108] Certain particular offences resulted in the enactment of a minimum ten-year sentence for obtaining or attempting to obtain property under the pretence of authority of the NRC, Executive Council, or the Chairman or any member thereof.[109] Thus the Subversion Decree was merely the culmination of a trend.

One case needs mention. In *Arthur* v. *The Republic*[110] the applicant had been convicted and sentenced to a term of imprisonment. He filed an appeal to the Court of Appeal, and was then released on bail, but failed to appear in court for the hearing of the appeal. The appeal was therefore dismissed, and he was arrested and taken to prison to serve his sentence. He now applied for an order that his appeal be re-entered for hearing. He filed a supporting affidavit explaining that he had not known that he should watch the *Gazette* or the notice board at the court to learn the date set for the appeal hearing. The Supreme Court Rules, 1962,[111] contained no provision for re-entering a criminal appeal, although they did for civil appeals. Nevertheless, the court held that, by virtue of its inherent jurisdiction to do substantial justice, especially in matters affecting the liberty of the individual, it had a discretion to grant the application. In this case it would be granted.

SUCCESSION AND ADMINISTRATION OF ESTATES

There was some development of the case-law on the customary law will. In *Hausa* v. *Hausa*[112] the plaintiffs claimed to be entitled to inherit certain property on intestacy. The defendants claimed that the deceased had made either a gift *inter vivos* or a will of the property in favour of one of them. It was held that the defendants had failed to prove a gift or will, but two members of the Court of Appeal took the opportunity to discuss earlier cases on the requirements of a customary law will. Bentsi-Enchill, J.S.C., in a judgement already noted for another of its aspects, noted that Ollennu, J., had laid it down as a requirement that the beneficiary formally accept the gift by presenting a thank-offering. He observed:[113] 'Speaking for myself, I should have had no difficulty in upholding the validity of the gift by will if there had been credible evidence proving that it had been witnessed by two responsible and disinterested persons.' He then proceeded, in the passage noted earlier , to support the view by analogy with other legal systems. Apaloo, J.S.C., held:[114] 'I think the purely evidentiary requirement of witnesses is desirable and if they are independent and disinterested, that should suffice.'

Unfortunately the court which decided *Hausa* v. *Hausa* was unaware of, and so could not comment on a relevant decision of the High Court delivered three months earlier. In *Abenyewa* v. *Marfo*[115] Taylor, J., after reviewing the existing authorities at length, concluded:[116]

'It is my view that the requirements of a valid customary will are as follows:
(1) Only the self-acquired property of a testator of sound mind can be disposed of by samansiw [customary will];
(2) The disposition must be made in the presence of witnesses one of whom at least it seems must be a member of the testator's family and the witnesses must be told that the bequests are his samansiw to take effect after his death;
(3) The family of the testator must know and consent to the disposition.
(4) There ought to be an acceptance of the gift evidenced by the offering of aseda or the exercising of acts of ownership or any act from which an acceptance can be inferred depending on the circumstances of the case.'

It would seem that requirements (2) and (3), and possibly (4), as formulated by Taylor, J., are contrary to the *dicta* in *Hausa* v. *Hausa*. They were not followed by Edward Wiredu, J., in *Abadoo* v. *Awotwi*,[117] although in that case *Hausa* v. *Hausa* was not brought to the court's attention. Wiredu, J.'s findings as to the essentials of a customary law will were:[118]

'(a) The declaration must be made in anticipation of death; i.e. it must be a death-bed declaration or the declarant must be in immediate fear of death;
(b) The declaration must be in respect of the self-acquired property of the declarant;
(c) The declaration must be made in the presence of witnesses (preferably including some members of the declarant's family);
(d) The witnesses present must hear the subject-matter of the declaration and understand it as representing the dying wishes of the declarant, and be able to know who received what in order to testify about the same.'

He expressly dissented from Taylor, J.'s, views that members of the family must witness the will, that the family's knowledge and consent were necessary, and that acceptance by the beneficiary ought to be listed as a requirement. On the question of the family's consent, he said:[119]

'For some time now the customary law has undergone considerable changes . . . The requirement of the family's consent to perfect any form of alienation is no longer good law and is now dead and buried. No attempt should therefore be made with respect to resurrect it. With this apart, that requirement does not reflect the present social changes which are now apparent in the Ghanaian society about modes of acquisition of property which are unlike the past when individual members of the family had to till portions of family land and at times even with the substantial assistance from members of the family . . .'

The case-law also evidences the growing concern with the rights of a man's dependent children on his death intestate. The general principles established so far indicate that a man's family inherits his property. Where the family is a matrilineage, it does not, of course, include his children. However, dependent children in such a case are entitled to be maintained and educated by the family from the estate. In granting letters of administration the courts normally exercise their discretion in favour of the 'successor', the individual appointed by the inheriting family to manage the estate. This practice was confirmed in one case.[120] However, in another, where the successor had not even buried the deceased before collecting the latter's final monthly salary, and had shown no interest in the education or maintenance of the six children of the deceased, the court granted letters to the widow, saying: 'The interest of the children in this case must to me be considered to be of paramount importance.'[121] The primacy of the children's rights was asserted in a further case, where it was said *obiter* that the successor was 'bound in law to utilize the money in the estate towards the maintenance and education of the children of the deceased even to the last pesewa.'[122] Thus even if the legislature does not intervene to modify matrilineal inheritance, it is possible that the courts will develop the means of protecting the children's expectations.

CONFLICTS OF LAWS

The steady stream of interesting cases in this area continued. *Hausa* v.

Hausa needs mention again. As already seen, it was held that the deceased had not disposed of his property by gift *inter vivos* or will, so that the law of intestacy fell to be applied. The question then arose as to which law of intestacy was appropriate. The property was a house in Navrongo, Ghana. The father of the deceased had been a Hausa from Kano, Nigeria, who settled at Yariba in Ghana. The deceased himself was born in Yariba, and lived all his life in Ghana. The High Court held that 'succession of the Hausas the *lex domicile* of [the deceased] is patrilineal and that of the Kassena-Nankani the *lex situs* of the property follows the same pattern.' Bentsi-Enchill, J.S.C., in a passage concurred in by the rest of the Court of Appeal, held that this holding was questionable 'in so far as it implied that [the deceased] had a domicile in Hausaland'. Even his father could have been held to have acquired a Ghanaian domicile. He concluded:[123]

> 'A holding that he had a Ghanaian domicile and had become a member of the Kassena-Nankani community among whom he settled and died in Navrongo would therefore have been the more reasonable conclusion, leading to the application of the Kassena-Nankani customary law rules of succession to this case.'

It would seem that the point in issue was not one of private international law. Under that law Ghanaian law was applicable as the *lex situs*. The question was rather one of internal conflicts. The question was, assuming that under Ghanaian law the personal law of the deceased was applicable, what had been his personal law? An interesting implication of both the High Court and the Court of Appeal judgements was that Hausa law could be applied in Ghana as a personal law. The decision of the Court of Appeal also suggests that permanent settlement in a given area may be taken as evidence that the propositus has adopted the customary law of that area as his personal law. However, this important question of the circumstances in which a person's personal law changes was again not fully discussed, perhaps because the evidence on it was scanty in this case.

Youhana v. *Abboud*[124] was a claim to the estates of two Lebanese brothers, each of whom had died intestate leaving immovable property in Ghana. It was agreed that the law of Ghana, as the *lex situs,* must apply. One party argued that the appropriate Ghanaian law was the customary law of the places where the properties were situated. The court held rather that it was the personal law of the deceased, on the authority of the Courts Act, 1971,[125] s. 49(1). (*Sed quaere.* The deceased had died in 1957 and 1967, when other provisions applied.) The deceased had never acquired Ghanaian domicile or nationality, despite long residence in Ghana.[126] There was no evidence that they by their acts adopted any Ghanaian family. Therefore no particular system of customary law could be said to be their personal law, and common law must apply. This decision gives a few hints (but little more) as to the mode in which a new personal law may be acquired. It also gives some support to the view that the personal law of a foreigner is presumed to be common law, not customary law.

A question of private international law arose in *Société Générale de Compensation* v. *Ackerman.*[127] This concerned a contract of employment between the plaintiff, an Israeli national, and the defendants, an external French company. The work was to be done in Ghana, and the plaintiff's salary, other than his living expenses, was to be payable in France in

French currency. There was no express agreement as to the governing law. The Court of Appeal held that the proper law of the contract, in the light of principles established in Commonwealth decisions, was Ghanaian law. It held further that the trial court had been procedurally wrong to award damages in French currency, since such an order could not be enforced by the ordinary process of execution in Ghana, and the plaintiff, having made use of the Ghanaian legal machinery to seek a remedy, must take it in Ghanaian currency.

PROPERTY, TORT AND OTHER AREAS OF PRIVATE LAW

In these areas two important statutes prepared by the Law Reform Commission were enacted during this year. The English statutes of limitation previously in force were replaced by the Limitation Decree, 1972,[128] modelled largely on the English Limitation Act, 1939. This development was important for its convenience, providing for the first time a single, accessible, well-drafted law of limitation. In addition the decree substantially changed the law in one respect, by expressly bringing customary-law rights within its scope.[129] It will be some years before the detailed effects of this are clear. However, two points emerge immediately: the statute puts an end to the principle that long, adverse possession of land never gives title in customary law; and in many cases where a defence would hitherto have been based on estoppel by acquiescence the decree will now be relied upon, the elements of limitation being more easily established.

Secondly, the Mortgages Decree, 1972,[130] partly codifies the law on its subject.[131] (It is doubtful whether the customary-law pledge is affected.)[132] Its overriding scope is established by sections 1 and 2, which provide in part:

'1. (1) A mortgage for the purposes of this Decree is a contract charging immovable property as security for the due repayment of debt and any interest accruing thereon or for the performance of some other obligation for which it is given, in accordance with the terms of the contract . . .
2. A mortgage of immovable property shall only be capable of being effected in accordance with the provisions of this Decree, and every transaction which is in substance a mortgage of immovable property, whether expressed as a mortgage, charge, pledge of title documents, outright conveyance, trust for sale on condition, lease, hire-purchase, conditional sale, sale with right of repurchase or in any other manner, shall be deemed to be a mortgage of immovable property and shall be governed by this Decree.'

The decree requires mortgages to be evidenced in writing, and implies various covenants. It provides for the remedies of the mortgagee on default, and abolishes foreclosure and sale other than judicial sale. It sets out the principles of priorities, from which are excluded consolidation and the *tabula in naufragio* instance of tacking.

Several cases concerned hire-purchase agreements for motor vehicles. In *Donkor* v. *Owona Farkye Brothers Transport*[133] the plaintiff had taken a vehicle from the defendants. The agreement between them provided for the payment of the purchase price in more than five instalments, which brought it within the definition of a hire-purchase contract in the Sale of Goods Act, 1962.[134] However, the agreement expressly provided for the application of s. 75(2), which allows parties to an agreement for the sale of goods exceeding G£1,000 in price to exclude Part VIII, which regulates hire-purchase transactions. When more than half the purchase price had been paid the plaintiff defaulted, and the defendants seized the vehicle and refused to release it on payment of the arrears. The plaintiff now sued to recover the total payment he had made. The defendants relied on the terms of the contract, which provided for seizure without repayment in such circumstances. The court held that all contracts for the sale of goods in Ghana must be within the framework of the Sale of Goods Act. Even though the parties might contract to exclude Part VIII, they could not entirely exclude the Act. This was implied by the words of the Act, and required by public policy and equity. The parties were not bound by s. 69, which was in Part VIII, and prohibited seizure without recourse to the courts when more than half the price had been paid. But they were bound by s. 57, which was not in Part VIII, and which provided that, where the seller recovered possession of the goods, the buyer was entitled to recover the sums he had paid. The court further held that the Act had not abolished the distinction between hire-purchase contracts and other forms of contracts for the sale of goods, although the agreement in the present case could not be enforced as a hire-purchase agreement under the Act.

In *Taylor* v. *S. Y. Sasu and Sons*[135] Part VIII applied. The vehicle was seized just before half the price had been paid. It was subsequently released to the buyer, who paid further instalments bringing the total to more than half the original price. Then the sellers seized it again. The buyer now sued under s. 69, but the sellers contended that they had released it on the first occasion under a new agreement providing for the payment of the remainder of the price, and that they had not received half the price specified in the new agreement. The Court of Appeal held that the second agreement had not been proved on the evidence, and that the original agreement had therefore remained in force. Apaloo, J.A., indicated the attitude of the court when he said:[136]

'It is difficult to escape the conclusion that the object of the so-called fresh agreement was to defeat the protection which section 69 of the Sale of Goods Act, 1962, conferred on the weaker of two contracting parties. In such a situation, a court should, I think, be slow in finding that a party has succeeded in setting at nought clear legislative intent and should decline to so find unless the evidence is compulsive of that conslusion . . . It would take a lot to persuade me that our law would sanction two sales of the same vehicle by the same vendor to the same purchaser by two successive hire-purchase agreements having two different hire-purchase prices.'

A similar policy of protecting operator-purchasers of vehicles against financiers was shown by the Court of Appeal in *Sasu* v. *Nyadualah,*[137] although there the court held that there was not a hire-purchase agreement. The respondent had acquired a used vehicle from a third party, and borrowed money from the appellant to put it on the road. Work on it was completed while the respondent was in hospital, and the appellant released the vehicle to the respondent's brother in return for the latter's signature on a hire-purchase agreement in the latter's name. The respondent was then 'pressurized' (as the court put it) to sign the agreement as a guarantor. The appellant later seized the vehicle. The court held that the respondent was entitled to recover it. The 'agreement' was not binding between the parties, because each knew that the respondent was the owner. The appellant had merely made a loan, and had a right *in personam* to repayment, not a right *in rem* in the vehicle.

Several cases concern problems of third party insurance for motor vehicles. The Motor Vehicles (Third Party Insurance) Act, 1958 (No. 42) provides that no motor vehicle is to be used without an insurance policy in respect of third party risks. S. 6 provides that such a policy must be one which 'insures such persons or classes of person as may be specified in the policy in respect of any liability which may be incurred by him or them . . .' S. 8 nullifies any condition in such a policy which provides 'that no liability shall arise under the policy . . ., or that any liability so arising shall cease in the event of some specified thing being done or omitted to be done after the happening of the event giving rise to a claim under the policy'. Controversy has arisen over the insertion of 'named driver' clauses in such insurance policies. The insurance companies frequently insist on such clauses, which provide that the operation of the policy shall be restricted to occasions when the vehicle is being driven by a particular, named person. (Indeed, their frequency is such that in one case a person driving under the perfectly adequate cover of a fully comprehensive policy was charged and convicted with driving under a policy in which his name did not appear; the conviction was, of course, set aside on appeal.[138]) However, it happens with depressing regularity that policies are so restricted, the vehicles are then driven by other persons, and are involved in accidents. The insurers then repudiate liability, which usually means that any injured third party has no chance of obtaining compensation. The validity of the named driver clause has been questioned from time to time, and the matter was fully discussed in *Pokua* v. *State Insurance Corporation*.[139] Bentsi-Enchill, J.S.C., in a dissenting judgement, held it invalid. He argued that the Ghana Act, although based on British legislation, should be construed independently, because the British legislation had been found unsatisfactory, and French law had long ago reached a different conclusion. The object of the Act would be defeated by upholding the clause, and a proper interpretation of the entire Act revealed that it was invalid. He cited numerous British decisions both to demonstrate the policy to be followed in Ghana, and to show that the Ghanaian legislation need not be construed in the same way as the British. The majority of the Court of Appeal (Amissah and Sowah, J.J.A.) held that the named driver clause was, on the wording of the Act, valid. They discussed and rejected the arguments of Bentsi-Enchill, J.S.C., but both suggested that the law was in need of reform.

The need for reform was repeated in *Shell Co of Ghana Ltd* v. *Sarpong*.[140] There the appellants had sold a petrol tanker on hire-purchase terms, the purchaser undertaking to insure it. He failed to do so, and his driver negligently injured the respondent. The Court of Appeal held that the appellants had not 'caused or permitted another person' to drive the vehicle while uninsured, and so were not in breach of the terms of the Act. The court regretted that this meant the respondent might get no compensation, and suggested that an institution similar to the British Motor Insurers Bureau would be desirable in Ghana.

Fan Milk Ltd v. *State Shipping Corporation,* mentioned in the *Annual Survey* for 1971 on the question of jurisdiction, was decided on the merits this year.[141] The court had previously decided that the Ghanaian courts had jurisdiction in this case concerning the carriage of goods by sea, and that Ghanaian and English law did not differ in any material particular on the matter in issue.[142] The court now applied English authorities exclusively to determine liability. By a bill of lading made subject to the English Carriage of Goods by Sea Act, 1924, and the Hague Rules scheduled thereto, the defendants had acknowledged shipment on board their vessel of the plaintiffs' goods in apparent good order and condition. There was no dispute that the goods were delivered damaged. It was held that the plaintiffs were entitled to sue in tort, the action on the case having been extended to such cases by *Hayn* v. *Culliford*[143] and subsequent English cases. Where the goods arrived in a damaged condition the onus was on the bill of lading holder to prove that the damage occurred on board the ship. If, however, the shipper had issued a clean bill of lading he had admitted that they were shipped in good order and condition and sufficiently packed. There was no evidence of any inherent vice or defect in the goods. Protection clauses in the bill of lading which were wider than those allowed in the Act were void. Therefore the plaintiffs succeeded.

Reference has already been made to *Mechanical Lloyd* v. *Croft,*[144] and the decision there on the circumstances in which a private party may sue for breach of a statutory regulation.

Finally, an interesting case in the law of torts is *Anthony* v. *University College of Cape Coast.*[145] The plaintiff was a respected married woman with a prominent social position. Her photograph was taken at a function of a benevolent society with her consent, and published in a religious newspaper. Subsequently it was published without her consent by the defendants in the form of postcards inscribed 'Traditional hairdo in Ghana', and sold at the defendants' bookshop. The plaintiff sued for libel, pleading an innuendo that she had consented to the exhibition and sale of her photograph, that she had done so for gain, and that she was of base, weak and mean moral character. Evidence was heard from persons including the plaintiff's son, husband and a business customer. They spoke of their own reactions to the exhibition of the postcards, and of those of Fanti society, to which they and the plaintiff belonged. The court held that this evidence proved the innuendo, and awarded damages of ¢2,750 (about £1,000 sterling). It might be questioned whether the test of what is defamatory ought to have been the opinion of Fanti society, rather than of right-thinking members of Ghanaian society generally. Moreover, if the latter is the correct standard, one wonders whether its determination is not a question of law, rather than of fact to be proved by evidence. The case is also notable for a short passage in the judgement which adds that the publication was an invasion of the plaintiff's privacy, and concludes:[146] 'In my judgement the plaintiff has two strings to her bow either in the defamation as proved or damages for an invasion of her privacy and legal right.' If this is followed, Ghanaian law will have acquired a new tort not yet developed in England, although well established in the USA.

NOTES

1. National Redemption Council (Establishment) Proclamation (Amendment) Decree, 1972 (NRCD 1)
2. Proclamation, ss. 4, 5 and 6
3. *Id.*, s. 7
4. *Id.*, s. 8. Mr E. N. Moore, previously President of the Bar Association, was appointed Attorney-General and Commissioner for Justice
5. *Id.*, s. 24
6. *Id.*, s. 25
7. NRCD 58
8. *Id.*, s. 1
9. *Ibid*
10. *Id.*, ss. 5 and 6
11. *Id.*, s. 7
12. *Id., passim*
13. Proclamation (Amendment) (No. 2) Decree, 1972 (NRCD 124)
14. NRCD 2
15. National Redemption Council (Forfeiture of Assets) Decree, 1972 (NRCD 5)
16. National Redemption Council (Forfeiture of Assets) (Amendment) Decree, 1972 (NRCD 33)
17. CA 12
18. NRCD 6
19. Foreign Travel (Exit Permits) Decree, 1972 (NRCD 7), repealed by the Foreign Travel (Exit Permits) (Repeal) Decree, 1972 (NRCD 65)
20. Assets and Bank Accounts Decree, 1972 (NRCD 8); Custodian of Assets Decree, 1972 (NRCD 12), replaced by the Custodian of Assets Decree, 1972 (NRCD 28)
21. Amendments to the list in the Schedule to the decree were by Legislative Instrument. 34 amendments (some removing names) were made in 1972.
22. Arms and Ammunition Decree, 1972 (NRCD 9)
23. National Redemption Council (Indemnity) Decree, 1972 (NRCD 13)
24. Act 380
25. Criminal Code (Amendment) (No. 2) Act, 1971 (Repeal) Decree, 1972 (NRCD 21)
26. Industrial Relations (Amendment) Decree, 1972 (NRCD 22)
27. Statutory Corporations Decree, 1972 (NRCD 14); Universities (Government Appointees) Decree, 1972 (NRCD 29); Centre for Civic Education (Dissolution) Decree, 1972 (NRCD 35)
28. Investigation and Forfeiture of Assets Decree, 1972 (NRCD 19)
29. Commission of Inquiry (Award of Import Licences, Government Contracts, etc.) Decree, 1972 (NRCD 55), replacing NRCD 52 with the same title
30. Proclamation, ss. 16 and 17
31. Commission of Inquiry (Bribery and Corruption) Decree, 1972 (NRCD 3)
32. Commission of Inquiry (Bribery and Corruption) (Powers of Commission) Decree, 1972 (NRCD 83)
33. Licensed Buying Agents Control Decree, 1972 (NRCD 56)
34. State Proceedings Decree, 1972 (NRCD 59)
35. Statutory Corporations Act, 1964 (Amendment) Decree, 1972 (NRCD 120)
36. National Redemption Council (Defamation by Newspapers) Decree, 1972 (NRCD 67)
37. National Security Council Decree, 1972 (NRCD 16). See also the Private Security Organizations (Revocation of Licences) Decree, 1972 (NRCD 31)
38. NRCD 68
39. Prevention of Crime Act, 1970 (Act 347); Prevention of Crime (Amendment) Decree. 1972 (NRCD 123)
40. Act 370
41. Proclamation, s. 23
42. Lands Commission Decree, 1972 (NRCD 24)
43. Chieftaincy (National House of Chiefs) Election Rules, 1972 (LI 746)
44. Chieftaincy (Proceedings and Functions) (Traditional Councils) Regulations, 1972 (LI 798)
45. Special Action Unity Decree, 1972 (NRCD 80)
46. Armed Forces (Amendment) (No. 2) Decree, 1972 (NRCD 125)
47. Act 359

48. Local Administration (Amendment) Decree, 1972 (NRCD 138)
49. Act 361
50. NLCD 333. Ghana Nationality (Amendment) Decree, 1972 (NRCD 134)
51. NRCD 90
52. The words 'not less than' were inserted by the Subversion (Amendment) Decree, 1972 (NRCD 93)
53. Subversion (Amendment) (No. 2) Decree, 1972 (NRCD 131)
54. Courts (Amendment) Decree, 1972 (NRCD 101)
55. *CFAO v. Zacca* [1972] 1 GLR 366 at 393-94
56. Criminal Procedure Code (Amendment) Decree, 1972 (NRCD 121)
57. See e.g. note 52 above
58. Thus NRC Decrees 3, 4 and 10 merely continue in existence Commissions of Inquiry established under the 1969 Constitution by Constitutional Instruments
59. See NRC Decrees 54, 96 and 114
60. Act 372
61. The original list contained 39 items. Four and part of another were removed by the Limitation Decree, 1972 (NRCD 54), mentioned below. The Courts (Amendment) (No. 2) Decree, 1972 (NRCD 137) removed a further 10
62. [1972] 2 GLR 209
63. At 212
64. [1972] 2 GLR 469
65. At 481
66. Act 360
67. At 486-87
68. [1973] 1 GLR 268
69. Acts 71 and 334
70. At 269-70
71. At 270-71
72. [1973] 1 GLR 326
73. [1959] GLR 49
74. NLCD 84
75. The judgement says (at 332) that *Karimu v. Ghassoub,* CA 27 July 1970 (1970) CC 104, had ceased to have effect. Clearly this is an error for *Sarpong v. Atta Yaw* [1964] GLR 419. *Karimu v. Ghassoub* was the 1970 decision which held *Sarpong v. Atta Yaw* binding
76. [1973] 1 GLR 25
77. At 27
78. *In re Arthur* [1972] 1 GLR 435
79. *Agbemashior v. State Insurance Corporation* [1972] 1 GLR 65
80. Act 32
81. *Lynes Quashie-Idun v. Gbedemah* [1973] 1 GLR 191
82. The others were: *Attoh-Quarshie v. Okpote* [1973] 1 GLR 59; *Arthur v. The Republic* [1973] 1 GLR 205, mentioned below
83. NRCD 64
84. Act 366
85. NRCD 17
86. NRCD 32
87. NRCD 114
88. Prices and Incomes Board Decree, 1972 (NRCD 119)
89. Petroleum Products Decree, 1972 (NRCD 76)
90. Lands Commission Decree, 1972 (NRCD 24)
91. *Ibid*
92. State Proceedings Decree, 1972 (NRCD 59)
93. NRCD 95.
94. NRCD 132
95. Timber Operations (Government Participation) Decree, 1972 (NRCD 139)
96. NRCD 136
97. NRCD 90
98. The Subversion (Amendment) (No. 2) Decree, 1972 (NRCD 131) inserted 'cocoa' in this paragraph
99. NRCD 131 (above) deleted the word 'cocoa' from this paragraph
100. NRCD 131 (above) substituted for this paragraph the following: 'steals any drug, medicine, or pharmaceutical preparation, substance or material from a Government hospital, health post or clinic'
101. Price Control Decree, 1972 (NRCD 17)
102. Price Control (Amendment) Decree, 1972 (NRCD 39)
103. NRCD 44
104. Foreign Exchange (Amendment) Decree, 1972 (NRCD 69). The Foreign Exchange

(Amendment) (No. 2) Decree, 1972 (NRCD 79) removes a minor point of doubt
105. Criminal Code (Amendment) (No. 2) Decree, 1972 (NRCD 53)
106. NRCD 76
107. Suppression of Robbery Decree, 1972 (NRCD 11)
108. Criminal Code (Amendment) Decree, 1972 (NRCD 50)
109. Criminal Code (Amendment) (No. 2) Decree, 1972 (NRCD 53)
110. [1973] 1 GLR 205
111. LI 218
112. [1972] 2 GLR 469
113. At 480
114. At 486
115. [1972] 2 GLR 153
116. At 167
117. [1973] 1 GLR 393
118. At 415
119. At 412
120. *Kumah* v. *Ankoma* [1972] 2 GLR 134
121. *Owusu* v. *Kisiwa* [1972] 2 GLR 99 at 102
122. *Rhule* v. *Rhule* [1973] 1 GLR 41
123. [1972] 2 GLR 469 at 485
124. [1973] 1 GLR 258, discussed in a note at (1974) 11 UGLJ 97
125. Act 372
126. *Abu-Jaudeh* v. *Abu-Jaudeh* [1972] 2 GLR 444, emphasizes the difficulty of proving an acquisition of Ghanaian domicile
127. [1972] 1 GLR 413
128. NRCD 54
129. S. 30(3)
130. NRCD 96
131. See generally Kludze, 'The Modern Ghanaian Law of Mortgages' (1974) 11 UGLJ 1
132. *Id.* at 5–7
133. [1973] 1 GLR 152
134. Act 137
135. [1973] 1 GLR 176
136. At 185
137. [1973] 1 GLR 221
138. *Chokosi* v. *The Republic* [1973] 1 GLR 29
139. [1973] 1 GLR 335, discussed (1973) RGL 90
140. [1973] 1 GLR 249
141. [1972] 2 GLR 1
142. [1971] 1 GLR 238
143. (1879) 4 CPD 182
144. [1973] 1 GLR 268
145. [1973] 1 GLR 299, discussed in a symposium at (1973) 5 RGL 17
146. At 311

CHAPTER TWO

NIGERIA

C. O. Okonkwo and E. I. Nwogugu

CONSTITUTIONAL LAW

There was not much significant constitutional legislative development ir 1972.

PROFESSIONAL BODIES

The Professional Bodies (Special Provisions) Decree, No. 3 of 1972, amends the provisions of the existing legislation relating to the practice of some professions in Nigeria by Nigerians only. It vests in the Head of State power to permit the practice in Nigeria of any of the professions set out in the schedule to the decree by persons other than citizens of Nigeria. The professions affected are law, medicine, dentistry, midwifery and nursing, engineering, surveys, architecture, accountancy and any other technological or scientific discipline. The Decree also provides that the Head of the Federal Military Government may lay down conditions under which such persons may set up the practice of such professions.

IMMIGRATION

The Immigration (Amendment) Decree, No. 8 of 1972, makes fresh provisions with respect to the issue of visas or permits for entry into Nigeria. Foreigners wishing to enter Nigeria are now required to apply for visa or entry permit to the appropriate Nigerian diplomatic mission abroad. Heads of such missions are authorized under the Decree to issue visitors permits and certain specified classes of visa or permits. Where there is no Nigerian diplomatic mission in a country, applications are to be directed to a government performing consular functions for Nigeria in that country or if no such agreement exists, to such diplomatic mission as may be designated by the Federal Commissioner for External Affairs. All applications by persons seeking entry into Nigeria for the purpose of taking up employment must be referred to the Federal Ministry of Internal Affairs in Lagos.

STATUTORY CORPORATIONS

The Medical Research Council of Nigeria Decree, No. 1 of ·1972, established the Medical Research Council of Nigeria as a body corporate charged with the responsibility of advising the Nigerian Council on Science and Technology and through it the various governments in Nigeria on national science policy in respect of research and training in the medical sciences. The Council is to be one of the major Research Councils under the general umbrella of the Nigerian Council for science and technology.

The National Electric Power Authority Decree, No. 24 of 1972, establishes the National Electric Power Authority as a body corporate charged *inter alia* with the duty to generate or acquire supply of electricity and to provide bulk supply for distribution within or outside Nigeria. The new body is an amalgam of the former Electricity Corporation of Nigeria and the Niger Dam Authority which before the Decree controlled the Kainji Dam.

The Second All Africa Games Decree, No. 26 of 1972, established a body known as the Organizing Committee of the Second All-Africa Games as a body corporate. The Committee was given the power to make all necessary arrangements for the success of the Second All-Africa Games scheduled to take place in Lagos in January, 1973 and it was given the exclusive function of making arrangements for the manufacture, printing, publication and sale of any souvenirs connected with the games.

The Nigerian Mining Corporation Decree, No. 39 of 1972, set up the Nigerian Mining Corporation as a statutory corporation. The corporation is empowered to engage in prospecting for, mining and refining minerals of various kinds found in Nigeria with the exception of coal and petroleum.

In both the Midwest State and the Benue-Plateau State a State Marketing Board is created by the Midwestern Nigeria Marketing Board Edict, No. 1 of 1972, and the Marketing Board Edict, No. 8 of 1972, respectively. The Boards are *inter alia* to purchase or otherwise acquire produce within the respective States. Both States have also created state-owned newspapers through the Midwest Newspapers Corporation Edict, No. 18 of 1972, and the Benue-Plateau State Printing and Publishing Corporation Edict, No. 6 of 1972. The Midwest Government has also created a Rural Electricity Board under the Rural Electricity Board Edict, No. 6 of 1972. The Board is charged with the responsibility *inter alia* of establishing and managing electricity undertakings in those parts of the State where the Electricity Corporation of Nigeria (now NEPA) does not at present maintain any electricity undertakings or installations.

EDUCATION

The Head of State who is the Visitor to the two federal universities—Ibadan and Lagos—is given additional powers by the University of Lagos (Amendment) Decree, No. 12 of 1972, and the University of Ibadan (Amendment) Edict, No. 13 of 1972. Henceforth the Visitor is empowered to conduct visitation of the University or direct that such a visitation be conducted by such persons and in respect of such affairs of the University as he may direct. The visitation is to be ordered as often as circumstances may require not being less than once every year.

Under the amendment the power to appoint and remove the Chancellors and Vice-Chancellors of the Universities is also vested in the Visitor. A Vice-Chancellor is to be appointed or removed by the Visitor acting after consultations with the Council. This change replaced the old system whereby the Vice-Chancellor was appointed by the University Council. The Vice-Chancellors of the two Universities are now to hold office for four years in the first instance and shall be eligible for re-appointment for a second term of three years. Thereafter they are no longer eligible for appointment until at least four years have elapsed.

The Students Loans Board Decree, No. 25 of 1972, establishes the Students Loans Board as a body corporate with power to maintain and administer the Nigerian Universities Revolving Loan Scheme. Under the Decree, no person shall be entitled to a loan unless he is a student in, or has been accepted as a student of, a University or other approved institution of higher learning in Nigeria. The Decree provides for the method of repayment of loans granted and requires the Board to prepare a yearly estimate of its income and expenditure for the consideration and approval of the Federal Executive Council.

The Loans to Students (Recovery) Decree, No. 21 of 1972, provides for the recovery of loans from the emoluments of persons to whom such loans have been granted. It makes an employer answerable for deductions made from emoluments and prescribes a penalty in the event of failure by such employer to make such deductions or properly to account for same. The Decree also applies to the recovery of a loan from self-employed persons.

The school year for schools and colleges other than higher educational institutions has been altered by the School Year (Variation) Decree, No. 29 of 1972. Previously the school year began in January of each year and ended in November or December. Under the Decree, the school year is to begin in the month of September of each year and end in the month of June or July of the following year. The change-over took effect from 1973.

The Nigerian Educational Research Council Decree, No. 31 of 1972, established the Nigerian Educational Research Council. The Council is charged with responsibility to undertake, promote and co-ordinate educational research programmes of various kinds throughout Nigeria. The Council, unlike other similar Research Councils set up by the Federal Government, is to function independently of the Nigerian Council for Science and Technology.

The Petroleum Training Institute Decree, No. 37 of 1972, established the Petroleum Training Institute for training and research in the oil technology and the production of technicians and other skilled personnel required to run the oil industry.

FUNDAMENTAL RIGHTS

The question of the infringement of the individual's right to a fair hearing under s. 22(1) of the Constitution was raised in *Alhaji Audu Bida* v. *Commissioner of Revenue.*[1] In that case, the plaintiff claimed the sum of £24,317. 15s. 0d from the defendant as arrears of income tax due from the defendant from 1965 to 1970. In support of the claim, which was brought under s. 43 of the Personal Tax Law,[2] the plaintiff called one witness, an Inspector of Taxes in the plaintiff's office who tendered a certificate which, the witness said, was signed by the Commissioner of Revenue of the North Central State. This certificate was admitted under s. 43(3) of the Personal Tax Law which provides that:

'In any suit under subsection (1) the production of a certificate signed by any person duly authorized by the Commissioner giving the name and address of the defendant and the amount of tax due from him shall be sufficient evidence of the amount so due and sufficient authority for the court to give judgement for the said amount.'

The defendant in his statement of defence denied liability and maintained that he had always paid his due taxes. He also contended that 'the method prescribed by the Personal Tax Law for proof, namely s. 29(1) read with s. 43(3), is inconsistent with the Constitution of Nigeria, and to the extent of that inconsistency is void.' The trial judge held that the certificate was evidence that the amount set out therein was due from the defendant.

The defendant appealed to the Supreme Court on the ground *inter alia*, that the words 'sufficient evidence' and 'sufficient authority' in s. 43(3) of the Law meant that the production of the certificate was conclusive evidence in itself and that there was nothing the defendant could do to rebut it. He was therefore unable to put forward his case and his right to a fair hearing under s. 22(1) of the Constitution was thereby infringed. The Court held that s. 43(3) of the Law made the certificate merely *prima facie* evidence, that is, 'enough evidence, if the defendant does not adduce evidence to rebut it, for the court to give judgement for the plaintiff.' It does not make the certificate conclusive evidence by estopping the defendant from calling evidence. The subsection, therefore, does not, in the court's opinion, infringe the requirement of a fair hearing laid down by s. 22(1) of the Constitution.

The extent to which a court is precluded from enquiring into the validity of any instrument made by or under a Decree or an Edict was examined by the Supreme Court in *Chief Adejumo* v. *Colonel Mobolaji Johnson (Military Governor of Lagos State).*[3] Sometime in 1969, pursuant to the provisions of s. 4(1) of the Investigation of Assets (Public Officers and other Persons) Decree, No. 37 of 1968, the respondent set up a Commission of Enquiry to enquire into the assets of some public officers including one Adenrele Adejumo, the appellant's son. Following the report of the enquiry, the respondent made an Order[4] by virtue of the powers conferred on him and in particular by virtue of s. 8(3) of Decree No. 37 of 1968 implementing some of the recommendations of the Commission. The Order *inter alia*, forfeited several real estate said to belong to Adenrele Adejumo which became vested in the Military Governor of Lagos State. Pursuant to the Order the property of the appellant was seized and confiscated to the State. He then commenced this proceeding by way of an order of *certiorari* to challenge the validity of the Order.

The trial judge refused to grant the relief sought by the appellant and he appealed to the Supreme Court. Counsel for the respondent filed a preliminary objection notice to the effect that the Supreme Court had no jurisdiction to hear or determine the appeal and that any decision of the court granting the relief sought by the appellant shall be null and void. The objection was based on the provisions of s. 1 of the Federal Military

Government (Supremacy and Enforcement of Powers) Decree, No. 28 of 1970. In support of the objection, it was urged that the implication of the Constitution (Suspension and Modification) Decree, No. 1 of 1966, was to make the provisions of a Decree or an Edict (in so far as such provisions of the Edict are not inconsistent with a Decree) override the provisions of the Federal Constitution, 1963. S. 6 of the 1966 Decree was aimed at ensuring that any Decree or Edict cannot be questioned in a court of law. Some doubts as to the ambit of s. 6 were cleared by Decree No. 28 of 1970. The Order, it was argued, was administrative in nature and therefore was protected by the provisions of Decree No. 28.

The appellant's main contention was that the Order was invalid *per se* for being made in excess of jurisdiction or in circumstances in which the respondent was incompetent to make it under Decree No. 28 of 1970 the definition section of which provides that:

'The reference to any Decree or Edict includes a reference to any Instrument made by or under such Decree or Edict.'

It was argued that the Order was not covered by this provision because it was not made by or under the relevant Edict. Reliance was placed on dicta in the celebrated case of *Anisminic Ltd* v. *Foreign Compensation Commission,*[5] to the effect that where an Order sought to be challenged was made in excess of jurisdiction, it would not enjoy the protection of any preclusive legislation forbidding a judicial review of its provisions. In rejecting counsel's argument the court pointed out that in the *Anisminic's case,*

'. . . the House of Lords was concerned with the interpretation of a particular statutory provision peculiarly worded and probably equally peculiarly oriented.'[6]

The court was of the opinion that the kernel of the issue was the meaning and effect of Decree No. 28 of 1970. It had no doubt as to the purport of the Decree which is as follows:

'The first part of the Decree . . . establishes and otherwise confirms the already existing ouster of the jurisdiction of courts of law in respect of a Decree or an Edict or other cognate acts in law comprehended by the definition section, that is to say s. 1(3). With respect to the second part of Decree No. 28 of 1970 even if it be arguable and indeed argued that that part assumes the possibility of a court assuming jurisdiction with respect to one or the other of the matters envisaged on the ground of manifest excess or incompetence or other type of invalidity (and we make no pronouncement on this point), that part declares (and this is the word used and presumably deliberately so used) any such pronouncement in exercise of such assumed jurisdiction and having the tendencies therein described to be null and void.'[7]

Applying this interpretation the court held that it could not hear the appeal. It was the view of the court that—

'By virtue of the provisions of Decree No. 28 of 1970 one can only attack an Edict if it is inconsistent with a Decree and as by virtue of s. 1(3) of Decree No. 28 of 1970 an instrument made by or under an Edict is given the same protection as the Edict under which the instrument is made, the same principle must apply to the instrument as would apply to the Edict itself.'[8]

Consequently, since the Order was made under an Edict it was protected by the provisions of Decree No. 28 of 1970.

ADMINISTRATIVE LAW

The Local Government (Transfer of Functions) (Amendment) Edict, No. 20 of 1972 (Midwestern State), transferred to the Midwestern State Local Government Service Board the functions of the appointment, promotion, discipline and transfer of the junior staff of local government bodies in the State. These functions were formerly performed by the Local Government Councils and Joint Boards.

In the Western State the Local Government Reform (Interim Provisions) Edict, No. 18 of 1972, made provisions in respect of local government reform in the State. It established a new one-tier Local Government Council system in place of the existing three tier local government council system. Consequently the previous 114 local government councils and provisional authorities in the State were replaced with only thirty-nine Local Government Councils. This change-over took effect from 1 April, 1973. The Edict also dealt with incidental matters including the appointment of Committees and staff for Local Government Councils and the power to give directions to such Councils.

The South-Eastern State Development Edict, No. 7 of 1972, established for that State a Development Administration System. The system involves community development and the aim as set out in s. 42 of the Edict is as follows:

'The fundamental aim of community development is the purposeful removal of obstacles to the rational utilization of such of the natural resources of a community as are capable of exploitation by the common effort of its inhabitants, conditioned by the financial resources at its disposal including such Government assistance, in cash or in kind or both, as the Military Governor, with the approval of the Executive Council may deem necessary, having regard to the nature, complexity or extent of a community project.

By community action through the Development Administration system the community shall participate directly or indirectly in the several areas of Government activity for its economic and social progress and the citizen shall become increasingly aware and associated with the implementation of the policy and understand the working of the established machinery of the Government.'

The basic territorial unit of the development administration is the Development area. This unit consists of a number of villages which have a natural social nexus and occupy contiguous territories and which, in the opinion of the Military Governor, may effectively be developed as a unit for the purposes of the Edict. There are 167 Development Areas, 15 Development Council Areas and 42 County Development Areas in the State. The State Military Governor may, by instrument published in the Gazette, establish an Area Development Committee in every Development Area, an Urban Development Committee in every Urban Development Area, and a County Development Council in every County Development Area. The chairman of a Council or Committee shall be selected annually from among their own number by the councillors and committee men while a Clan head shall be appointed President of a Development Council by the Military Governor.

The functions of a Development Council or an Area Development Committee may cover one or more of the following subjects—agriculture, animals, building and other structures, forestry, liquor, markets, public health, registration of persons, roads, street, waterways and public order.

Under the Edict, the office of the Co-ordinator of Development Administration is created. All officers of the Development Administration shall be responsible, in the exercise of their functions, to the Co-ordinator and through him to the Military Governor. The Co-ordinator is also the Chairman of the Central Development Committee based at the State headquarters. The Committee is to 'review the development progress, decide on priorities, resolve difficulties that may have arisen in the execution of development activities and serve as a forum for discussion and exchange of experience.'[9]

The Market Authorities (Establishment) Edict, 1971[10] of the East Central State established in each of the three largest urban areas of the State—Aba, Enugu and Onitsha—a Market Authority which is a body corporate. A market authority is charged with responsibility for the development, construction and management of markets and motor parks in its area of authority.

In the North-Eastern State the Bauchi Local Authority (Modification of Native Law and Custom Relating to the Selection of the Emir Bauchi) Order, 1972[11] which came into force on 21 February, 1972 modifies the Bauchi native law and custom relating to the selection of a person to be the Emir of Bauchi. Under the Order, an emir is to be appointed by an electoral college consisting of (a) the Senior Councillor and the Portfolio Councillors of the Bauchi Local Authority; (b) the five traditional title holders, i.e. (i) Galadima (ii) Madaki (iii) Sarkin Yaki (iv) Wambai (v) Ajiya, and (c) the Chief Imam of Bauchi.

The chairman of the electoral college is to be elected by members of the college from among themselves. The quorum for a meeting is two-thirds of the membership. The Order also deals with the procedure for nomination of candidates and election.

LEGAL SYSTEM

Under the Legal Practitioners (Amendment) Decree, No. 36 of 1972 the Supreme Court was included in the list of courts in which the right of audience by legal practitioners may be prohibited or restricted. Following this Decree, the Chief Justice of Nigeria made the Supreme Court Practice and Procedure Order, 1972.[12] The order provides that except in special cases where the Supreme Court gives its permission in writing, a legal practitioner of less than seven years' standing at the Bar may not appear in any cause or matter before the Supreme Court except as a junior to a legal practitioner of at least seven years' standing at the Bar. The order also makes it obligatory for counsel or their juniors to be present in the Supreme Court whenever a reserved judgement is to be delivered. Failure to observe this rule will be regarded as an act of disrespect to the court.

The Constitution (Amendment) Decree, No. 5 of 1972, amends s. 112 and s. 113 of the Constitution of the Federation relating to the appointment and removal of the Justices of the Supreme Court of Nigeria. Under the Decree, the Chief Justice of Nigeria shall be appointed by the Head of the Federal Military Government while the justices of the Court shall be appointed by the Supreme Military Council, acting after consultation with the Advisory Judicial Committee. The Chief Justice of Nigeria may be removed from his office or appointment by the Head of the Federal Military Government and a Justice of the Supreme Court may be removed from his office or appointment by the Supreme Military Council acting after consultation with the Advisory Judicial Committee.

In the Midwestern State, the Magistrates' Courts (Amendment) Edict, No. 26 of 1972, created new categories of Magistrates for the State—Chief Magistrate, Senior Magistrates Grade I, Senior Magistrates Grade II and Magistrates.

CONTRACT

In *Alhaji Mohammadu Inuwa Jajira* v. *Northern Brewery Co Ltd,*[13] the High Court—Kano (Jones, S.P., and Wali, Ag. J.) dealt with the construction of an agreement of which it said: 'We have studied this agreement. It is of a type we have not seen before . . .' The essence of the agreement was indeed of the common type whereby an employer advances money to an employee for the purchase of a vehicle which advance is repayable by instalmental deductions from the employee's salary.

The agreement in this case was made between an employee, the plaintiff borrower, and his employer, the defendant Company. The document stated that the borrower had applied for 'an advance' of £245 to buy a Vespa Scooter, that the company shall grant 'a loan' to the borrower repayable in 36 equal monthly instalments of a fixed sum; that so long as the loan remained unpaid the borrower shall not sell, assign, pledge, charge or part with possession of the scooter. There were conditions about the borrower insuring and keeping it in good condition and allowing the company access to it for inspection. There was a provision that until full repayment of the loan with interest the scooter would remain the property of the company which also had a right to terminate the agreement and retake possession of the scooter if the borrower defaulted in complying with any of the terms of the agreement.

While the plaintiff was remanded in custody on a criminal charge he asked a friend to take charge of the scooter for him but the company took possession of it. At that time the plaintiff had paid two instalments and none was outstanding. When he was released from custody the defendant terminated his appointment and refused to give him back the scooter. The plaintiff then sued to recover it. The writ called the agreement a hire purchase agreement but the statement of claim called it an agreement for a loan to purchase a scooter. .

The trial judge found that the defendant company purchased the scooter and remained owner of it under the agreement while the plaintiff remained borrower of the scooter until complete repayment; that the defendant seized the scooter by virtue of the clause in the agreement empowering it to do so if the plaintiff parted with possession of it. He found also that the transaction was conditional on the continued employment of the plaintiff by the defendant because the repayments were due out of salary (although this was not stated in the agreement). He held therefore that the defendant company was right in taking possession but he did not state what the nature of the agreement was, i.e. whether it was one of hire purchase or of loan.

On appeal, the Appeal Court first of all embarked on an examination of the nature of the agreement pointing out that 'it is the real transaction, the substantive transaction, which is to be looked at rather than the form of the document in which it is embodied.' It held that the transaction was not a hire purchase agreement because there was no bailment of the scooter since a bailment contemplates the return of the goods. On the contrary, 'the real transaction was a loan of (money) upon the security of the Vespa which plaintiff bought with the money lent.' The defendant's retaking possession of the scooter was a breach of the agreement 'for while it is true that they had the property in the Vespa, it is a necessary implication of . . . the agreement that so long as plaintiff complied with the agreement, he should have possession of the Vespa . . .' His asking a friend to look after the scooter while he was in custody was not a breach of the term forbidding him to part with possession.

Furthermore, although the agreement provided that until repayment, the scooter 'shall remain' the property of the defendant, the Court refused to give the word 'remain' its normal meaning 'in view of the total nature' of the transaction. It was the plaintiff who purchased the scooter with money given to him as a loan and the property in it would be his but for the agreement. Property in it was given to the company only by the agreement and 'it could not therefore "remain" with the company because it had not been with the company before.' It was the property of the company only so long as the agreement was in existence. The agreement could terminate either by completion of all its terms or by fundamental breach. The defendant in taking possession of the scooter committed a fundamental breach. 'With that breach, their property in the Vespa ceased. On the evidence, we cannot see that any act of defendant company was thereafter necessary to give plaintiff the property in the Vespa.' The plaintiff was therefore held entitled to the Vespa or its value assessed at £245 which was the amount of the loan.

No reduction for depreciation was made because as the Court held there was no evidence on which to base an assessment of depreciation. There being no counterclaim for the outstanding balance of the loan, no order for repayment was made.

In *George Chargoury* v. *M. Adebayo*,[14] the High Court of Lagos State (Taylor, C.J.) considered the question whether a punter who signed an agreement on a coupon to the effect that—

'I have read and agreed (if this coupon is accepted by you) to the Rules and Conditions. I am over 21.'

could be heard to say that he did not in fact read the Rules and Conditions because none were shown to him. Distinguishing the Railway ticket cases the learned Chief Justice held that in the absence of fraud or misrepresentation the punter could not retract the statement and it made no difference that he did not read the Rules and Conditions.

One of the many contractual problems that arose after the civil war concerned claims under life insurance policies. Owing to severance of normal communications, many people in the three Eastern States were unable to pay the annual premiums due on their life policies during the war years. After the war, many of these people claimed the surrender value of their policies but in some cases the question arose as to whether the policies had lapsed.

One such case was *Anunike* v. *Crusader Insurance Company (Nigeria) Ltd.*[15] After the war the plaintiff who had not paid any premiums on his life policy for the three war years 1967, 1968 and 1969 demanded the surrender value of his policy. The defendant company wrote to him, *inter alia,* as follows:

'When a policy has been in force for two years, it acquires a surrender value against which unpaid premiums are advanced in accordance with the non-forfeiture regulations of your policy, condition No. 2. When the surrender value is exhausted the policy automatically lapses.'

Since the unpaid premiums exceeded the paid premiums the defendant refused to pay him anything.

In an action by the plaintiff for a declaration that the application of condition 2 of the Policy was harsh, unconscionable and contrary to the public interest and that he was entitled to the surrender value of the policy the High Court Onitsha (Oputa, J.) held that since non-payment of the premiums for the war years was due to circumstances beyond the plaintiff's control and which were not in the contemplation of the parties, it would be harsh, unconscionable and inequitable to apply condition 2 of the policy to him. He was therefore held entitled to the surrender value.

In *The Lion of Africa Insurance Company Ltd* v. *Stella Anuluoha,*[16] the Supreme Court held that under s. 6(1)(*b*) of the Motor Vehicles (Third Party Insurance) Act (Cap. 126) it is only persons being carried for hire or reward who are required to be covered by a policy of insurance and that a person being given a lift in a private car, even if he is awarded damages against his host cannot require it to be satisfied by his host's Insurance Company under s. 10(1) of the Act.

It was held in *Bamidele* v. *The Nigerian General Insurance Co Ltd,*[17] that although in a proper case an Insurance Company will be liable if its agent misappropriates a premium paid to him by a proposer, this will not be so where there is collusion between the agent and the proposer and the premium was not paid to the company. It was held also that an accident policy is vitiated for non-disclosure of a material fact if the proposer's occupation is falsely stated to be that of green-grocer and horticulturist instead of a daily paid labourer. 'At least the fact that the deceased (proposer) was a dialy paid labourer and not a horticulturist and greengrocer could have influenced the computation of the premium.'

TORT

The Fatal Accidents Law (Amendment) Edict, No. 2 of 1972, of the Benue-Plateau State has amended the Fatal Accidents Law (Cap. 42) to provide for a uniform standard of assessment of damages. The definition of immediate family in s. 2(c) which includes, persons entitled to the award of *diya* prescribed by Moslem law for involuntary homicide is now replaced by a provision which covers persons entitled to share in the estate of the deceased person under Moslem law. S. 7(1) of the principal law has been repealed and replaced by a new section. Whereas under the old law the principles applicable to assessment of damages differed according to whether the deceased was, or was not subject to native law and custom (principles of customary law applied in assessing damages in the case of the former), under the amendment the method of assessment is the same for everyone but native law and custom if applicable to the deceased is relevant only in deciding which members of the immediate family of the deceased are entitled to share in the damages and in apportioning the shares among them.

In the tort of defamation qualified privilege does not apply to a statement uttered before an illegal court. So where the defendant alleged before a village gathering convened to try an issue of theft, that the plaintiff stole his cocoyams, it was held that the statement was not privileged.[18]

In *Daniel Ibeanu* v. *Josiah Uba*,[19] Egbuna, J., considered the correct procedure where defamatory words are spoken in a vernacular language. The defendant spoke words in the Ibo language which in English meant:

'Josiah, Josiah, you brought the thieves with whom you stole my goat and you have now come to ask me.'

The record of proceedings contained only the English version of the statement. The plaintiff successfully sued the defendant in the Magistrate Court for defamation. On appeal, it was held, allowing the appeal, that the acual words spoken by the defendant in Ibo language should have been stated in evidence as he said it and then an English translation of it furnished by an interpreter sworn as a witness. In the circumstances there was no proof of the actual words spoken by the defendant.

COMMERCIAL LAW

The most important piece of legislation in the field of commercial law was the Nigerian Enterprises Promotion Decree, No. 4 of 1972. The main objective of the Decree is to place the economy of the country in the hands of Nigerians by forbidding aliens from undertaking or participating in certain specified businesses and providing for increased Nigerian participation in others.

The Decree has two schedules. The first schedule contains a list of enterprises which are exclusively reserved for Nigerian citizens or associations.[20] The list includes such enterprises as advertising agencies and public relations business, all aspects of pool betting business and lotteries, bread and cake making, municipal bus services and taxis, retail trade (except within departmental stores and supermarkets) and tyre retreading.

The second schedule contains a list of enterprises which are partially barred to aliens. This list includes beer brewing, boat building, construction industries, furniture making, manufacture of bicycles, printing of books, shipping, travel agencies and wholesale distribution.

Aliens are forbidden to be owners of part-owners of any business in schedule 2 if the paid-up share capital of the business does not exceed ₦400,000.00 or the turnover does not exceed ₦1,000,000.00. If the paid-up share capital or turnover exceeds the above sums, then there must be not less than 40% equity participation of Nigerian citizens or associations in the business.

The Decree sets up a body known as the Nigerian Enterprises Promotion Board which has power 'to advance and develop the promotion of enterprises in which citizens of Nigeria shall participate fully and play a dominant role.'[21] It also has power to advise the Federal Commissioner for Industries on policy guidelines for the promotion of Nigerian enterprises. The Decree also sets up in each State a Nigerian Enterprises Promotion Committee with the function of assisting and advising the Board on the implementation of the Decree and of ensuring that the provisions of the Decree are complied with by aliens carrying on business in the State.

There are heavy penalties for any one who contravenes the provisions of the Decree and, in particular, for anyone who acts as a front or purports to be the owner or part-owner of a business in order to defeat the object of the Decree.[22]

31 March, 1974 was fixed as the date on which all existing businesses must conform with the provisions of the Decree but there have been two extensions for periods of six months each. Under the Decree aliens were not compelled to sell their businesses to Nigerians. They could either do that or wind them up. Not surprisingly there were some efforts to evade the provisions of the Decree but the vigilance of the Nigerian press paid dividends. The objective of the Decree appears to have been satisfactorily achieved. Various aspects of the nation's economy are now in the hands of Nigerian citizens. To achieve 40% equity participation by Nigerian citizens in schedule 2 enterprises the share capital or turnover of which exceeds the stipulated sums numerous, companies made their shares available to the public on the stock market. And in nearly every case the issue was over-subscribed.

One might criticize the decree for failing to provide that shares in such businesses must be offered to the public and not sold privately. For it seems that a few individuals were able to acquire very large shares in some companies which sold their shares privately—investment opportunities which if available to the eager Nigerian investing public would have made for more egalitarianism.

In its effort to wipe out corruption, the Federal Military Government, having discovered that certain persons and organizations did acquire shares in the Nigerian Pools Company Limited by dubious and irregular means and without paying therefor, passed the Nigerian Pools Company Limited (Take-Over) Decree, No. 20 of 1972, which forfeited all the shares and vested them in the Government free of all encumbrances. The names of affected shareholders were struck off the register of members and the name of the Federal Military Government substituted therefor. Aggrieved persons are forbidden to institute legal proceedings in respect of anything done under the decree; neither could a court enquire into whether the human rights provisions of the Constitution have been violated as a result of the forfeiture of the shares.

The Companies (Amendment) Decree, No. 32 of 1972, now places in the priority list of debts payable by a company in winding up, all outstanding contributions payable to the National Provident Fund in respect of a worker, being contributions outstanding for not more than 12 months immediately before the winding up.

The Banking (Amendment) Decree, No. 45 of 1972, has amended the Banking Decree, No. 1 of 1969, with respect to the eligibility of a company to carry on banking business in Nigeria. Under the amendment, no banking business can be carried on in Nigeria except by a company incorporated in Nigeria which has a valid licence granted by the Federal Commissioner for Finance authorizing it to do so, and the objects of which (as set out in the memorandum of association) have been duly approved by the Commissioner before its incorporation. The Decree also contains provisions forbidding bank managers from being interested, directly or indirectly, in any advance, loan or credit facility without declaring to the bank the nature of their interest and prescribes other safeguards to prevent abuse of office by bank managers.

The Price Control Regulations, 1972,[23] which are made under the Price Control Decree, 1970, make it compulsory for the seller of any price-controlled commodity to display the price of that commodity in such a manner as to be clearly visible to any prospective buyer thereof. There are similar conditions relating to the sale of books and wholesale transactions and penalties are provided for breach of the Regulations.

There was not much commercial legislation in the States. In the East Central State, the Registration of Business Premises Edict, No. 14 of 1972, provides for the registration of premises on which any company, firm or individual carries on business in the State. Premises on which a Government or its agency carries on business in the State are among those exempted from being registered.

COMPANIES

In *Starcola (Nigeria) Ltd* v. *Madam Taibatu Adeniji and ors,*[24] the applicants sought a declaration *inter alia,* that they were entitled to be subscribers of the memorandum of association of the respondent company and a consequential order to rectify the Company's register of members so as to include their names. Their case was that they had agreed with the second respondent to promote a new company (the first respondent) and to subscribe to its memorandum of association and be allotted shares in the company; that the second respondent registered the company and, with one other person, subscribed to the memorandum of association without informing the applicants. There was uncontradicted evidence that the applicants made cash contributions towards the promotion of the company.

The trial judge held that as the applicants were promoters of the company they were entitled to be subscribers of the memorandum of association and that by virtue of s. 26(1) of the Companies Decree, No. 70 of 1968, they were deemed to be members of the company. He therefore ordered that the register of members be rectified under s. 115 to include their names.

On appeal to the Supreme Court it was held that the learned trial judge was wrong in holding that s. 26(1) applied to the case. 'What s. 26(1) is dealing with is a subscriber to the memorandum and it provides that such person automatically becomes a member of the company and must be entered in the register accordingly. S. 26(1) does not deal with a person, if there be such, who is entitled to be a subscriber.' As the applicants did not in fact subscribe to the memorandum of association, s. 26(1) had no application to them.

Dealing with rectification of a register of members under s. 115 so as to include a person as a member, the court held that there must be an agreement to allot to such a person a specified number of shares whether fully paid up or not, which there was not in the instant case. The appeal was allowed and the case was sent back for re-trial by another judge.

In *The Matter of Paper Conversion Co (Nigeria) Ltd* v. *In the Matter of Companies Decree, 1968 re Bentworth Finance (Nigeria) Ltd,*[25] the High Court of Lagos State (Savage, J.), considered whether a company could be wound up on a petition in respect of a disputed debt. The petitioner had sued the company for a sum which included the amount of the debt and then presented the petition for winding-up while the action was still pending. The learned judge held that 'a winding-up order will not be made on a petition in respect of a debt which is *bona fide* disputed by the company, at any rate where there is no evidence that the company is insolvent.' Considering the fact that great damage might be done to a solvent company by a winding-up petition in respect of a debt which the company is able and willing to pay if established, but which is *bona fide* disputed, the learned judge made an order restraining the petitioner from taking any further proceedings on the petition whether by advertisement or otherwise.

And in *In the Matter of Italcom (Western Nigeria) Ltd,* and *In the Matter of the Companies Decree 1968,*[26] the High Court of Lagos State (Odesanya, J.) following English decisions held that a winding-up order will not be made on the petition of a shareholder whose shares are fully paid unless he shows a sufficient interest, i.e. that the company is solvent and that after payment of its debts and liabilities there will remain surplus assets for distribution among the shareholders. Therefore the petitioner in the instant case was held to have no *locus standi* because his petition alleged that the company was insolvent and an injunction was granted restraining him from advertising the petition.

TRADE MARKS

The question when is a trade mark deemed to be 'calculated to deceive' under s. 25 of the Trade Marks Act[27] was considered by the Supreme Court in *Bell Sons and Co* v. *Godwin Aka.*[28] The applicants applied for registration of a trade mark for their product, castor oil. The objectors opposed the application on the ground that it so resembled their registered trade mark for the same product, castor oil, as to be calculated to deceive. Both marks contained 'the same words expressed to be applicable to and descriptive of castor oil, the same colour combination and orientation of design.' The only difference was that the objectors' trade mark contained the letter 'B' in black colour while that of the applicant contained the letter 'A' in red colour, both letters being of the same size and character.

The trial judge, relying on minor differences, such as that the letters 'A' and 'B' are different in shape, held that the trade marks were not similar. On appeal, the Supreme Court held that the trial judge paid 'little attention to the possibility of deception at which the law strikes.' A trade mark 'is to be deemed "calculated to deceive" when by the representation which it presents, a customer, whether literate or not, going only by his recollection of an already registered trade mark, is not unlikely to mistake one for the other. Whether a mark is potentially capable of being so mistaken for another one is a question of fact to be decided after a comparison of one with the other . . .'[29] This a salutary decision in a country where many people are still illiterate.

In another trade mark case,[30] the Supreme Court held that where a plaintiff seeks to have the defendant's registered trade mark expunged from the register on the ground that it is identical with his own registered trade mark and it appears that the defendant had used the trade mark for many years and acquired a good deal of reputation in the same market, in circumstances which show that the plaintiff openly acquiesced in the concurrent use of the identical trade mark, he will be deemed to have surrendered his right to question the user, for it would be unjust to ask the defendant to stop using the mark.

BANKING

Negligence and the standard of care required of a banker were considered in *United Nigeria Insurance Co* v. *Muslim Bank (West Africa) Ltd.*[31] A customer opened a savings account at the defendant bank in the name of O.O. with an initial deposit of three pounds. Two days later he stole and paid into this account a crossed cheque for £550 drawn by the plaintiff's in favour of the real O.O. and marked 'Not negotiable—A/c Payee Only'—with a forged endorsement purporting to have been made by the real O.O. The defendants having collected the cheque from the plaintiff's bank, the customer withdrew part of the money. In an action by the plaintiffs against the defendants for negligence, the trial judge held that the defendants were not negligent. On appeal, the Supreme Court held that the conduct of the defendants fell below what was expected of a reasonable banker for they were 'negligent in not obtaining satisfactory references when opening the savings account (for O.O.) or when the latter came to deposit the cheque for £550 two days later especially as they had failed to make an initial inquiry about the prospective customer.'[32]

REVENUE LAW

Two Decrees dealing with taxation are worthy of attention. The Finance

(Miscellaneous Taxation Provisions) Decree, No. 47 of 1972 amends the Companies Income Tax Act, 1961, and allows a deduction for loss incurred by a company in a year of assessment to be allowed from profits made in a subsequent year. It introduces new rates of taxation on companies profits, (i.e. 40% for the first ₦10,000.00 of the profits and 45% for the profits in excess of that sum); abolishes deduction of tax by companies from dividends payable to shareholders; brings stocks and shares within the provisions of the Capital Gains Tax Decree, 1967; and abolishes the Super Tax Decree, 1967.

The Income Tax (Armed Forces and Other Persons) (Special Provisions) Decree, No. 51 of 1972 deals with the taxation of the income of members of the armed forces, persons employed in the Nigerian Foreign Service and with taxation of Nigerian pensions and dividends payable overseas. The taxes are collected by the Federal Board of Inland Revenue which pays them into the Consolidated Revenue Fund of the Federation. The Government credits an equivalent sum of money to the Distributable Pool Account for distribution among the States.

LABOUR LAW

In *P. Z. and Co Ltd* v. *Ogedengbe*,[33] the Supreme Court held that where a contract of employment does not stipulate the length of notice required for termination, the employee is entitled to reasonable notice having regard to his length of service and his position in the employment. So where the plaintiff who had worked for over eight years and had risen to the rank of shopkeeper had his employment terminated with one month's salary in lieu of notice, it was held that the trial judge was right in holding that three months' notice was reasonable in the circumstances.

And in *Lilian Ajiboye* v. *Dresser Nigeria Ltd*,[34] where the plaintiff was employed as a secretary typist and was earning £100 a month at the time her appointment was terminated, Adefarasin, J., held that owing to the temporary nature of her appointment a month's notice was reasonable in the circumstances.

CRIMINAL LAW

The defence of obedience to superior orders is one on which there is a dearth of case law in Nigeria. This defence was considered by the Supreme Court in *The State* v. *Pius Nwaoga*.[35] During the civil war the accused who was an officer in the 'biafran army' was ordered by his superior officer to lead two other officers behind the federal lines near Enugu and identify the deceased to those officers who were to kill him. The reason for the mission, as was alleged by his superior officer, was that the deceased who was formerly a 'biafran' soldier was given a substantial sum of money to reopen a hotel in Enugu for the benefit of members of 'biafra organization of freedom fighters' and that he diverted the money to the operation of his contract business in Enugu which was then in the hands of Federal troops. The accused complied with the orders and was subsequently charged with murder after the civil war. He pleaded obedience to superior orders. Rejecting this defence the trial judge said:

'In the case before me the order to eliminate the deceased was given by an officer of an illegal regime; his orders therefore are necessarily unlawful and obedience to them involves a violation of the law and the defence of superior orders is untenable.'

On appeal, the Supreme Court, while it did not 'necessarily disagree with the conclusions reached by the learned trial judge' preferred to uphold the conviction on the ground that as the accused went into Federal territory in plain clothes appearing to be a member of the peaceful private population and committed an offence therein, he was liable to punishment like any other civilian.[36]

In another case, *Ededey* v. *The State*,[37] the question of obedience to superior orders, was referred to indirectly on the question whether certain witnesses were accomplices. A few months after the end of the civil war, money belonging to the wife of the accused was stolen at Aba in the East Central State. He, being the acting Chief Superintendent of Police in charge of Aba, ordered the Mobile Police force under him to go into a looting spree in the town, with himself participating. He was charged *inter alia,* with robbery and stealing and was convicted. On appeal to the Supreme Court it was argued that certain witnesses who testified for the prosecution and who were subordinate officers acting under and obeying the instructions of the accused should have been treated as accomplices whose evidene ought to have been corroborated.

The Supreme Court, having held that neither s. 7(*b*) nor s. 10 of the Criminal Code applied to them, stated that 'rather the conditions operating in the area of the country concerned at the material time taking into consideration the actual acts or performances of those witnesses seem to justify the application to them of the provisions of s. 32(*b*) of the Criminal Code.' The secton exculpates a person which he is bound by law to obey, '*unless the order is manifestly unlawful*'.

It is submitted with respect that the subordinate police officers could not have been protected by s. 32(*b*) if they had been charged jointly with the accused for the order was manifestly unlawful. Indeed nothing could be more unlawful to a police officer than an order to pillage and plunder the very citizens he is charged with the duty to protect, in order to recoup a loss sustained by the superior officer's wife—conduct which the trial judge described as 'the pinnacle of piracy and a very grave official scandal'.[38]

The defence of *bona fide* claim of right contained in s. 23 of the Criminal Code is frequently raised in cases in which malicious damage to property is charged. In rural communities, where two people or groups are asserting rival claims to land, it is usual for one party or group to destroy crops planted by the other on the land in an honest assertion of a claim to the land. S. 23 provides as follows:

'A person is not criminally responsible, as for an offence relating to property, for an act done or omitted to be done by him with respect to any property in the exercise of an honest claim of right and without intention to defraud'.

This provision does not contain any requirement of reasonableness but Nigerian courts have sought to import this requirement into the section, holding that if the defendant's conduct in destroying property on land is unreasonable, the defence will not avail him.[39] A recent example of this attitude is *Commissioner of Police* v. *Adokiye Okpaku,*[40] the facts of which were said by the Chief Justice of the Rivers State to be 'commonplace, unfortunately, in the district'. For several years there had been a longstanding dispute over a piece of land between the Okari family and the Okpaku family. A series of civil suits in the Native Court and Magistrate Court ended in favour of the Okpaku family. Members of the Okari family, the unsuccessful contestants, subsequently built a house on the land. Members of the Okpaku family partially destroyed the house and were charged with malicious damage to property. Their defence of *bona fide* claim of right was upheld by the magistrate.

On appeal by the prosecutor, the High Court of the Rivers State (Holden, C.J.) while accepting that the 'respondent had a sincere claim of right made in good faith' held nonetheless that the defence of claim of right failed because the conduct of the respondents in partially destroying a completed building was unreasonable. Distinguishing *Ejike* v. *Inspector General of Police,*[41] in which it was held that destruction of 526 blocks on disputed land was reasonable, the learned Chief Justice said:

'. . . The destruction of cement blocks could be said to represent the simplest way of preventing the building of a house where it should not be built. The destruction of a completed building, roofed and fitted with doors and windows, cannot in my view be considered a reasonable way in which to prevent unauthorized occupation of the land. The occupation has taken place and is an established fact. Legal means are therefore the only means available to bring the occupation to an end.'

This decision may be criticized in two respects. First, it was wrong to introduce the element of reasonableness which is not contained in s. 23.[42] Second, the learned Chief Justice did not consider whether the disputed land having been adjudicated to the respondents, the house itself could be said to belong to them on the principle *'quicquid plantatur solo, solo cedit.*[43] In *Ukaegbu* v. *Commissioner of Police,*[44] Aniagolu, J., dealing with the defence in s. 23, rightly observed that:

'. . . the element of reasonableness would not come into a situation in which the ownership of the land in dispute had been declared to be in the prisoner, for in that case the ownership of the fixtures on the land remain vested in him. He could destroy the entire thing at will.'[45]

CRIMINAL PROCEDURE

S. 368(3) of the Criminal Procedure Act (Cap. 43) provides that a person convicted of a capital offence shall not be sentenced to death if in the opinion of the court he has not attained the age of seventeen years. In *R* v. *Bangaza,*[46] the Federal Supreme Court held that the time for determining the age of the accused was the time of conviction and not the time when the offence was committed. This resulted in the conviction of the appellants in 1959 for murder committed in 1950 when they were quite below the age of seventeen. This decision was not received without criticism and in fact the Federal Supreme Court itself in *R* v. *Bangaza* did suggest an amendment of the section. The East Central State has now amended s. 368(3) of its Criminal Procedure Law (Cap. 31) to override the decision in *R* v. *Bangaza*. The Criminal Procedure Law (Amendment) Edict, No. 22 of 1972, now provides that the sentence of death shall not be passed on a person who has not attained the age of seventeen years 'at the time the offence was committed'.[47]

Where an accused person pleaded guilty to a charge and the prosecutor having stated the facts, the trial magistrate recorded that:

'The Prosecutor states the facts as contained in the charge.'

the Lagos High Court (Taylor, C.J.) held in *Ojetola* v. *Commissioner of Police*[48] that this method of recording the facts was wrong. 'That is not what is required of the Court. The Court is required to take down the statement as stated by the prosecutor as the evidence he would lead if the accused had pleaded Not Guilty. When the Court reads those facts, it is to ask the accused what he has to say to those facts, and after that to decide whether the facts together with the answer of the accused warrant a finding of guilt. If not, a plea of Not Guilty is to be entered and the trial is to proceed.' The defect was held not cured by the statement in the *allocutus* and the conviction was quashed.

CIVIL PROCEDURE

In the Benue-Plateau State, the Chief Justice of the State, pursuant to powers conferred upon him by the Area Courts Edict, No. 4 of 1968, has made elaborate rules of civil procedure which are applicable to all area courts in the state. The rules which are known as the Area Courts (Civil Procedure) Rules, 1972,[49] cover all aspects of civil procedure applicable to area courts and contain schedules of forms and fees.

And in the North Eastern State, the Chief Justice, in exercise of the powers conferred upon him by s. 65 of the Area Courts Edict, No. 1 of 1968, has made rules known as the Upper Area Courts (Appeals) Rules, 1970,[50] which are deemed to have come into operation on 31 December, 1970. The rules which apply to appeals against decisions of any area court grade I, II or III in criminal and civil cases deal with the procedure for initiating appeals to an upper area court, the time for appealing and the forms and fees for appeals.

In *A. M. Soetan* v. *Total Nigeria Ltd*,[51] the Supreme Court held that where a plaintiff discontinues his action without leave of the Court before hearing under Order 44 Rule 1(1) of the Supreme Court (Civil Procedure) Rules, 1945, the proper order to be made is one striking out the case and not an order of dismissal for the plaintiff should be free to bring fresh proceedings in future if he so wished.

And in *A. U. Amadi* v. *Thomas Aplin & Co Ltd*,[52] the Court dealt with a matter of practice and procedure which it considered 'of considerable importance', namely the application of Order 34 of the High Court Rules of Eastern Nigeria which deals with amendment of proceedings. In an action for breach of a contract of sale of goods the plaintiff brought a motion on notice, before trial, to amend his pleadings to include an allegation that the defendant did not supply the goods ordered by the plaintiff. On the day fixed for for hearing the motion, the trial judge having rejected a request for adjournment by the plaintiff's counsel, dismissed the motion without hearing counsel on it on the ground that it would 'alter the whole nature of the case' and was unreasonable at that stage.

On appeal, the Supreme Court held that it is wrong under Order 34 for a judge to refuse a party's application for leave to amend his pleadings at any stage of the proceedings before judgement where the facts sought to be pleaded are such as would enable issues to be properly joined on the question in controversy between them unless the applicant is acting *mala fide* or by his blunder has caused injury to the other party which cannot be compensated for by costs or otherwise. In the instant case the conduct of the trial judge was an infringement of the maxim *audi alteram partem* and a denial to the plaintiff of a fair trial.

The principle upon which a counsel ought to be prevented from acting against the interest of a client for whom he had been a solicitor was discussed in *Adesetan* v. *Thomas*.[53] In that case after the plaintiff had given evidence in examination in chief, her counsel submitted that counsel for the first defendant in the case should not continue to appear in the case because he had acted for the plaintiff in respect of the subject matter of the proceeding and his continued participation in the suit would be contrary to professional ethics.

The trial judge referred to quotations from *'Conduct and Etiquette at the Bar'* by W. W. Boulton, pages 28-29, and the judgement in *Earl Cholmondeley* v. *Lord Clinton*[54] as laying down the principle on which a counsel should be barred from acting against the interest of his client for whom he had acted previously as a solicitor. He found that counsel for the first defendants prepared the power of attorney by which the plaintiff appointed the first defendant as attorney to act for her in matters mentioned in the Power of Attorney. Counsel for the first defendant also prepared the deed of assignment which was the subject matter of the suit. Furthermore the said counsel invited the plaintiff to a peace meeting with the first defendant in his office. Lastly when the plaintiff mortgaged her leasehold property to the second defendant, counsel for the first defendant was then solicitor to the plaintiff and helped the plaintiff in paying some of the mortgage money to the second defendant and kept some of the receipts for the payments with him.

The judge held that counsel for the first defendant should not continue to act for him in the suit when he had previously acted for the plaintiff in regard to the document which was the subject matter of the action. It was evident to the court that the counsel in question would be a material witness for either the plaintiff or the defendant and that the interests of the plaintiff and the defendant were in conflict.

In *Oyeyemi Olowosoke* v. *Isaiah Oke*,[55] the Supreme Court dealt with the right of appeal from the Western State Court of Appeal to the Supreme Court. The respondent's counsel had raised a preliminary objection on the ground that the appeal was not properly before the court because the appellant did not obtain leave to appeal either from the Supreme Court or from the Western State Court of Appeal as required by s. 117(4)(c) with the modification in s. 127(1)(a) of the Constitution of the Federation, No. 20 of 1963.

S. 117(4)(c) provides as follows:

'Subject to the provisions of sub-sections (2) and (3) of this section, an appeal shall lie from decisions of the High Court of a territory to the Supreme Court with the leave of the High Court or the Supreme Court in the following cases . . .
(c) decisions in any civil or criminal proceedings in which an appeal has been brought to the High Court from some other court.'

S. 127(1)(a) provide that if a state legislature creates a Court of Appeal to hear appeals from the High Court then the reference to the High Court in s. 117(4)(c) should be read as if it were a reference to the Court of Appeal. In the present case the matter seemed plain enough because the appellant had appealed from the High Court to the Court of Appeal.

Counsel for the appellant however relied on s. 117(2)(a) which he argued conferred on the appellant a right to appeal as of right. That section with the modification required by s. 127(1)(a) reads as follows:

'(2) an appeal shall lie from decisions of the Western State Court of Appeal to the Supreme Court as of right in the following cases—
(a) final decisions in any civil proceedings before the Western State Court of Appeal.'

The Supreme Court, having examined the relevant provisions of the Constitution, i.e. ss. 117(2)(a), 117(4)(c), 115 and 127(1)(a), came to the conclusion that in civil or criminal proceedings an appeal lies from decisions of the Western State Court of Appeal only with the leave of that Court or of the Supreme Court in all cases in which an appeal went to the Court of Appeal from the High Court. The Court said:

'. . . any other interpretation of s. 117(2)(a) and 117(4)(c) read together with s. 127(1)(a) would amount to making appeals from the Western State Court of Appeal automatic, thus depriving that court, or the Supreme Court of the power, in appropriate cases, of any form of control over appeals from the Western State Court of Appeal. We think that this would be an unacceptable, and indeed unprecedented, result.'

EVIDENCE

S. 8(e) of the East Central State Commissions of Inquiry Law (Cap. 24) empowers Commissioners 'to admit any evidence, whether written or oral, which might be admissible in civil or criminal proceedings'. The Commissions of Inquiry Law (Amendment) Edict, No. 20 of 1972, has now replaced this provision with a new one which empowers the Commissioners 'to admit any evidence, whether written or oral, notwithstanding that such evidence might have been *inadmissible* in civil or criminal proceedings before a court, and to act on such evidence'.

One cannot help commenting that this is a retrograde piece of legislation especially when it is recalled that these Commissions of Inquiry are usually headed by High Court judges and that eminent legal practitioners take part in the proceedings.

In *Bassa Vorgho* v. *The State,* [56] the Supreme Court dealt with what it considered as 'an interesting point that does not appear to be covered, so far as we are aware, by any previous authority, either in Nigerian or in English law.' The question was whether a dying declaration which not only contained the cause and circumstances of the declarant's death but also the declarant's opinion of the killer's motive was admissible as evidence of such opinion. Soon after a gunshot, the deceased was heard to say *inter alia,* 'Bassa has killed me' and 'It was because of the drink I had that annoyed Bassa. That is why he shot me. Go and pay all the people I owe.' The defence was accidental killing. According to the appellant, the deceased held him from behind and as he turned, the gun he was holding went off and shot the deceased and also wounded the appellant in the right thigh.

The trial judge admitted the dying declaration, not only as implicating the appellant, but also as true of the facts stated therein, including the declarant's expression of opinion as to the appellant's motive for the killing. He held that the appellant killed the deceased deliberately and convicted him of culpable homicide punishable with death.

On appeal it was held that the trial judge was wrong to have admitted as true of the facts, the deceased's expression of opinion as to the appellant's motive, for this was going beyond the established scope of s. 33(a) of the Evidence Law, Cap. 40 (North) which deals with the admissibility of dying declarations. The Court having upheld the trial judge's rejection of the appellant's account of how the gunshot occurred, substituted a conviction for culpable homicide not punishable with death.

Under s. 32 of the Marriage Act, Cap. 115, a marriage may be proved by the production of a copy of the certificatee of marriage filed in the Registrar's office.

But in *Esther A. Osho* v. *Gabriel A. Phillips,* [57] the Supreme Court held that the production of a copy of an entry in an Anglican Church marriage register in Nigeria endorsed by an Archdeacon was sufficient proof of a marriage. For this it relied on a dubious interpretation of s. 116 of the Evidence Act, Cap. 62, as amended by the Adaptation of Laws (Miscellaneous Provisions) Order, 1964, which provides as follows:

'When any document is produced before any court, purporting to be a document which, by the law in force for the time being in any part of the Commonwealth would be admissible in proof of any particular in any court of justice in any part of the Commonwealth, without proof of the seal or stamp or signature authenticating it, or of the judicial or official character claimed by the person by whom it purports to be signed, the court shall presume—
    (a) that such seal, stamp or signature is genuine, and
    (b) that the person signing it held, at the time when he signed it, the judicial or official character which he claims,
and the document shall be admissible for the same purpose for which it would be admissible in the part of the Commonwealth where the document is produced.'

Before the 1964 amendment the section covered only documents produced in the United Kingdom and ended with the words 'shall be admissible for the same purpose for which it would be admissible in the United Kingdom'.

The Supreme Court held that the main object of the amendment was to extend the scope of the section to cover all parts of the Commonwealth and that the only way to give it a sensible meaning was by omitting the words 'where the document is produced'.

In the *State* v. *Emmanuel Okechukwu Madukolu,* [58] the High Court

Onitsha (Oputa, J.) dealt with proof of the voluntariness of a confessional statement. The accused was charged with murder and the only evidence against him consisted of two extra-judicial confessions. At the trial he denied making the statements, alleging that they were already written out and passed to him to sign and when he refused he was tortured in a manner which caused injuries to his finger and private part. A prison staff nurse confirmed that he treated the accused for the injuries described.

The learned judge examined the two statements and found that the accused made them. He pointed out that the proper objection would have been that the accused made the statements under torture and not that he did not make them. He then considered the 'interesting question . . . what happens where the proper objection was not taken but the evidence led supports that objection?' He held that the Courts aim at substantial justice and that no court is bound to act on inadmissible evidence. To be relevant and admissible, confessions must be proved by the prosecution to be voluntary. As the nurse's testimony tended to confirm the accused's allegation of torture, it was held that the prosecution had failed to prove that the confessions were voluntary. The accused was acquitted and discharged.

The learned judge then made observations on the procedure to be adopted when an accused is taken to a superior police officer with a confessional statement. In serious cases like murder the superior police officer has a duty to conduct an impartial inquiry to satisfy himself that the alleged confession was voluntary.

'In this regard it is necessary for those superior police officers to adhere to the former practice of writing down what questions they asked the accused and his answers thereto—questions as to the usual and necessary cautions, questions as to whether the accused in fact made the statement voluntarily of his own free will. In addition the statement should then be read to the accused sentence after sentence and the accused should also then be asked whether he wished to add to, or alter anything in the statement. His answer to this question should again be recorded. If the statement is to be interpreted to the accused it will be inadvisable and undesirable to use as interpreter the same constable who recorded the alleged confession—*The Queen* v. *Nnana Okoro* (1960) 5 F.S.C. 134. This is important because the mere presence and co-operation of the junior officer who recorded the original confession at the inquiry before the superior police officer may play on the mind of the accused and threaten him into giving answers he would not under a completely different setting have given. The presence and co-operation of the constable who recorded the alleged confession may have the effect of keeping alive, as it were, the original threat or promise. At the end of such inquiry the superior police officer should then sign the record he had made and the accused should also sign or thumb impress the same record. This procedure will eliminate every doubt as to what actually happened before the administrative officer or superior police officer as the case may be. It will also greatly assist the trial judge at the hearing.'

FAMILY LAW

The Revenue Collection (Miscellaneous Provisions) Edict, No. 7 of 1972 (East Central State), makes it a duty for each community council to encourage and require the inhabitants of its area of authority to register every birth, death or customary law marriage occurring in that area. Such council is required to keep and maintain a register of all births, deaths and marriages respectively occurring in its area of authority after the commencement of the Edict. The Edict prescribes the fees to be paid for the registration of the events. A marriage is registrable under the Edict by either party to the marriage. A community council is authorized under the Edict to issue a marriage certificate or a birth certificate or death certificate. Revenue accruing from the registration of marriages is to be paid into the government sub-treasury while the proceeds of other registrations are to be retained by the council.

The Lagos State (Applicable Laws) (Amendment) Edict, No. 11 of 1972, amended the principal legislation—that is, the Lagos State (Applicable Laws) Edict, No. 2 of 1968, by enlarging the number of the laws applicable to Lagos State as listed in the first schedule of the principal legislation. Under the principal Edict, the Western Region Administration of Estates Law[59] was made inapplicable to Lagos State, thus leaving s. 36 of the Marriage Act to govern the intestate succession of persons married under the Marriage Act. The amending Edict of 1972 altered the position by applying the Western Region Administration of Estates Law to Lagos State from 1 May, 1968.[60] The 1968 Law thenceforth governs intestate succession within Lagos State to the exclusion of s. 36 of the Marriage Act. Although the Edict did not specifically repeal or refer to s. 36 of the Marriage Act, the latter is to be regarded as being repealed by implication as intestate succession is a matter within state jurisdiction.

The Edict also made applicable within the Lagos State the Western Region Wills Law[61] but deleted the Administration (Real Estate) Act (Cap. 2).

The Western Region Administration of Estates Law is amended in its application to the Lagos State by the Lagos State (Adaptation of Laws) (Miscellaneous Provisions) Order, 1972.[62]

The Nasarawa Local Administration (Declaration of Afo Native Marriage Law and Custom) Order, 1972,[63] provides in a written form, a declaration of what in the opinion of the Nasarawa Local Administration is the native law and custom relating to marriage and divorce applying throughout the area of its authority to all persons who marry according to Afo native law and custom. The declaration was approved by the Military Governor of the Benue-Plateau State.

During 1972 Nigerian courts had the opportunity of interpreting some of the provisions of the Matrimonial Causes Decree, 1970.

In *Sogbetun* v. *Sogbetun*,[64] Adefarasin, J., held that the test of whether under s. 15(2)(c) of the Matrimonial Causes Decree, No. 18 of 1970, the respondent has behaved in such a way that the petitioner cannot be reasonably expected to live with him is objective and not subjective. In doing so, he accepted that the language of s. 2(1)(b) of the English Divorce Reform Act, 1969, is the same as s. 15(2)(c) of the Decree. Consequently he adopted the interpretation of the English subsection by Sir George Baker in *Katz* v. *Katz*[65] as applicable to s. 15(2)(c) of the Decree.

In *Johnson* v. *Johnson*,[66] Adebiyi, J., was of the view that in a decree of divorce obtained under s. 15(2)(f) of the Matrimonial Causes Decree, No. 18 of 1970—which requires a living apart of the parties for a continuous period of at least three years immediately preceding the presentation of the petition—there is no need to find that one of the parties was at fault.

In *Asomugha* v. *Asomugha*,[67] Adefarasin, J., held that an independent action for maintenance which is not connected with a matrimonial cause could be brought under s. 70 of the Matrimonial Causes Decree. In the opinion of the learned judge, s. 70 of the Decree is similar to ss. 22 and 23 of the English Matrimonial Causes Act, 1965, which enable parties to bring applications for maintenance independently of a divorce petition. The learned judge agreed with the decision of the Chief Justice of Lagos State in *Esua* v. *Esua*.[68]

Although this matter has not been settled by the Supreme Court, it is doubtful if the decision is right in view of ss. 2 and 114 of the Decree. By s. 2 the High Court of each State possesses jurisdiction to hear and determine matrimonial causes instituted under the Decree. This jurisdiction is circumscribed by the definition of 'matrimonial causes' under s. 114(1)(c) which is as follows:

'proceedings with respect to the maintenance of a party to the proceedings, settlements, damages in respect of adultery, the custody or guardianship of infant children of the marriage or the maintenance, welfare, advancement or education of children of the marriage being proceedings in relation to concurrent, pending or completed proceedings of a kind referred to in paragraph (a) or (b) above, including proceedings of such a kind pending at, or completed before the commencement of this Decree'

In *Oyedu* v. *Oyedu*,[69] the learned counsel for the respondent at the hearing of a divorce petition raised a preliminary objection to the effect that the petition was defective in that the affidavit verifying it did not follow at the foot or end of the petition but was separately headed on a separate document. He urged that the petition be struck out. Counsel for the petitioner argued that the affidavit and the petition were one single document even though the affidavit was headed separately and was contained on a separate piece of paper. The oneness of the two documents was shown by the fact that they were filed at the same time and day. It was further contended that by reason of the provisions of s. 113(4) of the Matrimonial Causes Decree, the English Matrimonial Causes Rules, 1968, applied and under the new rules it was not necessary to attach an affidavit to a petition. The 1968 rules modified the requirements of the English Matrimonial Causes Rules, 1957. It fell to be decided whether the Matrimonial Causes Rules, 1957, or the Matrimonial Causes Rules, 1968, applied to the East Central State.

The trial judge (Aniagolu, J.) found that as no new rules have been made under the Matrimonial Causes Decree, 1970, the English rules of practice applied in accordance with s. 112(4) of the Decree. By s. 11(1) of the High Court Law, 1963,[70] the High Court was vested with all the jurisdiction, power and authorities which were, on 30 September, 1960, vested in the High Court of Justice in England. By s. 16 of the High Court Law, the jurisdiction vested in the High Court was, as regards practice and procedure, to be exercised in the manner provided by any law or in default, in substantial conformity with the law and practice obtaining in England for the High Court of Justice as at 30 September, 1960. The judge, therefore, concluded that in observing the dateline of 1960 the Matrimonial Causes Rules, 1968, were not applicable in the State. Rather the rules of 1957 applied.[71]

In the opinion of the learned trial judge, s. 6(3) of the 1957 Rules requires that the affidavit in support of the petition shall be contained in the same document as the petition and shall follow at the foot or end thereof. As the petition did not comply with this requirement it was not properly before the court.

In *Sifo* v. *Sifo,*[72] the petition was presented on the grounds of cruelty and desertion. The respondent in his Answer and cross-petition denied the charges of cruelty and desertion but asked that the marriage be dissolved on the ground of the petitioner's adultery. In her Reply, the petitioner denied the adultery and urged that even if the adultery was proved it had been condoned by the respondent.

The petitioner adduced evidence that she had sexual intercourse with her husband in April and May, 1964. On 27 May, she travelled to England and remained there until September 1964. While in England, she wrote to the respondent in August, 1964, giving him the impression that she was expecting a baby for him. On her return to Nigeria in September she continued to have intercourse with the respondent until the child was born in March, 1965. Subsequently, she informed the respondent that the child was not his and then left the matrimonial home to cohabit with the co-respondent. According to the medical evidence it was probable that conception took place in May or July, 1964. In either case the child would have been delivered normally as was the case in March 1965. The learned trial judge held that the presumption of legitimacy of a child born during the subsistence of a valid marriage with its mother as laid down in the *Banbury Peerage Case*[73] is now a rebuttable one. Such presumption could be rebutted by evidence which showed that it was impossible or unlikely for the child to be legitimate (*Poulett Peerage Case*).[74] He held on two grounds that the respondent was not responsible for the pregnancy which led to the birth of the child in dispute. First, the petitioner left the matrimonial home after the birth of the child to live with the co-respondent to whom she said the child belonged. Secondly, the respondent had averred in his Answer that the petitioner had repeatedly uttered words to bastardize the child.

On the question of condonation, the judge believed that, though fully aware that the pregnancy which the petitioner brought back in September, 1965 did not belong to the respondent, she pretended that it was his until the child was delivered in March, 1965. It was, therefore, held that the plea of condonation failed. Damages were also awarded against the co-respondent for his adultery with the petitioner.

In *Osamwonyi* v. *Osamwonyi,*[75] the Supreme Court examined the relevance of consent and co-habitation in Bini (Mid-West State) customary law. The petitioner contracted a statutory marriage with the respondent in Lagos in June, 1967. In 1968, he petitioned for divorce requesting the Benin High Court to declare the 1967 marriage null and void. He alleged that in 1964 the respondent, then a spinster, married one Goubadia in Benin according to Bini Customary law. The said marriage was dissolved by the Customary Court No. 2, Benin, in August, 1967, and the court ordered the refund of the dowry. The petitioner then contended that at the time he married the respondent, she was already married to Goubadia by customary law and that marriage was subsisting under Bini customary law.

The respondent denied the customary law marriage. She explained that in contemplation of a statutory marriage in 1966 with Goubadia, he, unknown to her, went to her father and paid him a dowry of six pounds. On learning about the payment, she rejected any marriage proposal with Goubadia and told him so. The payment to the respondent's father was not accompanied by any Bini customary marriage rights.

The trial judge found that the consent of the bride-to-be was fundamental to the celebration of a Bini customary law marriage. He also held it established on evidence before him that the payment of dowry alone does not constitute a valid Bini customary law marriage. There must be cohabitation as well. He, therefore, concluded that as the respondent did not give her consent to the purported customary law marriage and no cohabitation took place, there was no valid customary law marriage with Goubadia which subsisted at the time of the statutory marriage.

On appeal by the petitioner, the Supreme Court dismissed the appeal and upheld the findings of the trial judge on the relevance of consent and cohabitation in Bini customary law marriage.

In *The Matter of the Marriage Act Chapter 115: Registrar of Marriages* v. *Igbinomwanhia,*[76] the caveators filed a caveat against the issue of the Registrar's Certificate to the respondents who intended to marry under the Marriage Act. They contended that the first respondent was lawfully married to Ohuimumen Igbinomwanhia and Iroghama Igbinomwanhia under Bini customary law and these marriages had not been dissolved at the material time. The caveators were the children of the first respondent and the two women. In reply, the first respondent denied being ever married to the two women under customary law.

It was brought out in evidence that the first respondent paid dowry in respect of the two women although he was not living with them at the material time. One of the women left the matrimonial home five years ago following some domestic disagreement. The other claimed that she was sent home to her parents.

Obaseki, J., found that the payment of dowry was an essential of a valid Bini customary law marriage. The marriage may be dissolved by the refund of dowry. But separation, irrespective of its length, does not under Bini customary law constitute divorce. It was, therefore, held that the first respondent was still married to the two women and the caveat was validly lodged.

The requirements for the celebration and dissolution of customary law marriages were considered in the case of *Okpanum* v. *Okpanum.*[77] In that case, the respondent had filed a notice of marriage under the Marriage Act, Cap. 115, between him and the co-respondent. The caveatrix entered a caveat against the issue by the Registrar of Marriages of a certificate pursuant to the notice of marriage. She alleged that she was lawfully married to the respondent in 1969 by native law and custom and that the marriage was still subsisting at the time of action. The respondent denied the existence of the marriage and contended that he had called a joint representative meeting of the two families at which he announced his intention not to proceed with the marriage. It fell to be decided whether a customary law marriage between the parties was concluded and if so whether it had been lawfully terminated by the respondent.

Agbakoba, J., held that to constitute a valid customary marriage there must be parental consent, mutual agreement between the parties to the marriage, the payment or part payment of dowry and the ceremonies recognized by the community as constituting a valid marriage. In the instant case, the necessary elements of a valid marriage were present and a marriage was, therefore, created. In the opinion of the learned judge, the marriage was not vitiated by reason of the fact that the amount of dowry paid, which was £120, was in excess of the limit of £30 prescribed by the Limitation of Dowry Law, 1956.[78] The statute merely provided a penalty for infringement and did not affect the validity of a marriage.

On the dissolution of the marriage, the learned judge held that to constitute a customary law divorce a formal or physical return of the wife was not necessary. The marriage may be terminated by renunciation of the wife and the dowry by the husband. But he emphasized that

'the renunciation or termination of the marriage by the husband must, however, be formal; a mere bluff or quarrelsome statements are not enough'.[79]

He concluded that the act of renunciation of the wife and dowry at the joint family meeting was enough to dissolve the marriage.

In *Nwankpele* v. *Nwankpele*,[80] the court was called upon to determine the validity of a marriage celebrated in London on 4 January, 1969. The petitioner alleged that she married the respondent in London in 1969. On their return to Nigeria in 1970 she came across a letter in 1971 addressed to her husband by a woman who described herself as his wife. On enquiry, she found a Marriage Certificate which showed that the respondent was married to some other woman at the Lagos Marriage Registry in September, 1968. There was no affirmative evidence that at the time the petitioner married the respondent, the first wife was alive.

The trial judge cited with approval the dictum of Hodson, J., in *MacDarmard* v. *A.G.*,[81] that there is no presumption of law as to continuance of life and each case is to be determined on its own facts. He took into account the fact that the first wife was at the time of her marriage in 1968 only twenty-one years old and the second marriage by the respondent took place only four months later. Moreover, there was nothing to show that she was not a woman of normal health so as to suggest a shorter expectation of life. Relying on the dictum of Sacks, J., in *Chard* v. *Chard*,[82] he held that the balance of probability was that the 1968 wife was alive at the time the second marriage was celebrated in 1969. He, therefore, declared the 1969 marriage void under s. 3(1)(a) of the Matrimonial Causes Decree, 1970.

In *Labode* v. *Labode*,[83] Odesanya, J., decided that under s. 15(2)(c) of the Matrimonial Causes Decree the plea of adultery without anything more will not support a plea of irretrievable breakdown of marriage. It must in addition be stated that:

'the petitioner finds it intolerable to live with the respondent.'

With regard to desertion under s. 15(2)(d) of the Decree, the judge observed that the Decree refers to the period immediately preceding the petition and not just preceding it. Consequently, it was not sufficient to plead in the cross-petition that the petitioner had deserted the respondent for a period of at least three years preceding the presentation of the petition.

SUCCESSION AND ADMINISTRATION OF ESTATES

In *Kafene Jeddo & Anor* v. *Imiko*,[84] the Supreme Court examined the application of the doctrine of 'relation back' in respect of the grant of letters of administration after the commencement of proceedings. The plaintiff sued initially as the next-of-kin of the deceased. After the hearing of the action began, the plaintiff obtained letters of administration in respect of the deceased's estate and sought by motion to amend the title of the action to show her as the administratrix of the estate. The motion was granted and the learned trial judge found that the plaintiff was entitled to the remedies sought as the administratrix of the estate.

The defendant appealed on the ground that the plaintiff's claim as amended should have been dismissed because, though the plaintiff recovered judgement as administratrix, 'she had no cause of action as such at the date of the issue of the writ of summons.'

It was found by the court that the decided English cases[85] show that:

'When the only wrong description in a writ of the plaintiff was as administrator or administratrix, the action was a nullity as it was invalid *ab initio* since the plaintiff had not got the representative status claimed at the time of the issue of the writ and the doctrine of 'relation back' to the death of the intestate (see *In the Goods of Pryse* [1904] P. 301 at 305) did not help when the original action was wrongly constituted.[86]

The Court distinguished the case before it from those in which the action was improperly constituted as was the position in the English cases examined. It found that in the present case the claim was for possession and an injunction restraining the defendants from trespassing and the plaintiff claimed in her writ of summons as next-of-kin of the deceased. This was not a wrong statement and she could so sue and therefore when the letters of administration were subsequently granted to her, the doctrine of 'relation back' could apply and she could then act as from the time of the intestate's death. As the action was originally properly constituted it was perfectly in order for the court to allow an amendment for her to sue as administratrix which she then was.

Osho v. *Phillips*,[85] involved the issue whether an illegitimate child can claim to be legitimate as a result of being treated as such—legitimacy by conduct. In that case, Solomon Phillips and Christiana Vaughan were married under the Marriage Act on 25 April, 1897 at Ogbomosho. There were four issue of the marriage, three of whom were the defendants in the suit. The plaintiffs who were born out of wedlock during the subsistence of the statutory marriage, claimed that they were brought up and educated by their natural father. Mrs Christiana Phillips died intestate in 1924 leaving considerable landed property in Lagos. Solomon Phillips who survived her, died intestate in 1939 leaving his wife's real estate intact. Letters of Administration in respect of the personal estate of Solomon Phillips were granted to two of the defendants who shared the estate among all the children of Solomon including the plaintiffs. Subsequently the plaintiffs sought a declaration that they, as children of Solomon Phillips, were beneficially and jointly entitled to share with the other children in the distribution of his estate. Furthermore, the plaintiffs asked the court to order an account of all proceeds received as rent from the landed properties of Solomon Phillips. At the trial it was urged on their behalf that:

'inasmuch as the 1st and 2nd defendants, as administrators of the estate of the deceased, had by their conduct manifested that the plaintiffs were the children of the deceased, they were estopped from putting up a line of defence running counter to that by now suggesting or maintaining that the plaintiffs were not the legitimate children of the deceased.'[88]

The conduct relied upon by counsel included the distribution of a portion of the personal effects of the deceased amongst the plaintiffs as beneficiaries and extending invitations to them to attend the family meeting of the deceased's children.

The Supreme Court had no hesitation in rejecting the plaintiffs' contention and held, on the authority of *Cole* v. *Akinyele*,[89] that the plaintiff's were illegitimate. It distinguished the case of *Ogunmodede* v. *Thomas*,[90] on which counsel for the plaintiffs relied, from the instant case. The decision has established beyond doubt that an illegitimate child cannot by mere force of the conduct of others in treating him as a legitimate child acquire that status. However, such a child may be legitimated, if the facts permit, either by *legitimatio per subsequens matrimonium* or by acknowledgment.

The Supreme Court had to decide in *Fatoye Ojule & Ors* v. *Fatola Okoya*[91] whether a residuary devise to the defendant is adeemed by the subsequent gift *inter vivos* to him of part of the property comprised in the residuary devise. In that case the plaintiffs were the children of the testator who, by a will dated 25 November, 1939, devised all his real property except No. 34 Denton Street, Ebute Meta, Lagos. This property was devised generally to all the children in equal shares. The defendant was the grandchild of the deceased.

During his lifetime the testator treated all his grand-children, including the defendant, as his children. He also conveyed, during his lifetime, a portion of the property at No. 34 Denton Street to the defendant and one Abiodun Okoya in February, 1941. The plaintiffs contended that the interest given to the defendant in the general devise in the testator's will was adeemed and or satisfied by the subsequent gift *inter vivos* of a part of the residuary estate. The court of first instance held that the residuary devise in favour of the defendant did not adeem by the subsequent gift, *inter vivos,* to them of part of the same property comprised in the testator's will. On appeal, the Supreme Court upheld the decision at first instance pointing out that:

'The plaintiffs have not shown that the defendant had any claim on the testator, for they failed, as the learned Chief Justice pointed out in his judgement, to prove that the testator was *in loco parentis* to the defendant whereby he was bound to maintain him or to set him up in life. Surely, the doctrine of ademption was conceived in equity so that of many children or those to whom a testator stood *in loco parentis,* one should not at the expense of the other or others take a double portion (See *In re Tussaud's Estate, Tussaud* v. *Tussaud* (1878) 9 Ch. D. 363). Hence the relationship grounding the obligation to provide a portion must be established and a failure to do this is undoubtedly fatal to the case of the appellants.'⁹²

In *Egenti* v. *Egenti,*⁹³ one of the objections raised by counsel for the defendant who entered a caveat against proof of the will of one Daniel Ogachukwu Egenti (deceased) was that one of the witnesses to the said will was an infant. He contended that since an infant cannot make a will under s. 7 of the Wills Act, 1837 (a Statute of general application in Nigeria) he could not attest a will. In rejecting this submission the trial judge pointed out that if it was the intention of the legislature that an infant should be incapable of attesting a will, it would have stated so clearly and specifically.

In *Kareem & Ors* v. *Ogunde & Anor*⁹⁴ the Supreme Court held *inter alia,* that the native law and custom whereby a Yoruba person's children are entitled to succeed in Lagos to his property on his death intestate has been firmly established by numerous cases and does not have to be proved by evidence. The Court will, therefore, take judicial notice of that customary law.

Oshilaja & Anor v. *Oshilaja & Ors,*⁹⁵ raised in a neat form the problems arising from the customary rights relating to the administration of and succession to the money in a bank, articles of trade, and the real property of a childless and intestate Yoruba man who died leaving a wife married under Yoruba customary law. The other survivors were an uncle, i.e. the first plaintiff, a cousin, i.e. the second plaintiff, and two nephews, i.e. the second and third defendants.

The plaintiff claimed against the defendants the revocation of letters of administration granted to the latter, a fresh grant of such letters to them and an account. The deceased and the first defendant were married under customary law in 1941. There was no issue of the marriage. Out of the proceeds of joint trading by the deceased and the first defendant they bought five landed properties in Lagos. On his death, the deceased also had substantial amounts of money in his bank accounts. As a result of a family meeting held after the death of the deceased, the three defendants obtained Letters of Administration in respect of the deceased's estate. The plaintiffs claimed that under Yoruba customary law they were entitled, to the exclusion of the defendants, to administer the deceased's estate.

It was found by the learned judge that the decision of Jibowu, J., to the effect that under Yoruba customary law a widow is not entitled to administer her late husband's estate has not been followed in the subsequent cases of *Abigail Ayiwe & Anor (Executors of the Estate of Ige George Deceased)* v. *Ramotu Fajore,*⁹⁶ *Re Whyte,*⁹⁷ and *In the Matter of the Estate of Joseph Asaboro, Deceased*⁹⁸ He held that:

'Yoruba sentiment would now frown upon the idea of exclusion of this loyal and industrious wife from the administration of the intestate estate of her deceased husband.'

The court accepted the evidence of an Oba (a sole witness) that a widow could administer the estate of her husband, evidence which the judge found to be 'compatible with principle and authority and certainly with public policy, natural justice, equity and good conscience at least in the special circumstances of this case'. It was also found that under Yoruba customary law the nephews of the deceased have a share in his estate and are entitled to administer it.

With regard to the first defendant's interest in the estate, the learned judge accepted that under Yoruba customary law a widow cannot inherit her deceased husband's property. He found that this custom has become so notorious by frequent proof in the courts that it has become judicially noticeable.[99]

The learned judge pointed out that if the properties of the deceased had been inherited by him from his father or a paternal ancestor it would have reverted to his paternal relations on his death without issue. Similarly, the properties would go to maternal relations if they came from that side. In his opinion, the decided cases show that Yoruba customary law reserves the property of a childless intestate deceased for his maternal relations in preference to his paternal relations. He emphasized that in the present case the properties in dispute did not come from either branch of the deceased's family but were the self-acquired properties of the deceased and not inherited in any way. It was held that the letters of administration to the defendants were validly granted and that the first defendant (the widow) was a joint owner of the estate of her late husband with the other two defendants.

It seems that the learned judge in this case made strenuous efforts to uphold the interests of the widow principally because she was a joint owner of the properties which composed the deceased's estate. The joint ownership of property in an urban area is one of the results of social change which was not envisaged under the old customary law. It seems therefore that the judge did the right thing in applying such rules as would do justice to the widow in terms of modern thinking in society.

In *Ejiamike* v. *Ejiamike*,[100] the court was called upon to determine the position of the 'okpala' (head) of the household at Onitsha (East Central State) and that of the widow of the deceased in respect of the deceased's estate. The plaintiff claimed, as head of the Oscar Obi-Ogbolu Ejiamike family of Onitsha, an account of all rents and other income collected by the defendants from the family property and payment over to him of the amount found due to him on such account. He also sought an injunction restraining the defendants from dealing with any part of the said property. The first defendant was one of the widows of the deceased, Oscar Obi-Ogbolu Ejiamike, and the others were her children by the said Ejiamike and half brothers of the plaintiff. On the death of Oscar Ejiamike intestate, the defendants managed and administered his estate.

The trial judge found that in accordance with Onitsha customary law, on the death of a father his eldest son or 'okpala' assumes the headship of the family. All the property of the deceased vests in the 'okpala' whose duty it is to manage and administer the estate for the benefit of himself and his other male relations—brothers and half brothers. The widow is not entitled to administer the estate of her late husband except where the 'okpala' is an infant. Although the 'okpala' is accountable to his brothers, the latter have no right to oust him or take up themselves or share in the administration of their late father's estate without the consent of the '*okpala*'. If the younger brothers are dissatisfied with the administration of the estate they may sue for an account or else for partition. For the purposes of such partition each mother and all her male children constitute one unit. He refused to find that the incident of '*okpalaship*' in Onitsha is repugnant to natural justice, equity and good conscience and he upheld the plaintiff's claim.

LAND LAW

The Public Lands Acquisition Law (Amendment) Edict, No. 9 of 1972 (Mid-Western State), amends s. 2 of the principal law by including among the purposes for which the state may compulsorily acquire private land, the 'obtaining [of] control over land required by any company or industrialist for industrial purposes.' This modification was a sequel to the decision of Obaseki, J., in the High Court, at Warri in *Chief David Ereku & Ors* v. *The Military Governor of Mid-western State of Nigeria and Ors.*[101] In that case, the plaintiffs sought a declaration that the notice of acquisition and the compulsory acquisition of their land near Warri in 1969 under the Public Lands Acquisition Law, Cap. 105, was unconstitutional, *ultra vires* the Public Lands Acquisition law, irregular and null and void. The plaintiffs contended that they had entered into negotiations with a foreign oil company for a lease of the land. Before the negotiations were completed the Government of the Mid-West State published a notice of intention under the Public Lands Acquisition Law to acquire the same piece of land compulsorily. The notice indicated that the land was required by the government for 'public purposes absolutely'. Having acquired the land the government then granted it to the same oil company that had partly negotiated for it. It was held that:

> 'The public purpose for which the Government can compulsorily acquire lands are clearly defined in s. 2 of the Public Lands Acquisition Law Cap. 105 and does not include acquisition for the purpose of making a grant of it to a third party . . .'[102]

The court rejected the argument that the grant of the lease to the foreign company was in accordance with the public purpose for which the land was acquired because the objects of the company were in consonance with the declared objectives of the government to advance the industrial and economic development of the state.

ROAD TRAFFIC

Motor traffic problems have been the concern of many states in Nigeria and there are a number of laws dealing with motor traffic. The most elaborate of these was the Road Traffic Edict of the Mid-western State.[103] It repeals the Road Traffic Law, Cap. 113, and makes detailed provision for such matters as licensing and registration of vehicles, the licensing of drivers and the control of traffic. There are provisions dealing with civil and criminal liabilities of drivers and owners of vehicles.

The Highways (Removal of Obstructions) Edict, No. 8 of 1972, of the Mid-western State provides for the removal of obstructions from specified highways in the state. The cost of removing an obstruction is recoverable from the owner or person responsible for leaving it on the highway. An obstruction is deemed to vest in the State Government which may sell or dispose of it as it deems fit. The owners may, on application to the appropriate authority recover the sum realized from sale after deduction of necessary expenses.

The Highways (Removal of Obstructions) Edict, No. 9 of 1972, of the Kano State which applies to all highways in the state (except federal highways) is similar to the Mid-western State Edict.

NOTES

1. [1972] 1 All NLR 191
2. Cap. 94 Laws of Northern Nigeria, 1963.
3. [1972] 1 All NLR 159.
4. No. 13 of 1969.
5. [1969] 2 AC 147.
6. [1972] 1 All NL 9, 159 at p. 168.
7. At p. 169.
8. Ibid.
9. S. 106
10. No. 2 of 1972
11. NESLN 6 of 1972
12. LN 64 of 1972
13. Appeal No. K/IA/1972 (unreported)
14. CCHCJ/10/72 at p. 30
15. [1972] 2 ECSLR 27
16. [1972] 2 ECSLR 298
17. CCHCJ/7/72 at p. 51
18. John Agoaka v. Lovinah Ejiofor [1972] 2 ECSLR 109
19. [1972] 2 ECSLR 194
20. S. 4
21. S. 1(2)
22. Ss. 10, 11, 12
23. LN 70 of 1972
24. [1972] 1 All NLR 49
25. CCHCJ/12/72 at p. 20
26. CCHCJ/3/72 p. 14
27. Cap. 199
28. [1972] 1 All NLR 33
29. The Supreme Court also held that where part of a Trade Mark is disclaimed under s. 16, the registered proprietor is not thereby prevented from complaining of the appearance of the disclaimed part on the applicant's mark.
30. Elektrotechnische Fabrik Schmidt and Co otherwise Daimon-Werke Gmba v. Bateria Slany Narodni Podnic [1972] 1 All NLR 139
31. [1972] 1 All NLR 314
32. At p. 321
33. [1972] 1 All NLR 202
34. CCHCJ/7/72 at p. 57
35. [1972] 1 All NLR 149; [1970-71] 1 ECSLR 17
36. They relied on Oppenheim's International Law 7th Ed. Vol. 2 p. 575
37. [1972] 1 All NLR 15
38. At p. 23
39. See Ejike v. I.G.P. [1961] 5 ENLR 7; C.O.P. v. Iffie W/14CA/70 (unreported) Midwest High Court; Nwachukwu v. C.O.P. [1970-71] 1 ECSLR 110. But see Iroaghan v. I.G.P. [1964] MNLR 48
40. PHC/13CA/72 (unreported)
41. [1961] 5 ENLR 7
42. Cf. Glanville Williams: Criminal Law: The General Part p. 310: 'The conclusion is that reasonableness is irrelevant—except, of course, as having an evidential bearing on the question of whether the belief existed.'
43. See Francis v. Ibitoye (1936) 13 NLR 11; Oso v. Olayioye [1966] NMLR 329
44. [1972] 2 ECSLR 207

45. At p. 210
46. (1960) 5 FSI; See *Oladimeji* v. *R* [1964] 1 All NLR 131.
47. For a similar amendment of the Criminal Procedure Act in its application to Lagos, see The Criminal Justice (Miscellaneous Provisions) Decree, No. 84 of 1966, s. 5
48. CCHCJ/7/72 at p. 29
49. BPSLN 5 of 1972
50. NESLN 6 of 1972
51. [1972] 1 All NLR 1
52. [1972] 1 All NLR 409
53. CCHCJ/3/72 at p. 14
54. (1815) 34 ER 515
55. SC 144/1972 (unreported) of 3 November, 1972
56. SC 136/1971 (unreported) of 5 May, 1972
57. [1972] 1 All NLR 276
58. [1972] 2 ECSLR 623
59. WRL 1959 Cap. 1
60. S. 4(2) of Lagos State (Applicable Laws) (Amendment) Edict, No. 11 1972
61. WRL 1959 Cap. 133
62. LSLN 16 of 1972
63. BPSLALN 19 of 1972
64. CCHCJ/10/72 at p. 97
65. [1972] 3 All ER 219
66. CCHCJ/9/72 at p. 109
67. CCHCJ/7/72 at p. 63
68. M/3/70 (unreported)
69. [1972] 2 ECSLR 730
70. Cap. 61
71. The same conclusion was reached by Agbakoba, J., in *Adibuah* v. *Adibuah* [1971] 1 ECSLR 127 at p. 132
72. CCHCJ/1/72 at p. 52
73. (1811) S & S 153
74. [1903] AC 395
75. SC 295/69 (unreported) 6 October, 1972
76. Suit No. B/16M/72 (unreported) High Court, Benin, 5 August, 1972
77. [1972] 2 ECSLR 561
78. Cap. 76 Laws of Eastern Nigeria, 1963
79. [1972] 2 ECSLR 561 at p. 565
80. CCHCJ/2/72 at p. 101
81. [1950] 1 All ER 497
82. [1955] 3 All ER 721
83. CCHCJ/2/72 at p. 107
84. [1972] 1 All NLR 260
85. *Ingall* v. *Moran* [1944] 1 All ER 97 at p. 101; *Hilton* v. *Sutton Steam Laundry* [1945] 2 All ER 425; *Burns* v. *Campbell* [1952] 1 KB 15; *Finnegan* v. *Cementation Company Ltd* [1953] 1 QB 688; *Stebbings* v. *Holst & Co Ltd* [1953] 1 WLR 603; *Bowler* v. *John Mowlem & Co* [1954] 1 WLR 1445
86. At p. 268
87. [1972] 1 All NLR 276
88. At p. 286
89. (1960) 5 FSC 84
90. FSC 337/1962 of 10 March, 1966
91. [1972] 1 All NLR 385
92. At p. 388
93. CCHCJ/3/72 at p. 204
94. [1972] 1 All NLR 73
95. CCHCJ/10/72 at p. 11
96. (1939) 15 NLR 1
97. (1946) 18 NLR 70
98. Suit No. AK/4/70
99. See *Angu* v. *Attah* (1921) Privy Council (1874-1928) 43; *Suberu* v. *Sunmonu* (1957) 2 FSC 33
100. [1972] 2 ECSLR 11
101. Suit No. W/58//969
102. See also *Chief Commissioner, Eastern Provinces, Nigeria* v. *S. N. Ononye & 5 Ors* 17 NLR 142
103. Although titled Road Traffic Edict, 1971, the Edict is No. 3 of 1972 and came into force on 1 February, 1972

CHAPTER THREE

SIERRA LEONE

H. M. Joko Smart

CONSTITUTIONAL LAW

THE PRESIDENT

The Office of the President continued to grow in stature during the year under review. By the Presidential Style and Titles Act, 1972[1] the President was empowered to use the style and title of 'President of the Republic of Sierra Leone, Supreme Head of State, Commander-in-Chief of the Armed Forces, Fountain Head of Unity, Honour, Freedom and Justice.'

In order to pave the way for the introduction of indigenous honours and titles in replacement of the British honours which had hitherto been conferred on Sierra Leone nationals, the National Honours and Awards Act 1972[2] was passed. The Act enabled the President to make provision by warrant for the grant of titles of honour, decorations and other dignities and awards, save the conferrment by warrant of the title of 'chief'. Except with the prior consent of the President, citizens and members of the public service or of the armed forces of Sierra Leone could no longer accept honours, titles or decorations (except those pertaining to education, a profession or a scientific body) from an authority of a country other than Sierra Leone. Although this provision closed the long history of British titles and honours, decorations already in existence were permitted to continue being used.

ELECTORAL PROVISIONS

The Constitution (Amendment) Act, 1972[3] repealed s. 28(8) of the Republican Constitution and put the registration of voters and the conduct of parliamentary elections in all the constituencies in the country under the direction and supervision of the Electoral Commission. Furthermore, the Electoral Commission was given the mandate to review and revise the register of voters in each constituency at least once biennially.

It should be recalled that the Electoral Provisions (Political Parties) Act[4] of the previous year prevented a member of Parliament who had gained his seat under one party ticket from crossing over to another party without first resigning his seat and seeking a re-election under the banner of the party with which he now wished to be associated.

It soon dawned on the ruling APC Government which believed that a one-party system of government was the one which suited the needs and aspirations of the people of Sierra Leone that such a law would not only militate against that policy but also prevent sympathizers in the opposition party from joining them. In any event, the general election of May 1973 was imminent and it was felt in government circles that if these sympathizers were allowed to 'cross-carpet' without first surrendering their seats, it would be a symbol of unity which the ruling party would hold out to the nation in the elections. The previous law was therefore repealed by the Electoral Provisions (Political Parties) (Repeal) Act, 1972.[5] As events of the next year demonstrated, this repeal paid dividends.

FUNDAMENTAL RIGHTS AND FREEDOM OF THE INDIVIDUAL

Apart from a few intermissions from 21 November 1968 to the period under review, the country was virtually run under a state of emergency. The Public Order Act, 1965[6] had, however, provided that before there could be a suspension of fundamental rights and the freedom of the individual, Public Emergency Regulations made to that effect should be approved by a resolution passed by the House of Representatives. Such Regulations stipulated the period during which they should operate. As it was not always convenient for Parliament to meet and renew the Regulations at the exact time when they ceased to have effect, a period was bound to intervene during which any interference with fundamental rights and freedoms would be tantamount to their infringement contrary to the Constitution. In order to achieve validity and for the sake of convenience, Parliament therefore, enacted the Indemnity Act, 1972[7] and the Public Order (Amendment) Act 1972.[8] Save for Petitions of Right, The Indemnity Act disabled any person whose fundamental rights or freedoms had been infringed from the 1st day of October 1971 to the 20th day of May, 1972 from instituting any action or legal proceeding whatever against the person who infringed those rights and freedom if the perpetrator acted under the authority of the President or a Minister and did so in good faith and in the execution of his duty or in the public interest.

A certificate of the Attorney-General that anything was done by or under the authority of the President or a Minister or was done by any person in the execution of his duty would serve as conclusive evidence to that effect. Moreover, the onus of proof that something done by or under the authority of the President or a Minister was not done in good faith rested on the complainant.

The Public Order (Amendment) Act, 1972 repealed s. 40 of the principal Act and replaced it by a new s. 40 which reads as follows:

'40(1) (a) Every Regulation made under section 38 shall, without prejudice to the validity of anything lawfully done thereunder, remain in force until the expiration of the date when the Resolution passed by Parliament declaring the existence of a state of public emergency, ceases to have effect.

(b) Every Order or Rule made in pursuance of any Regulation mentioned in paragraph (a) shall, without prejudice to the validity of anything lawfully done thereunder, cease to have effect at the expiration of the period mentioned in paragraph (a) during which such Regulation was in operation.

(2) Any such Regulation, Order or Rule may, without prejudice to the validity of anything lawfully done thereunder, at any time be amended or revoked by resolutions passed by Parliament.'

Following up this Amendment, the Public Emergency Regulations, 1972[9] were made much in similar terms and content as previous Regulations pertaining to the same issue.

An important statute passed during the period under review and dealing with the apprehension of illegal immigrants into the country was the Non-Citizens (Registration, Immigration and Expulsion) (Amendment) (No. 2) Act.[10] The background to this legislation was that the unfavourable economic and political situations in some of the other West African Countries compelled the nationals of these countries to enter Sierra Leone illegally in pursuit of jobs, wealth and a political asylum. The presence of these immigrants in the country has not only been inimical to the economic welfare of the indigenous citizens but also an embarrassment to the Sierra Leone Government whose avowed policy has always been the nurturing of friendly relations with the neighbouring countries. Speed is of the essence in dealing with the apprehension of illegal immigrants. The act therefore empowered any Immigration Officer, without a warrant and for the purpose of apprehending an illegal immigrant who may be found therein (a) to enter or board any vessel, aircraft, railway train, motor or other vehicle, and (b) to enter or board any vessel, aircraft, railway train motor or other vehicle, and (c) to enter any dwelling house, office, shop or any other building, as often as might be necessary. The power to enter must, however, be exercised sparingly and only when the officer has reasonable grounds for believing that an offence in contravention of the provisions of the Non-Citizens (Registration, Immigration and Expulsion) Act, 1965,[11] has been committed.

THE JUDICIAL AND LEGAL SYSTEM

The only innovations worthy of note in this area were the reorganization of the Rules Committee of the judiciary and the adaptation of existing laws to suit the change from a monarchical to a republican form of government.[12] The Chief Justice, who under the Constitution is head of the Judiciary, retains his position as Chairman of the Rules Committee, and he sits with the Attorney-General or his representative, two Justices of the Supreme Court, two Justices of Appeal, two Judges of the High Court, all of whom are selected by the Chief Justice, and two Legal practitioners nominated by the Sierra Leone Bar Association. The Chairman, the Attorney-General or his representative, one Justice of the Supreme Court or Justice of Appeal or Judge of the High Court and one legal practitioner constitute a quorum.

By the Laws (Adaptation) Act, 1972[13] laws in general made before the

Republican Constitution came into force were tidied up in order to render the constitutional changes meaningful. As typical examples, expressions like 'the Queen' or any other name or description of the Queen of England appearing in existing laws were replaced with the expressions 'the Government of Sierra Leone' or 'the State' as the context required; 'the President' took the place of 'the Governor-General' and the 'High Court' and 'Supreme Court' were substituted for the 'Supreme Court' and 'the Privy Council' respectively in the judicial system.

CRIMINAL LAW AND EVIDENCE

The Explosives (Amendment) Act 1972[14] has increased the penalty for being found in possession of or for using any explosives otherwise than under the provisions of the Explosives (Amendment) Act, 1955[15] where the person is convicted on information. The new penalty is a fine not exceeding Le5,000 (five thousand Leones) or imprisonment for a term not exceeding 10 years or both fine and imprisonment as compared with £500 fine and two years imprisonment under the 1955 Act. Another new development introduced by the amending Act is that the burden of proof that the possession or use of an explosive is lawful is cast on the person charged with the possession or use thereof.

In a similar vein as the Explosives (Amendment) Act, the Arms and Ammunition (Amendment) Act, 1972[16] has increased penalties for unlawful possession or use of arms and ammunitions without a valid and current licence, from £500 fine and/or two years imprisonment to a fine not exceeding Le5,000 and/or imprisonment for a term not more than ten years where a person is convicted on information.

CONTRACT

A stimulating case depicting how the differences between Quasi-contract, Contract and Agency may at times be confused is *Sahr Mendekia* v. *George Beresford-Cole*.[17] The facts of this case are as follows:
The plaintiff, Mendekia, bought a piece of land from the defendant, Beresford-Cole, and the defendant undertook to build a block of flats on the said land in return for the sum of Le14,000 paid by the plaintiff. A document relating to the transaction was drawn up in the following terms, signed by the defendant and the plaintiff:

> 'Received the sum of Le14,000 (Fourteen thousand Leones) from Sahr Lebbie Mendekia Esq., Farmer of 27 Yaradu Road, Koidu Town, Kono District in the Eastern Province of Sierra Leone being payment of the sum of Le24,000 (Twenty four thousand leones) for the costs of construction of a two-storey building with boys' quarters and car park to be built and constructed with the best labour and materials available within a maximum period of (6) six calendar months.
>
> I Sahr Lebbie Mendekia aforesaid for myself, my heirs and successors in title do hereby contract and agree with my agent George Beresford-Cole, Real Estate Agent, to pay him the balance of Le10,000 (Ten thousand Leones) in full on or before but not later than 28th February 1969 for the fulfilment of the purposes herein before contained. Dated in Freetown the 3rd day of December, 1968. Sgd George Beresford-Cole.'

On the one hand, the plaintiff fulfilled his own part of the agreement by paying the balance of the money within the stipulated time. On the other hand, the defendant did not complete the building at the time agreed upon. When that period expired he asked the plaintiff for a month's extension of time and it was granted to him. Nevertheless, on the 11 June, 1969 the defendant wrote to the plaintiff demanding more money than was already agreed upon, alleging that because of the rising cost of living he was unable to complete the construction at the original cost. When the plaintiff failed to meet this demand, the defendant completed the house but refused to surrender the keys thereto until the balance requested was paid. The plaintiff sued for damages for breach of contract and the defendant counter-claimed for the additional sum of money he expended on completing the building.

Before the trial Judge two main issues were raised by the parties. Counsel for the plaintiff maintained that the document quoted above (referred to at the trial as exhibit 'C') was a contract between the plaintiff and the defendant whereby the defendant agreed to build a house for the plaintiff in consideration of the sum of money stated therein to be paid by the plaintiff. The defendant's counsel contended that the document was a mere receipt for the sum of money stated therein and that the document did not represent a contract; therefore the only remedy open to the plaintiff, the defendant continued, was an action in quasi-contract for money had and received. The trial Judge, on the other hand, ruled that the document revealed a Principal-Agent relationship and he dismissed both the Plaintiff's claim and the defendant's counter-claim.

With respect, the view of counsel for the plaintiff is to be preferred. All the essentials of a valid contract were present in the document: there was a promise enforceable in law in that the parties agreed and intended to enter into legal relations; their agreement was supported by consideration on either side, and there was no vitiating element rendering the agreement a nullity. On the legal point raised by counsel for the defendant, one would submit that the facts of the instant case do not establish a known instance in which a court in any legal system which recognizes the principle has sustained an action in quasi-contract for money had and received. Such an action is based on the principle of unjust enrichment, i.e. that the defendant is in possession of some advantage which, according to natural justice, is unjust for him to keep.[18] Restitution cannot, however, be ordered if the result is to enable a person to make a profit out of his own wrong.[19] Applying these tests, one would clearly see that restitution of the money paid by the plaintiff would be beneficial more to the defendant than to the plaintiff who would then be left with a house which he could sell at a large profit; he would then be gaining as a result of his own wrong in failing to complete the house at the time agreed upon. So far as the legal issue raised by the learned trial judge is concerned, it is difficult to construe the relationship of principal and agent from either the document itself or the transaction in its totality.

In all known instances or agency there must be a third party with whom the agent enters into a legal transaction on behalf of his principal such transaction being a contract or the disposition of property. The instant transaction was one between the plaintiff and the defendant although if the defendant had wanted he could have delegated the performance of his part of the contract while the resultant responsibility rested solely on him.

When the case went on appeal, the Court of Appeal rightly held that there was a contract and not agency and dismissed the issue of quasi-contract.

Allowing the appeal of the plaintiff, the Court of Appeal, in a judgement delivered by Tejan, J., who after finding in favour of a contract, put the legal position with respect to agency quite clearly: 'I have not been able to find any passage in exhibit 'C' which gives the slightest indication that it creates the relationship of principal and agent between the appellant and respondent . . . In the case of Agency, the relationship creates a situation whereby the agent is able to affect the principal's legal position in respect of strangers. There is nothing in exhibit 'C' which could be interpreted to the effect to give the respondent authority either express or implied to affect the appellant's legal position with a third party'.

TORT

The case of *Donald Siaka* v. *Sierra Leone Diamonds Ltd*[20] did not establish any new principle in the law of tort but is yet a vivid example of the application of the defence of *volenti non fit injuria* to an action for personal injuries. The plaintiff was an employee of the defendants whose business was buying rough diamonds and polishing and selling them. His specific duties were concerned with the polishing of the diamonds. Certain pieces of diamonds were stolen from the defendant's place of business by some unknown person or persons. In order to remove suspicion and probably to discover the thief, some of the employees including the plaintiff invited a 'juju-man' to the defendants' premises in order to perform some weird occult practices. To achieve his purpose, the 'juju-man' lit a stove, put on it a pot containing a liquid which looked like oil, and requested each of the employees who had invited him to dip their hands into the pot and recover a stone which he had put in it. He alleged that if a person putting his hand into the pot was not the thief, the liquid in it, although it was being heated, would feel icy-cold and would leave his hands unscathed. The plaintiff plunged his right hand into the pot in order to remove the stone but instead of the contents of the pot being icy-cold as it was alleged, his hand was severely burnt. Prior to this act by the plaintiff another employee had refused to dip his hand into the pot despite repeated requests by the 'juju-man' to do so and the said workman had been asked to stand aside. In an action by the plaintiff against the defendants for personal injuries on the ground that since the 'juju-man' performed on their premises, the defendants were vicariously liable for the assault to the plaintiff, the High Court held that the defence of *volenti non fit injiria* was available to the defendants and dismissed the action. On appeal, the Court of Appeal upheld the judgement of the Court below and went further to consider *obiter* the question whether the defendants would have been vicariously liable for the acts of the 'juju-man' if the plaintiff had not voluntarily assumed the risk in dipping his hand into the pot. The answer was in the negative because, in the words of Cole, C.J., 'the performance in question giving rise to the action was neither part of what the appellant (plaintiff) was employed by the respondents (defendants) to do nor was it incidental thereto'.

A master's duty of care at common law to his servants, expounded in the English cases of *Smith* v. *Baker and Sons*[21] and in *Wilsons and Clyde Coal Co Ltd* v. *English*,[22] was considered in the Sierra Leone Case of *Ibrahim Yatteh* v. *Sierra Leone Development Co Ltd*,[23] but the Sierra Leone case has a further-reaching effect than that arrived at by the English decisions. The facts of the Sierra Leone Case are these: Ibrahim Yatteh, the plaintiff, a man of low literacy, was employed by the defendants to work on conveyor belts at first under supervision and instruction with a view to being upgraded to the post of a chargehand. After a reasonable period of training under an expatriate supervisor and although the plaintiff did not make much improvement, he was promoted to the post for which he was being trained notwithstanding his low literacy and the warning of his examiner to his employers that the plaintiff must improve his literacy before any further advancements. A week after his promotion, the plaintiff was injured in an accident while performing his duties as a chargehand. His hand was caught in a conveyor belt while he, together with two other employees, was trying to remove a stone which had got stuck in the belt. The plaintiff brought an action against his employers for failing in their common law duty to provide a competent staff and safe system of work. The action was dismissed by the High Court and the plaintiff went on appeal. It is the decision of the Court of Appeal that is of the utmost importance for our present purpose. The Court found the defendants negligent not in providing a competent and proper person to superintend and direct the work done by the plaintiff. The defendants were also held culpable for employing an incompetent servant in the person of the plaintiff. What is rather startling and, perhaps, a stretching of the rules advanced in the English cases herein referred to, is the imposition of liability on the master for the incompetence of his servant resulting in injury to the servant himself and not another servant. Was the rule in the *Baker* and *Wilsons and Clyde* cases not invented to deal with the situation whereby the failure of a master to provide competent staff results in injury to another servant other than the one whose incompetence is in issue? The Sierra Leone Court of Appeal did not seem to address itself to this question but applied the rule to all servants alike. This indeed, is a novelty.

Osman Koroma v. *D. A. Tweede and D. B. Iscandri*[24] was a case in which the trial judge found that the negligence of the defendant in colliding with the plaintiff was contributed to by the negligence of the plaintiff, but the judge did not apportion the liability as provided for by the Law Reform (Law of Tort) Act, 1961.[25] The Court of Appeal set the law right by apportioning the liability accordingly.

COMMERCIAL LAW

By far the most important change in the sphere of commercial law was brought about by the Business Registration Act, 1972.[26] It became obligatory for every business carried out in Sierra Leone to be registered in accordance with s. 5 of the Act. This section read together with s. 4 made provision for the Registrar-General of Sierra Leone and his Deputy, upon the payment of the prescribed fee, to register any business if satisfied (a) that the particulars contained in the application for registration are correct; (b) that the prescribed application form contains the name, address and nationality of the proprietor of the business, the nature of the business, the date of commencement of the business if the business is already in existence, the date of registration of the business if the business is already regisered, the capital employed in the business, the turnover of the business and, if the business is in the nature of a partnership or a company, the name, address and nationality of each partner or shareholder and their respective contributions to the capital of the business; (c) that the business is registerable under the provisions of the Act. A copy of every application for registration of a business must be sent to the Commissioner of Income Tax in order to ensure that the proprietor is up-to-date with the payment of his income tax. Upon registration, a certificate is issued which must be renewed annually not later than 31 January. A later amendment[27] provided also that a licence should be obtained from the Registrar-General in addition to the certificate of Registration. The licence should also be renewed annually.

The Non-Citizens (Registration, Immigration and Expulsion) (Amendment) Act, 1972[28] dealt *inter alia* with business and professional activities of non-citizens. S. 3 of the Act amended S. 40 of the Principal Act by adding a new subsection 3 which empowered the President by Order to set up a Committee for the purpose of advising and making recommendations on the employment of non-citizens in business and the professions.

REVENUE LAW

Significant changes were made in Revenue Law. The Income Tax (Amendment) Act,[29] has exempted the whole income, public or private, of the President and half the official salary of the Vice-President and Prime Minister from income tax. The Commissioner of Income Tax cannot now make deductions in respect of a contribution to a pension, provident or other society or fund made by an employer for his employees unless all the contributions in respect of persons who are citizens of Sierra Leone are invested in Sierra Leone; no tax-holiday relief can be granted to a new company incorporated and controlled in Sierra Leone if more than fifty per cent of its shareholders or members are non-citizens of Sierra Leone or the company is controlled by such persons or more than fifty per cent of the share capital of the company is held beneficially by or on trust for non-citizens of Sierra Leone. The penalty for non-payment of tax within the prescribed period of assessment is increased by ten per cent of the tax payable; a penalty for non-payment is levied only if the tax charged and payable exceeds Le25 and the penalty is not in excess of Le5.

Emphasis is laid on 'Sierra Leonization' in employment. It has been the policy of Government to encourage Sierra Leone citizens not only to engage in business but also to be employed by foreign business concerns in positions where the Sierra Leoneans are as suited as foreigners. As it is also the policy of Government to encourage foreign capital which is needed for the economic growth of the country, and since most of the country's large commercial enterprises are controlled by non-Sierra Leoneans, Government has considered it proper to strike a balance between the interest of the investor and that of the country by maintaining the *status quo* while at the same levying a pay-roll tax on an employer in whose employment there is a non-citizen of Sierra Leone. The Pay-roll Tax Act, 1972[30] now requires every employer, except the President, charitable institutions, diplomatic and consular missions to pay a pay-roll tax of Le100 annually in respect of every employee who is not a citizen of Sierra Leone.

Minor amendments were made to the Entertainments Tax Act, 1971[31] by the Entertainments Tax (Amendment) Act 1972.[32] The most significant was that Night Clubs, Casinos and gaming houses now pay the same rate of tax as other chargeable entertainments for an admission to such entertainments which is ten per cent of the admission fee.

SUCCESSION

A very interesting matter that cropped up in this area of the law was whether the 'Administrator-General' was one and the same person as 'Official Administrator', thus being the person on whom the estate of a Mohammedan dying intestate devolves as provided for by s. 9(1) of the Administration of Estates Act, 1960. This matter was considered in the case of *Alhaji Abdul Wahid Biakieu* v. *The Administrator-General*.[33] It should be recalled that in a previous case[34] dealing with the same subject-matter, i.e. the estate of one Kultimi Deen, who died intestate of the Mohammedan Faith, in which the same plaintiff was involved, the Court of Appeal had decided another point of law, which was that s. 9(1) of the Administration of Estates Act[35] superseded s. 9 of the Mohammedan Marriages Act[36] and that the Official Administrator was the primary person on whom the estate of a Mohammedan dying intestate should devolve. In the instant case this legal point was no longer contested but the plaintiff contended that the Administrator-General who had hitherto believed himself to be the same person as the Official Administrator was wrong in that belief and was therefore not the competent person on whom the estate should devolve. For ease of reference it is necessary to quote s. 9(1) of the Administration of Estates Act once more. It reads:

'The estate of every person dying intestate after the date of operation of this ordinance (Act) shall devolve upon the Official Administrator: Provided that upon the grant of letters of administration under the provision of this Ordinance (Act) shall devolve upon the Official Administrator: Provided that and be vested in the person or persons to whom letters of administration has been granted as aforesaid.'

As it can be clearly seen the section refers to 'Official Administrator' and not 'Administrator-General.' The Administration of Estates Act became law on 1 January 1946. Thereafter, certain changes had been effected in the Office of the Official Administrator up to the time when the instant case came for trial but these changes were not reflected in the then existing law. First, the Office of Administrator and Registrar-General was created by an Order of the 1961 Independence Constitution dated 15 April 1964 and published as Public Notice No. 28 of 1964. This Order constituted for Sierra Leone 'the office of Administrator and Registrar-General which shall include the function of the Registrar of Trade Marks.' The Order also appointed to that office 'the public officer presently holding the office of Official Administrator and Registrar-General.' Incidentally, the public officer who at that time held the office of Official Administrator was thereafter elevated to the bench and was now one of the Justices before whom the present case came on appeal in the Court of Appeal.

The High Court decided that the 'Administrator-General' referred to in Public Notice No 28 of 1964 was the same person as the 'Official Administrator' mentioned in s. 9 of the Administration of Estates Act. But the Court of Appeal was reluctant to endorse this decision. It held that when Mr Percy Davies (as he then was) was appointed to the Office of Administrator and Registrat-General he was already Official Administrator and since his existing post was not abolished or substituted for by his appointment as Administrator and Registrar-General, he was deemed to have held two offices from the date of appointment, viz. 'Official Administrator' and also 'Administrator-General'. But when the present incumbent of the post of Administrator-General was appointed, the Court opined, he was not also appointed Official Administrator which post had fallen vacant with the elevation of Mr Percy Davies to the bench.

As it happened, however, the present Administrator-General had been performing the duties of the Official Administrator thinking that he was competent to do so.

Holding that in the absence of an Official Administrator as prescribed by Law, Letters of Administration should be granted to the plaintiff/appellant who was the elder brother of the deceased, the Court of Appeal, per Forster, J.S.C., observed that 'remedial steps would have to be taken by the appropriate authority to rectify whatever errors in the execution of their duty, the subsequent holders to the first of the office now held by the respondent (i.e. Administrator-General) had made, by consequential legislation or otherwise as may be advised by the Honourable Attorney-General.' Following the ruling of the Appeal Court Parliament enacted the Administration of Estates (Amendment) Act, 1972.[37] This Act replaced the words 'Official Administrator' with the words 'Administrator and Registrar-General' wherever the former words appeared in the Administrator of Estates Acts, thus clarifying the issue that when the office of Administrator General was created it was intended to be the Office also responsible for the duties of the Official Administrator. Another matter that was also clarified was that the Administrator and Registrar-General became a corporation sole, having perpetual succession, who may sue and be sued in his corporate name. This second clarification became necessary because Mr D. E. M. Williams, the holder of the office of Administrator-General and the respondent in the instant case, was ordered by the Court of Appeal to pay the costs of the litigation in his personal capacity. Fortunately for Mr Williams, Parliament saved his skin as the Amendment Act was made retrospective dating back to 14 May 1964.

An interesting question in civil procedure which came up for consideration of the Court of Appeal during the year under review is whether a plaintiff against whom a judgement has been obtained in default of appearance is entitled to apply to the trial Court to have that judgement set aside and the case relisted for trial instead appealing against the dismissal of the action. The question arose in the case of *Maria C. Parkins and Anor* v. *Amadu Jalloh & Ors.*[38] The appellants were the plaintiffs in the High Court against whom judgement was obtained in default of appearance. Thereafter, their counsel moved the Court to have the case relisted but the application was refused on the ground that the proper step to take was to appeal against the order dismissing the action. The plaintiffs appealed to the Court of Appeal against the refusal. The rule of the High Court under which counsel for the Plaintiffs/Appellants sought to have the case relisted by the High Court was Order XXV rule 12 which reads as follows:

'Any verdict or judgement obtained where one party does not appear at the trial may be set aside by the Court upon such terms as may seem fit, upon an application made within six days after the trial or within such time as the Court or a judge may allow.'

The Appeal Court applied two English decisions, namely *Vint* v *Hudspith*[39] and *Armour* v *Bate*[40] on the point at issue and answered the question in the affirmative.

In criminal procedure, a noteworthy change in the jury system was effected by the Criminal Procedure (Amendment)Act, 1972.[41] For the first time in the history of Sierra Leone women became eligible for jury service.

INTERNATIONAL LAW

The Wild Life Conservation Act, 1972[42] has enabled effect to be given in Sierra Leone to the International Convention Relating to the Protection of Fauna and Flora in such Natural State, 1933 as amended by the International Convention for the Protection of Fauna and Flora of Africa of 1953.

The Rural Area (Amendment) Act, 1972[43] has exempted from the payment of rates all premises occupied by foreign consular or diplomatic missions whether the premises are for official use or residence. The exemption is made subject to reciprocity by Foreign states in which there are Sierra Leone consular and diplomatic missions.

EDUCATION

The most notable legal development in the field of education was the re-constitution of the University of Sierra Leone. With the establishment of the University of Sierra Leone in 1966, the two constituent Colleges, Fourah Bay College and Njala University College, remained virtually independent of each other. Save for a titular Vice-Chancellorship which office was occupied biennially by the Principal of each College and save that the degrees awarded by both Colleges were in the name of the University, each institution was run by its Principal, a College Council, a Senate, and an Academic Board. In short, the University of Sierra Leone was up to the period under review, basically a federal institution.

The background of each College might have set the pace for such an arrangement: Fourah Bay College was founded in 1827 by the Church Missionary Society as a training centre for candidates for Holy Orders in the Church of England. In 1876, the College was affiliated to the University of Durham in England. With the growing demands for higher education in Sierra Leone, the central Government played a more active role in the affairs of the College and in agreement with the Church Missionary Society the Fourah Bay College Act, 1950 was passed yielding to Government the responsibility for the College. Nine years later, the College was constituted a University College by Royal Charter with the Queen of England as Visitor. It has been offering courses in Arts, Economics, Pure and Applied Sciences.

Njala University College is of more recent origin, established by an Act[44] of the Sierra Leone Parliament in 1964. With the spread of education into the Provinces of Sierra Leone the need was felt for a second institution of higher learning based therein. Njala, a town some 130 miles from the capital city of Freetown in the Western Area where Fourah Bay College is situated, was chosen as the location for the new University College probably because of its rural and agricultural advantages. The College has been offering courses mainly in Agriculture and Education.

After this outline of the history of the two Colleges we may now return to the University of Sierra Leone as a legal entity.

Although it was basically responsible for financing the University since its inception, Government had had very little say in the general administration of the University. The federal system was proving uneconomical and it was feared that if each College was allowed to go as it pleased there might be duplication of many activities—something that was least desirable in a developing country with a modest budget. Government, therefore, set up a Commission on higher education to study, *inter alia*, the system of higher education and make recommendations for its improvement. When the Commission submitted its report, a Government White Paper was published in 1970. The first implementation of the educational policy contained in this White Paper was the University of Sierra Leone Act, 1972.[45]

The structure of authority within the new University indicated that Government is prepared to assume greater responsibility for the affairs of the two Colleges. The President of Sierra Leone becomes the Chancellor of the University. There is to be a University Commission appointed by Government and entrusted with the responsibility of keeping under review—(a) the facilities for university education, (b) plans for the development of the University and (c) the financial needs of University education. This Commission and other important bodies of the university, namely, the University Court, the Board of Trustees and the Standing

Committee are manned in the majority by officials and nominees of the Government.

More uniformity is achieved by the abolition of the Council and the Academic Board of each constitutent College and their replacement by a Standing Committee. The Vice-Chancellor becomes the Chief Academic and Administrative Officer of the University and he is no longer the Principal of any of the Colleges. But the Pro Vice-Chancellor still remains as Principal of one of the Colleges and the office is held biennially by each Principal. A new office, that of Pro-Chancellor, is also introduced. According to the Act, the Pro-Chancellor should be a person of high academic distinction appointed by the Chancellor; he is Chairman of the University Court and his duties include functions delegated to him by the Chancellor. The Chancellor, Pro-Chancellor, the Vice-Chancellor, the Pro Vice-Chancellor, the Court and Senate altogether constitute the authorities of the University. Of these, although the Chancellor is 'head', the 'supreme authority' is the Court while Senate is the 'supreme academic authority'.

There is no change in the existing Faculties of the University namely, Agriculture, Arts, Economics and Social Studies, Education, and Pure and Applied Sciences. There is, however, provision for the establishment of new Faculties but such establishment can be made only by the Court.

An important move to ensure uniformity in the holding of the property of both Colleges is the establishment of a Board of Trustees. All proprietary interests of the University which were hitherto vested in the Councils of the respective Colleges are now held by this Board.

The new constituted University promises to be a symbol of national unity in the field of education and, in addition to academic attainment, to be a place for the building up of a national identity and the promotion of economic and social advancement of the peoples of Sierra Leone. This is best borne out in s. 8(1) of the 1972 Act which sets out the main objects of the University as follows: to

'(a) provide instruction in such branches of learning as it may think fit and make provision for research and for the advancement and dissemination of knowledge in such manner as may be determined by it;
(b) provide as may be determined by it external services (extension), for persons who are not regularly enrolled in the University;
(c) grant degrees, diplomas and certificates and make such other awards of the University;
(d) preserve academic freedom and prevent discrimination in teaching and research, in the admission of students, the appointment of staff and in the granting of degrees, diplomas certificates and other awards;
(e) preserve, enrich and develop the cultural heritage, the economy and welfare of the Republic of Sierra Leone in particular and humanity in general, holding out the benefits to all persons without discrimination.'

NOTES
1. Act No. 30 of 1972
2. Act No. 3 of 1972
3. Act No. 13 of 1972
4. Act No. 15 of 1971
5. Act No. 24 of 1972
6. Act No. 46 of 1965
7. Act No. 4 of 1972

8. Act No. 5 of 1972
9. Public Notices Nos. 36 and 58 of 1972
10. Act No. 20 of 1972
11. Act No. 41 of 1965
12. See The Courts (Amendment) Act,'1972; Act No. 2 of 1972
13. Act No. 29 of 1972
14. Act No. 7 of 1972
15. Act No. 15 of 1955
16. Act No. 10 of 1972
17. Civ. App. 12/72 (unreported) judgement delivered on 11 July 1973. The Supreme Court on 28 October 1974 affirmed the decision of the Court of Appeal. The present writer had concluded this survey before the Supreme Court's decision. It may therefore be necessary to mention this case again in a subsequent survey
18. See dictum of Lord Mansfield in *Moses* v. *Macferlan* (1760) 2 Burr. 1,005, 1,012
19. See Goff and Jones, *The Law of Restitution* (1966), p. 23
20. Civ. App. 18/71 (unreported); judgement delivered on the 25 May 1972
21. [1891] AC325; See the speech of Lord Herschell at p. 362
22. [1938] AC57; See the speech of Lord Maugham at pp. 78 & 86
23. Civ. App. 19/71 (unreported); judgement delivered on 15 February 1972
24. Civ. App. 16/71 (unreported); judgement delivered on 18 February 1972
25. Act No. 33 of 1961
26. Act No. 17 of 1972
27. Act No. 9 of 1973
28. Act No. 9 of 1972
29. Act No. 23 of 1972
30. Act No. 16 of 1972
31. Act No. 17 of 1971
32. Act No. 14 of 1972
33. Civ. App. 6/72 (unreported); judgement delivered on the 23 June 1972
34. See *Annual Survey of African Law*, Vol. IV 1970, p. 59
35. Cap. 45 of the Revised Laws of Sierra Leone, 1960
36. Cap. 96 of the Revised Laws of Sierra Leone, 1960
37. Act No. 19 of 1972
38. Civ. App. 32/71 (unreported); judgement delivered on 2 March 1972
39. (1885) 29 Ch D 322
40. [1891] 2 QB 233
41. Act No. 12 of 1972
42. Act No. 27 of 1972
43. Act No. 6 of 1972
44. Njala University College Act 1964, Act No. 18 of 1964
45. Act No. 22 of 1972

CHAPTER FOUR

THE EAST AFRICAN COMMUNITY

Margaret A. Rogers

The past year has seen little legislative activity in the East African Legislative Assembly but the Reports placed before the Assembly by the Corporations have been debated thoroughly and resulted in some constructive suggestions and solutions. The progress of the Community towards the aims declared in Art. 2 of the Treaty for East African Co-operation have been given much emphasis in several speeches and a review of economic integration activities up to the end of 1972 will be published early next year. The initial planning period for the common services was from 1969–72 and the necessity of having to plan and submit estimates for the period from 1973–76 has involved the Community's officials in extensive consultation and consideration of the future of the Community. There seems little doubt that economic co-operation will be strengthened over the next three years in spite of the disparate developments within the Partner States. On 8 February 1972 President Nyerere of Tanzania in an address to the East African Legislative Assembly said:

'The institutions and the fact of co-operation in East Africa have been under great strain since the coup in Uganda in January 1971. They survived and it is very good that they did so, for the break-up of the East African Community would not only mean an economic loss; it would also be a terrific setback to the Community's long term objectives . . . There is a distinction between the responsibilities each Partner State has as a member of the Community and the political relations of the Partners one to another. If we all hold fast to that distinction and, regardless of our bilateral disputes, work to strengthen the Community where we can, then East Africa will come through this crisis stronger and better equipped to deal with the real problems of the development of its peoples.'

However, one area in which it has been agreed that regionalisation must take precedence over intra-national co-operation is that of income tax. In both Kenya and Tanzania, budget statements for the financial year 1972/73 make reference to the proposed regionalization of the East African Income Tax Department. For some time now, consideration has been given to the best methods for rationalising and improving the machinery for the collection of direct taxation within the Community. An Income Tax Mission, arranged by the International Monetary Fund at the request of the Partner States has been visiting East Africa during the course of this year and has made a series of recommendations to the East African governments relating to the establishment of national income tax departments. It seems likely that these recommendations will be accepted and that next year we shall see legislation to this effect.

After many years of successful operation, East African Airways Corporation has recently encountered serious financial problems. Future trends in the development of the Corporation are at present being considered by a Select Committee of the East African Legislative Assembly set up in 1971 to examine the accounts of the Corporation. On domestic operations, decisive action appears necessary to reduce costs and increase revenues and steps have recently been taken to strengthen East African Corporation's management, finance and marketing services. A long-term plan for the development of East African Airways is expected to be presented to the Board of the Corporation within the immediate future.

CONTRACT AND TORT

The case of *Kyobe* v. *East African Airways*[1] arises out of a claim for damages for breach of a contract of service by a former employee of East African Airways Corporation. The appellant, Wilson Kyobe, formerly a Ugandan Government servant, was employed as general manager by the respondent corporation with effect from 1 September 1964. The post of general manager of the corporation was created by s. 6 of the East African Airways Act, 1963 and the appellant's appointment was duly approved by the Authority as required by the section. In 1967 the East African Airways Corporation Act (Cap. 16) set up the present Corporation and under s. 29(1) of that Act, the assets and liabilities of the Corporation established under the 1963 Act were transferred and vested in the present respondent Corporation. The issue in the case before the court was whether the appellant's appointment as general manager still existed after the 1967 Act came into force.

The 1967 Act makes no provision for a general manager but it does provide for a director-general. The President of the Court of Appeal in the course of his judgement said:

> It is a fact that the new post of director-general does appear to a great extent to have taken the place of that of general manager but there are considerable differences between the establishment of the post in the respective Acts. Thus the director-general is now a member of the Board of Directors while the general manager was not; but the main difference is now in their respective duties. The authority and power of the general manager were such as given him by the Corporation (s. 6 of the 1963 Act). In the 1967 Act the control and the executive management of the Corporation is now vested in the director-general and he is given certain other specific powers.

> The judge, in considering whether the appellant's position had been abolished by statute, relied on the fact that the appellant had a vested right to notice and also the fact that s. 24(3) of the 1967 Act specifically provided that persons in the service of the previous Corporation are deemed to be appointed

to the service of the Corporation established by the 1967 Act. I am of the view that the judge was correct in finding that the appellant's appointment continued with the respondent after the 1967 Act came into force.'

The President discussed the effect of the repeal of the 1963 Act on the post of general manager and concluded that although the post had been abolished, the contract of employment between the respondent and the appellant remained. By virtue of s. 24(3) of the 1967 Act persons in the service of the previous Corporation on the day of the coming into force of the Act were deemed to have been appointed on that day to the service of the Corporation created under the new Act. The appellant was clearly a person in the service of the previous Corporation and there appeared to be no reason for limiting the provisions of the sub-section to persons appointed by any specific method or under any specific section of the 1973 Act.

As the appellant's contract did not provide for the termination of his service with the respondent the President held that it would be subject to termination on reasonable notice. The appellant contended that reasonable notice should be a period of twelve months and in the cross-appeal, the respondent contended that it should be three months. The judge in the Court below had reached the conclusion that a period of six months would constitute reasonable notice in the circumstances and the President of the Court of Appeal confirmed this conclusion.

On the termination of his service with the Corporation, the appellant had received a payment of £4,033. 15. He claimed that this was a gift in recognition of his services and had nothing to do with the amount to which he was entitled by way of damages for wrongful termination of his contract. He claimed that he was now entitled to recover salary for the period of reasonable notice together with all other subsidiary benefits arising out of his contract of service. The respondent had led evidence in the Court below to the effect that they had paid him his salary in full up to the date of termination plus (a) salary for the nineteen days earned vacation leave which was due to him, (b) a refund of both the respondent Corporation's and his own contributions to the pension fund and (c) allowed him to remain in a Corporation house free of rent for a period of over seven months after the termination of the contract. In addition, they paid him the sum of £4,033. 15.

The judge in the lower Court had found that the appellant's claim for salary in lieu of notice had already been settled in full and disallowed his claim in that respect. In regard to the subsidiary claims made by the appellant there was no evidence before the Court to prove his entitlement to any of these special amounts. The President dismissed the appeal with costs to the respondent and also dismissed the cross-appeal with costs to the appellant, Mustafa, J., agreed.

The Vice-President in his judgement dissented on one issue, viz., that the appointment of the appellant as general manager was frustrated by the enactment of the 1967 Act. The Vice-President did not agree with the judge in the Court below when he concluded that the office of director-general was a redesignation of the office of general manager and had no doubt that the office of general manager had come to an end with the coming into operation of the 1967 Act. In considering the effect of s. 24(3) which provided that persons already in the service of the previous Corporation were deemed to have been re-appointed to the service of the new Corporation, the Vice-President agreed that the effect of the provision was to save the contracts of employment of all the Corporation's servants by deeming re-appointment. However, the Vice-President did not see how the appellant could be deemed to be re-appointed to an office which no longer existed. This difficulty did not arise in regard to the appointment of other employees. The appointment of a general manager was always on a different footing from that of all other employees of the Corporation. The appellant was appointed to a statutory office and was not an employee assigned to a particular post. At the moment immediately after the 1967 Act came into force he had no office and therefore his contract of service must have ended. The Vice-President would have allowed this ground of cross-appeal.

Two interesting decisions arise out of the Kenya case of *Queen's Cleaners and Dyers Ltd* v. *East African Community.*[2] In the first case, on a preliminary point, Mr Justice Trevelyan considered the effect of a plea of guilty to a charge of driving a motor vehicle without due care and attention under s. 49 of the Traffic Act[3] on the evidence led in a subsequent suit for negligence. The defendant had pleaded guilty to the statutory offence but in the civil suit he denied negligence. S. 47A of the Evidence Act[4] reads:

'47A. A final judgement of a competent court in any criminal proceedings which declares any person to be guilty of a criminal offence shall, after the expiry of the time limited for an appeal against such judgement or after the date of the decision of any appeal therein, which ever is the latest, be taken as conclusive evidence that the person so convicted was guilty of that offence.'

The judge held that the expression 'conclusive evidence' in s. 47A means evidence that cannot be the subject matter of dispute, qualification or challenge. It would be wrong to admit evidence to show why the plea of guilty was tendered for that would go to qualify if not to nullify what the legislature has declared to be conclusive. But where contributory negligence is concerned, it is different; for the Court must investigate whether one or other or both of the parties were at fault so as to apportion the damage according to the relative importance of their acts in causing the damage and their relative blameworthiness. To establish a claim in negligence simpliciter the degree of blame thereof is immaterial for if a person is negligent in the smallest degree it is enough to fix that person with liability. Applying s. 47A, the conviction spells out negligence and that concludes the matter. What s. 47A does is to make it impossible to hold that the person so convicted was not negligent at all; the court may find that his blameworthiness was small but it cannot find that he had none. The Court accordingly held that the defence could not lead evidence as to why the defendant had pleaded guilty to the criminal charge. Although the conclusion of the Court appears to be a reasonable interpretation of the provisions of s. 47A and its application to the facts of the case, one sentence in the judgement does appear to be misleading. To establish a claim in negligence simpliciter it is not enough to show negligence in the smallest degree in order to fix liability; the plaintiff must show a sufficient degree to negligence to breach the standard of care required in the particular circumstances.

The Court dealt, thereafter, with the main claim which was for damages against the East African Community as the first defendant, the former Minister for Finance and Administration to the Community, Mr Odero-Jowi, as the second defendant and a driver in the employ of the Community as the third defendant. As a result of a collision between a car driven by a director of the plaintiff firm and one driven by a Mr Kamau, the plaintiff suffered damage and claimed against each of the three defendants. The claim against the first and the second defendants was in the alternative; against the first defendant as the owner of the vehicle and as the employer of the third defendant or against Mr Odero-Jowi should the third defendant be held not to have been acting within the course of his employment with the first defendant. The Court held that the third defendant was, by reason of his negligent driving entirely to blame for the accident and that there was no contributory negligence by the plaintiff.

The court then had to consider the question of vicarious liability. The facts before the Court were that on 8 July 1969 Mr Odero-Jowi wrote a letter to the Secretary General of the East African Community stating that he was, that day, going on thirty days leave and he left Arusha with his official car and driver. While they were in Nairobi, on 27 July, the driver asked for leave to return to Arusha to visit his family and was given permission to do so. Another driver, Mr Kamau, was instructed by Mr Odero-Jowi to take the regular driver to the bus terminal and it was on the way there that the collision occurred. On those facts, the first defendant, the East African Community claimed that the third defendant was at the relevant time in Mr Odero-Jowi's particular employ.

Mr Odero-Jowi was appointed a Minister in the Community as from 1 December 1967 by a letter of that date which stated that his appointment was being made under Art. 49 of the Treaty for East African Co-operation and that it was subject to a Statement of Conditions of Service; one such condition made it clear that Mr Odero-Jowi had no right to take his car and driver with him when he went on leave. The judge also held that Mr Odero-Jowi was entitled to thirty days leave. By a Gazette Notice which appeared in the *Kenya Gazette* on 1 August 1969 Mr Odero-Jowi was shown to have been appointed Kenya's Minister for Economic Planning and Development with effect from 24 July 1969. Mr Justice Trevelyan found that Mr Odero-Jowi ceased to be a Minister of the Community on 24 July 1969 and that the fact that he had earned leave extending beyond that time did not affect the issue.

The Court then went on to consider the law in regard to a master's liability for the torts of his servant and Mr Justice Trevelyan said:

'A master is liable for his servant's tort which he has authorized or subsequently ratified and he is also liable for it when it was committed in the course of his employment. In the present case there is no suggestion that anyone authorized the third defendant's tort so we need say nothing about that . . . This leaves for consideration whether Mr Kamau was acting in the course of his employment with the Community or with Mr Odero-Jowi when the accident occurred . . . But what I think is at the core of the problem before us is the ostensible authority with which Mr Odero-Jowi was or had been clothed . . . In other words, what we have to decide is whether Mr Odero-Jowi, though (in my finding) not at the time a Minister in the Community, had ostensible authority to instruct Mr Kamau to take Mr Ombwodo to the omnibus terminus and whether Mr Kamau should have obeyed that instruction.'

The judge considered the authorities and concluded:

'So too in the present case do I believe that when the accident occurred the third defendant was acting as the first defendant's servant. The fact that Mr Odero-Jowi had no business to give him the order that he did is of no consequence to us. It is true that, so far as we know, no one in terms ever said to the third defendant "You will obey Mr Odero-Jowi's orders at all times" but the latter was the Minister responsible, if not for all the transport in the Community as one witness said, at least for the department in which Mr Kamau worked and there was no reason for him to doubt his authority. It was simply his duty to obey orders given him in the ordinary matters of his service . . .
    . . . But Mr Odero-Jowi was no longer a Community Minister when he gave his instruction. Nonetheless it makes no difference. He had been clothed with the authority and neither Mr Ombwodo nor Mr Kamau knew that he had been divested of it. He still had the official car and its driver and the official Gazette had not yet been published (though I doubt whether it would have been adequate notice had it been published before the accident) and no one, as far as we know had told either driver that he was no longer their political head. It will be recalled that Mr Kamau said "I do not question a Minister's instructions". He was given an order to drive the car, his job with the Community was to drive cars and, as I believe, it was his duty, not knowing the change of circumstances to have obeyed Mr Odero-Jowi's orders.'

The Court held that the third defendant was acting within the scope of his employment with the first defendant and gave judgement for the amount claimed and interest against the first and third defendants. The plaintiff was given costs against the first and third defendants and the second defendant costs against the first defendant.

CUSTOMS AND EXCISE

The limitation of an action under the East African Customs and Transfer Tax Management Act[5] was raised as a preliminary point in the case of *Ramji* v. *Customs and Excise.*[6] The Plaintiff had paid Shs. 18,000/- import duty on 19 April 1968 on a consignment of 12 cases of printed cotton piece goods purportedly imported into Kenya at Mombasa in April, 1968. The plaintiff claimed that in fact the consignment was never imported into Kenya and that the import duty was paid in error. He claimed a refund under s. 123(1)(*b*) of the East African Customs and Transfer Tax Management Act.[7] S. 123(1)(*b*) so far as is relevant reads as follows:

'123(1) Subject to this section, and to any regulations, the Commissioner General may grant a refund . . .
    (*b*) of any import or export duty or transfer tax which has been paid in error.
    (2) No refund of any import or export duty or transfer tax, or part thereof shall be granted under sub. s. (1) unless the person claiming such refund presents such claim within a period of twelve months from the date of the payment of the duty.'

The relevant regulation governing the submission of such a claim is regulation 139(*a*) of the East African Customs Regulations which reads as follows:

'139(*a*) Any person claiming a refund of any duties which have been overpaid shall submit to the proper officer at the place where the duty was paid an application therefor in the form No. C.54, in duplicate, together with such evidence of overpayment as the Officer shall require.'

On 5 December 1968, well within the limitation period, the 'proper officer' received a completed form C.54 from the plaintiff. However, the officer requested evidence of non-importation and the plaintiff obtained a certificate from the shippers dated 4 March 1969 which stated that the consignment had not landed from the relevant vessel at any port in Kenya or Tanzania. This certificate did not satisfy the officer and he requested further evidence from the plaintiff. The claim was not supported by satisfactory evidence by 28 June 1969 and counsel for the defendant took the preliminary point that the action was time-barred as regulation 139 required the claim to be made and the evidence to support it to be given within twelve months from the date on which the duty was paid. Mr Justice Mosdell held that the words 'together with' in the regulation were synonymous with 'as well as' and were not intended to signify contemporaneity. To construe the words in such a sense would produce an absurdity. The plaintiff could not supply the evidence at the time of the submission of the claim form as he did not know what evidence might be required by the 'proper officer'. The objection in law as to limitation was overruled.

In the case of *Riachand Khimji & Co* v. *Attorney General*[8] the Court held that the right to confiscate goods under s. 158 of the East African Customs and Transfer Tax Management Act[9] vested only in persons in the service of the Customs (other than a labourer) or in a police officer. A chief inspector of explosives had no such right.

EAST AFRICAN COURT OF APPEAL

New Rules for the Court of Appeal for East Africa have been promulgated by the President of the Court of Appeal[10] and replace the Eastern Africa Court of Appeal Rules which are revoked by Rule 114.

The right of audience of advocates is dealt with in Rule 25 and this provides that the Attorney General and the Solicitor General for each of the Partner States and the Counsel and Deputy Counsel to the Community shall have the right of audience before the Court and shall take precedence over all other advocates. As between themselves, the Attorneys-General and the Counsel to the Community shall take precedence according to the dates of their respective appointments and the Solicitors-General and the Deputy Counsel to the Community take precedence in like manner after them. However, the Attorney-General and the Solicitor-General for any Partner State shall take absolute precedence when appearing in their own capacity in their own State in any application or appeal arising from that State. Other legal officers of the

Governments of the Partner States or of the East African Community have the right of audience before the Court in all proceedings within the scope of their official duties. The right of audience extends to all advocates who are entitled to practice before the superior court of any of the Partner States, with the exception of any who may have been struck off the roll or is under suspension from practice in his own State, although he may be entitled to practice in another Partner State.

The procedure for the listing of authorities to be quoted in Court is set out in Rule 26. An advocate who intends to rely on the judgement of any reported case or to quote from any book must lodge a list of the titles of such cases or books with the Registrar of the Court and must furnish a copy of the list for the other party or parties to the case at least twenty four hours before the hearing of the case. If an advocate wishes to rely on unreported cases he must produce a certified copy for the Court and for the opposing party.

One of the processes which varies considerably from that in the Court of Appeal in England is set out in Rule 63. Under this Rule the appellant must in a criminal appeal lodge a memorandum of appeal in quintuplicate with the Registrar within fourteen days of receiving the record of appeal. The memorandum must set out under distinct heads, numbered consecutively, without argument or narrative, the grounds of objection to the decision appealed against, specifying, in the case of a first appeal, the points of law or fact and, in the case of another appeal, the points of law, which are alleged to have been wrongfully decided. The memorandum must be served on the respondent. Under Rule 65, the appellant may also lodge a statement in writing of his arguments in support of the appeal. A similar provision in regard to civil appeals may be found in Rule 84.

The following are the relevant extracts in regard to the payment of fees:

'102. Subject to the provisions of rules 110 and 112 the fees set out in the Second Schedule shall be payable in respect of the matters and services therein set out:

Provided—
(a) that no fees shall be payable upon any appeal from a superior court acting in its original jurisdiction in a criminal case, or on any application in connection with any such appeal or for the supply of the copy of the record of appeal to any party to any such appeal;
(b) that no fee shall be payable by the Government of any of the Partner States in respect of any criminal application or appeal;
(c) that copies of any documents may be issued without fee to such persons as the President may nominate or at such reduced fee as the President may direct.

THE SECOND SCHEDULE
(Rule 102)
FEES

PART I: Fees in connection with applications, other than applications relating to criminal appeals from a superior court in its original jurisdiction and other than applications under rule 112.

Item No.

1.	Upon loding a notice of motion	shs. 50
2.	Upon lodinging an affidavit, other than an affidavit annexed to a notice of motion	shs. 5
3.	Upon giving notice under rule 54 (1)	shs. 100

PART II: Fees inconnection with criminal appeals

4.	Upon lodging a notice of appeal from a superior court in its appellate jurisdiction	shs. 50
5.	For preparing the record of appeal, for each folio or part thereof- for the first copy	shs. 3.50
	for each additional copy	shs. 1

PART IIi: Fees in connection with civil appeals

6.	Upon lodging a notice of appeal	shs. 100
7.	Upon lodging a notice of address for service or a notice of change of address	shs. 5
8.	Upon lodging a memorandum of appeal—against an interlocutory decision against a final decision	shs. 250

(i) where the appeal is against an award of money or the refusal to make such an award or against a decision as to the ownership of or en-titlement to the possession of property: if the amount of the money (exclusive of any interest awarded thereon) or the value or the property

(a) does not exceet Shs. 10,000 — Shs. 400

(b) exceeds Shs. 10,000 — for the first shs. 10,000, shs. 400; and for each subsequent shs. 2,000 or part thereof up to shs. 210.000. shs. 20; and for each subsequent shs. 2,000 or part thereof, shs. 10; but so that the fee shall not exceed shs. 20,000.

(ii) in any other case — shs. 400, with an additional fee of shs. 400 for each day or part of a day of hearing after the first, but so that the fee shall not exceed shs. 4,000

9.	Upon lodging a notice of cross-appeal	shs. 100

Item No.

10.	Upon lodging a notice of grounds for affirming the decision	shs. 5
11.	Upon lodging a notice withdrawing an appeal, or a notice of cross-appeal, or a notice of grounds for affirming the decision	shs. 5

PART IV: Miscellaneous

12.	For serving any document in connection with any civil application or appeal, in addition to all necessary expenses of travel—	
	where the person to be served resides or has his place of business within the city or town where the Registry or a sub-registry of the Court is situate	shs. 4
	in any other case	shs. 6
13.	For sealing an order in any civil application or appeal	shs. 10
14.	For preparing certified copies of any document for each folio or part thereof—	
	for the first copy	shs. 3.50
	for each subsequent copy	shs. 1

PART V: Fees in connection with the taxation of costs

15.	Upon lodging a bill of costs for taxation	shs. 5
16.	For the certificate of the result of a taxation	shs. 10
17.	Upon applying for a reference under rule 109	shs. 20

SCALE OF COSTS

1.	For instructions to file a notice of appeal	shs. 60
2.	For instructions to act for a respondent where an appeal is subsequently instituted where no appeal is subsequently instituted, to cover all costs arising out of the notice of appeal, other than disbursements and those of any application to the superior court or the Court	shs. 60 shs. 100
3.	For drawing a notice of motion	shs. 30
4.	For drawing an affidavit, for each folio or part thereof, exclusive of exhibits	shs. 10 with a minimum fee of shs. 20
5.	For drawing a notice of appeal	shs. 15
6.	For drawing a notice of address for service	shs. 10
7.	For drawing a memorandum of appeal	shs. 150
8.	For drawing a notice of cross-appeal	shs. 75
9.	For drawing a notice of grounds for affirming a decision	shs. 50
10.	For drawing an order, for each folio or part thereof	shs. 10 with a minimum fee of shs. 20
11.	For drawing a bill of costs, for each folio or part thereof	shs. 5
12.	For drawing any other necessary document to be filed or used in the Court, for each folio or part thereof	shs. 5

13.	For making any necessary copies, for each folio or party thereof—	
	for the first copy	shs. 3.50
	for each subsequent copy	shs. 1
14.	For attendance at the Registry	shs. 10
15.	For attending on the Registrar	
	for the first 15 minutes	shs. 25
	for each subsequent 15 minutes	shs. 15
16.	For attending on a Judge in Chambers	
	for the first 30 minutes	shs. 100
	for each subsequent 30 minutes	shs. 50
17.	For attending in Court, where the matter was listed but not reached, for each day	shs. 100
18.	For attending in Court on the hearing of any application or appeal	
	for the first 30 minutes	shs. 150
	for each subsequent 30 minutes	shs. 50
19.	For attending in Court to hear judgement	shs. 50

INCOME TAX

The Minister of Finance of Kenya, introducing his budget speech in the National Assembly on 15 June 1972 announced that the three Partner States had agreed to the separation of the administration of taxation and that amendments to that effect would be introduced soon. It may well be that by the time this volume is available to the public that this transition will already have taken place. In the meantime, certain minor amendments are published to the East African Income Tax (Management) Act, 1958.[11] A new basis for the valuation of housing supplied by an employer to an employee is set out in a new sub-section to s. 5(1)(b) of the main Act. The new paragraph (v) reads as follows:

'(v) the value of premises provided by an employer for occupation by his employee for residential purposes, and such value, excluding the value of any furniture or other contents so provided, shall be deemed to be—
(A) in the case of a director of a company, other than a whole-time service director resident in Kenya or in Uganda, an amount equal to fifteen per cent of his world income, excluding the value of such premises;
(B) in the case of any other employee resident in Kenya or in Uganda, an amount equal to fifteen per cent of the gains or profits from his employment, excluding the value of such premises;
(C) in the case of a director of a company, other than a whole-time service director resident in Tanzania, an amount equal to fifteen per cent of his world income, excluding the value of such premises, or £2000, whichever is the lesser;
(D) in the case of any other employee resident in Tanzania, an amount equal to fifteen per cent of the gains or profits from his employment, excluding the value of such premises, or £2000, whichever is the lesser.
Provided that—
(A) where any person occupies such premises for part only of a year of income then the value, ascertained under the foregoing provisions, shall be reduced by such proportion as may be just and reasonable having regard to the period of occupation and the yearly rate of world income or gains or profits from employment, as the case may be;

(B) where the employee pays rent to his employer for such premises the value, ascertained under the foregoing provisions, shall be reduced by the amount of such rent;
(C) where part only of any premises is so provided, the Commissioner-General may reduce the value, ascertained under the foregoing provisions, to such amount as he may consider just and reasonable.'

In 1971 a new s. 53 was substituted for the previous provision and this is followed by a new s. 53A which deals specifically with the Selective Income Levy payable in Uganda. It provides that such levy shall be allowed as a credit in respect of persons resident in Uganda against Income tax payable in Uganda currency for the year of income in which the dividend is received provided that: 'where during the year of income in which the dividend is received, the person receiving the dividend has no liability, or has insufficient liability to income tax, under this Act, to offset the amount of the levy against, no credit of that levy shall be allowed, and any income tax liability for that year of income shall then be payable in full.' The wording is not as clear as it might be but the intent of the proviso is understandable.

One further provision in the amending Act is to be found in s. 16. Item 42 of Head A of the First Schedule of the principal Act is amended so that there are separate provisions for (a) Kenya and Uganda and (b) for Tanzania. The provisions deal with exemptions from the payment of tax on management or professional fee or any royalty.

In the case of *K. Ltd* v. *Income Tax*[12] the company concerned was incorporated in 1948 and in 1954 purchased a plot of land at Kisii and erected a building thereon. The building comprised shops and flats which were let out to tenants and the income of the company at all material times consisted solely of the rents received from the tenants. The capital of the company was acquired partly by contributions from shareholders and partly by a bank loan, which was granted on the condition that no profits should be distributed by way of dividend until the loan was paid off. The company, realizing that if no dividends were distributed it would become liable for tax on the accumulated profits, declared dividends but in order to comply with the condition in the bank loan agreement, it retained the sums payable to shareholders, merely crediting them to the accounts of the shareholders. After a period of eleven years, a number of shareholders threatened to sue the company if the dividends declared in the five preceding years were not paid forthwith. A compromise was reached whereby the shareholders agreed to forbear from instituting proceedings against the company if the company agreed to the conversion of dividend credits into loans in consideration of the company paying interest on the said loan amounts, backdated for the previous five years.

In its return of income for the relevant year, the company claimed to deduct from its total income the amount of interest credited under the agreement to the accounts of the shareholders in respect of the unpaid dividends. The commissioner refused to allow the deduction and the company appealed to the local Income Tax Committee. The Committee confirmed the assessment but stated that the members felt that the intention behind the shareholders' action was that the money must be accepted as a loan and interest was allowable under s. 14(3)(*a*) of the East

African Income Tax (Management) Act, 1958.[13] The company appealed against the decision and the Commissioner appealed against that part of the decision which held that the credits to the balances of the shareholders should be accepted as a loan and that the interest on that loan should be an allowable deduction under the provisions of the Act.

The substance of the case for the company was that the bank overdraft should be regarded as loan capital used in the creation of an income-earning asset. The company would never have obtained overdraft facilities unless it had agreed to pay interest. Payment of interest to the bank was accordingly directly incurred for the purpose of obtaining income. The overdraft was progressively reduced out of the company's profits and the reason why dividends were not paid to shareholders was that the company was using the amounts which were payable as dividends to reduce the overdraft. In other words, the bank loan was being replaced by a shareholders' loan. When the shareholders threatened to sue for their unpaid dividends, the only way in which the company could retain the money as a loan from the shareholders was to agree to pay interest. The interest payable to the shareholders should therefore be regarded in the same light as interest payable to the bank, i.e. as part of the income earning asset and as a charge directly incurred in the creation of the company's income.

The court held that the interest payable on the original bank loan no doubt fell within the description of an expenditure incurred for the direct purpose of producing income but found it difficult to see how interest required to be paid on a loan made subsequent to the completion of the income-earning asset could be so described. If expenditure incurred in resisting an application for winding-up is not incurred for the direct purpose of the production of income, as was held in the *Buhemba Mines*[14] case, then by parity of reasoning it would appear that money agreed to be paid to the shareholders to induce them not to take proceedings against the company is equally not expenditure incurred directly for the purpose of producing income. The company's appeal was dismissed and the Commissioner's appeal allowed.

The case of *Income Tax* v. *Rasiklal*[15] arose out of a claim by the respondent for child allowances in respect of his brother and sisters who were residing with their parents in India. He claimed that he remitted money regularly for their support and that his parents were not in a position to maintain his brother and sisters. The respondent claimed that the said brother and sisters, although resident in India were within his custody and the Commissioner refused to accept that custody, within the meaning of s. 44 of the East African Income Tax (Management) Act,[16] could arise in those circumstances. This was the first time that the meaning of the word 'custody' as contained in the provisions of the East African Income Tax (Management) Act had come up for decision and Mr Justice Biren in his judgement said: '. . . we have limited the meaning or definition of the word 'custody' to when used in connection with children. The section which we are interpreting has gone much further and qualified the word 'custody' by stating at paragraph (b):

'any other child who was under such age who was in his custody by virtue of any custom of the community to which he belongs.'

It is common ground that during the year of assessment the taxpayer had been remitting Shs. 500/- monthly to his parents for the maintenance and education of his brother and three sisters. It is also not disputed that his brother and three sisters are receiving full time education . . . the parents of the taxpayer, on account of their infirmities and poverty, have delegated their responsibility for the care and maintenance of these children to the taxpayer, in other words, they have abdicated their natural right to the custody of these children to the taxpayer, who apart from that has submitted that, as the eldest son of his parents, in view of their infirmities and their financial standing, their responsibilities in respect of his brother and sisters, according to the custom of their community, devolve on him . . . possibly the most material factor in this case is that there is a certificate from the Shree Hindu Manda to the effect that in accordance with the custom of their community the children with whom we are concerned are under the custody and maintenance of the taxpayer.'

Although the court agreed with the Commissioner's submission that the taxpayer could not be said to have physical custody of the children, they were all, according to the custom of his community to which they belong, in the custody of the taxpayer and he was therefore entitled to the child allowances in respect of them.

The question of a director's expenses was the subject of the case of *Income Tax* v. *M. Ltd.*[17] There the respondent company was incorporated in Kenya in 1963 and the shares were issued and held wholly and equally by Mr Jit Singh and his wife. These two, together with their son were the sole directors of the company. For the years prior to the year ending 31 May 1967 the company's accounts showed no expenditure on overseas travel but in the year of income 1967 there was expenditure of Shs. 6,146/- on return passages for Mr and Mrs Jit Singh to India. In all the relevant years, including the year ended 31 May 1967, the accounts of the company showed remuneration to the directors but the remuneration had never before included expenditure on overseas travel. The Commissioner contended that the expenditure on the sum of Shs. 6,146/- was not director's remuneration and therefore not allowable as a deduction under the East African Income Tax (Management) Act.[18] Mr Jit Singh admitted that he and his wife went to India solely for health reasons and while there he did no business on behalf of the company. The court held that his trip to India did not satisfy the requirement that the relevant expenditure was incurred wholly or exclusively in the production of the company's income for the year of income 1967. The court allowed the appeal by the Commissioner with costs and ordered the Commissioner's assessment made upon the respondent to be restored.

The case of *Income Tax* v. *Holdings Ltd*[19] decided that in terms of s. 58(c) of the East African Income Tax (Management) Act[20] as it applied before the 1970 amendment the entire dividend received from resident companies should be deducted from the chargeable income and not the net dividend after deducting expenses. This was a 'tax loop-hole' which had now been removed.

Two further tax cases are *Income Tax* v. *Kagera Saw Mills Ltd*[21] which deals with the interpretation of paragraph 27 of the 2nd Schedule of the East African Income Tax (Management) Act[22] and *Income Tax* v. *R.M. and Another*[23] which deals with the extension of time for the filing of an appeal by the Commissioner.

NOTES

1. [1972] EA 403
2. [1972] EA 229
3. Cap. 403 (K)
4. Cap. 80 (K)
5. Cap. 27 (EA)
6. [1972] EA 154
7. Cap. 27 *ibid*
8. [1972]EA 536
9. Cap. 27 *ibid*
10. Subsidiary Legislation 1972
11. Cap. 24 (EA)
12. [1972] EA 112
13. Cap. 24 *ibid*
14. *Commissioner for Income Tax* v. *Buhemba Mines*, 2 EATC 333, [1957] EA 589
15. [1972] EA 150
16. Cap. 24 *ibid*
17. [1972] EA 509
18. Cap. 24 *ibid*
19. [1972] EA 128
20. Cap. 24 *ibid*
21. [1972] EA 387
22. Cap. 24 *ibid*
23. [1972] EA 459

CHAPTER FIVE

KENYA

Eugene Cotran and Margaret Rogers

CONSTITUTIONAL LAW

No legislation on this subject was passed in 1972, but three cases of some interest were decided.

In *Attorney-General* v. *Oluoch*[1], the Court of Appeal considered the scope of s. 4(5) of the Government Proceedings Act (Cap. 40) which provides:

'(5) No proceedings shall lie against the Government by virtue of this section in respect of anything done or omitted to be done by any person while discharging or purporting to discharge any responsibilities of a judicial nature vested in him, or any responsibilities which he has in connection with the execution of judicial process.'

The facts were that the respondent claimed damages against the appellant for wrongful arrest and wrongful detention in respect of the actions of two magistrates and two police officers. It was clear from the plaint that the magistrates were acting as magistrates and the police officers were executing their warrants. There was no allegation that they had not acted in good faith. The trial judge refused to strike out the claim, but on appeal, the Court of Appeal held that in the absence of an allegation of bad faith, s. 4(5) fully protects the appellant since the acts done were in the discharge of judicial functions.

In *Matalinga and Others* v. *Attorney-General,*[2] Simpson, J., considered the meaning of s. 82(3) of the Constitution which defines discrimination, as follows:-

'In this section, the expression "discriminatory" means affording different treatment to different persons attributable wholly or mainly to their respective descriptions by race, tribe, place of origin or residence or other local connexion, political opinions, colour or creed whereby persons of one such description are subjected to disabilities or restrictions to which persons of another such description are not made subject or are accorded privileges or advantages which are not accorded to persons or another such description.'

The plaintiffs sued the defendant for a declaration that certain medical assistants be treated equally with respect to salary and other privileges. They claimed, *inter alia,* that the distinction between two salary scales in contrary to s. 82 of the Constitution. Simpson, J., held that the dis-

discrimination alleged does not fall within s. 82(3).

In *Ismail* v. *Attorney-General*,[3] the appellant applied for citizenship in December 1965, and in December 1969, he was informed that his application had been approved. No certificate of citizenship had been issued to him when in May, 1970, the fee for registration as a citizen was increased from Shs. 50 to Shs. 2000. He paid under protest and sued for the recovery of Shs. 1950. The Court of Appeal, reversing the judgement of Mosdell, J., in the High Court, held that the date of registration must refer back to the date when the appellant was entitled as of right to be registered as a citizen, i.e. when the lower fee was chargeable and 'his right could not be prejudiced or whittled away by any clerical or administrative act on the part of the Immigration Department.' (per Mustafa, J.A.)

LEGAL SYSTEM

In *Mayers and Another* v. *Akira Ranch Ltd. (No. 2)*,[4] the Court of Appeal considered the vexed question whether the Kenya Courts are bound by decisions of English Courts on the Common Law given prior to the date of reception in Kenya. The Court was adamant in asserting its judicial independence by asserting that though such decisions would be given the highest respect, they would feel free to depart from them if they considered them to be wrong. The Court said:

'Mr Slade, in the course of his argument, submitted that decisions of the English courts given prior to 1898 on the interpretation of the common law are binding on this Court and not merely persuasive. With respect, I cannot agree. There have been cases where the English courts after that date have held that earlier decisions were wrong. I think it would be quite absurd if we were to be bound by decisions of English courts which we think wrong and which have, in England, been held wrong, or which may in the future be held wrong there. In my opinion, we should treat the pre-1898 English decisions on the common law with the highest respect, but I think we have the power to depart from any such decision if we are convinced that it was wrong and that there is no reason of judicial policy for continuing to follow it.'

MARRIAGE

In *K (otherwise B)* v. *K*,[5] the respondent was married to another woman by Kikuyu customary law at the time when he purported to marry the petitioner in the registrar's office under the Marriage Act (Cap. 150). Waiyaki, J., had no difficulty in finding that the subsequent monogamous marriage is null and void.

SUCCESSION AND ADMINISTRATION OF ESTATES

Re Kibiego[6] raised the interesting question of whether a widow is entitled to administer the estate of her deceased husband when he died subject to customary law. Madan, J., had no hesitation in holding that whatever customary law has to say on the subject, the widow is the most suitable person to be granted letters of administration. The learned judge said:

'This matter has come before me on a reference by the registrar for two reasons. The first raises the question whether the widow of an African of the Nandi tribe who died intestate may apply for a grant of letters of administration. A glimmering of the law relating to administration of a Nandi's estate is referred to in Restatement of African Law by Cotran, Vol. 2, p. 115 who states, at p. 116, that on intestacy the family elders will always appoint the eldest son of the deceased as administrator. I think it is this statement of the law which made the registrar consider the propriety of grant of letters of administration to the widow . . . Whatever Cotran's source of Nandi law may be, I am of the opinion that in today's Kenya, in the absence of a valid reason such as grave unsuitability, a widow of whatever race living in the country, is entitled to apply to the court for the grant of letters of administration, more so when the children, as in the instant case, are minors. A widow is the most suitable person to obtain representation to her deceased husband's estate. In the normal course of events she is the person who would rightfully, properly and honestly safeguard the assets of the estate for herself and her children. It would be going back to a mediaeval conception to cling to a tribal custom by refusing her a grant which is obviously unsuited to the progressive society of Kenya in this year of grace. A legal system ought to be able to march with the changing conditions fitting itself into the aspirations of the people which it is supposed to safeguard and serve.'

The learned judge could, of course, have easily discovered 'Cotran's source of Nandi law' if he had read the preface and introduction to Volume II of the Restatement of African Law. The investigation was, of course, an official one carried out with the assistance of Law Panels set up by the Government of Kenya for the purpose. I do not think it can be doubted that under the customary law of the Nandi (and for that matter of the majority of the Kenya tribes) the deceased's widow was *not entitled* to administer the estate. Quite the contrary, she was herself subject to inheritance in the sense that her fate had to be decided by the family members.

However, one has great sympathy with the learned judge in not liking this position. His comments are reflected in the views adopted by the Commission on the Law of Succession in 1968, to which we now turn.

It will be remembered that the Commission drafted a Bill to give effect to its recommendations.[6] An attempt was made to introduce the same draft Bill in the National Assembly in 1970, but this proved abortive.[7] Following the criticisms in Parliament, a few amendments were made to the draft and in 1972, the Parliament passed the measure as the Law of Succession Act (No. 14 of 1972).

There are two principal amendments made to the Bill drafted by the Commission: (1) *Illegitimate Children*. Following the criticisms in Parliament which followed from the recommendations of the Commission that illegitimate children should inherit equally with legitimate children, the Act makes it clear that an illegitimate child does not inherit any property except if the father expressly recognized him or accepted him as his child or if the father has in his lifetime voluntarily assumed responsibility for him.[8] (2) *Share of Widow on Intestacy*. In the new Act, in addition to giving the widow a life interest in the whole of net intestate estate, she is also entitled absolutely to 'the personal and household effects of the deceased'[9] which is defined in s. 3(1) as:

'clothing and articles of personal use and adornment, furniture, appliances, pictures, ornaments, food drink, utensils and all other articles of household use or decoration normally to be associated with a matrimonial home, but does not include any motor vehicle or any other thing connected with the business or profession of the deceased.'

The Act provides in s. 1 that it shall come into operation on such a date as the Minister may by notice in the Gazette appoint. He has not so appointed to date, so that although passed by Parliament, it is not yet operative. One hopes that it will not take as long to bring it into effect as it took to pass it!

Reverting to the judgement of Mandan, J., in *Re Kifiego*, it is clear therefore that the learned judge was not prepared to uphold the customary law even although the new law giving the widow the right to administer had not come into force. Although he does not say so, it is submitted that he could only do this in one of two ways: (a) either under the authority of s. 3(2) of the Judicature act, No. 16 of 1967, which enables the displacement of customary law if it is 'repugnant to justice and morality'; or (b) by applying the provisions of the Indian Probate and Administration Act, 1881, which by a decision in 1965[10] has been extended to Africans.

In *Re Kibiego*, there do not appear to have been rival claimants, but in a case where there are, the Court would have to choose between applying the approach in (a) or (b). The stand of Madan, J., if the rival claimants had been before him is, at any rate, clear.

COMMERCIAL AND INDUSTRIAL LAW

AGENCY

The case of *Victory Ship-handlers* v. *Leslie & Anderson*[11] arose out of claim for damages for breach of contract by a ships chandler for goods sold and delivered on the instructions of the defendant company. The Plaintiff had had previous dealings with the defendant and on the occasion in question, they had received a letter from the defendant asking them to supply a list of stores ordered by the captain and the chief steward of the Merchant Vessel *Mellina*. A delivery order was prepared by the company's manager on 8 August and sent with the goods to the vessel. Someone on the ship signed each page of the order as having received the goods ordered in good condition. The invoices were similarly signed on 10 August and the Captain added 'Prices according to the owner's agreement'. The invoices were made out to the Master and Owner of SS *Mellina* and on the next line 'M/S Leslie & Anderson (EA) Ltd', the defendant company. There was no payment.

A letter of demand from the plaintiff firm's advocates went to the defendant company for Shs. 22,815/25, 'being the price of goods sold at your order and delivered on MV *Mellina*. In reply, the defendant company stated that it had acted for the charterers of the vessel and not the owners and one M. L. Eustace was the man to look to for payment. The defendant company alleged that they appointed the plaintiff firm as chandlers on behalf of the charterers.

The judge found that the defendant company was the agent of the charterers of the ship, Bagazi de Merina Carrara Massa based in Italy, and that the owners of the ship were probably the Meldarf Shipping Company in Athens. It was not clear who should pay for the groceries for a ship's crew and passengers as between the owner, charterer or crew. The agents' principals were, in any case, foreign. A reasonable chandler in Mombasa would not supply a foreign vessel with goods until he knew that the funds were in Kenya if he had to look to the foreign principal for payment rather than the local agent. Shipping companies in Mombasa accept agencies when they are satisfied that the owners or charterers will pay the chandler's bills. The defendant had acted in this way on previous occasions and their letter to the plaintiff in the present case was in a similar form to those used on other occasions. In this case, the Greek shipping company had refused to pay the bills and the defendant as agents wished to avoid liability.

The defendant had not signed as agent for anyone or used any phrase which would exclude their personal liability. The plaintiff admitted that he knew that the defendant was an agent for a principal but that the principal was undisclosed when the contract was made and performed. The plaintiff also admitted that he had attempted to seek payment from M. L. Eustace but there was no clear evidence that they had elected to seek payment from him rather than from the defendant. The court held that there was nothing in the contract to contradict the presumption that the defendant incurred personal liability and judgement was given for the plaintiff.

CONTRACT

In the case of *Schwartz* v. *Gill & Co*[12] the plaintiff had been employed by the defendant on overseas terms which included a provision that he had the right to two months' leave every four years together with passages to England. The plaintiff contended that it was an implied term of the contract that if leave and passages were not taken he had the right to accumulate the entitlement or to be paid the money equivalent. He claimed the value of leave and passages not taken in 1963 and in 1967. Mr Justice Wicks said that the court would imply a term where it felt satisfied that failure to mention the matter was due only to the fact that it was felt wholly unnecessary to say what was obvious at the time to all parties concerned. On the other hand, a term would not be implied merely because the court thinks it would have been reasonable to have inserted it in the contract nor if the contract would be effective without the proposed term and it was not obvious that that was the intention of the parties at the time. Quoting the dictum of Scrutton, L.J., in *Reigate* v. *Union Manufacturing Co,*[13] the judge said:

> 'A term can only be implied if it is necessary in the business sense to give efficacy to the contract; that is, if it is such a term that it can confidently be said that if at the time the contract was being negotiated someone had said to the parties, "What will happen in such a case?" they would both have replied: "Of course, so and so will happen; we did not trouble to say that; it was too clear." '

The judge went on to consider the East African case of *Greenly* v. *Rootes*

(Kenya) Ltd,[14] and quoted with approval an extract from the judgement of
Law, J.A., as follows:

> 'For the appellant to succeed in his appeal we would have to imply a term into
> the contract that the appellant at his option could choose to be paid the value of
> the passages instead of being provided with tickets after three years' service
> whether he went on leave or not. I agree with the trial judge that it would be
> unreasonable to imply such a term into the contract between the parties.'

The court observed that the real question to be taken into account in
deciding whether or not to imply such a term into a contract was whether
it could be established from precedent which terms will be implied and
which will not. In this case the relationship between employer and
employees must be considered and a host of issues emerged. On passages,
the employer may have allocated a total sum for passages and that sum
not being expended on one employee would be spent on others. On leave
pay, the work accumulated, or was spread amongst employees not on
leave so that the work was done and the wage bill remained static. On
both passages and leave pay taken, employees returned refreshed and
their improved efforts generated increased profits which wrote off the
cost. In the circumstances, the court found that there was no term implied
into the contract that the plaintiff was entitled to claim money in lieu of
leave and passages and the case for the plaintiff was dismissed.

An interesting situation in regard to a contract for the sale of goods
arose in the case of *Potgieter* v. *Stumberg and Another (No. 2).*[15] The
appellant had granted the respondents an option to purchase an
undivided half share in his farm, including the livestock and movables.
The consideration for the option was a loan of £8,000 for the development
of the said farm. By a letter in October 1965 the respondents exercised the
option but no documents of transfer were executed in favour of the
respondents and in March 1966 the appellant's farm was sold by the
mortgagee on the appellant failing to pay the mortgage instalments. The
appellant then sold the livestock and movables without accounting
therefor to the respondents. The respondents claimed either that they had
become partners with the appellant or that they had become joint owners
of the livestock and movables and they claimed for an account. The judge
at first instance found that the respondents were joint owners as alleged
and ordered an account. The appellant appealed, contending that the
agreement to purchase half the livestock had been frustrated by the forced
sale of the farm and that the appellant had not consented to the joint
ownership of the livestock and movables by the respondents.

The Court found, firstly, that the option agreement was undoubtedly a
legal and enforceable agreement made for valuable consideration and that
it was validly exercised on 26 October 1965. The option then became a
contract for the sale of the land and the movables and livestock on the
land. The sale of the land to the respondents was not completed before the
mortgagee sold the farm in March 1966. The land was sold at an amount
insufficient to cover the amount outstanding on the mortgage and all that
remained to the respondents was their agreement to buy the movables and
livestock. One of the main issues in the case was whether any property in
the movables and livestock passed to the respondents. The appellant

contended that the sale of the farm by the mortgagee frustrated the agreement between the appellant and the respondent but the court found that as the option was exercised before the sale, no question of frustration arose. Mr Justice Mustafa considered s. 19 of the Sale of Goods Act[16] and stated that in his view the movables and livestock were definitely ascertained and known goods within that section. On the exercise of the option the respondents obtained an undivided half-share in all the movables and livestock then on the farm belonging to the appellant. The respondents themselves might not have known exactly what these goods were but these were definite goods known to the appellant and could be proved by evidence. Immediately on the exercising of the option the respondents acquired a joint interest and the property passed to them. The appeal was dismissed.

The case of *Sardarilal Ltd* v. *Gusii County Council*[17] dealt with a contract of a local authority and decided that the presumption of due execution of such a contract may be rebutted by evidence of lack of authority. Rectification of the contract was refused on the grounds that it will be ordered only when the contract as it exists correctly expresses the agreement between the parties in all other respects.

HOTELS AND RESTAURANTS ACT, 1971[18]

The Hotels and Restaurants Act was brought into operation on 1 February 1972 and the Minister of Tourism promulgated Regulations under s. 29 of the principal Act on 21 October 1972. The regulations provide *inter alia* for minimum standards in respect of lighting, ventilation or air conditioning; rooms must be of adequate size for their use; stairways, halls and exits must be kept lighted and unobstructed at all times. The Authority set up under the principal Act must be satisfied in regard to the size of the lounge and dining-room and in regard to the equipment supplied for use in the dining-room. Provision is made for the regular testing of the water supply to any hotel or restaurant and for the maintaining of adequate fire-fighting appliances. Every person carrying on any hotel or restaurant business is required to submit a financial report to the Authority as and when required. The following extract from regulation 6 gives an indication of the standards expected by the Authority.

(2) (*a*) a mirror and shelf, each of adequate size to the satisfaction of the Authority, shall be provided in every bedroom;
(*b*) a wash-hand basin shall be provided in each bedroom to which a private bathroom is not attached;
(*c*) all mattresses shall be inner sprung, foam rubber, or a satisfactory equivalent;
(*d*) one dressing-table shall be provided in every bedroom with at least one chair to each bed;
(*e*) mosquito nets shall be made available on demand;
(*f*) fresh bed linen shall be supplied at least twice a week and for every new guest;
(*g*) a key of the bedroom or suite shall be made available to the occupant of each bedroom or suite;
(*h*) clothes-hooks, clothes-hangers and wardrobe or hanging space for clothes shall be provided in each bedroom;
(*i*) drinking water shall be provided in bedrooms and bathrooms at all times and shall be made available in public rooms;

(3) (a) the ratio of bathrooms and separate water-closets to residents shall be at least one to ten;
(b) an efficient hot and cold water system, to the satisfaction of the Authority, shall be installed to serve every bathroom;
(c) every bathroom including appropriately appointed shower room shall be equipped with—
(i) a secure door fastening;
(ii) a towel rail, clothes-hooks and a chair or stool.
(d)(i) soiled towels and bath mats, shall be replaced with freshly laundered towels and bath mats each day the guest occupies a room;
(ii) soap shall be provided each day or as required;
(iii) one extra roll or package of toilet tissue in addition to that in use shall be provided in each toilet room or bathroom;
(iv) furniture and shelving shall be of impermeable material or finish.

INSURANCE

In the case of *Jubilee Insurance Co Ltd* v. *Ombaka*[19] in the High Court of Kenya the plaintiff, an insurance company claimed repayment by the defendant, the insured, of a sum of money which the insurance company alleged it had become liable to pay to a third party by virtue of the provisions of the Insurance (Motor Vehicles Third Party Risks) Act.[20] The facts of the case were that during the week-end of 2 and 3 January 1965, the defendant had gone to Nakuru, leaving his family at home in Nairobi and his motor car in the garage of his house. The defendant's son was at that time a schoolboy of about sixteen or seventeen years who had been learning to drive at his school and held a provisional licence. On the Sunday afternoon, the defendant's son wished to visit the nearby shops and taking the keys of his father's car he drove along the main Ngong Road. While doing so he had to swerve to avoid running into the back of a lorry which had braked suddenly and a car, approaching from the opposite direction, in order to avoid a collision drove into the ditch and a passenger in the vehicle, viz the third party sustained a fractured leg. It was not disputed that the accident was due to the negligence of the defendant's son and that he was at the time an unlicensed driver. The only fact in dispute is whether the defendant's son was driving with the defendant's permission, a point which is of importance in connection with the definition in the policy of 'authorized driver'.

The Court had no difficulty in finding on the facts that the defendant's son was, at the time of the accident, driving the vehicle without the defendant's permission. The policy contained the usual provision that the company would indemnify any authorized driver who was driving the motor vehicle in the event of an accident caused by or arising out of the use of the motor vehicle. The expression 'Authorized Driver' was defined in the policy as follows:

'any of the following:
The Insured:
Any person driving on the Insured's order or with his permission. Provided that the person driving is permitted in accordance with the licensing or other laws or regulations to drive the Motor Vehicle or has been so permitted and is not disqualified by order of a Court of Law or by reason of any enactment or regulation in that behalf from driving the Motor Vehicle.'

As the court found that the defendant's son was driving without the permission of the insured and without a valid driving licence, he was not an authorized driver within the definition.

However, the defendant contended that the third party had no right to the payment of any sum of money under or by virtue of the Act and that accordingly the plaintiffs were not entitled to recover from the defendant the amount paid by them to the third party. The policy contained an 'avoidance clause' which read:

> 'Nothing in this policy or any endorsement hereon shall affect the right of any person entitled to indemnity under this policy or of any other person to recover an amount under or by virtue of the legislation' (which by definition includes the Act).
> 'But the Insured shall repay to the Company all sums paid by the Company which the Company would not have been liable to pay but for the Legislation.'

The only provision in the Act which directly imposes upon an insurer an obligation to pay compensation to an injured party is set out in s. 10(1); if after a policy of insurance has been effected, a judgement is obtained against any person insured by the policy in respect of any type of liability which is required to be covered under s. 5 of the Act, then not-withstanding that the insurer may be entitled to avoid or cancel the policy, he, the insurer must pay the sum specified in the judgement to the injured party.

It was common ground that any liability which arose in this case was a liability which was required to be covered by a policy under s. 5 of the Act but the defendant pointed out that a precondition of the application of s. 10(1) is that a judgement should first have been obtained against a person insured by the policy and it was conceded that in this case there had been no such judgement. The court held that the absence of a judgement was fatal to the plaintiff's claim for repayment since the obligation under s. 10(1) had not arisen.

Although it was not necessary for the decision, the court went on to consider whether the liability to the third party was a liability in fact covered by the policy. Mr Justice Farrell discussed the majority decision in the 1966 Court of Appeal case of *New Great Insurance Company of India* v. *Cross*[21] which held that s. 8 of the Insurance (Motor Vehicles Third Party Risks) Act[22] makes ineffective a condition which provides that no liability shall arise under a policy so far as it relates to such liabilities as are required to be covered under s. 5(b) of the Act. The judge in the present case considered that although he was bound by that decision, he was not called upon to apply it more widely than the decision itself demands. That case was concerned with an unlicensed and disqualified driver driving with the permission of the insured and it was held that the proviso in the schedule of the policy dealing with disqualifications must be treated as a condition caught by the provisions of s. 8 and that the liability was covered because the condition excluding liability was ineffective. The present case, however, was concerned with an unlicensed driver driving without the permission of the insured. So far as his being unlicensed was concerned, the judge felt bound to hold that the similar proviso in the schedule to the policy excluding him from the definition of an 'authorized driver' is a condition which is invalidated by s. 8 and so must be ignored. However, it did not necessarily follow that the liability in the present case was covered by the policy since the driver was not only unlicensed but also unauthorized and it was by no means self-evident that the inclusion within the definition of an 'authorized driver' of 'any person driving on the insured's order or with his permission' is to be treated on the same basis as the proviso. The learned judge argued that the condition in the proviso was restrictive whereas the inclusion in the definition of 'any person driving on the insured's order or with his permission' effected an extension of the category of persons within the scope of the policy. This was a clear indication that the court would like to see a limitation to the application of the decision in the New Great Insurance case.

PASSING-OFF

An application for an interlocutory injunction gave rise to the case of *E. A. Industries Ltd* v. *Trufoods Ltd.*[23] As a preliminary point the respondent argued that an order rejecting an application for an injunction did not fall within 0.42, r. 1(1)(*q*) of the Civil Procedure (Revised) Rules of Kenya and that no appeal lay against such rejection. The court dismissed the preliminary objection and proceeded to hear the appeal. The application was brought in a passing-off action. Both parties were manufacturers of fruit drinks and the appellant company claimed that the respondent had changed the shape of the bottles which it used and the shape and design of the labels affixed to them in such a way that they so nearly resembled those of the appellant company as to be likely to deceive.

In stating the law to be applied in regard to interlocutory injunctions, the court held that the applicant had to show a prima facie case with a probability of success and that if the court was in doubt it would decide the application on the balance of convenience. An interlocutory injunction would not normally be granted unless the applicant might otherwise suffer irreparable injury which would not be adequately compensated by an award of damages. In the lower court the judge had held that the applicant would be unlikely to succeed in the suit and that in his opinion no reasonable ordinary shopper would be misled by the resemblances in the packaging of the two products. He concluded that the appellant company would not suffer irreparable harm if an injunction were refused and that if it succeeded in the action it could be adequately compensated by damages. On the other hand, he thought that the respondent company would suffer irreparable harm if its products were taken off the market from the time that it would take for the action to come to judgement.

The appeal court considered that there were three misdirections in the judgement of the court below, viz. (a) that the judge had concentrated his attention on the names that appeared on the labels and had not paid sufficient attention to the overall impression created by the bottles and their labels, (b) the judge said that he had taken judicial note that in Kenya to-day the vast majority of customers for the fruit drinks made by the parties would be sophisticated shoppers who could read the English language and (c) in dealing with the evidence of a woman shopper who said that she had picked up two bottles of fruit drink in a store believing them to be the goods of the appellant company and later realized that they were the product of the respondent, the judge said that he thought this was due to carelessness on the part of the shopper. In regard to (b) Mr Justice Spry held that the characteristics of the normal customer for fruit drinks was a matter for evidence and not for judicial note and that such evidence could be led at the hearing of the action if it were of assistance to the parties. In regard to (c) the Vice-President further held that carelessness on the part of the customer did not necessarily negative the deception. Almost every passing-off action is based on an assumption of some degree of carelessness on the part of customers and the question in any particular case is whether that degree of carelessness is reasonable in the circumstances. The judge was clearly wrong in holding that there was no likelihood of the applicant company succeeding. A prima facie case had been made out but the court was not prepared to say that the outcome was so certain one way or the other that the application ought not to be decided on the balance of convenience.

On the whole, the court felt that the harm the respondent would suffer as a result of an injunction, if it succeeded in the suit, would be likely to be greater and graver than that which the applicant would suffer by the refusal of an injunction, should the applicant succeed in the suit. The applicant would not suffer any loss that could not be sufficiently compensated by an award of damages. The appeal was dismissed but as the applicant company had had a measure of success in regard to the likelihood of its success in the suit, the court ruled that each party must bear its own costs of the appeal.

TRADE DISPUTE

The Kenya Government's policy of Africanization led to a claim for compensation for loss of a career in the case of *Bhogal* v. *International Computers (EA) Ltd.*[24] The plaintiff was employed by the defendant company as a computer operator and his work permit expired on 6 May 1970. On 10 September 1969 the defendant company wrote to the plaintiff advising him to make arrangements to leave Kenya on the expirty of his work permit and the plaintiff left the defendant's employment on 11 February 1970. The plaintiff claims that his employment was terminated as a result of the Government of Kenya's Africanization policy and that he is entitled to severance pay or compensation for loss of career at a rate of one month's salary for each year of service. The plaintiff based this claim on the award of the Industrial Court confirmed by the High Court of Kenya in *Re Motor Trade & Allied Industries Employers Association.*[25] Alternatively the plaintiff claimed that it was now a matter of custom for retirement benefits, calculated at the rate claimed, to be paid by employers whose services are terminated as a result of the policy of Africanization.

The court had little difficulty in holding that any award of the Industrial Court related only to the parties to the award and Mr Justice Madan quoted s. 10 of the Trade Disputes Act[26] as follows:

An award shall state to which parties and to which employers and employees comprised in the parties each of the provisions of the award related.'

Sub-s. (6) then provides *inter alia* for the award to be—

'an implied term of every contract of employment between the employers and the employees to whom the award relates.'

In regard to the claim that there was a custom for retirement benefits to be paid to employees whose services were terminated as a result of the policy of Africanization, the plaintiff had led evidence to the effect that three British Banks, East African Power and Lighting Co, Mackenzie Dalgety and Union Carbide (Kenya) Ltd were four specific companies which paid such retirement benefits. However, the Chief Assistant Executive Officer of the Federation of Kenya Employers gave evidence to the effect that the attitude of the Federation was that unless a company had made a special agreement with its employees there should not be any special benefits relating to Kenyanization; any consideration that was shown would be *ex gratia* and at the discretion of the employer.

The court held that there was no course of dealing generally known to all persons who normally enter into this business relationship; nor was it certain that the position of each of the parties affected by the usage must have intended to be bound by it. Chief Justice Wicks was relying on the judgement of Sir Charles Newbold in *Harilal* v. *Standard Bank*[27] where he stated:

'A trade usage may be provided by calling witnesses, whose evidence must be clear, convincing and consistent, that the usage exists as a fact and is well-known and has been acted upon by persons affected by it.'

The Chief Justice went on to hold that in the case before him none of these requirements had been satisfied and that there was no evidence of the custom or trade usage pleaded. Judgement was given for the defendant.

LAND LAW

In the case of *New Munyu Sisal Estates Ltd* v. *Attorney-General*,[28] the plaintiff company sued the Attorney-General for compensation in relation to a sisal estate taken over by the Government of Kenya. The Attorney-General admitted liability for compensation both under the Constitution and at common law. The relevant provisions of the constitution are given in the following extract:

's. 75(1)—
(a) The acquisition must be "necessary" in the interests of defence, public safety, public order, public morality, public health, town and country planning—there is no suggestion it was necessary for any of these purposes—or the development or utilization of the property in such manner as to promote the public benefit. No special attempt has been made to show that acquisition was for development or utilization for "public benefit" but it seems to be accepted that the acquisition of land for the purpose of settling squatters on it would be for public benefit.
(b) The "necessity" must be such as to justify any hardship to the owner. There is no evidence on this from either side but the necessity is not challenged.
(c) Provision must be "made by a law applicable to that . . . acquisition for the prompt payment of full compensation".'

The question arose as to where was the law applicable to the acquisition in this case and the court discussed the provisions of the Land Acquisition Act, 1968. Mr Justice Chanan Singh found two difficulties arose in applying that Act; first, the Land Acquisition Act applies only to land whereas the provisions in the Constitution apply to property in general and secondly, the Land Acquisition Act came into force on 23 August 1968 whereas the sisal estate in question was taken over 'in or about the months of November and December 1967'. The Indian Land Acquisition Act, 1894, applied to Kenya at that time and that Act does provide for compensation although not expressed as in 'the Constitution as 'the prompt payment of full compensation'. The Court was referred to s. 188 of the Agriculture Act which read as follows: 'Where land is acquired compulsorily under this Part, it shall be acquired under the Land Acquisition Act, 1894 of India and the purposes of this Part shall be deemed to be a public purpose within the meaning of that Act.' However, the judge held that the provisions for compuslory acquisition in the Agriculture Act did not exactly fit the circumstances in the present case and that there appeared to be no law to which his attention had been drawn under which it could be said with certainty the Government had acted in acquiring this farm.

In order to decide the measure of compensation the court applied the law which it considered most nearly fitted the case and that was to interpret the Constitutional provisions by using the definition of 'full compensation' contained in the Land Acquisition Act, 1968 on the basis that the similarity of the language used afforded some indication of Parliament's intention. The measure of compensation under the Land Acquisition Act, 1968 and that under the Indian Land Acquisition Act, 1894 is the same. The plaintiff had claimed the market value of the assets plus fifteen per cent for immovable assets and interest at nine per cent. The defendant had included interest at eight per cent in the sum deposited in court. The rate of interest in s. 28 and s.34 of the Indian Land Acquisition Act is six per cent but as the defendant had admitted liability the Court awarded interest at that rate.

An interesting point on the application of the consent requirements in the Land Control Act to the exercise of an option arose in the case of *Russell* v. *Principal Registrar*.[29] The appeal concerned agricultural land at Kitale registered under the Registration of Titles Act[30] in the name of Lands Ltd as lessee for the term of 999 years from 1 April 1957. The predecessor in title to the lessee granted a lease of the land to the appellant for the term of five years as from 1 November 1964 by a deed executed on 23 April 1965. By a further deed executed between Lands Ltd and the appellant on 12 February 1971, the term of five years was extended by a further two years from 1 November 1969. The lease contained provision for an option to acquire the whole estate or interest of Lands Ltd in the land and the improvements thereon at the sum of Shs. 122,040/-, such option to be exercisable at any time during the currency of the lease. The appellant exercise this option and a transfer of Lands Ltd's title and interest in the land was executed on 15 February 1971 in purported exercise of the option to purchase. The appellant duly applied to the Registrar of Titles for registration of the transactions and the Principal Registrar refused registration on the grounds that he was not satisfied that the necessary consents to these transactions had been obtained.

Mr Justice Law, in the course of his judgement said that the law relating to the granting of consents to transactions was, at the date of the consent relied upon by the appellant contained in s. 218 of Schedule 2 of the Kenya Independence Order-in-Council, 1963. The position had been complicated by the enactment of the Land Control Act in 1967[31] which prohibits the giving of consent to disposals of agricultural land in favour of persons who are not citizens of Kenya. The appellant was not such a citizen but counsel for the respondent had admitted that if valid consents had been obtained to the original lease to the appellant in 1964 those consents would be valid for all purposes and would not be affected by the enactment of the Land Control Act, 1967. The only question for the Court was therefore whether the consent obtained to the lease covered consent not only to the transaction by way of lease but also to the exercise of the option to purchase and the option to renew.

For the appellant it was argued that an option to purchase creates in equity an interest in land and is an agreement to purchase land and that accordingly it was a transaction requiring consent within three months if it was not to be void under s. 218 above. That consent had been obtained. For the respondent it was submitted that all that had been obtained was consent to a lease containing two options, one to renew and the other to purchase. The person to whom the option is given is not bound to exercise it; in each case an irrevocable offer was made but until accepted no contract arose. An option represents no more than a contingent interest in land which does not crystallize until it is exercised. Counsel for the respondent further submitted that both options when exercised gave rise to transactions requiring separate consent and that consent was required at every stage.

The Court held that the consent given to the original transaction was to a lease containing two options; it was not consent to the transactions resulting from the possible future exercise of those options. When the stage was reached of exercising those rights and putting them into effect, then the appellant's rights became contractual and he became a party to the transactions resulting from that exercise, transactions which were quite different and separate from the options and which required consent under s. 218. Consent to the transactions of renewal of the lease and the purchase of the reversion had never been obtained.

Spry, V.-P., did not agree that the exercise of an option was a new transaction. However, he held that although the original lease contained an option to purchase exercisable during the currency of that lease, the lease lapsed and although the appellant entered into a renewal, the option agreement was not repeated. As the option had expired, the subsequent transfer of the interest to the appellant must have been a new transaction and therefore consent would be required. For differing reasons the appeal was dismissed.

In the case of *Panesar* v. *Balbir*[32] the respondent let premises to the appellant which he used for the manufacture of furniture. The respondent filed a suit for recovery of the premises and the appellants raised in defence the protection of the Landlord and Tenant (Shops, Hotels and Catering Establishments) Act,[33] alleging that the premises were a shop within the meaning of that Act. The case for the appellant was that the furniture made at the said premises was all sold either in bulk from the place of manufacture or in another shop nearby leased by the appellant.

The suit premises, according to the appellant were used to manufacture furniture to feed the retail shop and would therefore be part of a shop and 'occupied wholly or mainly for the purposes of a retail trade or business,' within the meaning of the said Act.

Mr Justice Mustafa held that the title to the Act refers only to shops, hotels and catering establishments and not to factories or premises for manufacturing goods. The court was not prepared to accept the proposition that as the suit premises were used to manufacture furniture to feed the retail shop they would form part of the said shop. The suit premises were not a shop within the meaning of the Act. The appeal was dismissed.

The case of *Obiero* v. *Opiyo and Others*[34] held that rights arising under customary law are not overriding interests within s. 30 of the Registered Land Act.[34]

The Statute Law (Miscellaneous Amendments) Act[35] contains minor amendments to s. 107(2) of the Government Land Act,[36] s. 33 of the Registration of Titles Act[37] and s. 63 of the Land Titles Act.[38] S. 14 of the Land Acquisition Act[39] is deleted.

NATIONAL CORPORATIONS

The National Construction Corporation Act[40] sets up a new Corporation 'to assist persons engaged in the construction industry and for purposes incidental thereto and connected herewith'. The Corporation is to be run by a Board of Directors constituted as follows:[41]

(a) not less than four nor more than six persons appointed by the Minister, being persons who, in his opinion, possess qualities likely to be of benefit to the Corporation and of whom—
    (i) at least one shall possess knowledge of accounting;
    (ii) at least one shall possess knowledge of civil engineering;
    (iii) at least one shall possess knowledge of building construction;
    (iv) at least one shall be an advocate;
(b) one shall be the Permanent Secretary to the Treasury;
(c) one shall be the Permanent Secretary to the Ministry for the time being responsible for matters relating to commerce and industry;
(d) one shall be the Permanent Secretary to the Ministry for the time being responsible for matters relating to housing; and
(e) one shall be the Permanent Secretary to the Ministry for the time being responsible for matters relating to works:
    Provided that any Permanent Secretary aforesaid may depute in writing any other person to be a director in his place.

The Board has powers of co-option.

The Board must appoint a General Manager approved by the Minister who will act in accordance with the general or special directions which may be issued to him by the Board.[42] The powers of the Corporation, in addition to those general functions set out in the Title are as follows:[43]

(3) without prejudice to the generality of subsection (2) of this section, the Corporation shall have power to—
    (a) engage in the construction industry;
    (b) manufacture, or deal in plant, tools, materials, nachinery and equipment used in connexion with the construction industry;
    (c) establish, equip and maintain educational and training establishments

for the benefit of persons employed or to be employed in the construction industry;
(d) furnish managerial, technical and administrative advice;
(e) enter into partnership with, or acquire the whole or any part of the interest in, any company or firm;
(f) invest money after consultation with the Treasury in any funds which, for the time being, trustees are authorized by law to invest, and to place money on interest-bearing deposit with any public body.
(g) award contracts through a Works Committee consisting of two members of the Board, and the General Manager.

The Corporation may make loans out of its funds to any person engaged in the construction industry upon such terms as to security, interest and repayment or otherwise and in such manner as the Board may deem fit.[44] Loans may also be made to any director, the General Manager or to any member of the staff of the Corporation.[45] The First Schedule to the Act sets out the covenants and conditions which must be implied in every mortgage executed to secure a loan by the Corporation. An annual report and an auditor's report must be submitted to the Minister within a period of six months from the end of each financial year and the Minister must lay the report before the National Assembly as soon as practicable.[46]

TAXATION

The Consumption Tax Act[47] is an Act to consolidate several taxes already provided for and to add further commodities intended for consumption within Kenya to liability to the tax. The Petroleum and Fuel Oil Tax Act[48] and the Beer, Cigarettes and Tobacco Tax Acts[49] are repealed and those commodities are listed in the Schedule to the new Act. The consumption tax is charged on both locally manufactured and imported commodities and those which have been added to the list are electricity, pneumatic tyres, car batteries, torch and transistor batteries, crown corks, cement, footwear, paint and fabrics.

NOTES
1. [1972] EA 392
2. [1972] EA 518
3. [1972] EA 275.
4. [1972] EA 347
5. [1972] EA 554.
6. Report of the Commission on the Law of Succession, 1968, Government Printer, Nairobi
7. *Annual Survey of African Law*, Vol. IV, 1970, p. 107
8. Compare s. 3(2) of Act with s. 3(3) of Commission's Draft Bill
9. Compare ss. 35, 36 and 40 of Act with ss. 35, 36 and 40 of Draft Bill
10. *Re: Maangi*, East African Law Journal, Vol. IV, p. 53.
11. [1972] EA 42
12. [1972] EA 1
13. [1918] 1 KB 592
14. EACA 31 of 1965 (unreported)
15. [1972] EA 370
16. Cap. 31
17. [1972] EA 255
18. No. 19 of 1971
19. [1972] EA 301
20. Cap. 405
21. [1966] EA 90
22. Cap. 405 ibid
23. [1972] EA 420

24. [1972] EA 55
25. [1970] EA 435
26. Cap. 234
27. [1967] EA 512
28. [1972] EA 88
29. [1972] EA 249.
30. Cap. 281
31. Cap. 302
32. [1972] EA 208
33. Cap. 301
34. [1972] EA 227
34a. Cap. 300
35. No. 15 of 1972
36. Cap. 280
37. Cap. 281
38. Cap. 282
39. No. 47 of 1968
40. No. 9 of 1972
41. s. 5(1)
42, s. 6
43. s. 15(3)
44. s. 20(1)
45. s. 20(2)
46. s. 23
47. No. 11 of 1972
48. Cap. 477
49. No. 24 of 1971

CHAPTER SIX

UGANDA

H. F. Morris

During 1972 interest in Uganda affairs in the international press was focused upon the legislation directed at those in Uganda of Asian origin who were not citizens of the country. The Immigration Act of 1969,[1] which replaced earlier immigration legislation, stated that, although entry permits, certificates or passes issued under earlier legislation would retain validity for twelve months, all non-citizens must thereafter possess the appropriate documents under the 1969 Act. The Immigration (Cancellation of Entry Permits and Certificates of Residence) Decree passed in August 1972[2] states that 'every entry permit or certificate of residence issued or granted under the provisions of the Immigration Act, 1969 to any person who is of Asian origin, extraction or descent and who is a subject or citizen of' the United Kingdom, India, Pakistan or Bangla Desh ceased to have any validity. The Minister might, however, by statutory order, reinstate any entry permit or certificate of residence cancelled or revoked under the Decree. An Asian who, although he was not a citizen of Uganda, was also not a citizen of any of the four stated countries would not come within the ambit of the legislation. The Decree was, accordingly, amended in September[3] and extended to any person who was of Indian, Pakistani or Bangla Desh origin, extraction or descent, whether or not he was a citizen of one of the four countries referred to above.

The Declaration of Assets (Non-Citizen Asians) Decree,[4] as amended,[5] states that no person leaving the country by virtue of the Immigration (Cancellation of Entry Permits and Certificates of Residence) Decree[6] may transfer any immovable property, bus company, farm land, livestock or business to any other person, or mortgage his immovable property. Nor, in the case of a company, might it issue new shares, change the salaries or terms of employment of its staff, or appoint new directors or vary the remuneration payable to its directors. Every 'departing Asian' must declare his assets and liabilities and must nominate a person to act as agent to sell his business or property. An application to purchase such property must be made on specified forms, and, except where the applicant is the Government or a state corporation, the Minister must, before sale, advertise the business or property. Where two or more applications are submitted, the Minister is to refer the applications to an advertising committee appointed by him. Where there is a dispute as to the price to be paid for the business or property, the Minister is to appoint valuers to determine this. Where the agent leaves Uganda or is unable to discharge his duties, the Minister appoints a trustee. An Abandoned Property Custodian Board is established. Property in respect of which no information or documents have been submitted vests in the Board, which also may, by statutory order, declare that property which has been abandoned or left in such a way that no adequate arrangement has been made for its proper management is to be vested in it. The Board is to manage such property and sell, or otherwise deal with, such property in the same way as the departing Asian would have done. The Board is to appoint valuers in respect of such property for which compensation may be payable. Appeal in respect of such valuation lies to a tribunal and from thence to the High court.

The Proceedings against the Government (Protection) Decree[7] provides that 'notwithstanding any written or other law, no court shall make any decision, order or grant any remedy or relief in any proceedings against the Government or any person acting under the authority of the Government in respect of anything done or omitted to be done for the purpose of maintaining public order or public security in any part of Uganda or for the enforcement of discipline or law and order or in respect of anything relating to, consequent upon or incidental to any of those purposes, during the period between the 24th day of January, 1971, and such date as the President shall appoint'. Similarly, the Proceedings Against the Government (Prohibition) Decree[8] protects the Government from proceedings in respect 'of wrongs committed by the Civilian Government for political motives' and no actions may be instituted by any person in respect of 'any wrongful arrest, false imprisonment, personal injury, loss of life suffered by that person or damage to his property (including its destruction) effected by or on the orders of the Government which was overthrown by the Military Government on the 25th day of January, 1971, against that person for or on account of holding, receiving or imparting political opinions contrary to the political opinions of that Government or for other cause whatsoever'.

Under the Newspaper and Publications Act, as amended by a 1972 Decree,[9] the Minister, if he is satisfied that it is in the public interest to do so, may, by statutory order, prohibit the publication of any newspaper for a specified, or indefinite, period.

CRIMINAL LAW AND PROCEDURE

The Penal Code Act (Amendment) Decree[10] was passed 'to prohibit the wearing of certain dresses which outrage decency and are injurious to public morals'. Any person of or over the age of 14 who, in a public place, wears a garment, skirt or shorts the hem line or bottom of which is three inches above the knee-line, or who wears a slit 'midi' or 'maxi' dress with a slit above the knee-line, or who wears 'short tight-fitting pants popularly known as hot-pants', is deemed an idle and disorderly person and is liable to a fine or imprisonment.

The Robbery Suspects Decree,[11] deemed to have come into effect on 1 June 1971, provides that where a security officer[12] has reason to believe that any person has committed, or is about to commit, robbery and he fails to submit to arrest, the security officer may use such force as is necessary to prevent his escape.[13]

Under the Armed Forces (Powers of Arrest) Decree of 1971[14] soldiers and prison officers had powers of arrest in respect of a wide range of offences.[15] This Decree was, however, stated to be in force for one year only and expired in March 1972. In October 1972, a new Decree, bearing the same name and in identical terms,[16] was passed and was stated to be deemed to have come into force in the preceding March.

TORT

In *Securicor* v. *Mugenyi*,[17] the respondent had been attacked and bitten by a guard dog on the premises of Grindlays Bank(U) Ltd to which the public had access. It was found that the dog had no previous record of attacking human beings; nevertheless, it was doing what it had been trained to do. It was held that when an animal *mansuetae naturae* is trained to attack human beings, it is, in practice, an animal *ferae naturae* and a person who takes it to a place to which the public have access has a duty to see that it does not cause injury; the owner is not entitled to the benefit of first bite to find out if the training has been successful, and the appellant had, therefore, rightly been held liable for the injury done.

In *Attorney-General* v. *Musisi*,[18] the appeal turned on the question whether exemplary damages could be awarded to a widow and her children in respect of her husband's death. The majority view of the Appeal Court was that the right to claim exemplary damages is a personal one inapplicable to cases brought under the fatal accidents provisions of the Law Reform (Miscellaneous Provisions) Act.[19] Spry, V.-P., however, drawing a distinction in this respect between aggravated and exemplary damages, held otherwise. This case is also of interest in that the trial judge had stated that, whereas some years ago life expectancy in Uganda was assessed at about 45 years, it was now nearer to 60 years. The Appeal Court, however, did not accept that there was evidence on record to justify such a conclusion. A similar question—this time concerning the length of a working life—was also considered in *Lusiya* v. *Kampala City Council*[20] and the court was unable to accept that a man of 28 had another 30 years of working life, preferring a figure of 20.

In *Sabani* v. *Crispus*,[21] the plaintiff sued for damages arising from the loss of the services of his wife who had died in hospital shortly after, and as a result of, an accident caused by the defendant's negligence. Having settled that the woman's death was immediate for the purposes of the claim, the High Court concluded that (in the absence of any East African decisions on the point) the principle established in *Baker* v. *Bolton*[22] was valid and had always been recognised by the law of Uganda, and that the plaintiff could not succeed in his claim.

SUCCESSION

The Succession Act,[23] originally passed as an Ordinance in 1906, did not, from the year of its enactment until 1966, apply to the estates of deceased Africans, succession to which was governed by customary law. In 1966, however, a large part of the Act was made applicable to all, but not the part dealing with intestate succession. In the following year, a Bill was published proposing to amend the Succession Act and to introduce a completely new set of provisions dealing with the distribution of property on intestacy, which would apply to all members of the community. These provisions, although they made some concessions to customary law, followed broadly the English-law pattern of distribution according to degree of consanguinity.[24] This Bill was never enacted, but it has clearly formed the basis of the Succession (Amendment) Decree of 1972,[25] although the provisions of the latter differ widely in many respects from those in the Bill.

The Decree *inter alia* replaces the existing provisions in the Succession Act dealing with the succession to property on intestacy. Apart from the deceased's principal residential holding, such property is divided in the following manner. Where there is a surviving customary heir,[26] a wife,[27] a lineal descendant and a dependent relative,[28] the customary heir receives one per cent, the wives receive fifteen per cent (in equal shares), the dependant receives nine per cent and the lineal descendants receive seventy five per cent. If there are no lineal descendants, the customary heir gets one per cent, the wife fifty per cent and the dependant forty nine per cent.[29] If none of these classes of persons, apart from the customary heir, survives the deceased, the estate is divided equally between those relatives in the nearest degree of kinship to him, and, failing these, the whole property belongs to the customary heir. Where there is no customary heir, his share goes to the 'legal heir', that is to say, 'the living relative nearest in degree to an intestate under the provisions set out in Part III of the Act.[30] The word 'child' and related terms are defined so as to include legitimate, illegitimate and adopted children. The residential holding normally occupied by the intestate as his principal residence, including household chattels, is to be held by the person appointed to administer the estate upon trust for the legal heir, subject to certain rights of occupancy to be enjoyed by the deceased's family and to terms and conditions set out in a schedule to the Decree.

The Decree also provides that if adequate provision has not been made by the deceased in his will for a dependent relative, then, on application, a court may order such reasonable provision as it thinks fit to be made out of the estate.

The Administration of Estates (Small Estates) (Special Provisions) Decree[31] was passed six months before the Succession (Amendment) Decree. The former provided that Part V of the Succession Act (dealing with the distribution of an intestate's property) and Part XXXI (dealing with the practice in granting and revoking probates and letters of administration) should not apply to the administration of small estates, that is to say estates the total value of which did not exceed sh. 100,000/-. Jurisdiction to grant probate or letters of administration in respect of letters of administration in respect of small estates was to be exercised by the various grades of magistrates' courts. S. 3 of the Decree stated that any person to whom letters of administration were granted should administer the estate 'in accordance with the custom relating to the succession of property of deceased persons of the class of which the deceased was a member'. S. 4 gave the magistrates' courts discretion as to whom letters of administration should be granted. The Succession (Amendment) Decree repealed sections 3 and 4, but not the provision that Parts V and XXXI of the Succession should not apply. It is, consequently, uncertain whether the new provisions of the Succession Act governing intestate succession or customary law (where appropriate) are applicable to these small estates.[32]

COMMERCIAL AND INDUSTRIAL LAW

The programme of nationalization inaugurated by the preceding regime in 1970[33] had been halted by the political changes at the beginning of the following year. 1972, however, saw, quite apart from the effect of the Immigration (Cancellation of Entry Permits) Decree (referred to above), a resurgence of nationalization policies. The Properties and Businesses (Acquisition) Decree[34] provides that all properties and businesses listed in the Schedule to the Decree[35] are to vest in the Government as from 18 February 1972. The Government is to pay compensation and a Board of Valuers is to be appointed. Appeal against valuation lies to a tribunal and from there to the High Court.

The State Trading Corporation Decree,[36] which repeals the Export and Import Corporation Act of 1970[37] and the National Trading Corporation Act of 1966,[38] establishes a State Trading Corporation. The Corporation has the sole right to import and export and to trade in such goods as are specified by the Minister by statutory order. If, in the conduct of its business, the Corporation requires the premises or equipment used by a former importer, exporter or trader, it may take possession for such period as is deemed necessary. The Minister may, by statutory order, prohibit or limit the export or import of any goods from or to any country if, in his opinion, such action is in the interests of the country. All the assets and liabilities of the Export and Import Corporation vest in the State Trading Corporation.

The Industrial Training Decree[39] establishes a Directorate of Industrial Training, consisting of a Director and such other officers (all of whom are to be public officers) as the Minister may determine. There is also to be an Industrial Training Council, which, at the request of the Minister, or of its own motion, may make recommendations to the Minister on any matter concerned with the Decree; investigate any dispute or other matter arising out of a contract of apprenticeship referred to it by the Director, and endeavour to settle such disputes amicably; and secure the greatest possible improvement in the quality and efficiency of industrial training. The Minister may establish a training levy, the proceeds of which would go into a Training Levy Fund and be used, for example, to meet the cost and maintenance of those attending approved training courses.

MISCELLANEOUS

The Atomic Energy Decree[40] establishes an Atomic Energy Control Board, consisting of a chairman and fourteen members. The Board is to make recommendations to the Minister on matters concerning the encouragement and promotion of the use of atomic energy, including those to ensure that all such activities avoid danger to the public or workers concerned. There is also set up a Radioisotope Advisory Committee, which advises the Board on matters referred to it and on such as fall within the sphere of technical competence of the Committee, on the requirements for the promotion of the use of radioisotopes in the best interests of the country and on requirements to ensure an adequate degree of public safety in their use. Any person wishing to use radioactive material or other sources of dangerous ionizing radiation must apply to the Board for an appropriate licence.

The Uganda Development Bank Decree[41] establishes the Uganda Development Bank for the purpose of promoting and financing development in the various sectors of the country's economy; furnishing managerial and administrative advice and services; providing finance in the form of secured loans; acquiring share holdings in any company; making funds available for reinvestment by selling any investment of the Bank; and drawing, accepting and endorsing bills of exchange for the purposes of the Bank. The authorised capital is 100,000,000 sh. There is to be a Credit Guarantee Fund consisting of contributions from Government, the Bank and any other source. The fund is to be applied towards assisting a 'marginal borrower'[42] to secure a loan from a bank or other credit institution.

DECREES PASSED DURING 1972

1 Distribution and Price of Goods Act (Amendment) Decree
2. Industrial Training Decree
3. Game Preservation and Control (Amendment) Decree
4. Armed Forces (Amendment) Decree
5. Hide and Skin Trade Act (Amendment) Decree
6. Civil Aviation (Government Aerodromes) Decree
7. Robbery Suspects Decree
8. Proceedings Against the Government (Protection) Decree
9. Penal Code Act (Amendment) Decree
10. Trial on Indictments (Amendment) Decree
11. Magistrates' Courts (Amendment) Decree
12. Atomic Energy Decree
13. Administration of Estates (Small Estates) (Special Provisions) Decree
14 Finance Decree
15 Supplementary Appropriation Decree
16 Appropriation Decree
17 Immigration (Cancellation of Entry Permits and Certificates of Residences) Decree
18 Exchange Control Act (Amendment) Decree
19 Proceedings Against the Government (Prohibition) Decree
20 Historical Monuments Act (Amendment) Decree

21 Fish and Crocodiles Act (Amendment) Decree
22 Succession (Amendment) Decree
23 Uganda Development Bank Decree
24 State Trading Corporation Decree
25 State Trading Corporation (Amendment) Decree
26 Armed Forces (Powers of Arrest) Decree
27 Declaration of Assets (Non-Citizen Asians) Decree
28 Produce Marketing Board (Exemption From Income Tax) Decree
29 Declaration of Assets (Non-Citizen Asians) (Amendment) Decree
30 Immigration (Cancellation of Entry Permits and Certificates of Residences) (Amendment) Decree
31 Civil Aviation (Government Aerodromes) (Amendment) Decree
32 Properties and Business (Acquisition) Decree
33 Social Security Act (Amendment) Decree
34 National Water and Sewerage Corporation Decree
35 Newspaper and Publications (Amendment) Decree

NOTES

1. Act 19
2. Decree 17
3. By the Immigration (Cancellation of Entry Permits and Certificates of Residence)(Amendment) Decree (Decree 25 of 1972)
4. Decree 27 of 1972
5. By Decree 29 of 1972
6. Referred to in the Decree as the 'departing Asian'
7. Decree 8 of 1972
8. Decree 19 of 1972
9. Newspaper and Publications (Amendment) Decree (Decree 35 of 1972), amending Cap. 305
10. Decree 9 of 1972
11. Decree 7 of 1972
12. Defined as a member of the armed forces, police force or the prison service
13. The Decree is discussed by D A Jenkins in 'Comments on Recent Legislation', *The Uganda Law Focus*, Vol. 1, pp. 31-8
14 Decree 13 of 1972
15. See 'Uganda' in *Annual Survey of African Law*, Vol. V, 1971
16. Decree 26 of 1972
17. [1972] EA 362
18. [1972] EA 217 and [1972] JAL 181
19. Cap. 74
20 [1972] EA 240
21. [1972] EA 319
22. (1808) Camp. 493
23. Cap. 139
24. See 'Uganda' in *Annual Survey of African law*, Vol. I, 1967, pp. 147-9
25. Decree 22
26. ' "Customary heir" means the person recognized by the rites and customs of the tribe or community of a deceased person as being the customary heir of that person'
27. 'Wife' means a person who, at the time of the deceased's death was validly married to him according to the laws of Uganda, or was married to him in another country by a marriage valid by the law under which the marriage was celebrated
28. ' "Dependent relative" includes (a) a wife, a husband, a son or daughter under eighteen years of age, or a son or daughter who is wholly or substantially dependent on the deceased; (b) a parent, a brother or sister, a grandparent or grandchild who, on the date of the deceased's death, was wholly or substantially dependent on the deceased for the provision of the ordinary necessaries of life suitable to a person of his station'
29. If only a wife or dependant survives, then the customary heir gets one per cent and the wife or dependant ninety nine per cent
30. Subject to certain modifications
31. Decree 13 of 1972

32. See Charles Kabagame, 'The Administration of Estates (Small Estates) (Special Provisions) Decree, 1972', *The Uganda Law Focus*, Vol. 1, p. 43
33. See 'Uganda' in *Annual Survey of African Law*, Vol. IV 1970, pp. 110-11
34. Decree 32 of 1972
35. The Minister may by statutory order amend the list
36. Decree 24 of 1972, amended by Decree 25
37. Act 4 of 1970
38. Act 18 of 1966
39. Decree 2 of 1972
40. Decree 12 of 1972
41. Decree 23 of 1972
42. Defined as 'a businessman with neither sufficient security nor previous ascertainable experience, and includes a businessman who, having been successful in a business at a certain level, wishes to make some rapid expansion of that business'

CHAPTER SEVEN

TANZANIA

James S. Read

In 1972, the first year of Tanzania's second decade of independence, the contrasting elements of national life were prominent: on the one hand there was the elaboration of Tanzanian socialist ideology and its practical implementation on a sweeping scale in the legislative framework for the 'decentralization' of Government administration; on the other hand, significant but uncharacteristic episodes of violence indicated the limitations and constraints which exist upon the radical policy objectives. The year was prefaced by the 'political murder' of a distinguished national leader, Dr Wilbert Klerruu, which was allegedly motivated by resistance to the policy of rural socialism embodied in the famous 'ujamaa villages'.[1] Only a week earlier a senior Minister had warned officials of the ruling party, TANU, of the threats posed by the nation's enemies who might even 'stage an invasion'.[2] On 7 April 1972 Sheikh Karume, ruler of Zanzibar since the revolution of 1964 and First Vice-President of Tanzania, was assassinated. In September 1972 serious armed conflict erupted around the border with Uganda, with the armed assault on towns in Uganda by supporters of former President Obote who were alleged to have mounted an invasion from Tanzania. During the last two weeks of September the Tanzanian lakeshore towns of Bukoba and Mwanza were bombed by Ugandan aircraft with a number of deaths and casualties. The Mogadishu Agreement of 5 October 1972, achieved through the mediation of the President of Somalia, brought a respite: Tanzania and Uganda agreed to withdraw their forces at least six miles from the border, to cease military activities and hostile propaganda and to return the other's nationals and property. It was against this turbulent background that important and far-reaching constitutional developments were set in train with the reorganization of government in Zanzibar and legislation for the decentralization on the mainland. The definition of the ideological imperatives by President Nyerere retained its continuity and consistency—the commitment to transformation to socialism, 'the only rational choice',[3] by means of self-reliance and participation.

PUBLIC LAW

DECENTRALIZATION: AT THE CENTRE
An early move towards the decentralization announced by President

Nyerere in January 1972 was the reconstruction of the Government which he announced on 17 February, with the appointment for the first time during the Republic of a Prime Minister—Rashidi M. Kawawa, who retained his existing office as Second Vice President, in which capacity he was already leader of government business in the National Assembly.[4] Mr. Kawawa was also, of course, the last Prime Minister of Tanganyika, having held office as such for most of the first year of independence until the inauguration of the Republic. Then he had been head of government under an independence constitution which provided for a modified version of the 'Westminster model' of cabinet government; but in 1972 the Constitution made no provision for the office of Prime Minister and no constitutional amenment was proposed: the President merely used his power to designate his ministers and determine their responsibilities but in doing so he created a hybrid form of 'executive dualism'[5] resembling the Constitution of France and its African derivatives: under the Interim Constitution of Tanzania executive power remains vested in the President. These changes were designed to recast the ministerial structure of central government to facilitate the forthcoming decentralization of responsibility. Central ministries were to be denuded of their departmental activities in the regions, and of many of their staff, remaining as national organs to plan and control national projects and to assist and advise the decentralized administration of government through the new regional and district structures. Other elements in this strategy involved the appointment of senior political leaders as regional commissioners; an increase in the relative power of the National Executive Committee of TANU and increased opportunities for Members of Parliament to be involved in development planning at all levels.

Legal niceties were not to stand in the way of policy implementation: it was perhaps debatable whether the President's delegation of functions to ministers and especially to the Prime Minister was entirely constitutional; the Constitution authorizes him to delegate his own functions only in case of absence or illness. However, a constitutional amendment passed at the end of the year but given more than nine months' retrospective operation to the date of the reorganization resolved the matter, adding a new section enabling the President to delegate his functions although without preventing him from exercising them himself.[6]

Associated with the decentralization was a curious move to democratize the process of planning for development. The National Assembly was, by a short Act,[7] given a new *alter ego* as the Planning Commission, composed of MPs only, two of them being appointed Chairman and Vice-Chairman by the President. The Planning Commission has the following functions:

(a) to participate in the formulation of plans for economic, commercial, industrial and social development of the United Republic;
(b) to consider plans for national development submitted to it by the various working parties and to make such recommendations thereon as the Commission may consider fit;
(c) to carry out such other functions in relation to development planning as the President may direct.

The Chairman can set up, and appoint members to, working parties: at least half the members of each must be MPs. It is apparently intended that the Commission should consider plans for national development submitted by the working parties; a designated Ministry, acting as the secretariat for the Commission, will communicate its decisions to the Government and TANU. It is surprising to learn that such a step was necessary 'to provide means for the participation of the people's representatives in the formulation of plans for the economic, industrial, commercial and social development of Tanzania'. Of course MPs are now also closely involved in planning at regional and local levels as members of the development committees discussed below and the formulation of national plans does not necessarily involve the legislative activity which the Constitution ascribes to Parliament. Nevertheless it is notable that the new separate capacity of this Commission was considered necessary in order to facilitate MPs' participation in national planning.

DECENTRALIZATION: IN THE REGIONS

Seven years after the inauguration of the single-party Constitution with its emphasis on participation and democracy, Tanzania in 1972 was still searching for an effective structure for regional administration and local government (matters not provided for in that Constitution otherwise than by authorizing the appointment of Regional Commissioners). The daunting problems involved in the search for appropriate means of 'administration for development' are known to most African states. In Commonwealth states these result not merely from the usual problems of development but in part also from the inheritance of administrative structure and practice from colonial government, with the pattern of 'indirect rule'—a model form of which was developed in Tanganyika —leaving a legacy of uneasy tension between the imposition of central control and the nurture of local initiative and participation, with representative local government in a merely embryonic stage. The history of regional administration and local government in Tanzania since independence has been probably the least successful aspect of one-party government with improvised changes, hesitant and sometimes retracted experiments, divergence in practice from the legal requirements and a continued lack of cohesion and efficiency.[8] District councils as institutions of representative local government have had a very chequered career since their late introduction in 1953; originally elections were rare since TANU candidates were usually returned unopposed and after independence a system of Ministerial appointment following informal elections was found more practicable than formal elections until the 1966 and 1970 local government elections when two TANU candidates competed for each seat on the lines of national Parliamentary elections. However, partly as a result of local financial and staffing difficulties, central Government had already in 1969 taken over from local authorities responsibility for major services such as education, health, water and roads and given them direct grants from Government in place of their former revenue sources in local rates. With the growth of TANU in size and strength of organization the local Party structure stood as an alternative local apparatus with its own authority and responsibility. (The Presidential Commission on the Establishment of the Democratic one Party State recognized in 1965 the existence of 'considerable confusion . . . between the role of TANU and that of the Local Authorities' and recommended the incorporation of the members of the District Executive Committees of the Party as ex officio members of the District Councils, with the elected councillors.[9] To this recommendation the Government added the proposal that the District Chairman of TANU should be the ex officio Chairman of the District Council[10] and this was given effect although the Commission's recommendation was abandoned as likely to prove unworkable.[11] Then there was the regional administration of central Government, led after independence by Regional and Area Commissioners— political officers but still, like their colonial predecessors, in a somewhat difficult relationship with the specialist officers who were responsible primarily to their respective Ministries and, particularly in the case of the Area Commissioner, in a somewhat awkward constitutional relationship with the district councils over which it was the Regional Commissioner who had the most direct control. Co-ordination between Party and regional administration was provided in some measure by the fact that the Commissioners were also appointed Regional and District Secretaries of TANU and thus also functioned as the chief executive officers of the Party in their respective areas.

These structures resulted in a cumbersome complexity in which the individual citizen might well not only be confused by the unsystematic distribution of functions among alternative agencies but might also find it almost impossible to participate effectively in the decision-making which most immediately affected his interests. Moreover the apparatus tended to divorce administration from development when in fact the true imperative in the situation demanded the closest integration between these. These weaknesses, and the general inadequacies of the official local government system, were the more serious in the light of the increasing emphasis placed upon the priority of rural development in the context of self-reliance since the Arusha Declaration of 1967, but even before that the institutions had in fact been created which were to provide the basis for the changes introduced in 1972.

Following a detailed study and report by professional international consultants, President Nyerere announced in January 1972 to the TANU National Executive Committee that a major reorganization of the administration of Government would be undertaken with a view to 'Decentralization', the title of his paper, published in May 1972, setting out detailed proposals.[12] He there stated the main thrust of the changes as being to increase the extent of local freedom for decision and action, while curing the difficultes noted above. However, despite the importance of this development in 1972, it was, like so many Tanzanian innovations, evolutionary rather than revolutionary for the basic pattern adopted for the new framework of administration, which has replaced the previous local government organs throughout Tanganyika, had existed for a decade within the old system in the development committees at village, district and regional level. The changes in 1972 provided for the reconstitution of these bodies, which had formerly rested upon administrative directions and practice, upon a statutory basis at district and regional level. The Regional and District Development Committees, presided over by the Regional and Area Commissioners respectively, included Party, local government and Parliamentary members together with specialist officers of the relevant Government departments. The Regional Development Committees were set up by administrative direction in 1962—their non-statutory basis being said to give them the adaptability needed for such an experiment; they approved nation-building projects proposed by District Development Committees and requiring financial assitance but, as there were no regional local government councils, they also discussed a wide range of subjects (although upon a merely advisory basis with regard to matters remaining within the executive responsibility of central Government or District Councils). District Development Committees were reconstituted in 1963 as committees of the District Councils, from which they were previously distinct, but with the Area Commissioners as Chairmen and all the departmental technical officers in the district as members, with the members of the Finance Committee of the District Council; strictly these Committees did not accord with the statutory requirement that two-thirds of the members of a committee must be elected councillors. After 1966 these Committees were known as District Development and Planning Committees. At the lowest level the Village Development Committees, effectively established from 1964 and incorporating the former elected village councils where they existed, were seen as the key 'organs of representative government at the village level' with diffuse but vital func-tions: 'All development activities of government in their areas concern these committees'.[13] The Chairman of the Village Development Committee was normally the elected Chairman of the TANU village committee and in other ways too the VDC was the basic unit for the integration of Government and Party at the local level. However, by 1969 it had been decided to abolish the VDCs and instead to establish Ward Development Committees as committees of the District Council at a higher level than the village. WDCs were the only development com-mittees to be given statutory powers of a limited kind, to enable them to initiate local development schemes with Ministerial approval and then to oblige local citizens to participate therein on a self-help basis.[14] A significant innovation was the establishment of the Regional Development Fund in 1967; this was administered by the develop-ment committees and, although relatively small—a total of Shs. 100 million was allocated to the Fund by 1972—it gave useful experience of developmentadministration both to central Government and to those involved locally at different levels.[15] Problems of capacity, communication and co-ordination were identified and this knowledge informed the scheme adopted in 1972 for decentralization.

The new framework of Government administration necessitated considerable adaptation and a lengthy transitional period. The experi-mental nature of the structure adopted is indicated by the title of the implementing Act—'The Decentralization of Government Administration (Interim Provisions) Act'[16]—which was expressly given a life of one year only, at the end of which new statutory provision was anticipated to make more comprehensive provision in the light of experience gained. Yet the implementation of the new system was to take very much longer than the year originally planned: although the President was empowered to extend the life of the Act by Proclamation, it was in fact by further amending Acts that the life of the Act was extended first for eighteen months to 31 December 1974 ('in order to complete the decentralization programme gradually without creating any unnecessary disruption of the local administration') and then for a further year, to 31 December 1975.[17] In fact the system was not brought into operation in the districts until 25 October 1974,[18] more than two years after the Act was passed.

The Act took effect at regional level at once but at district level only when an order by the Prime Minister brought it into effect there. (The 1974 Order applied to all districts.) When it was applied to a district, the old local authority—the District Council—was abolished and replaced by a District Development Council, chaired by the District Chairman of TANU, with the Area Commissioner and elected members of the old authority as members, together with constituency and (locally resident) National Members of Parliament. The Secretary is the District Development Director, a new official appointed by the President to act as chief district executive officer and thus replacing both the Area Secretary and the District Executive Officer. The District Development and Planning Committee is a committee of the DDC but is chaired by the Area Commissioner with the TANU District Chairman and the MPs who are on the DDC as members but with only ten (or a maximum of one quarter) of the elected councillors of the old District Council, elected by the DDC, and with a large official membership. The Act defines 'staff officers'—the District Planning and Personnel Officers and the Financial Controller—and 'functional officers'—the local technical officers responsible for the eight departmental activities (health, education, agriculture, natural resources, commerce and industry, ujamaa and co-operative development, public works, water and land development); these officers may all attend DDC meetings without voting but they are full members of the DDPC. The latter has the tasks of formulating projects and programmes for the DDC to consider and of supervising the implementation of approved projects and programmes; President Nyerere described it as 'the executive arm' of the DDC and it is therefore interesting to note the heavy dilution of the representative element in its membership. In fact, however, even the membership of the elected councillors in the DDC itself appears to be merely a device to preserve some continuity with the former system for it is provided that there will be no further elections to the DDCs as now constituted—vacancies will be filled by Ministerial appointment. (The position with regard to elections was announced to be a matter for review when the system is established.) DDCs will now plan and implement projects and programmes within the eight areas of former departmental interest noted above; they also inherit all the powers and functions of the old district councils; by-laws continue in force as if made not by the DDC but by the District Development Director. He also issues licences and permits (subject to the DDC's directions), yet, as finally implemented in 1974, the system gives to the DDC itself the power to make new by-laws (which take effect only after receiving Ministerial consent).[19]

Below the district level the Ward—or, as the case may be, Ujamaa-Development Committees will continue but they receive no new statutory recognition; each consists in principle of ten members elected from the area with the local TANU Chairman. Above the districts, Regional Development Committees are now established by the Act throughout Tanganyika, with a large appointed membership: the Regional Commissioner is Chairman, the new Regional Development Director (who has replaced the Administrative Secretary) is Secretary; and other members include all the Area Commissioners and District Development Directors in the Region. All these officers are appointed to their posts by the President. The RDC also includes all regional constituency members of Parliament (two Regions have ten constituencies each, two others eight, and the others seven or less so that the 'representative' element in the RDC is small) and the Regional and District Chairman of TANU (who are elected by the appropriate annual Party conference). The Minister may appoint four more (non-voting) members and the regional 'staff' and 'functional' officers may attend but not vote.[20] Each of the RDCs is essentially advisory with regard to district development projects although it formulates and implements development projects affecting the whole Region. Parliament now appropriates funds by regional votes for expenses and development expenditure: at this early stage of decentralization the Supplementary Appropriation Acts for 1972-73[21] show a wide diversity in the figures allotted, from Shs. 3,466,129 for Arusha to only Shs. 1,427,066 and Shs. 757,277 to the large Mwanza and Coast Regions respectively; Tabora was the only Region allotted separate development expenditure—Shs. 750,000 in addition to expenses of Shs. 1,731,667—but these figures do not show the whole of the financial allocations because, in this first transitional year only, the Minister for Finance was authorized to re-allocate to Regions funds originally allotted to other Ministers and Departments.[22]

The officials with executive responsibility at each level together form the 'Development Team' led by the Development Director and including the three 'staff' officers (Finance, Personnel and Planning) and the eight 'functional officers' who replace the former representatives of different central departments. The obvious analogy with the old 'district team' of colonial days which springs to mind is not a close one in view of the serious attempts at decentralization of responsibility made by the new scheme, for each 'Regional Directorate' (including the District Development Directors) forms a separate Department of Government in which the District Directorate is a Division; the Regional Development Director can exercise the powers of a Principal Secretary.

Thus an impressive and integrated administrative structure has replaced the previous array of authorities involved in regional administration and local government. Of course, the Party structure continues although there is little explicit co-ordination between the two; not surprisingly, the National Executive Committee of TANU was in 1972 considering strengthening the relevant TANU departments in response to the new system. It is clearly intended that District Development Councils will refer their draft development proposals to the TANU District Executive Committees for their approval of the policies (but not the details) involved. Furthermore, there is at regional level considerable overlap of membership between the RDC and the Regional Executive Committee of the Party; the elected TANU Chairman of the REC is a member of RDC, and the Regional Commissioner who presides over the RDC is a member of the REC, in his role as TANU Regional Secretary. Local MPs and the TANU District Chairmen are members of each body as are Area Commissioners (who, however, as TANU District Secretaries, have no votes on the REC). There is much less overlap between the membership of the District Development Council and the District Development and Planning Committee and the District Executive Committee of TANU, although the TANU District Chairman, the Area Commissioner and the local MPs are members of all three. However, within the districts the Ward Development Committees have a crucial role to play and it is the more anomalous that they are not specifically included in the new Act for by earlier statutory provision they are committees of the old local authorities which have now disappeared.[23] Yet the WDCs are also the point at which state and Party institutions most closely merge into one organ, just as the Government formerly tried to make the old VDCs which they superseded official TANU organs, by composing them of all ten-house cell leaders in the village.

This new framework of administration was essentially designed for the rural areas in which more than ninety per cent of Tanzanians live; how far could it be applied in urban areas? The special problems they raised were recognized by the exclusion from the application of the original Act of all areas governed by municipal or town councils.[24] However, with the passage of time before the Act was implemented at district level it was evidently accepted that there was no necessary reason to exclude the urban areas and in 1974 the Prime Minister exercised the power given him by the Act to amend the relevant legislation to enable him to order that any municipality and any town council area, including any part of these, should be taken out of that system of local government and be brought within the decentralization provisions, the respective elected councillors then serving as members of the new District Development Council.[25] The new scheme was then applied to the urban areas including even the old capital, Dar es Salaam, which was removed from the jurisdiction of the City Council as from 1 January 1974 and brought within the system of district administration forming a new Region divided into three new districts—Ilala, Kinondoni and Tameke.[26] Three other important towns were also divided into two districts each. The system of decentralized administration in Dar es Salaam is now similar to that elsewhere although, to ensure consistency, it is the Regional Development Director (instead of his District colleague) who is given power to make by-laws for these three districts and he is subject to the directions of the Regional Development Committee in so doing.[27]

How far will this new system achieve the important aims which inspired it? These, as stated by President Nyerere, included: decentralization from Dar es Salaam to increase local freedom in decision-making, while retaining national control of national projects; centralization locally between functional and political officers and between central and local government officers; the reduction of bureaucratic excesses and 'red tape', with the retention of sufficient central government guidance; the accessibility of responsible officers to the local people; the general equalization of development between the different Regions by providing help to needy areas; a new attitude whereby officials think not of 'administration' but of 'administration for development'. In short, the overall aims were greater efficiency combined with more democracy. Yet the scheme for the implementation of these aims appears to involve many paradoxes. The structure aims to regionalize the bureaucracy, bringing it nearer to the people; yet the effect may be to increase the directness and immediacy of impact of bureaucratic decisions. In particular, decentralization of government has involved centralization of staff: there is no longer a local government service for all these local officers are now employed and paid by central government as part of the public service whereas formerly local officers were employed by the district councils (although since 1963 all senior posts had formed part of the unified Local Government Service, appointments being made by the Local Government Service Commission). A further anomaly is that the new system has involved the immediate reduction in, and possibly the ultimate elimination of, participation in decision-making by elected representatives. The President indicated that the new DDCs will in fact be in direct consultation with the people, and the citizen will be able to approach directly a local official with real responsibility. Of course the local responsibility and powers are now much increased, and the voice of the people is heard through the TANU organs. The President has drawn an analogy between the new organization in each district and Region and the organizations of central Government—the Regional and Area Commissioners being equivalent to Ministers, the Development Directors their Principal Secretaries, responsible particularly for the preparation and implementation of annual plans for all aspects of development in their areas. (The budget allocations for the regional votes in 1974-75 clearly indicate the measure of decentralization that has been achieved in financial responsibility: recurrent expenditure allocations vary widely between the twenty Regions, from Shs. 73,286,400 for Tanga to Shs. 30,153,300 for the small new Rukwa Region; development expenditure appropriations were topped by Dar es Salaam (Shs. 23,063,000) with Rukwa again the lowest (Shs. 9,460,000).[28] President Nyerere himself does not see this as the transfer of a rigid bureaucratic system from the capital, but as a means of entrusting responsibility to more and more people—and, as an inevitable corollary, weakening the capacity of Ministers to answer in the National Assembly for specific local developments. On the other hand, the new system increases the importance of the role of MPs at the regional and district levels. (Will difficulties arise when Ministers shed their executive roles when participating in their regional and district committees?)

Decentralization—in this form involving 'deconcentration' as well as 'devolution'[29]—thus has a rather special connotation in Tanzania. While, as the President suggests, attitudes are more important than structures, this scheme may prove to have been 'decentralization' with 'bureaucratization'. Few tears will be shed for the abolition of district and town councils; the development committee structure which has grown up alongside them had a relevance and dynamism upon which it may have been wise to build the new framework. But it may be questioned whether enough has been done to reverse the former trend towards the pre-eminence of officials in local decision-making. This is a novel approach to government 'administration for development' and its ultimate success is linked with the new District Corporations created in 1974 with wide-ranging functions in agriculture, industry, commerce, housing etc.[30] The statutory scheme betrays some abiguity of functions and obviously presumes supplementation by conventions: for example, in implementing district projects the RDC 'advises and assists', the DD 'plans and implements', the DDPC 'formulates projects' and 'supervises implementation'. Is there even some ambiguity as to the basic unit for de-centralization? The Regional structure is strong but its role weak so that the district is the key unit, where functional officers are concentrated. The Regional Development Director may have a difficult role as accounting officer who must pass on to the districts funds for district projects in the implementation of which the RDC can only 'advise and assist'.

Because of the strength and ubiquity of the official element in the new structure, it is appropriate to urge that the activities of one of Tanzania's most successful innovations—the 'Ombudsman', the Permanent Commission of Enquiry—should be extended by 'decentralization' of the Commission to provide a present and active friend to the citizen at regional level.

ZANZIBAR

The nature of the Union relationship and of President Karume's regime have been considered in previous volumes. 1972 opened with the curious affair of the Zanzibar prisons which were closed (or, in a sense, opened). What might be welcomed as an enlightened act of radical penal policy was qualified by the announcement on 7 January, by Aboud Jumbe as Minister of State, that the prisoners—600 of whom, excluding murderers and political detainees, were ceremonially released by Karume on 12 January, the eighth aniversary of the Revolution—would be conscripted into forced labour and had accepted freedom after signing an oath that they would submit to execution if they repeated their crimes.[31] On 23 January Karume announced the reprieve of nineteen conspirators sentenced to death in 1971 for plotting against the ruling Revolutionary Council; they would instead work in rehabilitation centres—for example, as cattle herders—for up to ten years. He also announced a new Decree which would permit citizens to kill anyone whom they believed to be plotting to overthrow the Government.[32] Subsequent events were to demonstrate that his anxiety was not ill-founded; his assassination on 7 April 1972 marked a turning point in the history of independent Zanzibar and throughout the rest of the year the islands were adjusting to the new situation. Aboud Jumbe, a former teacher, was elected President of the ruling Afro-Shirazi Party (ASP) and Chairman of the Revolutionary Council, and, under the Interim Constitution of Tanzania, he was then appointed First Vice-President on 12 April; Hassan Moyo was appointed as his Minister of State. The closed prisons were soon reopened to admit hundreds of detainees suspected of complicity in a plot and a number were also detained on the mainland.[33]

Chairman Jumbe was widely expected to set a new style for the Zanzibar leadership, with some amelioration of his predecessor's austerity. One of his early tasks was the reorganization of governmental structure. An early decision was the division of Zanzibar into five, instead of three, regions.[34] The regional and area commissioners were appointed ASP secretaries, to promote integration of party and government. The main effects of changes accomplished by the end of the year, including the new Zanzibar constitution, were to assert the primacy of the ruling ASP and to make the Revolutionary Council an instrument of its policies—in aim thus paralleling the corresponding developments in Tanganyika in recent years which have emphasized the dominance of the ruling party, TANU. The supreme organ under the ASP Congress, which met for the first time in December 1972, is the new Political Committee of nine members appointed by the ASP President who is its chairman. Its position as both the Cabinet of Government and the principal Committee of the Party is not free from ambiguity: ministries have been made departments of the Party, and the Political Committee can call for witnesses and reports from Party and Government departments. The Committee has general authority over the implementation of Party policy but it can also modify policy in consultation with other Party organs. The ASP Congress passed a mixture of resolutions: to execute clove smugglers by firing squad; to nationalize cinemas; to purge former members of defunct parties formerly opposed to ASP, and other opponents, from Party, Government, Police, Defence Forces etc.[35]

Ultimately over eighty persons were charged with treason, including several plots between April 1968 and April 1972 and involving complicity in Karume's assassination. Most of these were tried by a People's Tribunal of three members in a lengthy trial which commenced in 1973; eighteen, detained on the mainland, were tried in absentia, the Tanzanian Government declining to send them to the islands for trial without assurances of fair trial procedures including legal representation. Nine pleaded guilty and gave evidence for the prosecution after being sentenced to death. Judgement was given on 15 May 1974: seventeen were acquitted and against six more the court found there was no case to answer. Four were convicted of misprision of treason and forty-four of treason, including thirteen of the eighteen tried in absentia, amongst them a former Tanzanian Cabinet Minister. In all twenty-nine were sentenced to death. Appeals were heard at the end of 1974.[36]

THE PUBLIC SERVICE

Tanzania's evolving strategy for 'government for development' involves an increasing element of mobility in the public service. In 1972 the laws were amended to facilitate the movement of public officers to political roles as Members of Parliament or to posts in parastatal organs, as well, of course, as the integration of the former local government service in the public service, paradoxically as part of the decentralization reforms. The Constitution was amended to facilitate the combination of political and public office by removing the disqualification formerly imposed on public officers from standing for election as constituency Members of Parliament.[37] The Constitution had previously allowed such officers to offer themselves as candidates in the primary election but now they need no longer resign their offices in order to stand as candidates in the General Election or to take their seats if elected. Moreover the reverse is also possible so that Members of the National Assembly may be appointed to public office without losing their Parliamentary seats. The offices specified in this amendment include all civil service and judicial offices and offices as Area Commissioner, or in the Unified Teaching Service, the Unified Co-operative Service, the Police Force, National Service or Tanzania Peoples' Defence Force.

A significant amendment to the Pensions Ordinance was designed to facilitate the movement of officers between the public service and the parastatal organizations, by safeguarding their pension rights on retirement from either after service in the other.[38] The protection applies to an officer who left the public service after 1 January 1954 in order to join a parastatal organization and who did so join within a month of leaving Government service. On retirement he retains his entitlement to a pension based on his period in the service of Tanzania. For this purpose 'parastatal organization' is widely defined to include any corporation (excluding the East African Community, its corporations and any registered company unless Government or a parastatal owns fifty per cent of the issued share capital), TANU and its organs and a registered trade union.

It has already been noticed that the decentralization programme has involved the expansion of the civil service by the absorption of many members of the former Local Government Service. When the decentralization system came into force (in 1974) every local authority employee—under a contract of service or by appointment to the Local Government Service—was deemed to have been appointed to the service of the United Republic; however, such officers are not automatically entitled to the terms of employment and superannuation benefits of public officers although the rules governing termination of appointment in the public interest and disciplinary offences do apply to them. The Prime Minister was empowered to make regulations governing the terms of employment of these officers, including their superannuation, without of course extinguishing their rights to their deposits in the Local Authorities Provident Fund.[39]

Africanization policies within the organs of the East African Community were ventilated and considered in an interesting case in the Tanzania High Court.[40] The plaintiff, a Tanzanian citizen of Asian origin, sued the East African Posts and Telecommunications Corporation, by which he had been employed, for a declaration that he had been compulsorily retired and was therefore entitled to the benefits stipulated for premature retirement. He had in fact been given notice of compulsory retirement and protested that this violated the non-racial policies of the Tanzanian Government; the Corporation then had second thoughts and withdrew the notice but he asserted that it was too late, that he had made arrangements accordingly and would accept compulsory retirement. The

Regional Director for Tanzania agreed to this but from the headquarters of the Corporation in Kampala came an opposite view cancelling the notice of retirement. Biron, J, observing that 'innumerable lies' had been told in the course of the hearing, rejected the suit. He noted a decision of the Board of Directors of the Corporation in 1969 that, while the policies of Africanization would continue, they would no longer apply to non-African citizens of partner states, who could indeed be recruited on permanent terms subject to the approval of the General Purposes Committee for each appointment. However, this decision conflicted with Establishment Circular 40B of 1962, issued under the direction of the Authority, and even if it could override that Circular the decision had not in fact been implemented, being honoured more in the breach than in the observance and never brought to the notice of officers of the Corporation. A change of policy was, however, instituted by the Director-General's Personnel Circular No. 2B of 1971, ending compulsory retirement in the interests of Africanization and the eligibility of citizens of partner states for premature retirement. The Court of Appeal, upholding the decision, held that the Corporation's agreement to allow the appellant to retire prematurely did not constitute a binding contract and could later be withdrawn, being merely the gratuitous grant of a request. The Corporation would, however, have been liable if, between the giving of notice and its withdrawal, the employee had acted upon it to his detriment.

The High Court has held also that no court has jurisdiction to hear a suit for wrongful dismissal by a Service Commission of one of the East African Corporations.[41] Mfalila, J, has held that, although most suits against the Government must be brought under the Government Suits Ordinance, 'suits under the Employment Ordinance can by clear provision of that Ordinance be brought under the provisions of that Ordinance as if the Government was a private employer'. In the instant case, therefore, he held somewhat surprisingly that it was correct for a dismissed employee to sue the Regional Fisheries Officer who had employed him.[42] A former local government officer has succeeded in obtaining damages for wrongful dismissal, plus his and the employer's contribution to the provident fund, where the proper procedure prescribed by the Regulations, and the principles of natural justice, had not been followed.[43]

PARASTATALS

Several new parastatal organizations were established in 1972. The State Mining Corporation, set up by Presidential order, has comprehensive functions in the exploitation of minerals.[44] It can prospect, mine, produce, refine, grade, cut, store, supply, buy, sell and distribute minerals; it can acquire shares or interests in any other company or undertaking engaged in this area. The authorized nominal capital is Shs. 100 million in 10,000 shares, which can be held by the United Republic only. The initial paid up capital is Shs. 65 million. The Corporation is run by a Board of seven to eleven Directors appointed by the Minister with a Chairman and General Manager appointed by the President. The shares held by the National Development Corporation in four companies were transferred to the Corporation.[45]

The newly established Tobacco Authority of Tanzania has a key role to play for it will effectively control the development of a crop which has been spectacularly successful, production increasing from 2,700 metric tons in 1961 to 21,400 in 1970. The Authority,[46] replacing the Tanganyika Tobacco Board set up in 1963, now controls the export of tobacco and its products by issuing permits and may, by Ministerial orders, be given control of the planting and/or of the marketing of tobacco in any area. Where an order is in force it becomes illegal to plant tobacco without a licence from the Authority, the maximum fine for contravention being Shs. 5,000 with the possibility also of imprisonment for two years. No local enabling order is required before the Authority can give, with Ministerial consent, binding directions, subject to a similar penalty, as to many details of tobacco production including preparation of the ground for planting, harvesting, grading, packing, manufacturing, storing, processing and marketing. Compulsory marketing orders may be made with the Minister's consent, requiring all tobacco to be sold to the Authority or a specified person and at a price fixed by the Authority, which also recommends to the Minister the rate of levy to be imposed, the proceeds of which form part of the Authority's financial resources. It maintains a register of growers and of land planted with tobacco, supervises cultivation and harvesting, inspects plantations, negotiates processing agreements, organizes arrangements for the transportation and purchase of the crop, supervises research programmes, participates in manufacturing and supervises programmes for the development of the industry. As usual with such bodies, the Minister can give general directions to the Authority.

The Tanzania Housing Bank was established[47] to promote housing development (i.e. the development of sites and the construction of residential or commercial buildings) by providing finance: it is enjoined to mobilize local savings and external resources for this purpose and to operate savings, time and term deposits accounts, making loans or equity finance available to any person for housing development and giving technical, financial and other assistance to provide owner-occupied housing schemes and building programmes in ujamaa villages, and helping other organizations engaged primarily in housing development for the benefit of the Tanzanian people. The Bank must implement Government housing and building policies, promoting the use of local materials and the construction of houses suited to local conditions 'to foster the minimizing of building costs, prices at which houses may be sold and rents at which they are let'. The Bank is controlled by a Chairman appointed by the President and a Board of eight to twelve Directors appointed by the Minister for Finance from persons with knowledge and experience in economic and financial matters, town planning, estate management, building or other relevant fields. The Minister, after consulting the Board, appoints the General Manager. The authorized share capital is Shs. 100 million in 100 shares allotted to the Government; if the Board, with the Minister's approval, increases the capital the President may direct that additional shares be held by a specified parastatal. Financial criteria for the Bank's operation are prescribed in detail: the General Revenue Fund must reach half the authorized capital stock before any dividend can be paid and borrowing by the Bank for ordinary operations must not exceed three times the aggregate of the Fund plus the issued share capital. Special Funds may be held for special operations. The Bank's own investments in equity financing are restricted to institutions a substantial portion of whose operations are similar to those of the Bank; there is a limit to the investment of ordinary funds. The Bank must finance projects that are 'economically viable, socially desirable and technically feasible'. It can terminate its operations by a resolution approved by the Minister; in that event Government would be liable to all creditors to the extent of the unpaid capital stock. The President is empowered to transfer not only any asset or liability of a parastatal to the Bank but also any employee thereof. The President can also transfer to the Bank all the shares in any 'parastatal company', i.e. one of which the Government or any parastatal holds fifty per cent of the issued share capital—reasonable compensation is then payable to the deprived shareholders. These powers of transfer had to be exercised within six months of the commencement of the Act which was later fixed as 1 January 1973.[48] When the Bank came into being on that date it did in fact take over, by such an order, all the assets and liabilities of the Permanent Housing Finance Co.[49]

Overshadowing these new developments in the field of parastatals was the rising tide of public and official anxiety about one of the most important of the parastatals established in the wave of nationalization which in 1967 followed the Arusha Declaration. The problems of the State Trading Corporation, with its extensive and central responsibilities in the trading life of the nation, were such that the tide overwhelmed it. Recurrent serious shortages of essential goods, including staple foods such as meat, sugar, maize and salt, during 1971 led to the appointment of a Select Committee of six, to investigate the shortages and make recommendations, by a unanimous resolution of the National Assembly on 31 January 1972.[50] An Open General Licence published in March, 1972 confirmed the STC's monopoly of the import of a wide range of consumer goods (confectionery, beer, soap, various foods etc.).[51] Yet widespread criticism of the organization and efficiency of the Corporation could no longer be withheld: severe strictures voiced by an inter-Ministerial Committee were followed by the announcement in October 1972 of a complete restructuring of the national trading system: the STC would be divided into a number of new companies, six at national level (three dealing with specialist items—pharmaceuticals, hardware, industrial and agricultural goods—and three with bulk imports—foods; household supplies, domestic appliances) with one trading company for each Region.[52] This decentralization of the national commercial network, while in keeping with the policy of government decentralization, multiplies demand for management and allied skills when lack of skilled personnel continues as an important constraint upon efficiency in many areas.

One of the most interesting innovations of Tanzania in the field of parastatals is the Tanzania Legal Corporation, established in 1971 'to provide legal services to parastatal organizations . . . and . . . to Government . . .' It was intended from the start that the Corporation would ultimately be authorized to make its services available more widely—for example, to private individuals—and an unusual case of 1972 precipitated that extension of its powers. In *W. v. Income Tax*[53] the Corporation sought to represent in the High Court an appellant who had earlier been appointed by the Court receiver of certain immovable property on the motion of the Permanent Housing Finance Company (Tanzania) Ltd, a parastatal organization for which the Legal Corporation was authorized to act but which was not a party to this appeal. For the Commissioner-General of Income Tax it was submitted that the Legal Corporation had no right of audience on behalf of W., an individual. Although the Finance Company was entitled to the considerable sums of money at issue if the appeal succeeded, Mwakasendo, Ag J, held that this did not create a client-advocate relationship between the appellant and the Legal Corporation, which therefore had no *locus standi* in the case. This decision of July, 1972, illuminating the inconvenience of the limitations imposed at its birth upon the Legal Corporation, which was already prepared to act for individuals, prompted a wide extension of the Corporation's powers a month later by an amendment which now allows it, 'subject to the directions of the Attorney-General, to provide legal services to members of the public on such terms and conditions as the Chief Corporation Counsel may deem fit'.[54]

An important study of parastatals and the law in Tanzania was published during 1972 and is included in the Bibliography at the end of this chapter.

JUDICIAL SYSTEM

Despite the tendency to restrict the jurisdiction of the courts by the statutory withdrawal of various matters involving administrative discretions from review by them, the volume of work for the courts continues to increase. The pressure on the High Court was reflected by a constitutional amendment of 1972 which increased the maximum number of judges who may be appointed from eight to fifteen; an unlimited number of acting judges may also be appointed.[55] It is also notable that an unprecedented number of judicial decisions were reported for 1972, in the established *East African Law Reports* and in the *High Court Digest* and in the inaugural volume of the new series of *Tanzania Law Reports*, dated 1973.[56] Another sign of pressure of work on the judiciary was an amendment to the Magistrates Courts Act to enable the Minister responsible for justice, after consulting the Chief Justice and the Attorney-General, to confer on a resident magistrate the appellate jurisdiction normally vested in the High Court, in relation either to a class of cases or to a particular case (but not, of course, in relation to any judgement of his own as magistrate).[57] Orders were in fact made conferring such jurisdiction on certain resident magistrates.[58]

The close interest of the ruling party, TANU, in the local

administration of justice is demonstrated in the new regulations which govern the appointment of assessors, who are important members of primary courts.[59] Each court now has a panel of thirty to forty members nominated annually in the first instance by Branch Executive Committees of TANU. The District Executive Committee considers 'the merits and suitability' of each nominee, approves a list and sends it to the District Magistrate for transmission to the magistrates of the primary courts, whose responsibility it is to propose a roster giving each assessor equal opportunity to hear cases. The roster must be approved by the TANU district secretary. An assessor can be removed at any time by the District Executive Committee for inability or misbehaviour. An assessor is disqualified from sitting on any case in which he has a pecuniary or other interest. Assessors share with the magistrate in deciding 'all matters before a primary court'; Kisanga, J, has held that this includes the sentence to be imposed after conviction.[60] Although it is expressly permitted for a court to continue a trial with only one assessor, if the original two assessors are replaced by another two during a trial the proceedings are invalid if they merely continue from that point and it is irrelevant that the accused made no objection.[61]

IMMIGRATION

The new Immigration Act,[62] which came into force on 1 June 1972, replaces the old Act which had taken effect just before the Union with Zanzibar eight years previously. The new Act is clearly intended to apply to Zanzibar as well as Tanganyika, immigration being one of the 'Union matters' within the jurisdiction of the Parliament of Tanzania; yet it appears that Zanzibar has continued its separate control of immigration within the United Republic even after 1972. The new Act makes a number of changes of importance in immigration law and procedures. It abolishes the former exemption of many Africans from immigration controls. The old Act did not apply 'to any African' but the term was defined as 'a member of a tribe indigenous to' territories bordering Tanganyika, and Southern Rhodesia; the new Act applies to all non-citizens but Africans who were as such exempt from the old Act and ordinarily resident in Tanzania were exempted by subsequent Ministerial order from control under the Act for a specified period in order that they might apply for the appropriate permits or passes (at a reduced fee).[63] Refugees from certain neighbouring states and from South Africa, Namibia and Rhodesia were indefinitely exempted by the Minister from the regime of permits and passes.[64]

The 1972 Act introduces a new system with three types of residence permits. Under the old Act there were two classes of entry permits—'Class A' permitting entry for approved purposes without security and 'Class B' permitting entry for approved purposes with security provided by either a financial deposit or a bond sufficient to cover the cost of repatriation; a 'B' permit was really intended to operate temporarily pending application for an 'A' permit. In the new Act the old 'Class B' permit becomes a 'Class A' residence permit for persons engaging in business, trade, a profession, agriculture or mining specified therein, the old 'Class A' permit being abolished. A new 'Class B' permit is now authorized for a person who has been offered specific employment in, and of benefit to, Tanzania. A new 'Class C' permit may be granted to other persons. These residence permits are granted, and conditions may be imposed thereon, in the discretion of the Principal Immigration Officer who may at any time cancel (or vary the conditions of) a permit if he considers it in the public interest to do so, such cancellation being subject to the Minister's confirmation which is final. In any case no permit can be given for a longer period than three years initially or for a total period after renewal exceeding five years. There is also now an appeal to the Minister against the Principal Immigration Officer's refusal of a permit; the Minister's decision is final and is expressly not subject to review by any court. Noncompliance with any condition attached to a permit now results in its immediate expiry and may cause forfeiture of any security provided. Unless exempted by the Minister, everyone entering Tanzania must possess a valid passport.[65]

A number of incidental changes were made by this Act to the law relating to 'prohibited immigrants', no doubt to remedy defects in the old law which had come to light. In particular, the rules are extended with regard to a person whose entry is legal but whose continued presence becomes unlawful—for example, because his permit has been cancelled or revoked or because he has been declared a prohibited immigrant by the Minister or Principal Immigration Officer as an undesirable (the PIO's order requires confirmation by the Minister whose decision is final). Powers of arrest are extended to apply to a person whose presence has become illegal since his original entry. A person arrested must normally be brought before a magistrate without delay but (by a new provision) not if he has been declared a prohibited immigrant in Tanzania when he may be kept in custody until deported. The Minister has general authority to prohibit, in his absolute discretion, not merely as before the entry into, but now also the presence within, Tanzania of any non-citizen or class of non-citizens, and to make deportation orders for prohibited immigrants and non-citizens, 'whose continued presence in Tanzania is, in the opinion of the President, undesirable'. In any proceedings under the Act the burden of proving lawful presence now lies on the person asserting it, as the burden of proving alleged citizenship continues to do.

Enforcement provisions are strengthened under the Act. Immigration officers' powers to search ships, aircraft or vehicles are extended to allow searches of any building; the offence of failing to answer an immigration officer's 'lawful and reasonable question', or giving a false answer, no longer has the qualifying provision entitling a person to refuse to answer an incriminating question. It is now an offence to employ a non-citizen who has no appropriate permit and the Minister can prescribe the information to be given by employers regarding their employees' citizenship, work, qualifications and experience and their training schemes for citizens. Maximum penalties under the Act are substantially increased: thus where no specific penalty is stated offences carry a maximum sentence of three years imprisonment or a fine of Shs. 30,000 or both (under the old Act one year or Shs. 10,000 or both).

INDIGENIZATION

Immigration policy is one aspect of the Government's endeavour to promote 'indigenization' of staff in public and private sectors. Other Governments have pursued the same aim by various means, but Tanzania's approach has been more subtle and gradualistic than blunt expulsion or imposed time limits. In 1972 a financial sanction was introduced to prod temporizing employers towards introducing proper training schemes for their local staff. The new 'Training Levy'[66] must be paid monthly by every employer of a non-citizen at a rate of ten per cent of the chargeable emoluments of every non-citizen employee. Substantial penalties (twenty-five per cent of the unpaid levy after twenty-one days, ten per cent of the balance unpaid every thirty days subsequently) are payable for dilatoriness. The Minister can exempt any employer who shows that he is making *bona fide* efforts for the training and employment of citizens for offices held by non-citizens. To prevent evasion the Act ingeniously provides that a non-citizen partner in a business or profession is deemed to be employed thereby unless the Minister, being satisfied that he 'has made a significant contribution to the capital' and 'that it is in all respects a *bona fide* partnership', exempts the partnership to the extent of the non-citizen partner's share of the profits. 'Chargeable emoluments' were originally defined as chargeable income for income tax purposes, but second thoughts prevailed and a retrospective amendment[67] redefined the term to embrace all emoluments—'the salary, allowances and other income accrued in or derived from the United Republic in respect of any employment'. For a non-citizen partner the phrase means his share of profits plus any chargeable income as an employee, if any, with a deemed 'minimum' of Shs. 20,000 if his chargeable emoluments are less than that. The Principal Secretary to the Treasury is the Commissioner of Training Levy.

NATIONAL ECONOMIC AND SOCIAL DEVELOPMENT

COMPANIES: GOVERNMENT FINANCIAL CONTROLS

Extensive powers to control the finances of companies with regard to dividends and investments were granted to the Minister for Finance by a new Act,[68] the main purpose of which is to facilitate regulation of dividend levels and the uses of cash flows to serve the national interest especially with regard to national investment planning; other purposes include conservation of foreign exchange. The scheme of control introduced has several aspects. Firstly, dividend limitation was imposed on all companies: for any financial year dividends declared must not in aggregate total more than the amount by which the company's net worth exceeds 125 per cent of the par value of the paid up share capital at the end of that year; nor must they exceed the average annual profits in the preceding three years or eighty per cent of the profits in the immediately previous year (or in the current year for a new company), whichever is the larger. The Minister can authorize the payment of larger dividends, specified by him, with prior approval by resolution of the National Assembly.

Secondly, special dividend controls are available over certain 'specified companies': in addition to the general dividend limitation, the Minister can order any of these companies to limit its dividends further, to an aggregate not exceeding a prescribed percentage of the company's 'approved net worth', or he can order the company to declare and pay dividends and may then prescribe a minimum aggregate for such dividends as a percentage of 'approval net worth' (but within the general rules of dividend limitation). 'Net worth' is defined as the difference between the value of all assets and the value of all liabilities at the end of the financial year; 'approved net worth' means the net worth shown by the latest properly audited balance sheet plus the portion of profits which the Minister is satisfied has been spent subsequently (but before the commencement of the year for which dividends are proposed) in specified ways (i.e. in reducing any loan from the National Bank of Commerce or by investment in Government securities or authorized investments). In this way the Act facilitates a measure of investment control with regard to retained earnings; a Ministerial order has limited dividends of specified companies to an aggregate of twenty per cent of 'approved net worth'.[69]

Thirdly, specified companies must submit to the Minister, at least thirty days before each financial year, 'cash flow budgets' setting out estimated receipts, within a prescribed period, in specified Government Minister can, before the year starts or within three months of receiving the the budget, order the company to invest a prescribed portion of its estimated receipts, whithin a prescribed period, in specified Government securities or other investments. Where such an order has been made a statement of actual cash flow must be submitted within three months of the end of the year. Regulations have prescribed other detailed returns required from specified companies and the Treasury Registrar is empowered to demand these also of any other company.[70]

The Act specifies thirty-six companies including oil, motor and transport, manufacturing and processing companies (in some of which the Government has a controlling interest) and also some national corporations established under the Companies Ordinance—e.g. the National Insurance Company of Tanzania Ltd—or under a special statute—e.g. the National Bank of Commerce. The Minister for Finance can vary the Schedule which names these companies and more than seventy more companies have been added by him to the list.[71] The Act thus attempts a cure for the weaknesses of investment policy shown by parastatal organizations, amongst others, in the past; indeed, the cash flow budget requirements also apply to four statutory bodies specified in the second part of the Schedule: the Lint and Seed Marketing Board, the National Agricultural Products Board, the Tobacco Authority and the Registrar of Buildings; the Tanzania Tea Authority was later added.[72] The Minister can specify what are 'authorized investments', either generally or for a specified company.[73] In deciding whether to exercise his powers, the Minister may consider the national interest or the interests of shareholders. There can be no winding-up of a specified company, whether by resolution or court order, without the Minister's consent.

Finally, special controls are introduced for 'foreign companies'—those incorporated outside Tanganyika. No such company can transfer outside Tanganyika, or appropriate for distribution to its members, more than the 'prescribed portion of its local profits' in any financial year. 'Local profits' are those 'arising from or attributable to its business in' Tanzania; the 'prescribed portion' thereof is a portion not exceeding the average annual local profits in the preceding three years or 80% of the local profits in the immediately preceding year, whichever is greater. Furthermore, the Minister for Finance can oblige a foreign company to incorporate locally in Tanganyika if he is satisfied that it is carrying on a substantial business there and that local incorporation is in the national interest. He must consult the Minister responsible for legal affairs before making such an order, which may require the company to transfer all its local business, assets and liabilities to the new local company and itself to cease to trade in Tanganyika. (He may, however, expressly allow the foreign company to carry on some business and to retain specified local assets and liabilities.) Special provision is made to allow the foreign company to be the sole member of the new local company. Contravention of a Ministerial order by the foreign company is an offence incurring a maximum penalty of Shs. 10,000 per day. The maximum penalty for other offences under the Act by companies is Shs. 50,000; the Attorney-General's consent is required for any prosecution. The Act was made retrospective for more than two months before the date when assent was given (18 August 1972), to 15 June 1972: the first order for local incorporation was made in respect of a Danish company on the date the President assented to this measure.[74]

PRICE CONTROL

A simple measure, passed to counter price increases in certain goods manufactured in Tanganyika, was also given two months' retrospective effect to the date of first publication of the Bill. The Act[75] forbids any manufacturer, wholesaler or retailer to sell or offer for sale a specified product at a price higher than he normally sold such product at immediately before the 'effective date' (which is 15 June 1972 for those products specified in the original schedule: tyres, tubes and pangas, jembes and ploughs and similar agricultural implements; the Minister for Finance can vary the list and add other local products to it). Where a product is first manufactured after that date, the Price Controller can approve the price. The Price Controller can authorize price increases by the manufacturer and it is a defence for a seller to satisfy the court that he was merely passing on to his customer the additional cost he had paid for the product. The maximum penalties for breach of the Act are a fine of Shs. 20,000 or imprisonment for five years or both. A principal or employer is liable to be punished unless he satisfies the court that he knew nothing of the breach and could not, by the exercise of reasonable diligence, have had knowledge. The DPP's consent is required before a prosecution is instituted.

BUSINESS LICENSING

The comprehensive licensing system for the control of businesses of almost every kind in Tanganyika, effective from 1 September 1972,[76] while it is a far-reaching scheme of Government control of commerce and professions appropriate in an aspiring socialist state, in fact replaces with important but not fundamental changes the old system of trades licensing which was first introduced by the colonial government in 1927.[77] A business licence is required, and must be exhibited, by every person carrying on business (as principal or agent); each licence specifies the place of business and different licences are needed for different businesses carried on at the same place, or for the same business carried on at different places (although a subsidiary licence, at a reduced fee, may be granted for any place other than the principal place of business and no offence is committed in respect of an unlicensed 'subsidiary' of a licensed business if no licence fee is prescribed for the appropriate subsidiary licence). Every licence expires on 31 March annually. Very little of this so far is new. However, the licence fees prescribed by the schedule are much increased—usually at least doubled; they range from Shs. 6,000 for banking and Shs. 5,000 for electricity distributors or builders with an annual turnover exceeding Shs. five million to Shs. 2,000 for specified professions, Shs. 500 for a commercial traveller and Shs. 400 for a broker. The system applies to most kinds of businesses, the few exempted by the Act including farming or market gardening (including the sale of own produce) and certain businesses for which particular Acts prescribe special controls: trophy dealing, itinerant traders, the licensed liquor trade and mining. In general no licence is required if no fee is prescribed; however, the schedule includes a residual head of fees payable for any business not specifically provided for and the only business for which no fee is prescribed is that of a 'specified profession' in the full-time employment of the Government, the Community, a co-operative or parastatal (including technical assistance officers). The Minister can appoint any public officer or other authority to act as a licensing authority generally or for a specified area or category of businesses; where a parastatal organization is appointed the Minister can allow it to retain licence fees paid for its own use. A penalty of fifty per cent of the relevant fee is payable if the licence is not taken out within twenty-one days of the commencement of business or the expiry of the previous licence. Before issuing a licence the authority must be satisfied that any non-citizen applicant is lawfully present in Tanganyika and is authorized to carry on the business by a valid immigration permit or pass under the Immigration Act, 1972; it would appear therefore that those exempted from the controls established by that Act (e.g. refugees) may not obtain business licences. The President can restrict the number of business licences in any area of any class or limit any class of licences in any area to a parastatal organization. Maximum penalties for offences under the Act are a fine of Shs. 15,000 and, or in the alternative, imprisonment for two years; but the maximum penalty is a fine of Shs. 2,000 only if the offence was committed within twenty-one days of the expiry of the previous licence or the commencement of business.

A significant novelty in the new system lies in the considerable discretionary powers given to the Principal Secretary. The old law had no provision for revocation; now he can revoke the licence of any person convicted by a court of an offence against the Act, or the price control legislation, or decency or morality, or national security or economy or involving moral turpitude or the non-payment or evasion of any tax or duty; moreover he can ban the person concerned from carrying on any business or specified class of business in Tanganyika for three years. A person can lose his licence in this way if the convict was his director, officer or employee and if the Principal Secretary is satisfied that the licensee knew of the offence or received a benefit from it. These powers are also available where the Principal Secretary has exercised his power to compound any offence instead of prosecuting in court.

As in other statutory schemes of control of economic and commercial activity in Tanganyika, the jurisdiction of the courts is effectively excluded: a person aggrieved by the refusal or revocation of a licence or by a disqualification imposed by the Principal Secretary can appeal to the Minister who may delegate his functions to an Appeals Committee of two or more persons appointed by him; but the Committee is advisory only and the Minister is not bound to accept its view. Appeal against the fee assessment lies to the Principal Secretary. Advocates are not allowed to appear on appeals.[78]

The Minister has overriding power to revoke any licence or disqualify any person from carrying on any business if, in his opinion, it is in the public interest to do so. His decision is final and beyond judicial review: although he is required to consult with the Attorney-General and obtain the President's consent, a court must presume that this was done.

EDUCATION AND TRAINING

Two important new bodies were set up in 1972 to provide for the training of the key personnel needed to serve Tanzania's development needs. The nationalization of banks in 1967 and of insurance business in 1967-8 presented serious problems of staffing, particularly as earlier training programmes had been restricted in scope and as, immediately after nationalization, expansion of the respective services was undertaken. The nationalized businesses had considerable success during their crucial first years in the staff training programmes, but without the advantage of specialized local training institutes. Thus the National Bank of Commerce, with an expansion in the number of its senior staff of almost eighty per cent between December 1967 (1,211) and June 1971 (2,151), had reduced the proportion of non-citizen staff from 28.6 per cent (344) to eleven per cent (247). Over much the same period the staff of the National Insurance Corporation had grown from sixty to 580, including only eight expatriates.[79]

Training is now centralized in the Institute of Finance Management[80] which trains and examines students in the principles, procedures and techniques of banking, insurance, finance management and related subjects. Two Examination Boards—for Bankers and Insurers respectively—were established, connected with the Institute, and the Council of the Institute, after consulting the relevant Board, makes decrees regulating entry to and study at the Institute.

The success of the decentralization programme must depend to a large extent upon the quality of management available at district level; with such extensive distribution of executive authority over a wide range of development activities, Tanzania faces unprecedented pressure upon her reserves of skilled administrators and managers. Moreover the new system, designed as it is to invoke new attitudes of leadership and participation, demands managers with a novel combination of skills and training. Training for these tasks will fall within the scope of the Institute of Development Management, established in 1972[81] on the basis of former institutions (especially the Local Government Training Centre) and charged to promote social, economic and political development through training in 'specified subjects'—which are: management, accountancy, secretarial practice, public administration, the administration of justice, local government and rural development. The Institute also conducts research into 'the operational and organizational problems and training needs' and provides consultancy services to Government and other public authorities. The Minister can refer matters of administrative reform to the Institute for its advice. The Governing Body of the Institute includes five Principal Secretaries, the Vice-Chancellor of the University, nominees of NUTA and the Co-operative Union and ten members appointed by the Minister, with a Chairman appointed by the President.

Each of the seventy-two secondary schools in Tanzania, and the twenty-two Colleges of National Education, now has an Advisory Board established by Ministerial order to bring participation into the control of education.[82] Membership of each Board is controlled by the Minister who appoints five of the possible total of twelve members and who must also approve the Regional Education Officer's choice of four others. Each Board advises the Director of National Education and the Headmaster, and can discuss any topics of educational policy.

LABOUR

A new Ministerial order regulates wages and terms of employment, stipulating a minimum wage of Shs. 240 per month for all urban employees and for employees of commercial and industrial undertakings in rural areas.[83] For others the minimum wage is Shs. 140 per month. A Minimum Wage Board was established to review minimum wages and terms of employment.[84]

A highly unsatisfactory state of the law emerged from two cases, one of which indeed was not decided by the High Court because of the difficulty. The Security of Employment Act[85] excludes the jurisdiction of the courts regarding summary dismissal but certain employees are excluded from the provisions of that Act: thus an employee is exempted who 'in the opinion of the labour officer, is employed in the management of the business of his employer'.[86] The result is that the discretionary decision of a labour officer may determine the jurisdiction of the court and that obvious difficulties arise where the labour officer has made no decision. In one case Onyiuke, J., commented on the unsatisfactory state of the law when he stayed an action by a former hotel restaurant manager, to enable either party to obtain a labour officer's opinion.[87] In a later case Biron, J., was able to distinguish that precedent on the facts—the plaintiff had been employed as a sales trainee and it would have been a waste of time to stay the proceedings when there were no possible grounds upon which a labour officer could have held that he was employed in management.[88]

PROFESSIONS

The legal regulation of professions was extended with modern provisions designed also to promote professional development and Government control. Accountants and auditors were not previously subject to legal regulation; now the new National Board of Accountants and Auditors provides registration machinery and arranges qualifying examinations.[89] The Board can also provide opportunities for training and arrange conferences, seminars, publications etc. It consists of six to fifteen members, up to twelve of whom are appointed by the Ministers for Finance, Commerce and National Education. Accountants and auditors must be registered by the Board before carrying on business or undertaking employment: the Board's Registrar maintains three registers—of Authorized Accountants, Authorized Auditors and Approved Accountants respectively. Approved Accountants may be employed but may not engage in private practice. The Board must be satisfied not only that the person is qualified—either by membership of an approved institute or by passing its own examinations—but also that his 'professional and general conduct' make him a fit and proper person for registration. An approved accountant may either have professional qualifications or a certificate from his employer that he is experienced in specified fields of accountancy. The Board has disciplinary powers and can penalize improper, disgraceful or grossly negligent professional conduct, or offences under the Act, in various ways—e.g. by caution, suspension or removal from the register. Unless there has been a conviction the Board must conduct its own inquiry for which it is given certain judicial powers although the person concerned is not entitled to legal representation. Appeals from the Board's decisions—whether to refuse registration or to exercise disciplinary powers—lie to an Appeals Board whose decision is final and not subject to review.

The Act imposes obligations upon other persons too: every body of persons, whether or not incorporated, engaged in any trade, business or profession with assets in Tanganyika exceeding Shs. ten million in value or a gross annual turnover in Tanganyika exceeding Shs. five million, is now obliged to employ at least one authorized auditor or accountant (on pain of a maximum fine of Shs. 50,000). Furthermore, 'no person shall submit his income tax return to the appropriate authority unless such return has been prepared or certified by an authorized auditor or an authorized accountant'; the maximum penalty is a fine of up to Shs. 20,000 and two years imprisonment but there are exceptions including persons whose whole income is from employment or totals less than Shs. 150,000 annually. Will it be a defence that no accountant was available, in view of the shortage of accountants in Tanganyika?

Another Act[90] establishes the National Board of Architects, Quantity Surveyors and Building Contractors, to regulate the activities and conduct of these persons by maintaining a register, conducting examinations, providing opportunities for study and training and arranging conferences, seminars, publications etc. The Registrar appointed by the Board keeps the three registers. An applicant for registration as an architect or quantity surveyor must be a member of a recognized institute or hold a recognized academic qualification, as well as being a fit and proper person. It is interesting therefore to note how a person may be qualified for registration as a building contractor: he must satisfy the Board that he is 'experienced in works involving construction of buildings or other structures' and is 'a man of upright character'; registration may be refused if it would be 'against the national interest'.

The Board also has disciplinary powers and can caution, suspend or 'disbar' any person convicted of an offence under the Act or found by an inquiry held by the Board guilty of improper, disgraceful or grossly negligent professional conduct. Appeal lies to an Appeals Authority whose decision is final. It is an offence for any unregistered person to carry on business as an architect, quantity surveyor or building contractor. A body of persons—whether or not incorporated—can be registered as a building contractor but not in the other categories.

CRIMINAL LAW AND PROCEDURE

MINIMUM AND MAXIMUM SENTENCES

The most distinctive, and certainly the best known, Tanzanian contribution towards the solution of the problem of rising crime rates now experienced by most nations was the Minimum Sentences Act, 1963 which imposed a scheme of minimum penalties for a wide range of offences.[91] Widely criticized outside Tanzania, mainly for its wooden combination of minimum sentences of imprisonment with corporal punishment in two instalments (at the beginning and end respectively of the imprisonment), the Act had been widely welcomed within Tanzania. After a few years of the experiment, Government changed its mind but its attempt to repeal the corporal punishment element in 1969 was defeated in Parliament.[92] 1972 is notable as the year in which the mandatory corporal punishment was discarded with the replacement of the original Act by the Minimum Sentences Act, 1972;[93] this came into operation on 1 March 1972 but as from the date of enactment—8 February 1972—no corporal punishment was to be inflicted on a person convicted of an offence scheduled under the old Act. The dropping of indiscriminate, mandatory corporal punishment is a welcome reform; however, it is balanced by increases in the minimum sentences of imprisonment for most offences involved which are likely to impose heavy strains upon the Tanzanian penal system. Thus for the majority of offences listed in the first schedule the minimum sentence goes up from two to three years, for cattle stealing the sentence is raised from three to five years and for robbery from two to seven years.[94] The list of offences affected has been extended to include obtaining by false pretences where Government property is involved. Minimum sentences for minor offences under the Stock Theft Ordinance[95] remain unchanged at six months or one year. Furthermore, the Act provides for enhanced minimum sentences in certain circumstances: if the court is satisfied that the convict was previously convicted of a like offence, or of another scheduled offence, or of any other offence against property, within the previous seven years, the minimum sentence is five years imprisonment as it is if the value of the property obtained or attempted to be obtained, or the value of the advantage gained, sought or offered in corruption cases exceeds Shs. 5,000.

The old Act was especially designed to protect Government property but the schedule did not extend to include offences against the property of the public corporations or of the East African Community or its corporations. The new Act alters this, with a new approach to the mode of definition: the term 'specified authority' is adopted to indicate the body theft of whose property, or by whose employee, will attract the minimum sentences and the term is given a wide definition: it includes not only the Government, local authorities, the East African Community and its corporations and institutions, trade unions, TANU (including its organs and affiliates) but any corporation established otherwise than under the Companies Ordinance: but any 'subsidiary company' established under that Ordinance but owned as to at least fifty per cent of its issued share capital by one or more of the 'specified authorities' is included. (Under the old Act, employees of a company wholly owned by Government were held not to be public servants for the purposes of the Act.[96]) In the list of scheduled offences the opportunity has been taken to include expressly not merely the offence of obtaining an advantage without consideration, contrary to s. 6 of the Prevention of Corruption Act, 1971,[97] but also the offence of obtaining an advantage without adequate consideration defined by the same section (thus reversing the position established by the Court of Appeal in *Haining* v. *Republic* when it held that the specification of the former offence did not include the latter).[98]

A significant feature of the original Act was the very restricted discretion which it allowed to a sentencing court to reduce the minimum sentences: the new Act enlarges the discretion in one way and reduces it in another. The discretion will still arise only if the person convicted is a first offender and the value of the property in the offence is no more than Shs. 100/-; but it is no longer necessary for the court then to find and record that there are also 'special circumstances', which previously enabled the court to choose between either corporal punishment or a suitable term of imprisonment. Now the court can pass any sentence which it could have imposed if the Act had not been passed, if, 'having regard to all the circumstances of the case, it is just and equitable so to do'. The editor of the *Tanzania Law Reports* has argued that this latter phrase merely imports the usual principle of sentencing, not a specific requirement necessary for the discretion to arise: he fairly criticized a High Court judgement which still referred to 'special circumstances' as a relevant factor and which moreover failed to recognize the offender's low age as a ground for leniency.[99] However, now no discretion to reduce the minimum sentence will arise in cases of robbery, cattle-stealing or corruption. Three months after the Act came into operation Mfalila, J., had to determine an application by the State for the enhancement of sentence in the case of two men who had been convicted of offences of corruption on 20 October

1971. Probation orders had been made and these were clearly illegal under the old Minimum Sentences Act; the circumstances were such, however, that the court could have exercised its discretion to impose sentences of imprisonment of any length under the old Act although under the new Act now in force no discretion exists for such offences so that counsel for the Republic now asked for minimum sentences of three years' imprisonment to be imposed. The learned judge held that he was bound to apply the Act which was in force at the time of the original sentences and in the special circumstances he imposed sentences of one day's imprisonment.[100] The usual considerations apply to the determination of bail applications where a scheduled offence is charged.[101]

The Act retains the original provision requiring a court which convicts a person of a scheduled offence to award compensation to the owner of any property obtained by the offender as a result of the offence, although the corruption offences are now excluded from this provision; such an order can be made at any time after the sentence has been imposed, but only in the presence of the offender, and can be filed in the appropriate district court and then be executed as a civil decree of that court. An accompanying Act makes a number of amendments to the Penal Code and the Criminal Procedure Code.[102] The main effect achieved by this Act is a substantial inflation of the maximum sentences which may be imposed for various offences: the increases include, for example, for theft, from five to seven years imprisonment; for stealing by a public servant, from seven to fourteen years; for fradulent false accounting, from seven to fourteen years; for arson, from fourteen years to life imprisonment; for robbery, from fourteen to twenty years; for housebreaking and burglary, from seven to twenty years. Such sweeping increases, 'across the board', can surely be reflected ultimately only in increasing numbers of prisoners, and therefore in increasing costs of prisons, over future years. The Criminal Procedure Code is amended to prescribe maxima for the aggregate of separate sentences imposed for several offences at one trial. Sentences of imprisonment will continue to take effect consecutively, unless otherwise directed, but a magistrate shall not sentence a person convicted of two or more offences to consecutive sentences of imprisonment exceeding in aggregate eight years (or ten years if one of the offences carries a maximum sentence exceeding five years), or to fines exceeding in aggregate Shs. 15,000 (or double the maximum fine which is possible, if one of the offences carries a maximum fine exceeding Shs. 10,000).

NEW CRIMES

Responding to recent events, Parliament defined three new offences by amendments to the Penal Code during 1972. Widespread temporary shortages of various basic commodities occurred during 1971-72 and the potentially dangerous social consequences prompted the introduction of the most interesting new offence: 'hoarding' by a trader.

'Where a person who carries on the business of selling goods of any description, either wholesale or retail, and having such goods in stock, refuses to sell the whole or any quantity thereof to any person offering to purchase the same, shall be guilty of an offence.' (sic)[103]

This is a notable instance of Parliament characterizing certain commercial conduct as antisocial and imposing a draconian penalty: the maximum sentence prescribed is a fine not exceeding Shs. 100,000, or imprisonment not exceeding fourteen years or both and the court may also forfeit all goods of the same description as the goods in question in the convicted person's stock at the date of the offence. The definition of the offence involves a number of detailed elements such as the definition of when a person is deemed to be carrying on the business of selling goods. Then, he is deemed to have goods in stock if he has any quantity in any premises under his control or management or is the owner of them or has the right to dispose of any quantity by sale. He is deemed to have refused to sell if 'he offered the goods for sale at a price or subject to a term or condition which, in the opinion of the court, having regard to all relevant circumstances, was unreasonable'. Various defences are set out: that the goods did not belong to him and that he had no right to dispose of them and that he advised the complainant or investigating officers at the earliest possible opportunity of the owner's identity; or that the goods had already been sold to another person; or that the goods were for his own use or were being used in connection with his business; or that he is a wholesale trader and that the offer to purchase was not by a retailer or was for a quantity too small to justify a wholesale transaction. A final defence enables a trader to sell his goods equitably at times of shortages: it is a defence if he agreed to sell a limited quantity only and refused to sell more in order to ensure a fair distribution to all customers having regard to the scarcity of the goods in question.

The Penal Code has also been amended to provide for 'hijacking' or other interference with aircraft flights:

'Any person who—
(a) performs an act of violence against a person on board an aircraft in flight if that act is likely to endanger the safety of that aircraft; or
(b) destroys an aircraft in service or causes damage to such an aircraft which renders it incapable of flight or which is likely to endanger its safety in flight; or
(c) places or causes to be placed on an aircraft in service, by any means whatsoever, a device or substance which is likely to destroy that aircraft, or to cause damage to it which would render it incapable of flight, or to cause damage to it which is likely to endanger its safety in flight; or
(d) destroys or damages air navigation facilities or interferes with their operation, if any such act is likely to endanger the safety of aircraft in flight; or
(e) communicates information which he knows to be false, thereby endangering the safety of an aircraft in flight,
shall be guilty of an offence and shall be liable on conviction to imprisonment for a term not exceeding twenty years.'[104]

The consent of the Attorney-General is necessary for a prosecution. A person may be prosecuted for the offence even if it was committed outside Tanganyika but conviction or acquittal elsewhere shall be a defence unless the aircraft was registered in, or owned by a resident of, Tanganyika.

A third new provision redefines the offence of killing animals with intent to steal the skin or carcass or any part thereof, which carries the same penalty as theft but is now deemed to be cattle stealing (and therefore within the scope of the Minimum Sentences Act) if the animals concerned are within the wide definition of 'cattle'.[105]

GENERAL POINTS OF CRIMINAL LAW

General provisions concerning the criminal liability of employers, principals and officers of corporations were included in the new Interpretation of Laws and General Clauses Act[106] which, with few minor changes, replaced the Interpretation and General Clauses Ordinance[107] first enacted in 1928 but subject to much accretion by amendments over the years. These provisions were not, however, new, having appeared in all recent statutes with penal provisions. It is thus now provided generally that for an offence committed by a corporation, any director or officer concerned with the management of the corporation's affairs at the time of the offence may be charged and convicted unless a contrary intention appears; the accused will escape conviction if he satisfies the court that he had no knowledge of the commission of the offence and could not by exercising reasonable diligence have had such knowledge. Similar rules apply to define the liability of the principal or employer where the offence is committed by a person as agent or employee. The Bill for this Act included a clause enabling the Attorney-General to exercise the DPP's functions under any Act; but this was amended before passage of the Bill so that the Act makes a narrower provision, empowering the Attorney-General to nominate a Law Officer to exercise the DPP's functions when he is absent from Dar es Salaam or incapable through illness or otherwise to act.

Where a person has been convicted of an offence against an Act which had in fact been replaced by a new Act at the date of the offence, can the conviction stand? In a criminal revision case Biron, J., noted a number of local precedents in favour of amending the charge and conviction, for example, where the conviction was under a new Act which had not yet come into force. But in all those cases the new law was in similar terms to the old one; here the accused had been convicted of possessing 'moshi', a local brew, against which there had been an absolute prohibition under the old law, while the new law, introducing a new policy, penalized only unlicensed possession. This difference meant that a failure of justice could not be ruled out if the conviction were upheld and it was therefore quashed.[108]

Several cases decided during 1972 concerned the position of police officers in relation to the criminal law. Biron, J., held that where money was taken by a police officer during an unlawful search, he was properly convicted of theft by a public servant, for the money came into his possession by virtue of his employment albeit illegally.[109] Mnzavas, J., quashed convictions imposed for obscene language likely to cause a breach of the peace where the only persons who heard the words used were police officers, who were most unlikely to have caused a breach of the peace.[110] The power of a Gazetted police officer to summon any potential witness to the police station for questioning has been extended to any police officer in charge of a police station.[111]

On the definition of attempted crimes, Mnzavas, J, has held that it was attempted murder where the accused had spread a substance on his victim's drinking straw, admitting the intention to kill although the substance used was not in fact deadly;[112] while Kwikima, Ag J, held that it was not attempting to obtain by false pretences where the accused had filled in a Post Office Savings Bank withdrawal form with a discrepant signature and for an amount greater than was shown in his passbook as his balance.[113]

An interesting case arose on the application of the definition of the offence of conversion not amounting to theft. A transport company driver took a vehicle for an errand involving a seven mile journey and was not seen again for several days, reporting that the vehicle had been wrecked in an accident sixteen miles beyond his authorized destination. The trial magistrate found as a fact that he should have returned the vehicle on the same day and that he had no authority to extend his journey. For the appellant it was argued that he was not guilty of conversion if his possession of the vehicle was lawful at its inception—an unauthorized detour would not be an offence. Onyiuke, J, held that the lawfulness of the original custody was not the only question to be asked: if the driver has completed his authorized journey and then drives off for his own purposes that may, and in the instant case did, amount to a fresh and separate taking justifying conviction.[114]

GENERAL POINTS OF CRIMINAL PROCEDURE

Biron, J., has emphasized the need for proper procedure to be followed by a magistrate who considers that a person is guilty of contempt of court in his view: a charge must be framed and the accused called upon to show cause why he should not be convicted.[115] Mwakasendo, Ag. J., has followed two earlier precedents and held it to be a fatal duplicity of charges to allege failure to pay the statutory minimum monthly wage over a period of thirty-nine months: each failure in a particular month should be the subject of a separate charge and if only one were charged the prosecution could give the statutory 'notice of intention' to the accused that, on conviction, evidence of his like contravention during the year preceding the date of the offence would be given.[116]

The power to order forfeiture in a criminal case usually involves a judicial discretion to be exercised in the light of the particular facts; while it is desirable that a sentencing court should state reasons for a forfeiture order, its failure to do so is not necessarily fatal.[117] When should a court, in sentencing an offender, award compensation to his victim? This question has long been seen to raise an important issue as to the purposes of the system of criminal justice, and to reflect divergences between the integrated processes of traditional African law and the specialized distinction between civil and criminal cases and procedure in the common law. In two cases the Court of Appeal set aside compensation orders made under s. 176 of the Criminal Procedure Code, emphasizing that such orders are discretionary and that, while they may be made on the initiative of the court, it is a requirement of natural justice that the persons affected thereby—esecially the convicted persons—be given an opportunity to show cause why such orders sould not be made.[118] The editor of the *Tanzania Law Reports* argued, to the contrary, that 'trial courts should be encouraged to make compensation orders' to avoid leaving the victim with a 'civil remedy more theoretical than real' (because of his likely lack of knowledge and resources to pursue it). The legislature has recognized the problem to some extent by making the award of compensation mandatory in certain circumstances (e.g., under the Minimum Sentences Act or s. 284A of the Penal Code).

Where a wife was sentenced to eighteen months' imprisonment for causing grievous harm to a co-wife with whom she shared the husband, El Kindy, J, wisely reduced the sentence on revision so as to release her immediately. Although violence was increasing locally, he pointed out that imprisonment would aggravate the situation between wives who have to live together: this was a case where reconciliation and settlement would have served a better purpose.[119]

'Justice deferred is justice denied'—many accused persons, not only in Tanzania, would echo that sentiment in view of the dilatoriness of trial procedures to which they have been subject. But what power does a magistrate have to expedite a tardy prosecution? In a case where, after many adjournments of a part-heard trial, the prosecutor was absent, the magistrate treated the prosecutor as the complainant and held that there was no case to answer. The state appeal was allowed by Mwakasendo, Ag. J., who ordered a trial de novo before another magistrate: the magistrate was held to have been in error in closing the case for the prosecution himself and in finding that there was no case to answer (a finding which, as Parker, L.C.J., has prescribed in an English practice note here cited with approval, is appropriate only if either a vital element of the offence remains unsupported by evidence or the prosecution evidence is manifestly unreliable or has been discredited by cross-examination). The learned judge emphasized the importance of reducing the law's delays; but his suggestion that 'The Criminal Procedure Code is sufficiently comprehensive in its provisions to enable any enterprising magistrate to bring to an end any case the determination of which he considers has been unduly and inexcusably delayed' provoked a learned response from the editor of the *Tanzania Law Reports* suggesting that it is by no means clear that the magistrate has adequate discretion in this situation.[120]

EVIDENCE

The Court of Appeal has emphasized that, where the prosecution seeks to rely on a confession, the burden of proof 'is entirely on the prosecution to prove that it was voluntary' and a conviction of murder was quashed where the trial judge appeared to have put the burden on the accused to prove that his statement was not voluntary.[121] The exclusion of confessions made to police officers does not necessarily extend to exclude confessions made to a ten house cell leader although he may appear to exercise police powers; but a ward executive officer actually has powers of arrest and is therefore to be equated with a police officer, a confession to him being therefore inadmissible.[122]

A novel point arose before El-Kindy, J. A trial in the lower court had been interrupted by a change of magistrate; the new magistrate had correctly heard all the witnesses de novo but he did not use their previous testimony as a basis to cross-examine them as to credibility. The learned judge held that that previous testimony was to be equated with depositions and it was therefore a serious error by the magistrate not to cross-examine in this way once it had become clear that there was inconsistency between the two statements.[123]

Mnzavas, J., after considering the numerous precedents, some of which conflict to some degree, has emphasized the majority view that a conviction of a sexual offence on the uncorroborated evidence of a complainant will almost invariably be set aside on appeal unless it is clear that the trial magistrate directed himself on the need for corroboration and was satisfied of the complainant's veracity. (The view of Biron, J., in a 1969 case, that the trial magistrate's failure to direct himself on the need for corroboration was 'not necessarily fatal' Mnzavas, J., held to have been 'based on the particular circumstances in the case'.)[124]

FINANCE

TAX LAW

A new Act consolidates the law governing the taxation of motor vehicle registrations and transfers but the new, higher, rates of tax reflect the notable developments in the national policy of car ownership.[125] The registration tax on new vehicles is now twenty per cent (up to 1200 cc), twenty-five per cent (up to 2000 cc), thirty per cent (up to 2250 cc) and forty per cent (over 2250 cc). Taxes on transfer of used cars vary according to capacity and period of registration; within the first three years of registration—when permission for any transfer must be obtained from the appropriate committee under the controls introduced in 1971—the tax ranges from Shs. 500 to Shs. 1500; the highest rates are imposed on transfers of vehicles which have been registered between three and six years, reflecting the freedom of disposition and the relative newness of such vehicles, ranging in stages from Shs. 1500 (not exceeding 1200 cc) to Shs. 5000 (exceeding 2250 cc). After six years of registration the tax rates decline although it remains higher than in the first three years until after the vehicle has been registered for nine years.

A new Act replaces the old one which imposed a levy on a person occupying hotel accommodation; now the hotel levy is imposed on hotel charges received by the owner who must collect it at a rate of twelve per cent of the 'room and breakfast charge.[126] The Commissioner for Hotel Levy can, however, by notice require a hotel owner to pay the levy at ten per cent of the total charge received where a single payment includes meals other than breakfast; the Commissioner's order is final subject to an appeal to the Minister.

The Finance Act[127] included a number of changes in tax rates, amending several Acts including the Customs Tariff Act, 1969, varying rates of customs and excise duties, the Sales Tax Act, 1969, raising the rates of sales tax payable and the Entertainment Tax Act, 1970 which is amended to enable the Minister to exempt an entertainment, in place of the general exemption for educational entertainments as decided by the Commissioner. The tax on electricity consumption introduced in 1968 was abolished. A new Stamp Duty Act[128] consolidated the law with some minor amendments, mainly procedural. Now, however, for any payment, property, bill of exchange etc. worth Shs. 50 or more a duly stamped receipt must be given and new rates of duty for receipts were introduced, the basic rate being Shs. 0/50 cents for each Shs. 500 up to a maximum of Shs. 40 duty.

The Income Tax (Allowances and Rates) Act, 1972[129] replaced with minor changes only the 1971 Act, with effect from the tax year 1971; the rates of allowances etc. are unchanged but there is now provision for the application of double taxation agreements and a new Third Schedule imposes a non-resident withholding tax at basic rates of 12½ per cent on dividends and interest, twenty per cent on royalties, management or professional fees.

EXCHANGE CONTROL

In place of the abortive Bill of 1971, which would have replaced the Exchange Control Ordinance,[130] extensive amendments to that Ordinance were enacted in 1972,[131] designed in part to achieve some of the objectives of that Bill. The amendments enable the Bank of Tanzania to demand relevant information from any person including details of assets owned and bank accounts outside Tanzania. Enforcement provisions are strengthened and a special exception is made to the Evidence Act, which normally excludes as evidence confessions made to police officers, to allow the proof in evidence of confessions made to police officers of senior rank in proceedings under the Ordinance. The penalty for contravention of the Ordinance is increased to a maximum fine of Shs. 100,000 (or, if foreign currency is involved, ten times the value if that is greater) or imprisonment up to fourteen years or both. Evasion of controls by false invoicing is attacked by the definition as a serious offence (carrying the above penalties) of the export of goods for a consideration less than the fair and reasonable value unless the accused satisfies the court that the Bank knew all the circumstances and consented or that the difference between the value received and the fair and reasonable value 'is within the range which a prudent man of business would consider to be a reasonable commercial risk'. There is a complex definition of 'fair and reasonable value' including, for exported goods, the export price in Tanzania or at least ninety-five per cent of the maximum price which such goods would have realized if exported to the USA or the UK, whichever is greater; the prices indicated can be certified by the Principal Secretary to the Ministry of Commerce and Industries.

A new 'constructive' offence is introduced by the amendments: the accused is charged with being reasonably suspected of being unlawfully in possession of foreign currency and is guilty if he fails to satisfy the court that he lawfully owns, possesses or controls the foreign currency or that he does not own, possess or control it or that the document or article found in his possession or control and reasonably suspected of being evidence of unlawful possession or ownership of foreign currency does not relate to any foreign currency; the maximum penalty is a fine of Shs. 50,000 or imprisonment for five years or both. Prosecutions under the Ordinance require the consent of the Director of Public Prosecutions; the Governor of the Bank of Tanzania has power to compound offences concerning foreign currency not exceeding Shs. 2000 in value.

BANKRUPTCY LAW

Two interesting bankruptcy cases concerned the rescission of receiving orders. In a case which came before the Court of Appeal in a very confused state it was held that 'the burden on a debtor seeking rescission of a receiving order when it was made by consent must be exceptionally heavy'; absence of misconduct by the debtor is a condition for rescission but not a ground therefor; the fact that there is only one creditor is relevant only if that one concurs in the application for rescission.[132] In another case a receiving order had been made on the debtor's own petition; three months later a creditor applied for rescission of the order, alleging certain formal defects in the original petition (viz, that the petition was neither signed nor attested and had been presented more than three days after the submission of the 'statement of affairs'). Biron, J., held that the defects were curable and that under the Bankruptcy Ordinance it was mandatory that proceedings should not be invalidated by a formal defect unless it causes substantial injustice: although here the creditor would suffer by the absence of a surety, that was not an injustice occasioned by the defect. Biron, J., had held that, as the Bankruptcy Ordinance had been amended in 1958 to allow a court to rescind an order 'at any time', it prescribed a period for the rescission—albeit unlimited in time—and the periods prescribed by the Limitation Act were therefore excluded.[133]

FAMILY LAW

An important point under the new Law of Marriage Act, 1971[134] arose when a wife, petititioning for divorce, did not first follow the procedure for attempting reconciliation involving designated Marriage Conciliatory Boards, which is normally a mandatory preliminary stage in the new process for matrimonial remedies. It was argued that the husband had beaten the wife and threatened to kill her if she tried to end the marriage and s. 101(f) was invoked which provides exemption from the reconciliation procedure 'where the court is satisfied that there are extraordinary circumstances'. Onyiuke, J., held that, while it is not necessary to obtain the leave of the court before filing a petition in reliance on this sub-section, the court's discretion is to be exercised sparingly, when it is clear beyond reasonable doubt that reference to a Board is not a practical proposition. In the instant case he declined to apply s. 101(f), holding that the matters alleged by the wife were precisely the sort of issues that a Board would investigate, especially as the husband was apparently anxious to preserve the marriage.[135]

Application of the new Act also affected a father's claim for compensation from the seducer of his daughter—the damages claimed being the amount of payments received by the father from the man to whom she was betrothed and repaid after the girl had become pregnant by the defendant. The primary court awarded the father the full compensation sought but the district court reduced the amount by Shs. 148 which was a sum for the girl herself, applying the Declaration of Local Customary Law, s. 13, which distinguishes mere gifts which are not returnable by custom from the 'bridewealth' proper. However, Mwakasendo, Ag. J., noting that the Law of Marriage Act expressly supersedes any custom or Islamic law where it applies, held that the district court should take further evidence as to whether the Shs. 148 was a gift conditional on the marriage being contracted in which case it would be returnable under the Act (s. 71) whatever the old custom may have been.[136]

Rights to the custody of an adulterine child were briefly considered by Kwikima, Ag. J., in *Mgowa Madole* v. *Mgogolo Dododo:* his terse judgement summarily rejected the woman's application that her child, born before she divorced her former husband, should be granted to her present husband, the father of the child. The learned judge rejected the application in strong terms:

> 'Her request is immoral and no court of law would countenance it. It is settled custom amongst the patrilineal tribes of Tanzania, the Wagogo being among them, that all children conceived during wedlock belong to the husband. Anyone who sires a child adulterously cannot be heard to claim it. Even if such were not the accepted custom, the ethics of our present time would not tolerate an adulterer benefitting from his sin to the detriment of his cuckold. It would be adding insult to injury. This appeal has no merit whatever . . .'[137]

In a tax appeal concerning permissible allowances for children under the income tax legislation, the Court of Appeal held that evidence of Hindu custom (in the form of an unchallenged certificate of the Hon General Secretary of the Shree Hindu Mandal of Dar es Salaam) whereby elderly or sick parents may delegate responsibility for their children to their eldest son, with evidence of acts associated with such responsibility and of actual payments to the children, was sufficient to support a finding of custody.[138]

Interesting questions of Islamic law arose in *Zainabu* v. *Mohamedi*[139] where Kwikima, Ag J, took 'judicial notice of the well-known fact that most if not all indigenous Muslims . . . are Sunni Muslims of the Shafii sect' and regretted the 'confusion' which has reigned in the Tanzania High Court when, because of the dearth of case law or text-books on Sunni Shafii law, authorities have been accepted from India where Muslims 'are mainly Shias who do not recognize the "Sunna" (the sayings of the Prophet)'. In the instant case a primary court, on the application of a wife, had ordered her husband to pronounce a divorce by talak: she alleged physical cruelty which had driven her away but Kwikima, Ag. J., held that Sunni Shafii law does not recognize the concept of constructive desertion and that the wife was seeking a remedy unknown to Islamic law. While a court could grant divorce, there was here insufficient evidence to prove cruelty, for it was not established that the beating of the wife by the husband exceeded the limits of 'chastisement' permitted by Islamic Law. Indeed, the judgement indicates that the wife, by leaving the husband and refusing to return, was herself guilty of disobedience and therefore 'nashiza' and disentitled to maintenance.

TORT

Biron, J., has accepted the celebrated rule regarding negligent misstatement, in *Hedley Byrne & Co Ltd* v. *Heller,*[141] as good law in

Tanzania. Where an officer of the National Insurance Corporation had told the plaintiff that a car driver was insured by the Corporation, it was held that the latter was liable in damages to the plaintiff for the full amount of his judgement debt against the driver which was now unenforceable, for lapse of time, against the actual insurer.[142]

A respondent has been held liable for the destruction of his neighbour's garden by fire which was blown by strong winds from his own grass-burning on land owned by the appellant who had consented to the respondent's occupation. Bramble, J., allowing the appeal against the Resident Magistrate's decision, held that the respondent was negligent in failing to guard against a foreseeable eventuality. The defence of 'Act of God' was rejected in the circumstances.[143]

Liability for the seduction of an unmarried daughter was considered by Kwikima, J.: he held that no action lies in enticement or loss of virginity although damages might be recoverable if the enticer took the girl away to live in concubinage, for then he would have deprived the father of his bride-price as well as of his daughter.[144]

BIBLIOGRAPHY

A notable publication of the year was a special issue of the Eastern Africa Law Review, edited from the Faculty of Law, University of Dar es Salaam, and devoted to 'Public Enterprise and Law in Tanzania'. (Vol. 5, Nos. 1 and 2). The contents present a wide-ranging, critical analysis by lawyers and other specialists. Topics discussed include the political economy of parastatals, the organizational relationships and control of parastatals, management agreements including the control of managing agents, patents and the transfer of technology and some comparative aspects of Kenya and Tanzania. There is a useful bibliography of legal sources and other material.

NOTES

1. For further details see C. Legum, ed, *Africa Contemporary Record 1969-1970*, p. B 189, pp. B191-3; *ACR* 1970-71 p. B 169; *ACR* 1972-73 p. B 254
2. *Keesing's Contemporary Archives*, Vol. 18, 1971-72, 25124
3. J. K. Nyerere, *Freedom and Development* (Dar es Salaam, 1973), p. 382
4. G. Notice No. 41
5. B. H. Selassie, *The Executive in African Governments* (London, 1974), discusses various forms of executive structure including (Ch. 2) types of 'dual executive'.
6. Interim Constitution (Amendment) Act 1972, No. 29, assented to on 23 November 1972 and deemed to have come into operation on 17 February 1972
7. Planning Commission Act 1972, No. 28
8. There are a number of relevant studies, e.g. William Tordoff, *Government and Politics in Tanzania* (Nairobi 1967), ch. IV, pp. 95-135; Henry Bienen, *Tanzania: Party Transformation and Economic Development* (Princeton, 1967, Expanded edition 1970), esp. ch. IX, pp. 307-333; K. W. von Sperber, *Public Administration in Tanzania* (Munich 1970), pp. 69-101; S. Dryden, *Local Administration in Tanzania* (Nairobi 1968); Diana Conyers, 'Organization for Development: The Tanzanian Experience' *J. Ad. Overseas*, XIII, July 1974, pp. 438-448
9. Report of the Presidential Commission on the Establishment of a Democratic One-Party State (Dar es Salaam 1965), para. 73
10. Proposals of the Tanzania Government for the Establishment of a Democratic One-Party State (Dar es Salaam 1965), Government Paper No. 1 of 1965
11. See Tordoff, *op. cit.*, pp. 124-6
12. Extracts from the paper appear in: *ACR* 1972-73, pp. C 161-5; J. K. Nyerere,

Freedom and Development (Dar es Salaam 1973), pp. 344-50; M. Minogue and J. Molloy, *African Aims and Attitudes* (London 1974), pp. 97-101

13. Rashidi Kawawa, Second Vice-President, quoted by Bienen, *op. cit.* p. 349; the previous quotation from Bienen, p. 350
14. See *Annual Survey of African Law*, Vol. III, 1969, pp. 135-6
15. Paul Collins, 'Decentralisation and Local Administration for Development in Tanzania', *Africa Today*, Vol. 21, No. 3, 1974, pp. 15-25 and 'The Working of Tanzania's Rural Development Fund: A Problem in Decentralization', *E.A.J. Rural Dev*, Vol. 5, Nos. 1 & 2, 1972
16. No. 27
17. No. 9 of 1973; the quotation is from the 'Objects and reasons' published with the Bill; and No. 41 of 1974
18. Decentralization (Dissolution of District Councils) Order 1974, GN No. 252
19. *Ibid*, s. 3
20. They are not strictly members, as President Nyerere forecast in his paper
21. No. 36 of 1972 and Nos. 5 and 7 of 1973
22. No. 27 of 1972, s. 15
23. No. 6 of 1969
24. S. 7(7)
25. Decentralization (Amendment of Written Laws) Order 1974, GN No. 30
26. Establishment of Districts Proclamation, GN No. 41 of 1974; Establishment of Regions (Amendment) Proclamations, GN Nos. 42 and 43 of 1974
27. GN No. 252 of 1974, s. 3(c)
28. Appropriation Act 1974, No. 34
29. Conyers, *op. cit.*, footnote 8, p. 439
30. District Corporations Act 1973, No. 16
31. *Keesing's Contemporary Archives*, Vol. 18, 1971-72, 25124
32. *The Guardian* (London), 24 January 1972
33. *Keesing's Contemporary Archives*, Vol. 18, 1971-72, 25222, 25468
34. The Interim Constitution was amended accordingly to increase the number of ex officio seats in Parliament: Act No. 10 of 1972
35. *Keesing's Contemporary Archives*, Vol. 18, 1971-2, 25468
36. *Ibid, The Guardian* (London), 16 May 1974; 3 January 1975
37. Public Officers (Eligibility for Election as Constituency Members) Act 1972, No. 11
38. Pensions Ordinance (Amendment) Act 1972, No. 4
39. No. 27 of 1972, s. 9
40. *Hatimali Adamji* v. *East African Posts and Telecommunications Corporation* 1973 LRT n. 6; 1972 LRT n. 35, CA
41. *Railways Corporation (sic)* v. *Sefu* [1973] EA 327
42. *Thabit Ngaka* v. *Regional Fisheries Officer* 1973 LRT n. 24
43. *Kilala* v. *Mwanza D.C.* 1973 LRT n. 19
44. GN No. 163 of 1972
45. GN No. 229 of 1972
46. Established by the Tobacco Industry Act 1972, No. 7
47. By the Tanzania Housing Bank Act 1972, No. 34
48. GN No. 265 of 1972
49. GN No. 253 of 1972
50. On a private member's motion: *The Parliamentarian*, Vol. 53, 1972, pp. 242-3
51. GN No. 47 of 1972
52. For a full account see *ACR* 1972-3, pp. B 250-52, where doubts are fairly voiced as to 'whether decentralization will exacerbate or relieve the manpower problems'
53. *W.* v. *Income Tax* [1973] EA 187
54. GN No. 162 of 1972
55. Interim Constitution (Number of Judges) Act 1972, No. 32
56. Published by the Faculty of Law, University of Dar es Salaam, as was the *High Court Digest*
57. Written Laws (Miscellaneous Amendments) (No. 2) Act 1972, No. 31, adding a new s. 39A to the Magistrates' Courts Act 1963, Cap. 537
58. Extension of jurisdiction of certain Resident Magistrates Order 1973, GN No. 98
59. Primary Courts (Assessors) Regulations 1972, GN No. 223. For the role of assessors in primary courts see *Annual Survey of African Law*, Vol. III, 1969, pp. 137-8
60. *Rioba Nyachancha* v. *Republic* 1973 LRT n. 31
61. *Dominico Simon* v. *Republic* 1972 HCD n. 152
62. No. 8 of 1972, replacing the Act of 1963, Cap. 534
63. Immigration (Exemption) Order 1973, GN No. 208
64. Immigration (Exemption of Refugees) Direction 1973, GN No. 95
65. The African refugees mentioned above were exempted by GN No. 95
66. Imposed by the Training Levy (Imposition) Act 1972, No. 26. For the Training Levy

Regulations see GN No. 188 of 1972
67. Written Laws (Miscellaneous Amendments) (No. 2) Act 1972, No. 31
68. Companies (Regulation of Dividends and Surpluses and Miscellaneous Provisions) Act 1972, No. 22
69. GN No. 167 of 1972
70. Companies (Regulation of Dividends and Surpluses) Regulations 1972, GN No. 159
71. GN Nos. 160 and 258 of 1972
72. By GN No. 160 of 1972
73. The Authorized Investments Order 1972, GN No. 255 (replacing GN No. 246) specifies 'authorized investments' generally including net investment in current assets, productive fixed assets and ancillary fixed assets, subject to express limits
74. GN No. 161 of 1972; see also GN No. 67 of 1973
75. Locally Manufactured Products (Price Stability) Act 1972, No. 24
76. Business Licensing Act 1972, No. 25. For subsidiary legislation see GN Nos. 187, 189, 190, 195, 196 of 1972
77. Trades Licensing Ordinance, Cap. 208, originally No. 1 of 1927.
78. Business Licensing Regulations, GN No. 187 of 1972, s. 12.
79. J. K. Nyerere, *Freedom and Development* (Dar es Salaam 1973), pp. 317-20.
80. Institute of Finance Management Act 1972, No. 3, brought into operation on 10 March 1972 by GN No. 52. A Kiswahili translation of the Bill appears in GN No. 13 of 1972.
81. Institute of Development Management Act 1972, No. 15
82. GN No. 116 of 1972, made under s. 12 of the Education Act 1969, No. 50
83. Regulation of Wages and Terms of Employment Order 1972. This Order was first made as GN No. 139 of 1972; printing errors were corrected by GN No. 149 but the Order was replaced, with amendments and modifications, to improve its clarity, by GN No. 152 of 1972. A Kiswahili translation appeared as GN No. 208 of 1972
84. GN No. 136 of 1972
85. Cap. 574
86. The definition being derived from the Employment Ordinance (Exemption) Order 1961, GN No. 26.
87. *Jager* v. *Tanganyika Tourist Hotels and Oyster Bay Hotel Cordura Ltd* 1972 HCD n. 133
88. *Sankey* v. *Caltex Oil Tanzania Ltd* 1973 LRT n. 46
89. Auditors and Accountants (Registration) Act 1972, No. 33
90. Architects, Quantity Surveyors and Building Contractors (Registration) Act 1972, No. 35
91. Cap. 526. See James S. Read, 'Minimum Sentences in Tanzania' [1965] JAL 20-39
92. *Annual Survey of African Law, Vol. III,* 1969, p. 144
93. No. 1. A Kiswahili translation of the Bill appears in GN No. 16 of 1972
94. By a somewhat infelicitous piece of drafting: see *Namukonei s/o Lemenduli* v. *Republic* 1973 LRT n. 2
95. Cap. 422
96. *Bwogi* v. *Republic* [1973] EA 32
97. No. 16; see *Annual Survey of African Law,* Vol. V, 1971, pp. XX-XXX
98. [1970] EA 620
99. *Republic* v. *Selemani Mohamed* 1973 LRT n. 8; *Republic* v. *Marki* 1973 LRT n. 13
100. *Republic* v. *Omari and Anor* [1973] EA 29
101. *Jaffer* v. *Republic* [1973] EA 39
102. Minimum Sentences (Consequential and Incidental Provisions) Act 1972, No. 2
103. S. 194A of the Penal Code, Cap. 16, inserted by the Written Laws (Miscellaneous Amendments) (No. 2) Act 1972, No. 31
104. S. 318A of the Penal Code, inserted by the same Act
105. Ss. 268 and 279 of the Penal Code, as replaced by the same Act
106. No. 30 of 1972
107. Cap. 1
108. *R.* v. *Alli Litengine* 1973 LRT n. 52
109. *Rashidi* v. *Republic* [1972] EA 438
110. *Republic* v. *Kimanga* [1973] EA 42, following *Republic* v. *John* 1967 HCD 61
111. No. 31 of 1972, amending the Police Force Ordinance
112. *Republic* v. *Raphael s/o Songareti & Anor* 1973 LRT n. 22
113. *Republic* v. *Daniel s/o Chaula* 1973 LRT n. 3
114. *Lawrence s/o Maliki* v. *Republic* 1973 LRT n. 12
115. *Jairos* v. *Republic* [1972] EA 434; see also *Republic* v. *Ramadhani Abdallah* 1973 LRT n. 49
116. *Piru* v. *Republic* [1973] EA 44
117. *Republic* v. *Abdalla and Others* [1972] EA 68
118. *Haining and Others* v. *Republic* [1972] EA 133, CA; 1972 HCD n. 53. *Selemani* v. *Republic* [1972] EA 269, CA; 1973 LRT n. 5

119. *Julia* v. *Republic* [1972] EA 437
120. *Republic* v. *Selemani Mussa* 1973 LRT n. 47
121. *Ezekia* v. *Republic* [1972] EA 427
122. *Lundamoto and Mkonda* v. *Republic* 1972 HCD n. 44
123. *Bernado* v. *Republic* 1973 LRT n. 38
124. *Shabani s/o Hamis* v. *Republic* 1973 LRT n. 1
125. Motor Vehicles (Tax on Registration and Transfer) Act 1972, No. 21. The assent was given on 18 August but the Act was given retrospective effect from 16 June 1972.
126. Hotel Levy Act 1972, No. 23, replacing the Hotel Accommodation (Imposition of Levy) Act 1962, Cap. 475
127. No. 18 of 1972
128. No. 20 of 1972
129. No. 9; assent given on 11 May 1972, Act given retrospective effect from 18 June 1971
130. Cap. 294. For the Bill see *Annual Survey of African Law*, Vol. V, 1971,   ·000
131. Financial Laws (Miscellaneous Amendments) Act 1972, No. 12
132. *National and Grindlays Bank Ltd* v. *Shariff and Anor* [1972] EA 413, CA
133. *Re Licalsi. Ex parte City Painters* [1973] EA 48
134. No. 5. *Annual Survey of African Law*, Vol. V, 1971; James S. Read, [1972] JAL 19-39
135. *Zinat Khan* v. *Abdulla Khan* 1973 LRT n. 57
136. *Ngonyani* v. *Mbuguni* 1972 HCD n. 5
137. *Mgowa Madole* v. *Mgogolo Dododo* 1973 LRT n. 7
138. *Commissioner-General of Income Tax* v. *Rasiklal Joshi* 1973 LRT n. 26, [1973] EA 147, CA, upholding the decision of Biron, J: [1972] EA 150
139. [1973] EA 280
140. GN No. 222 of 1967; *Annual Survey of African Law*, Vol. I, 1967, pp. 185-7
141. [1963] 2 All ER 575
142. *Francis Ngaite* v. *National Insurance Corporation of Tanzania Ltd* 1972 HCD n. 13. The *Hedley Byrne* precedent has also been adopted in Kenya: *Winther* v. *Arbon Langrish & Southern Ltd* [1966] EA 292, per Harris, J
143. *Salim Omari* v. *Jackton Ongea* 1972 HCD n. 145
144. *Mapugilo* v. *Gunza* 1972 HCD n. 143

Abbreviations

ACR Africa Contemporary Record
EA   East Africa Law Reports
GN   Government Notice
HCD High Court Digest
JAL   Journal of African Law
LRT   Tanzania Law Reports

CHAPTER EIGHT

MALAWI

Mark Peters

1972 occasioned remarkably few changes in Malawi's law; and most of those that merit report are merely examples of government's effort to elaborate and amend, in minor ways, the large body of regulatory law that already exists. By promulgating the necessary subordinate legislation, government also began to implement the more ambitious legislative programme that was undertaken last year; but 1972's legislative quiescence is, for this review's purposes, the year's single most striking characteristic.

THE CONSTITUTION

The Constitution provides that whenever there is a vacancy in the office of the President, or whenever the President is, in certain circumstances, incapacitated, the functions of the office are to be performed by a Presidential Council, whose membership is to consist of the Secretary-General of the Party and two qualified Cabinet Ministers.[1] Amending legislation now provides that the Secretary-General of the Party shall be chairman of the Council and the two Cabinet Ministers members.[2]

The definition of 'Secretary-General' in s. 98 of the Constitution has also been changed.[3] The words formerly meant the Secretary-General of the Party, but now mean 'the person who is for the time being lawfully discharging the functions of the Secretary-General of the Party'. This amendment, though it may forestall uncertainty, was not in fact legally necessary: s. 29 of the General Interpretation Act[4] provides, in terms identical to those used in the amendment, that a reference to an office-holder, in any law including the Constitution, shall be read as referring to the person discharging the functions of that office.

The same amending legislation has also altered the constitutional qualifications for election to the Presidency.[5] The minimum age is now forty rather than forty-five years.[6]

All these amendments are addressed to the problem of succession, a problem that the Constitution, which makes no provision for a vice-president, awkwardly manages in a way that leaves room for much political slippage. The first two amendments, which marginally concern themselves with that aspect of the problem, in fact do little to anticipate the real difficulties that inhere in the succession provisions of the Constitution. It is to be doubted whether constitutional appointment of a chairman of the Presidential Council goes very far toward filling the vacuum created by lack of a vice-president, or whether the transfer of authority from defunct President to inchoate Council will, as a result, take place with greater simplicity or greater smoothness. Even as amended, the Constitution ensures that for a time there will be no-one in charge, no-one with even ostensible supreme executive authority; and in a country whose government is still striving for the substance of legitimacy, that time must be one of many perils.

The Army (Amendment) Act[7] has altered the structure of the civilian command of the Army. Responsibility for the command, discipline and administration of the Army is vested in the Army Council, whose membership formerly consisted of the Secretary to the President and Cabinet as chairman, the Commander and Deputy Commander of the Army, and the Secretary to the Treasury as members.[8] The amending act provides that the Minister, who is the President, shall now be chairman of the Council; the Secretary to the President and Cabinet and the Commander and Deputy Commander of the Army remain as members, while the Secretary to the Treasury has been removed.[9] The power to co-opt additional members, formerly given the Council collectively,[10] is now exclusively the Minister's.[11] Similar power is given the Minister to fill temporary vacancies in the Council's membership.[12]

The purpose and effect of the act are to give the President full control of the country's only military force.[13]

THE COURTS

Minor changes have been made in the jurisdiction of various courts.

The Loans Recovery Act[14] empowers a court that is hearing a case involving a claim for interest or similar charges to fix a reasonable sum in place of the amount claimed if that amount is considered excessive.[15] Until now this discretionary power has been exercisable only by the High Court and the Magistrates Courts. By changing the act's definition of 'court', the amending legislation extends the power to Urban and Grade A1 Traditional Courts.[16]

The Affiliation Act[17] has been amended in similar fashion. To make it clear that Magistrates Courts have jurisdiction to hear all cases arising under the act, the definition of 'court' has been made to comprehend all subordinate courts,[18] and now also includes Traditional Courts to the extent that any claim arising under the act may fall within their jurisdiction. At the same time, the scope of the Traditional Courts' jurisdiction has been delimited more precisely: a Traditional Court may make no order under the act 'whereby the aggregate of all monthly payments payable thereunder, or the lump sum awarded thereby . . . exceeds the limit of civil jurisdiction of such Court as specified in its warrant.'[19]

The criminal jurisdiction of the Traditional Courts has been amended in two minor respects.[20] All Traditional Courts have heretofore had jurisdiction to try any case arising under the Game Act.[21] The amending order now excludes from their criminal jurisdiction certain cases arising in respect of hunting within a game reserve.[22]

By the same order the Traditional Courts have been given jurisdiction to try cases arising under the provisions of the National Parks Act.[23] The order excludes their jurisdiction only in respect of cases arising under certan sections of the act that correspond to the exempted sections of the Game Act.[24]

An amendment to the Special Crops Act[25] has ousted the appellate jurisdiction of the courts. The act enables the Minister to revoke, suspend or refuse the issue of any licence required by the act; amending legislation now provides that the Minister's decision in such matters 'shall be final and shall not be questioned in any court.'[26] When introducing its bill in the National Assembly, government made the following statement regarding this perfunctory ouster:

> . . . in the past the Minister could not refuse a licence to any person or revoke or suspend any licence that was in existence without giving reasons for his refusal.
> This method, Mr Speaker, has been found unsatisfactory, and, therefore, this Bill is here to widen the powers of the Minister . . . This Bill, Mr Speaker, then is going to stop the courts to probe (sic) into the reasons why the Minister has refused or revoked or suspended any existing licence.[27]

The amendment is another example of government's unwillingness to be bound by traditional principles of administrative law.[28]

LOCAL GOVERNMENT

The list of occupations that district councils (and, where applicable, district commissioners) may control, regulate, supervise and license pursuant to the Local Government (District Councils) Act[29] has been newly augmented by government order.[30] The amendment may reflect the growing importance in rural areas of such occupations as photographer, curio maker and watch and radio repairer.

In similar fashion, government has enlarged the regulatory powers granted to city, municipal and town councils by the Local Government (Urban Areas) Act.[31] They are given the power 'to control and license creches and nursery schools,' and many now 'control, regulate, supervise and license' a long list of occupations that were previously outside the scope of their control.[32]

CIVIL PROCEDURE

In In re Dominion Earthworks (Swaziland) Ltd,[33] the High Court was asked on an ex parte application to issue an 'interim declaratory order' in respect of a dispute between the applicant and the Government of Malawi. The Court held that it was unable to make such an order. Although the Civil Procedure Act[34] grants the Court jurisdiction to issue declaratory orders against the Government in lieu of injunctions, the Court has no power, it held, to issue an interim declaratory judgement in lieu of an interim injunction. The Court accepted the reasoning of the decision in International General Electric Co. of New York v.

Commissioners of Customs and Excise[35] where the court said,

> When one comes to the question of a final injunction, no doubt a declaratory order may be made in lieu thereof, for that finally determines the rights of the parties; but it seems to me quite impossible to invent some form of declaration which does not determine the rights of the parties, but is only meant to preserve the status quo.

In *Nganisho* v. *Mtewa*[36] the High Court heard an application for leave to apply for the grant of an order of certiorari to remove into the High Court and quash a judgement and order made by a subordinate court. In his affidavit the applicant averred that the procedure prescribed by the subordinate court rules had not been followed in setting the action down for trial. The Court held that it had jurisdiction to grant leave to apply. In doing so it said:

> For a long time it was thought that certiorari did not lie to quash the judgements of inferior courts of civil jurisdiction, but in *R.* v. *Judge Worthington-Evans, Ex parte Madan*[37] a contrary view was taken.

Certiorari is now available in England whenever a lower court has acted outside its civil jurisdiction; and because the Statute Law (Miscellaneous Provisions) Act[38] gives the High Court power to make an order of certiorari in any case in which the High Court in England is so empowered, the decision in *Worthington-Evans'* case has enlarged the jurisdicition of the High Court of Malawi. The existence of a pending appeal, however, is a bar to the grant of leave to apply, the High Court held, for an applicant should not be allowed to pursue both an appeal and certiorari at the same time. In the event, because an appeal had been lodged, the application was adjourned until final determination of the appeal.[39]

PUBLIC FINANCE

The Customs and Excise Act[40] was amended in several minor respects for the purpose of clarifying certain provisions in the act and of facilitating its administration.[41] In two instances the power of customs officers to search and seize goods is slightly enlarged. Ss. 16(1)(*a*) and 146(1) of the principal act permitted officers to carry out certain searches and seizures on the strength of a reasonable belief that such was necessary. As amended, the sections permit these searches and seizures to take place on the ground of reasonable suspicion.[42] The word 'smuggling' has also been redefined to give it a broader, less particularistic meaning.[43] The other amendments of the act are merely technical in their nature.

The Income Tax (Amendment) Act[44] has consolidated the provisions of the Income Tax Act[45] and the Taxation Act[46] in a new Taxation (Consolidation) Act.[47] Technical changes have been made in ss. 86 and 120 of the Income Tax Act,[48] and s. 150, discussed below, has been given new content; but apart from these minor alterations, the provisions of the Income Tax Act remain the same. To them have now been added what formerly constituted Parts II and III of the Taxation Act, relating, respectively, to the imposition of a minimum and graduated tax.[49] In the course of their transposition some of the provisions of the Taxation Act have been redrafted in order to render their language slightly more elegant, but none of these alterations is of substantive effect. Part IV of the Taxation Act,[50] which related to the imposition of an assessed tax, has been repealed; it provided for collection of a rural income tax and had in fact already been rendered redundant by the Income Tax Act.

S. 150 of the Income Tax Act and ss. 7 and 25(2) of the Taxation Act enabled the Commissioner of Taxes to make regulations pursuant to each of the acts. S. 150 subjected the Commissioner's power to ministerial approval and the Taxation Act contained a general provision subjecting the Commissioner to the general directions of the Minister.[51] A new s. 167,[52] which now gives the Minister himself all power to make regulations has not, therefore, accomplished any substantial transfer of authority. A transitional amendment provides that subsidiary legislation made under the Taxation Act shall remain in operation until replaced or revoked pursuant to the consolidated act.[53]

Several changes, none of them substantial, have been made in the Finance and Audit Act.[54]

Its s. 22(3) and (4) empowers the Minister, 'where it is expedient in the public interest', to vary the total estimated cost of any project contained in the development estimates and to add any new item not otherwise provided for. But in the exercise of these powers, the Minister is prohibited from increasing the total estimated cost of development projects by an amount exceeding £200,000.[55] It is now provided that this increase shall not exceed K1,000,000 (£500,000).[56]

In similar fashion, the Minister's power to draw against foreign loans[57] without prior authorization of the National Assembly has been enlarged. Whereas he was previously authorized to draw no more than K400,000, the limit is now K1,000,000.[58]

S. 27 of the Finance and Audit Act authorizes the creation of sinking funds for the redemption of Treasury stocks and bonds. The section requires the Treasury to pay into such funds the amounts specified at the time any stocks or bonds are issued. An amendment to the section now permits the Treasury to pay into the sinking funds such additional sums as they may consider advisable.[59] The Treasury can, in short, make payments from the Consolidated Fund without the prior approval of Parliament save insofar as this act itself constitutes such approval.

SOCIAL WELFARE

The Handicapped Persons Act[60] came into operation on 1 October 1972.[61]

PROFESSIONAL QUALIFICATIONS

Parliament this year enacted the Engineers Act,[62] which repealed the Registered Engineers Act[63] and established a new Board of Engineers with general power to supervise the profession. The Board, a body corporate, with a membership whose majority is drawn from the public, private and academic sectors of the profession,[64] has been given broad powers as the sole qualifying and registering authority for engineers in Malawi. Among these powers are the following: to register engineers pursuant to the act, to establish educational standards and qualifications for the profession, and to exercise disciplinary control over it.[65] The Board is required to keep a register of engineers qualified to practise in Malawi, to approve educational institutions whose professional course in engineering is acceptable for purposes of the act, to prescribe examination syllabuses, to set and hold qualifying examinations, to prescribe canons of professional ethics and the disciplinary measures applicable for their infringement and to prescribe various technical rules regarding grades of competence.[66] The Board is also empowered to define the scope of the profession by prescribing the kinds of work that may be performed only by registered engineers.[67]

The act creates machinery for the maintenance of discipline within the profession. It establishes a Disciplinary Committee[68] and grants it power, subject to specified procedures, to make enquiries and to recommend to the Board the reprimand of any registered engineer or the cancellation or suspension of his registration.[69] Having considered the report and recommendations of the Committee, the Board must decide what disciplinary action is appropriate, and may, when reprimanding an engineer, order that he pay compensation for any damage caused the complainant by his default.[70]

An engineer whose registration has been suspended or cancelled can appeal from the decision of the Board to the High Court;[71] but no right of appeal is granted from the Board's decision to reprimand, even when the reprimand is accompanied by an order to pay compensation. This is an unfortunate omission, for the statute grants to a body of engineers the power to adjudicate matters within the realm of the law of tort and does so without setting forth the standards appropriate to assessing compensation. The statutory omission ought not, then, to be interpreted as ousting the court's supervisory jurisdiction.

The act provides that no person, other than members of the Board, is entitled to be informed of the contents of the disciplinary committee's report and recommendation.[72] But the High Court hearing an appeal may require evidence to be adduced by the appellant engineer and by the Board itself.[73] This latter provision must be taken to prevail over the former.

Part VII of the act contains criminal provisions that relate to the unlawful practice of engineering.[74]

The Professional Qualifications Act[75] has been amended so as to render it inapplicable to 'any profession where there is in force in respect of such profession any written law, expressly enacted for the purpose, which makes provision for qualification for membership of, and the right to practise, such profession in Malawi.'[76] In consequence, the act no longer applies, *inter alia,* to engineers and legal practitioners.

EDUCATION

The Industrial Training Act[77] reallocates the costs of operating apprenticeship schemes that have been undertaken pursuant to the Apprenticeship Act.[78] An Industrial Training Fund has been established[79] to which certain levies are payable by all employers of skilled workers and from which the costs incident to apprenticeship and industrial training schemes are to be met. Prior to passage of the act, costs incurred in the training of individual apprentices were assumed in part by government, in part by the participating employers. The act now provides that all employers of skilled labourers in trades to which the Apprenticeship Act applies shall be subject to pay a levy to the Fund calculated as a share of the total contribution required to cover the Fund's disbursements during the preceding six-month period.[80] Each employer's share is determined on the basis of the number of skilled labourers he employs in any of the prescribed trades. Self-employed persons who are not employers are also liable to pay the levy in respect of the trade in which they are themselves skilled.[81] Government's contribution, calculated in the same way, is provided for as a charge on the Consolidated Fund.[82]

S..7 authorizes the disbursements that are to be made from the Fund. Government and all employers and self-employed persons are entitled to be reimbursed every six months for all wages, calculated at the relevant minimum rates of pay, paid to every apprentice in their employ.[83] In addition, government is entitled to be reimbursed from the Fund for various related administrative costs and for one half of any amounts expended on supplementary industrial training programmes.[84]

S. 10 provides machinery for appeal that seems to be unique in Malawi law:

> Any person aggrieved by a decision by the Minister in respect of the amount of any levy demanded under this Act, or of any reimbursement made from the Fund, may appeal in writing to the Minister for a review of his decision, and the Minister, if he considers it desirable, may appoint a tribunal of not more than three persons to hear evidence and advise him thereon. The Minister's decision on any appeal under this section shall be final and shall not be subject to question or review by any court of law.

In order to compensate employers who, largely at their own expense, have undertaken to train apprentices under the terms of the Apprenticeship Act, a rather heavy-handed measure has been framed at the end of the act. S. 12 provides that, in respect of any contract of apprenticeship subsisting at the time the act comes into operation, the Minister may require an apprentice to remain in the service of his employer for a period not to exceed two years.[85] This period of extended (and forced) service is to be undertaken at such remuneration and on such terms as the Minister may determine. Either party to the contract, employer or apprentice, has a statutory right of appeal to the Minister against his exercise of these powers,[86] and the Minister may call the parties before him and may hear them in respect of any matter he deems relevant.[87] His decision is final and not subject to review by any court.[88] Failure to comply with any order made by the Minister pursuant to s. 12 is an offence punishable by a fine of K500.[89]

When the bill was read a second time in the National Assembly, a nominated European Member who purported to speak for private industry stated that employers, who sympathized with the object of s. 12, were rather apprehensive about its implementation.[90] Forced labour, he suggested, was not altogether desirable even from the employers' point of view; rather, it was an ineffectual way of permitting them to recoup their investment in apprentice trainees. The extent to which the Minister will make use of this peculiar power remains to be seen.

CRIMINAL PROCEDURE AND EVIDENCE

In the case of *Rep.* v. *Kasamba*[91] the High Court had to consider the propriety of the magistrate's calling witnesses on his own motion. At the close of the prosecution's case the defendant declined to call any witnesses in defence, and the magistrate then recalled several of the prosecution's for the purpose of elucidating the evidence that had already been led. The problem that this procedure presents had been dealt with in the earlier case of *Barnet* v. *R.*[92] There the court had had to consider cases which appeared to state conflicting rules with respect to the trial court's right to recall a witness. The older cases held that this should be done only when something had arisen *ex improviso* during the course of the trial. More recent cases had stated a broader rule; they held it incumbent on the court to call a witness whenever his testimony was essential to a just decision of the case. The *Barnet* court resolved the rule of the later cases into a restatement of that of the earlier ones and held, in effect, that a court should use this power sparingly and only when something has arisen *ex improviso*.

The High Court, ruling on the appeal in *Rep.* v. *Kasamba*, endorsed the decision of the court in *Barnet* v. *R.* and held that the procedure adopted by the magistrate in the case under review had not been irregular. He exercised a valid discretion, the Court said, in calling witnesses for the purpose of clarifying testimony that was already part of the record.

The appeal of *Saimon* v. *Rep.*[93] raised a question regarding the application of ss. 140 and 259 of the Criminal Procedure and Evidence Code.[94] Together these sections require that in every case the court shall render judgement and that

> every judgement shall . . . be in writing and shall contain the point or points for determination, the decision thereon and the reasons for the decision . . .[95]

The question before the Court was whether a judgement, confined to the pronouncement 'Found guilty and convicted on both counts', complied with the statutory requirement. A similar question had been considered in *Thompson* v. *Rep.*[96] and the Court there held that use of the word 'shall' in s. 140 was directory rather than mandatory; in consequence, failure of the magistrate to comply with the section's provisions was not itself sufficient to require setting aside a conviction.

In the *Saimon* case the Court disagreed; it said in a forceful obiter that the requirements of the section are to be taken as mandatory. But it was unnecessary for the Court to decide the question, because it held that regardless of whether the provisions of s. 140 are directory or mandatory, so signal a failure to comply with them as that in the present case was an irregularity sufficient to ground reversal. Yet in the event the Court affirmed the conviction having reviewed all the evidence, it held that non-compliance with s. 140 had in this case occasioned no failure of justice.

In the case of *Maliseke* v. *Rep.*[97] the High Court was confronted with the insurmountable difficulty of hearing an appeal after loss of the trial record. Thus rendered impossible of review, the conviction was quashed. The Court said that 'ordinarily' it would be proper to order a retrial, but declined to do so here in the light of the fact that the defendant had already served nearly half of what appeared to the Court to be an excessive sentence.

One minor amendment has been made to the Criminal Procedure and Evidence Code.[98] S. 15(1) of the Code requires that certain sentences imposed by subordinate courts shall be confirmed on review by the High Court. That requirement no longer applies to a sentence imposed on a first offender and suspended pursuant to s. 340.[99] The proceedings of the lower court must now be reviewed only if the offender should later be committed to serve the sentence previously suspended.[100]

CRIMINAL LAW

The case of *General Construction Co Ltd* v. *Rep.*[101] came on appeal to the Supreme Court of Appeal from the High Court[102] where the appellant company, a member of a partnership, had been held vicariously liable for a violation of the Explosives Act[103] committed by a servant of the partnership. The High Court held, first, that the partner/company was vicariously liable for the acts of partnership servants when such acts constituted offences of absolute liability, and, secondly, that s. 24 of the Penal Code,[104] which limits the liability of 'persons' concerned with the management of an association that has committed an offence, applied only to natural persons.

Both elements of the High Court's judgement were affirmed, but the Supreme Court had one additional contention to deal with: for the first time in the appeal it was argued that the offence committed in violation of s. 15 of the Explosives Act was not absolutely prohibited. That section makes it a criminal offence to manufacture explosives without a licence. Taking note of the evident purpose of the provision, the Court cited the decision of the English court in *Sweet* v. *Parsley*[105] and said:

> where a statute regulates a dangerous activity in which citizens have a choice as to whether or not to participate, the court may infer an intention in Parliament to impose penal sanctions requiring high standards of care to prevent the prohibited act.

This reasoning, the Court held, applies to the Explosives Act: one must obtain a licence or refrain from doing what the statute prohibits: the manufacture of explosives entails absolute liability irrespective of intention or negligence.

In *Katchitsa* v. *Rep.*[106] the High Court propounded the rule that governs sentencing in cases where the defendant has been convicted of the offence of causing death by dangerous driving.[107] The Court adopted the reasoning of the judgement given in the East African case of *Wanjema* v. *Rep.*[108] where the court accepted the rule of the English cases.[109] Imprisonment, the Court said, is only appropriate where some element of 'deliberate risk-taking' is present, 'though there may also be cases where evidence of conscious recklessness in the offender's driving will be enough . . .' In the instant case, the Court found that the defendant's driving at high speed on the wrong side of the road was sufficiently reckless to warrant the six-month sentence imposed by the magistrate.

The respondent in *Director of Public Prosecutions* v. *McLuckie*[110] had been prosecuted in magistrate's court for being a member of the Jehovah's Witnesses, an unlawful society, membership of which is a punishable offence under s. 66(*a*) of the Penal Code.[111]

For twenty-one years prior to his retirement the respondent had been a missionary who subscribed to the beliefs of the Jehovah's Witnesses. He had not actively engaged in missionary work after the society had been declared unlawful but had been arrested for having a large quantity of the society's publications in his possession. S. 67(3) of the Penal Code provides that possession of any of the literature of an unlawful society raises the presumption that the possessor is one of its members. Interpreting and applying this section, the magistrate held that mere private possession was insufficient to give rise to the presumption, but that the possession must amount to some outward demonstration or declaration of the possessor's allegiance.

The appeal of the Director, taken from the lower court's acquittal, was pursued on two grounds. It was argued first, that the magistrate had erred as a matter of law in holding that possession of books or pamphlets of an unlawful society is not *per se* sufficient to raise the presumption of the possessor's membership of the society, and secondly, that he erred as a matter of law in holding that adherence to the beliefs of the Jehovah's Witnesses is not equivalent to unlawful membership of the society. The respondent for his part argued that the Jehovah's Witnesses were not a society but merely an amorphous group who shared certain common beliefs, and that whatever his relationship to them, it could not be that of member of a society. The Court first took up this argument regarding the nature of the Jehovah's Witnesses as an organisation. Basing its judgement on evidence of the respondent's own activities, it held that,

> such an association of persons who are united by a common faith which they are organised to profess and propagate, 'and who are linked together by an organisation which despatches books and pamphlets and provides missionaries is clearly a society.

This established, the Court turned to the prosecution's two contentions.

Interpreting s. 67(3) of the Penal Code, the High Court held that bare possession of its literature gives rise to the presumption of membership of an unlawful society, and that no additional act is required to turn belief into crime under s. 66(a). The presumption may be rebutted by a 'preponderance of probabilities', but if the presumption stands, the court is bound to convict:

> I think the magistrate's remarks concerning the need for an outward demonstration of belief are misconceived in this context. The Statute makes the possession of literature sufficient, and from such possession alone membership is to be presumed until the respondent proves to the contrary.

The Court emphasised that the act prohibits the *membership* of unlawful societies: one may be a member of a religious body without making current witness of one's faith; indeed, an active profession of faith is only evidence of a membership that may be proved in other ways.

This last assertion led the Court to the second of the Director's contentions. It held that belief in the tenets of a religious body was not tantamount to membership of that body as a society. Belief and membership may or may not coincide, and the former is only evidence of the latter. The Court rejected the Director's argument on ground of fundamental principle:

> While in respect of the majority of crimes the law does enquire into the mental state of an accused person, it does so only where it is incidental to an overt act, and I know of no law in Malawi which makes a person criminally liable because of his bad mind where no act at all has occurred. Freedom to think and to hold opinions is not penalized by section 66(a) of the Penal Code, nor by any other enactment, and to hold to the contrary would do violence not alone to the language of the section but also to the fundamental principles of government and to good sense.

Having given its opinion on the law, the Court proceeded to review the evidence. It held that the respondent had adduced none that rebutted the presumption raised by s. 67(3): his refraining from any public protestation of faith was not sufficient evidence, at least not in light of the fact that he had for so long been a missionary and confessed to continued belief in the religious tenets of the society.

Impelled by an incident of airline piracy that was a rather remarkable cause célèbre here, Parliament this year enacted the Hijacking Act.[112] It deals comprehensively with offences against aircraft, motor vehicles, trains and water-borne vessels. Part II of the act pertains specifically to air transportation;[113] its important criminal provisions are contained in s. 3 which provides in part:

> Any person, whatever his nationality, who unlawfully—
> (a) on board any aircraft in flight—
> (i) by use of force or by threats of any kind, seizes that aircraft or exercises control of it;
> (ii) assaults any person, if such assault is likely to endanger the safety of that aircraft;
> (iii) assaults or interferes with any member of the crew of that aircraft in the performance of his duties; [or]
> (g) performs any other act which jeopardises or may jeopardise the safety of an aircraft in flight or of persons or property therein or which may jeopardise good order and discipline on board an aircraft in flight,
> shall commit an offence and shall be liable to imprisonment for life.

The section's other provisions define various related offences concerning the operation of aircraft and navigational equipment.

S. 4 extends the law's application to acts done outside Malawi.[114] Where any act that would have been an offence had it taken place in Malawi takes place on board an aircraft of Malawian registration, it is an offence contrary to the laws of Malawi though the aircraft is not within the country's territorial jurisdiction.[115] Similarly, by virtue of s. 4(2), where any of the offences specified in s. 3 of the act takes place on board a non-Malawian aircraft without the territorial jurisdiction of Malawi, it is deemed an offence committed within Malawi

> (a) if such aircraft lands in Malawi with the person who committed such act still on board;
> (b) if such aircraft is leased without crew to a lessee who has his principal place of business or, if he has no such place of business, his permanent residence in Malawi; or,
> (c) if that person is present in Malawi.[116]

For purposes of a court's jurisdiction, an offence referred to in s. 4(2) is deemed to have been committed wherever the accused happens to be.[117]

S. 6 applies the Extradition Act, 1968,[118] to the offences specified in s. 3 but it does so only in favour of countries who are also signatories of one or another of the international Conventions relating to air piracy.[119] Subject to that qualification, extradition for crimes committed on board aircraft is available in favour of the country whose aircraft it is, the country where the aircraft lands with the offender still on board, and the country of residence or business of the lessee of the aircraft by demise.

S. 7 of the act gives the commander of aircraft power to do whatever may be necessary to maintain order aboard the aircraft and to preserve its safety and that of its passengers. It also imposes on him certain duties in respect of any person whom he has restrained for the purposes mentioned above. The section is taken in its entirety from s. 3 of the Tokyo Convention Act, 1967 of the United Kingdom.[120]

Taking cognisance of the international character of the crimes with which it deals, the act makes special provision for the admissibility of evidence.[121] In proceedings for an offence committed on board an aircraft, the written statement of a person not to be found in Malawi may be admitted if it has been made on oath before the person charged with the offence and before an officer acting in the capacity of a judge, magistrate or consular official. The section reproduces almost all of s. 5 of the Tokyo Convention Act, 1967.[122]

Part III of the act applies to land and water transportation. S. 10 defines various offences against motor vehicles, trains and vessels, and corresponds in its essentials to the provisions of s. 3. As in the earlier section, the offences carry with them liability to imprisonment for life. S. 11 and s. 12 apply the statute to acts committed outside Malawi on board vessels and trains respectively; adapted in ways appropriate to the different modes of transportation, they correspond in concept and purpose to the provisions of s. 4.[123] In similar fashion, s. 13 reproduces the grant of jurisdiction made in s. 5. Part III contains no provision making the Extradition Act specially applicable to offences committed against land and water transportation, nor are there any extraordinary provisions relating to the admisibility of evidence at proceedings for such offences.

TRADE AND INDUSTRY

The Companies Act[124] continues to be the subject of legislative tinkering. Amending legislation now requires that companies incorporated in Malawi shall keep true accounts of their income and expenditure and of their assets and liabilities.[125] The appropriate books of account must now be kept at the company's registered office or at any other place in the country of which the Registrar has been given notice.[126] To give effect to these new requirements, the act requires that within two months of its commencement every existing company notify the Registrar of the place where its books are kept.[127] Failure to comply with this provision is punishable as an offence.[128]

The general effect of this new provision is to require domestic companies to keep financial accounts in the same manner as that already required of external companies.[129] Domestic companies need not, however, register their financial statements.

The amending act also enlarges the Minister's power to exempt external companies from the obligation to keep books of their local accounts. S. 274E requires that every external company periodically register these with the Registrar, but as originally enacted, the section permitted the Minister to exempt any external company from its application. By an amendment of s. 274F, which requires that these books of account be kept within Malawi, an exemption granted an external company under s. 274E now automatically exempts that company from the requirements of s. 274F.[130] In its effect, the amendment also exempts certain external insurance and banking companies from the provisions of the latter section. In addition, the Minister is empowered specifically to exempt any external company from the provisions of s. 274F.[131] These extended powers of exemption appear to have been required by discovery of the fact that many external companies find it extremely difficult, even impossible, to prepare separate accounts for their operations in Malawi.[132] The power has already been exercised in at least one case.[133]

S. 274E(3) of the Companies Act requires that external companies submit their local accounts to an approved auditor practising in Malawi. The substance of that requirement has now been extended to domestic companies:[134] the amending act provides that none but an approved auditor shall be appointed auditor of any company registered in Malawi.

S. 274G(1) as originally enacted permitted every external company to appoint a managing director from among the members of its local board of directors. This provision has been amended to require that every external company appoint a chairman of its local board.[135] No provision is now made for a separate managing director.

S. 274G(2) has been amended in order to enable external companies to vary the number of their local directors within the limits prescribed by s. 274G(1) and subject in certain cases to ministerial approval.[136]

Regulations governing presentation of accounts and various other matters affecting external companies have been issued under the act.[137]

The purpose of the Malawi Bureau of Standards Act,[138] to put the matter as generally as possible, is to permit government to insist that goods, whether produced or consumed in Malawi, satisfy minimum standards of quality. Several considerations bear on government's policy. It is obviously thought desirable to protect the public from shoddy and dangerous goods and to prevent industry from taking advantage of a society increasingly avid to consume. In addition, government is anxious that goods made in Malawi should compete successfully in the international market, and it recognizes that such competition must depend in some measure on the quality of what Malawi produces for export. Indeed, the same is true with regard to the ability of locally manufactured goods to compete in the domestic market. The problem of quality, then, has some effect on government's policy of import substitution just as it has on its policy of promoting exports.[139]

To effect these general purposes, both social and economic, the act contemplates the gradual introduction of standard product specifications, first by making it advantageous for producers to use official marks that assure consumers of some minimum standard of quality, and, secondly, by enabling government, presumably at a later stage, to make such standards compulsory. The vehicle for effecting this policy is the Malawi

Standards Board, a body corporate that is given general responsibility for administering the act.[140] Many of its functions are to be carried out through the medium of the Malawi Bureau of Standards, an unincorporated body whose general brief is to promote standardization in commerce and industry, to prepare specifications and codes of practice and to test commodities for any of the purposes set forth in the act.[141] The Board, for its part, is obliged to formulate general policy with a view to achieving these objects and generally to control and manage the Bureau.[142]

The Board has also been given the several crucial powers that relate to the promulgation and enforcement of standard specifications. It may declare any device to be a standardization mark in respect of any specifications, and thereafter the device may not be used as a trade or other mark except under permit and subject to the requirement that the commodities to which it is affixed comply with the relevant specifications.[143] From a decision of the Board to refuse the issue of such a permit, an administrative appeal lies to the Minister, whose decision is final and not subject to review.[144]

In addition, the Minister, on recommendation of the Board, is authorized to make any standard specification compulsory; and thereafter no-one may sell any commodity to which the specification applies unless it conforms with that specification.[145] Before giving notice that any standard is to become compulsory, the Minister is obliged to call upon all interested persons to lodge with the Board any objections they may have.[146] The Minister, having considered the Board's recommendation and any objections that have been made, must then act; his decision in the matter is final and not subject to review.[147]

The act also provides for creation of an inspectorate whose officers are granted broad powers to examine products, processes and manufactories for the purpose of enforcing conformity with compulsory specifications.[148] Misuse of any standardization mark and failure to comply with relevant compulsory specifications are offences punishable by fine and imprisonment.[149] But the act relieves offenders of absolute liability: it is sufficient defence to a charge made under the act that the defendant 'took all reasonable precautions against committing the offence' and gave the Board all the information he had regarding the person from whom he acquired the offending commodity.[150]

The government and Board are saved from any civil liability arising from the fact that a commodity has or is alleged to have complied with any compulsory specification or been sold under any standardization mark.[151]

Regulations have now been made to implement the Second-Hand and Scrap Metal Dealers Act, 1971.[152] Their provisions are merely technical and need not be described here.

Regulations prescribing forms and fees have been made under authority of the Automotive Trades Registration and Fair Practices Act, 1971;[153] and 30 September 1972 was appointed as the date for the act's coming into operation.[154]

The Milk and Milk Products Act, 1971, came into operation on 1 November 1972.[155]

NOTES

1. Constitution, s. 13(1)
2. Constitution (Amendment) Act, 1972, No. 10 of 1972, s. 3
3. *Ibid.*, s. 4
4. Cap. 1:01
5. Constitution (Amendment) Act, 1972, s. 2
6. Constitution, s. 10(2)(*b*)
7. No. 14 of 1972
8. Cap. 12:01, s. 8
9. Army (Amendment) Act, 1972, s. 2
10. Cap. 12:01, s. 8(4)
11. Army (Amendment) Act, 1972, s. 2
12. *Ibid.*, s. 2
13. See Hansard (Malawi) (unrevised), 1st Mtg., 9th Sess. (1972), p. 249 (hereinafter referred to as Hansard)
14. Cap. 6:04
15. *Ibid.*, s. 3
16. Statute Law (Miscellaneous Amendments) Act, No. 24 of 1972, s. 2, amending cap. 6:04, s. 2
17. Cap. 26:02
18. Statute Law (Miscellaneous Amendments) Act. No. 24 of 1972, s. 2, amending cap. 26:02, s. 2
19. *Ibid.*, s. 2, adding a new sub-s. 7 to s. 5 of cap. 26:02
20. Traditional Courts (Criminal Jurisdiction) (Amendment) Order, GN 166/72
21. Cap. 66:03
22. See *ibid.*, ss. 11 and 41(1), (2) and (3)
23. Cap. 66:07
24. See *ibid.*, ss. 7(1)(*c*) and 8(1), (2) and (3)
25. Cap. 65:01
26. Special Crops (Amendment) Act, No. 9 of 1972, s. 2, amending s. 6(3) of the principal act
27. Hansard, 3rd Mtg., 8th Sess., p. 653
28. See *Annual Survey of African Law*, Vol. V, 1971
29. Cap. 22:02, s. 29
30. Local Governments (District Councils) (General Powers) Order, 1972, GN 57/72
31. Cap. 22:01, s. 75
32. Local Government (Urban Areas) (General Powers) Order, 1972, GN 99/72
33. Cause No. 42 of 1972, 3 Feb. 1972
34. Civil Procedure (Suits by and against the Government) Act, s. 10
35. (1962) 2 All ER 399, at p. 401
36. Civil Cause No. 409 of 1972, 1 Dec. 1972
37. (1959) 2 All ER 457; and also citing *R. v. Judge Hurst, Ex parte Smith*, (1960) 2 All ER 385
38. Cap. 5:01, s. 16(2)
39. Citing *R. v. Barnes, Ex parte Vernon*, 102 LT 860
40. Cap. 42:01
41. Customs and Excise (Amendment) Act, No. 5 of 1972
42. *Ibid.*, ss. 6 and 12, amending, respectively, ss. 16(1) (a) and 146(1) of the principal act
43. *Ibid.*, s. 2, amending s. 2 of the principal act
44. No. 6 of 1972
45. Cap. 41:02
46. Cap. 41:01
47. Income Tax (Amendment) Act, 1972, s. 3
48. *Ibid.*, ss. 5 and 6
49. Taxation (Consolidation) Act, ss. 150-160 now incorporate the substance of the Taxation Act, ss. 9-20 (Part II) and ss. 161-166 incorporate the substance of ss. 21-26 (Part III). The Second Schedule of the Taxation Act is now the Thirteenth Schedule of the Taxation (Consolidation) Act
50. Ss. 27-39
51. Cap. 41:01, s. 3(2)
52. Income Tax (Amendment) Act, 1972, s. 8
53. *Ibid.*, s. 11(2)
54. Cap. 37:01
55. *Ibid.*, s. 22(5)
56. Finance and Audit (Amendment) Act, No. 18 of 1972, s. 2
57. Finance and Audit Act, s. 26A. See *Annual Survey of African Law*, Vol. V, 1971

58. Finance and Audit (Amendment) Act, 1972, s. 3
59. *Ibid*, s. 4
60. No. 48 of 1971. See *Annual Survey of African Law*, Vol. V, 1971
61. GN 159/72
62. No. 17 of 1972
63. Cap. 53:03
64. Engineers Act, 1972, ss. 3 and 4
65. *Ibid*., s. 11
66. *Ibid*., s. 12
67. *Ibid*., s. 13
68. *Ibid*., s. 29
69. *Ibid*., ss. 30, 31 and 33
70. *Ibid*., s. 34
71. *Ibid*., s. 34(9)
72. *Ibid*., s. 33(2)
73. *Ibid*., s. 33(11)
74. *Ibid*., ss. 38–41
75. Cap. 53:01
76. Statute Law (Miscellaneous Amendments) Act, 1972, No. 24 of 1972, s. 2, amending s. 3 of the principal act and adding a new s. 5
77. No. 20 of 1972
78. Cap. 55:06
79. Industrial Training Act, 1972, s. 6
80. *Ibid*., s. 5(2) and (4)
81. *Ibid*., s. 5(2) and (4)
82. *Ibid*., s. 5(3)
83. *Ibid*., s. 7(1) and (3)
84. *Ibid*., s. 7(1) and (2)
85. *Ibid*., s. 12(2)
86. *Ibid*., s. 12(4)
87. *Ibid*., s. 12(5)
88. *Ibid*., s. 12(8)
89. *Ibid*., s. 12(9)
90. Hansard, 1st Mtg., 9th Sess., p. 281
91. Crim. App. No. 150 of 1972, 24 Aug. 1972
92. 3 ALR (Mal.) 524
93. Crim. App. No. 45 of 1972, 27 April 1972
94. Cap. 8:01
95. *Ibid*., s. 140(1)
96. 5 ALR (Mal.) 264
97. Crim. App. No. 163 of 1970, 19 July 1972
98. Cap. 8:01
99. Statute Law (Miscellaneous Amendments) Act, No. 24 of 1972, s. 2, amending cap. 8:01, s. 15(1)(d)
100. *Ibid*., s. 2, amending cap. 8:01, s. 341
101. Crim. App. No. 4 of 1971, 3 Feb. 1972
102. Crim. App. No. 560 of 1970, 18 May 1971. See *Annual Survey of African Law*, Vol. V, 1971
103. Cap. 14:09, s. 15
104. Cap. 7:01
105. (1970) AC 132, at 163; also see *Lim Chin Aik* v. *The Queen*, (1963) AC 160, at p. 174
106. Crim. App. No. 58 of 1972, 21 Aug. 1972
107. Road and Traffic Act, cap. 69:01, s. 123
108. (1971) EA 493
109. See *R.* v. *Joliffe*, (1970) Crim. LR50
110. Crim. App. No. 126 of 1972, 17 July 1972
111. Cap. 7:01. See GN 235/67 and 127/69
112. No. 19 of 1972
113. It does not apply, however, to aircraft used in 'military, customs or police services'. *Ibid*., s. 9
114. No offence committed outside Malawi may be prosecuted without the consent of the Director of Public Prosecutions. *Ibid*., s. 14
115. This provision, together with s. 14, replaces s. 16 of the Aviation Act, 1970, No. 7 of 1970. See Hijacking Act, 1972, s. 16
116. Hijacking Act, 1972. s. 4(2)(a), (b) and (c)
117. *Ibid*., s. 5

118. No. 9 of 1968, to which a slight technical amendment has been made by the Hijacking Act, 1972, s. 15
119. These are the Convention on Offences and certain other Acts Committed on board Aircraft signed at Tokyo on 14 September 1963; the Convention for the Suppression of Unlawful Seizure of Aircraft signed at The Hague on 16 December 1970; the Convention for the Suppression of unlawful Acts against the Safety of Civil Aviation signed at Montreal on 23 September 1971. Hijacking Act, 1972, s. 2
120. 1967 c. 52
121. Hijacking Act, 1972, s. 8
122. 1967 c. 52
123. See fn. 114, *supra*
124. Cap. 46:03
125. Companies (Amendment) Act, 1972, No. 7 of 1972, s. 2, amending cap. 46:03, s. 3. A domestic company was previously given the option whether to adopt as a term of its articles of association the requirements that the new legislation now makes mandatory. Companies (Consolidation) Act, 1908 (UK) (8 Edward VII, cap. 69), s. 10(2), as amended and applied by the Companies Act, cap. 46:03
126. *Ibid.*, s. 2, amending cap. 46:03, s. 3
127. *Ibid.*, s. 3(1)
128. *Ibid.*, s. 3(2)
129. See Companies Act, s. 274F, as amended by Companies (Amendment) Act, 1971, No. 31 of 1971
130. Companies (Amendment) Act, 1972, s. 2.
131. *Ibid.*, s. 2, adding a new sub-s. (6) to s. 274F
132. See Hansard, 3rd Mtg., 8th Sess., pp. 651-3
133. See GN 95/72, granting an exemption pursuant to s. 274E(8) in favour of WENELA
134. Companies (Amendment) Act, 1972, s. 2, amending the Companies (Consolidation) Act, 1908 (UK) (8 Edward VII, cap. 69), s. 112
135. Companies (Amendment) (No. 2) Act, No. 15 of 1972, s. 3(a) and (b)(i)
136. *Ibid.*, s. 3(b)(ii)
137. Companies (External Companies Accounts) Regulations, 1972, GN 152/72; Companies (External Companies) Forms Regulations, 1972, GN 153/72
138. No. 23 of 1972
139. See, generally, Hansard, 1st Mtg., 9th Sess., pp. 304-6
140. Malawi Bureau of Standards Act, 1972, ss. 6 and 15
141. *Ibid.*, ss. 3 and 4
142. *Ibid.*, ss. 5 and 15
143. *Ibid.*, s.20
144. *Ibid.*, s. 22
145. *Ibid.*, s. 21(10)
146. *Ibid.*, s. 21(3)
147. *Ibid.*, s. 21(4)
148. *Ibid.*, ss. 24 and 25
149. *Ibid.*, s. 29(1)
150. *Ibid.*, s. 29(3)
151. *Ibid.*, s. 26
152. GN 73/72
153. GN 147/72
154. GN 151/72
155. GN 161/72

CHAPTER NINE

ZAMBIA

Muna Ndulo

CONSTITUTIONAL LAW

ONE PARTY STATE

A major constitutional amendment was enacted in the Constitutional (Amendment) Act (No. 5) of 1972.

In January of 1972 the government had announced its intention to set up a One Party System of government in Zambia. A Commission to recommend changes in the constitution was set up.

Act No. 29 of 1972 is the act that brings into force a one party system of government. The constitution is amended by the insertion after chapter II of a new chapter namely chapter IIA.

In the new chapter s. 12A provides:

> (1) There shall be one and only one political Party in Zambia, namely, the United National Independence Party. (In this constitution referred to as the party.)
> (2) Every citizen who complies with the requirements laid down, from time to time, by the constitution of the party shall be entitled to become a member of the party.
> (3) Nothing contained in this constitution shall be so constructed as to entitle any person to lawfully form or attempt to form any political party or organization other than the Party or to belong to or assemble, associate, express opinion or do any other thing in sympathy with such political party or organization.

Nkumbula v. *The Attorney-General* was an appeal from a decision of the High Court dismissing an application under s. 28 of the constitution for redress on the grounds that the provisions of certain sections of chapter III of the constitution were likely to be contravened in relation to the appellant.

The petitioner was the leader of the now illegal African National Congress Party. On 25 February 1972 the President announced that the cabinet had taken a decision that the future constitution of Zambia should provide for one party democracy. On 1 March the President, by statutory instrument No. 46 of 1972, set up a commission to consider and recommend changes in the Constitution of Zambia and matters related thereto necessary to bring about the establishment of a one-party system of government in Zambia. The petitioner was appointed to the Commission but declined to take his seat.

The Commission was appointed under s. 2(1) of the inquiries Act which states that:

The president may issue a commission appointing one or more commissioners to inquire into any matter in which an inquiry would, in the opinions of the president, be for the Public Welfare. The terms of reference of the commission were as follows:

(1) to consider the changes in

    (a) the constitution of the Republic of Zambia;

    (b) the practices and procedures of the Government of the Republic; and

    (c) the constitution of the United National Independence Party; necessary to bring about and establish One Party Participatory Democracy in Zambia.

(2) Consider all matters incidental to or connected with the aforesaid matter in general and in particular the following matters:

    (a) The nature of the presidency, methods of election including the important question of whether or not a presidential candidate shall be eligible for re-election, and if so, after how many terms.

    (b) The nature and structure of government in general including the relationship between cabinet, Parliament and the Central Committee of the party.

    (c) The nature and structure of Parliament itself and its relationship to, for example, the National Council of the Party.

(3) The relationship between various political and administrative elected and appointed bodies ranging from Village Productivity and Village Political section committees to the Cabinet and the Central Committees.

    (d) The code of leadership for parliamentarians and other leaders in order to qualify for various positions in which supreme power normally rested in the people, is exercised by them indirectly on behalf of the people.

    (e) The Supremacy of the party vis-a-vis Government administration.

    (f) The amount of freedom of the people to form pressure groups based on tribal loyalties or for particular purposes.

    (g) The role of the labour movement and other specialized organizations in the National in the formulation of Government policies.

    (h) The participation of Public servants in politics and Government.

    (i) The system of discipline in the party, government and Public Service.

    (j) Lastly the freedom of candidates to stand for elections at local or national level.

The petition alleged that the petitioner's freedom of expression guaranteed under s. 13, 22 and 25 chapter III of the Constitution has been, is being and is likely in the future to be hindered in that:

(i) Under a One Party State system the freedom which at present existed under the Constitution to form and belong to a political party is incompatible therewith and can no longer be expected to exist.   .

(ii) The Petitioner may express to the Commission neither in evidence to it nor in its deliberations as a Commissioner, were he to take his seat upon it, the views which he holds and could reasonably be expected to hold by virtue of the facts set forth in paragraph 2 (which are well known to the Respondent) in disagreement with the announced decision that a One Party State will be introduced in the Republic.

(iii) The Commission in contravention of ss. 13, 22 and 25 Chapter III of the Constitution may not hear by virtue of its own terms of reference, or alternatively, by its own deliberative act, refuses to hear, expressions of opinion contrary to the introduction of a One Party State. The Petitioner's freedom to assemble and to associate with other persons namely as a member and as leader of the African National Congress Party, guaranteed under ss. 13 and 23(1) Chapter III of the Constitution is likely to be infringed in that:

(i) The introduction of or the maintenance of orderly Government under a One Party System is incompatible with such freedom, or further or in the alternative.
(ii) The introduction of a One Party State will be contrary to the spirit of the Constitution.'

The appellant then claimed the following declarations:

(a)' A declaration that the Commission has the power to hear evidence in opposition to the introduction of a One Party State: and/or
(b) A declaration that the Commission is bound to hear such evidence.
(c) A declaration that any statement by or on behalf of the Government of the Republic of Zambia inhibiting any expression of opinion against the introduction of a One Party State is in contravention of the spirit of the Constitution and in particular ss. 13, 22 and 25 Chapter III thereof.
(d) Such other Order, Writ or Direction as shall to the Court seem appropriate for the purpose of enforcing or securing the enforcement of ss. 13, 22 and 25 Chapter III of the Constitution in relation to the Petitioner.
(e) A declaration that the introduction of a One Party State is contrary to the spirit of the Constitution and rights that are guaranteed to the Petitioner under ss. 13 and 23 Chapter III of the Constitution are likely to be infringed thereby.'

The matter was argued on the following bases:

1. That the appointment by the President of the Commission of inquiry under s. 2 of the Inquiries Act, Cap. 181, was *ultra vires* and null and void because the matters to be inquired into could not be 'for the Public Welfare' within the meaning of those words as used in the said section.
2. That if a One Party State were introduced, the appellant's rights under s. 23 (freedom of association) are likely to be infringed.

On the first ground the court took the view that the power is to set up a Commission of inquiry if in the opinion of the president it would be for the public welfare. The Court went on to say that the words 'in the opinion of the president' clearly make the matter one for the subjective decision of the president, and it has never been doubted that a decision made under a power expressed in such terms cannot be challenged unless it can be shown that the person vested with the power acted in bad faith or from improper motives or on extraneous considerations or under a view of the facts or the law which could not reasonably be entertained.

The appellants argued that it could never be for the public welfare to prepare to derogate from existing fundamental rights and freedoms. It was submitted that public welfare means the welfare of the individuals comprising the public and that to derogate from individual rights and freedoms could not be for their welfare.

The Court rejected this argument. It went on to say that the ordinary meaning of the 'Public' is the community in general as an aggregate the court also thought it unthinkable to suggest that the government of a country elected to run an ordered society is not permitted to impose whatever constitutional restrictions on individual liberties it regards as necessary to enable it to govern to the best advantage for the benefit of the society as a whole. For these reasons the court held that the president in setting up a Commission to inquire into the various matters specified in statutory instrument No. 46 of 1972 was acting within the powers contained in the inquiries Act.

On the second ground of Appeal, that the introduction of a One Party

State would infringe in particular s. 23 of the Constitution in its present form, the court took the view that it is not part of the function of the courts to issue warnings to the government as to the legality of its proposed actions. The President of the court of Appeal went on to say:

'In my judgement therefore s. 28(1) has no application to proposed legislation of any kind, far less to a proposal to amend Chapter III itself. I entertain no doubt whatever that this section applies only to executive or administrative action, (or, exceptionally, action by a private individual) and that this is so is underlined by the existence of the words "in relation to him". Thus, if there is on the statute book an Act of Parliament, or subsidiary legislation, which it is alleged contravenes the Constitution, it is not open to any individual to come to court and ask for a declaration to this effect; before the individual has *locus standi* to seek redress there must be an actual or threatened action in relation to him. For instance, if an individual is arrested under a provision of an Act which he alleges is *ultra vires* the Constitution, he may in addition to any other remedy open to him proceed under s. 28(1).'

Again, if an individual has good ground for believing that some executive or administrative officer will take some action prejudicial to him and in contravention of his rights under Chapter III of the Constitution, he may proceed under this section. Many examples might be given. For instance, a parent of a school child might have received a letter from the headmaster threatening expulsion if the child did not conform to certain rules; the parent need not wait for the actual expulsion but could invoke s. 28(1) if he alleges that to enforce such rules would contravene the provisions of Chapter III. Again, a trader might have received an intimation from an executive officer indicating that a recommendation would be made for the revocation of his trading licence if certain conditions were not complied with; the trader would have *locus standi* to proceed under s. 28(1) to determine whether the imposition of such conditions and the revocation of a licence on failure to comply therewith; the trader would be in contravention of his constitutional rights.

The Court also added that since no executive or administrative action had been taken in relation to the appellant and that it was not alleged that any such action was threatened; s. 28 could not be invoked.

JUDICIAL AND LEGAL SYSTEM

COURTS

The High Court Act[2] was amended by the High Court (Amendment) Act, No. 3 of 1972. The purpose of the amendment is to make it possible for a judge to deliver a judgement prepared by another Judge.

The Subordinate Courts Act[3] was amended by the Subordinate Courts (Amendment) Act, No. 4 of 1972. This amendment has the same objective in relation to Subordinate Courts as the High Court (Amendment) Act, 1972. S. 26B empowers the Chief Justice to direct that another magistrate deliver in open court the judgement prepared by the presiding magistrate where the presiding magistrate is, on account of illness, death, relinquishment or cesser of jurisdiction or any other similar cause, unable to deliver a judgement already prepared by him.

MAGISTRATE COURTS

The jurisdiction of magistrates in criminal matters were substantially increased by the Criminal Procedure Code (Amendment) Act, No. 6 of 1972. S. 7 of the code is amended by the substitution of a new section. The new section reads as follows:

(a) A Subordinate Court presided over by a Senior Resident Magistrate shall not impose any sentence of imprisonment exceeding a term of nine years;
(b) A Subordinate Court presided over by a Resident Magistrate shall not impose any sentence of imprisonment exceeding a term of seven years;
(c) A Subordinate Court presided over by a Magistrate of the first class shall not impose any sentence of imprisonment exceeding a term of five years.
(d) A Subordinate Court other than a court presided over by a Senior Resident Magistrate, a Resident Magistrate or a Magistrate of the first class shall not impose any sentence of imprisonment exceeding a term of three years;
Sentences passed by Magistrates other than the Senior Resident Magistrates and Resident Magistrates require confirmation by the High Court before they can take effect if they are in excess of two years.

S. 3 of the Criminal Procedure Code (Amendment) Act, No. 6 of 1972 provides that:

(1) No sentence imposed by a Subordinate Court presided over by a Magistrate of the first class (other than a Senior Resident Magistrate or a Resident Magistrate) exceeding two years imprisonment with or without hard labour shall be carried into effect in respect of the excess, until the record of the case or a certified copy thereof has been transmitted to and the sentence has been confirmed by the High Court.

INTERPRETATION

The Penal Code was amended by the Penal Code (Amendment) Act, No. 5 of 1972. The Amendment repealed s. 4 which provided that:

this Code shall be interpreted in accordance with the principles of legal interpretation obtaining in England, and expressions used in it shall be presumed, so far as is consistent with their context, and except as may be otherwise expressly provided, to be used with the meaning attaching to them in English Criminal law and shall be construed in accordance therewith.

In its place the following section is substituted:

This Code shall be interpreted in accordance with the principles of legal interpretation obtaining in England.

LEGAL PROFESSION

The Legal Practitioners Act[4] was amended by Act No. 13 of 1972. The Principal Act is amended by the insertion immediately after s. 7H of the following new sections:

7I upon the appointment of any person to the office of the attorney-general the rank and dignity of a State Counsel for Zambia may be conferred upon him by the President.
7) any practitioner wishing the rank and dignity of a state counsel for Zambia be conferred upon him shall submit his application, accompanied with the recommendation of his state counsel, in that behalf to the Attorney-General.

The amending act restricts the number of people who can be appointed to State Counsel to not more than three in a given year. (s. 2). The same section also provides that a person shall not be appointed as a state counsel for Zambia unless he is qualified for appointment as a puisne judge of the High Court. This qualification does not apply to an appointment of the Attorney-General as a State Counsel.

CRIMINAL LAW AND PROCEDURE

ABORTION

Act No. 26 of 1972 was passed to amend and clarify the law relating to termination of pregnancy by registered medical practitioners. The Act widens the grounds on which a lawful abortion may be performed. S. 3 provides that:

> Subject to the provisions of this section, a person shall not be guilty of an offence under the law relating to abortion when a pregnancy is terminated by a registered medical practitioner if he and two other registered medical practitioners, one of whom has specialized in the branch of medicine in which the patient is specifically required to be examined before a conclusion could be reached that the abortion should be recommended, are of the opinion, formed in good faith—
> (a) that the continuance of the pregnancy would involve—
>   (i) risk to the life of the pregnant woman, or
>   (ii) risk of injury to the physical or mental health of the pregnant woman or
>   (iii) risk of injury to the physical or mental health of any existing children of the pregnant woman, greater than if the pregnancy were terminated or
> (b) That there is a substantial risk that if the child were born it would suffer from such physical or mental abnormalities as to be seriously handicapped.

The Act goes on to provide that the termination must be carried out in a hospital unless termination is immediately necessary to save the life or prevent permanent physical or mental injury to the woman (s. 3(3)). It further provides that no person shall be under any duty to participate in any treatment (except in treatment which is necessary to save the life or to prevent grave, permanent injury to the physical or mental health of a pregnant woman) authorized by the Act to which he has a conscientious objection. The burden of proving conscientious objection rests on the person claiming to rely on it.

The Act has done much to liberalize the grounds on which an abortion can be performed. Previous to the Act, the law on abortion was that laid down by the *People* v. *Gulshan*.[5] The law in this case was substantially that laid down in the English case of *R.* v. *Bourne*.[6]

SENTENCING

Courts which sentence to imprisonment persons who are not citizens of Zambia and who are convicted of an offence under the Penal Code, or under any written law other than an offence relating to the driving of a motor vehicle set out in the Roads and Road Traffic Act or in any regulations for the time being in force made thereunder are required by the Penal Code (Amendment) Act, No. 2 of 1972, to forward to the minister responsible for the administration of the Immigration and Deportation Act the particulars of the conviction and sentence and all other personal particulars.

This is to enable the minister to deport the person. For under the

Immigration and Deportation (Amendment) Act, 1972, the minister, after receiving the particulars, is empowered to deport such person from Zambia.

LEGAL AID

The Legal Aid Act[7] was amended by Act No. 34 of 1972. The Amending Act permits an accused person to refuse legal aid which would otherwise be granted to him in furtherance of a legal aid certificate (s. 7). Where an accused person refuses legal aid the court is required to record reasons put forward by the accused person for the refusal.

PROPERTY

MINING

The Penal Code (Amendment) Act, No. 5 of 1972, also repeals and replaces chapter XXXIA of the Penal Code. The new chapter reads as follows:

288A(1) Any person who, without the written permission of the Chief Mining Engineer has in his possession or disposes of any diamond or emerald shall be guilty of a misdemeanour.
(2) For the purposes of this section—'Chief Mining Engineer' means the person appointed as such in pursuance of section six of the Mines and Minerals Act, 1969.
'Diamond' means any rough or uncut diamond and includes any diamond which has been partially cut, shaped or polished out of the rough;
'Emerald' means any rough or uncut emerald and includes any emerald which has been partially cut, shaped or polished out of the rough.
(3) Any police officer of or above the rank of Assistant Inspector may arrest without warrant any person reasonably suspected by him of having committed or of attempting to commit an offence under this section.
288B(1) When a person has been found guilty by a Court of an offence under section two hundred and eighty-eight A, in addition to any other punishment imposed on the accused person, the diamonds or emeralds in respect of which the offence has been committed shall be forfeited to the state upon such finding by the court.

RENT

An Act to make provision for restricting the increase of rents, determining the standard rents, prohibiting the payment of premiums and restricting the right to possession of dwelling houses was passed during 1972. The Rent Act, No. 10 of 1972, applies to all dwelling houses in Zambia whether or not the terms of the letting of such dwelling houses include the use in common with the landlord or other persons authorized by him of other rooms in or amenities of or portions of the building of which the said dwelling house forms a part or the grounds or gardens immediately adjacent thereto, and whether or not the terms of the letting include a provision for services or the use of furniture. S. 3(1) states that it does not however apply to (a) a dwelling house let or occupied by an employee by virtue, and as an incident, of his employment; (b) premises let by the government save as to the rent charged in respect of any authorized subletting of the whole or part thereof; (c) premises for which an inclusive charge is made for board and lodging and in respect of which a permit in that behalf has been issued under any law for the time being in force; (d) premises held by the tenant under a lease for a term certain exceeding twenty-one years.

S. 4 of the Rent Act empowers the High Court (in relation to premises for which the rent demanded exceeds three thousand six hundred Kwacha per annum) and a Magistrates Court (in relation to all other premises) to:

(a) determine the standard rent of any premises either on the application of any person interested or of its own motion.

(b) fix in the case of any premises, at its discretion and in accordance with the requirements of justice, the date from which the standard rent is payable;

(c) apportion payment of the standard rent of premises among tenants sharing the occupation thereof;

(d) where the rent chargeable in respect of any premises includes a charge for services in addition to the standard rent, fix the amount of such charge;

(e) make either or both of the following orders, that is to say:

(i) An order for the recovery of possession of premises whether in the occupation of a tenant or of any other person, and

(ii) An order for the recovery of arrears of standard rent, mesne profits and a charge for services.

(f) for the purpose of enabling buildings to be erected, make orders permitting landlords (subject to the provisions of any written law) to excise vacant land out of premises where such a course is, in the opinion of the court, desirable in the public interest.

(g) When the landlord fails to carry out any repairs for which he is liable, order the landlord to carry out such repairs;

(h) permit the levy of distress for standard rent;

(i) impose conditions in any order made by the court under the provisions of this section;

(j) upon the determination of any application or other proceedings, in his discretion, order any party thereto to pay the whole or any part of the costs thereof;

(k) exercise jurisdiction in all Civil matters and questions answering under the rent act;

(l) at anytime, of his own motion, or for good, cause shown on an application by any landlord or tenant, re-open any proceedings in which it has given any decision, determined any question, or made any order, and to revoke, vary or amend such decision determination or order, other than an order for the recovery of possession of premises or for the ejectment of a tenant therefrom which has been exercised:

Provided that—

(i) nothing in this paragraph shall prejudice or affect the right of any person under section seven to appeal to the Courts of Appeal from any such decision, determination or order as aforesaid, or from the revocation variation or amendment of any such decision, determination or order;

(ii) The powers on the Court by this paragraph shall not be exercised in respect of any decision, determination or order while an appeal therefrom is pending or in a manner inconsistent with or repugnant to the decision of the appellate Courts on such appeal.

The court has power by virtue of s. 5 of the Rent Act to investigate any complaint relating to the tenancy of premises made to it either by the landlord or a tenant of such premises. When the Court investigates any complaint or other matter under this section, it may make such order in the matter, being an order which it is by this Act empowered to make as the justice of the case may require. It is an offence under s. 6 to fail to comply with any lawful order or decision of the court after the expiration of the time allowed for an appeal, therefrom, or if any appeal has been filled after such order or decision has been upheld. A prosecution under this section cannot be instituted except with the consent of the Director of Public Prosecutions.

S. 7 provides that when any question is, under the provisions of this act, to be determined by the Court, the determination by the court shall be final and conclusive. There is a proviso to the section that an appeal from any such determination shall lie on any point of law, or of mixed fact and law to the Court of Appeal.

Under s. 8 it is the duty of the landlord of any premises to which this Act applies and of which the standard rent has not been determined by the Court, other than the premises which were let on the prescribed date, to apply to the Court for determination of the standard rent of such premises either before letting the premises or within three months of the letting or of the commencement of this Act, which ever is later.

S. 9 prohibits a landlord from receiving excessive rent. It provides that:

> Subject to the provisions of this Act, the landlord of premises shall not be entitled to recover any rent in respect thereof in excess of the standard rent.

The rent Act also restricts instances when rent can be increased, s. 11(1) provides:

> A landlord may, by notice in writing to the tenant, increase the standard rent of any premises, that is to say—
> (a) in the case of premises upon which the rates payable by the landlord have increased since the prescribed date—
> (i) by the amount of such increase, where the premises were let on or before the prescribed date; and
> (ii) by the amount of the increase in rates payable by the landlord since the premises were let, where they were let after the prescribed date;
> (b) In any case where the landlord has, since the prescribed date, incurred expenditure on the improvement or structural alteration of premises (excluding expenditure on redecoration or repair, whether structural repair or not) or in connection with the installation or improvement of a drainage or sewage system or the construction or making good of a street or road executed by or at the instance of a local authority, by an amount calculated expenditure so incurred.

There are then restrictions on the right to possession contained in s. 13 of the rent Act. S. 13 provides:

> No order for the recovery of possession of any premises or for the ejectment of a tenant therefrom shall be made unless—
> (a) Some rent lawfully due from the tenant has not been paid, or some other obligation of the tenancy (whether under a contract of tenancy or under this Act) so far as the same is consistent within the provisions of this Act, has been broken or not performed; or
> (b) The tenant, or any person residing with him, has been guilty of conduct which is a nuisance or annoyance to adjoining occupiers, or has been convicted of using the premises or allowing the premises to be used for a criminal or illegal purpose, or the condition of the premises has, in the opinion of the court, deteriorated owing to acts of waste by, or the neglect or default of, the tenant or any other person; or
> (c) The tenant has given notice to quit, and in consequence of that notice the landlord has contracted to sell or let the premises or has taken any other steps as a result of which he would in the opinion of the court be seriously prejudiced if he could not obtain possession; or
> (d) The court is satisfied that the tenant has sublet the whole or any part of the premises (such part being also premises to which this Act applies) for a rent in

excess of the rent recoverable under the provisions of this Act; or

(e) The dwelling house is reasonably required by the landlord for occupation as a residence for himself or for his wife or minor children or for any person bona fide residing or intending to reside with him, or for some person in his whole-time employment or for the occupation of the person who is entitled to the enjoyment of such dwelling house under a will or settlement, and the landlord has given to the tenant not less than twelve months notice to quit; and in such case the court shall include in any order for possession a requirement that the landlord shall not without prior approval let the premises or any part thereof within three years after the date on which the possession is to be given; or

(f) The premises are reasonably required by the landlord for the purpose of the execution of the duties imposed upon him by any written law, or for any purpose which, in the opinion of the court, is in the public interest; or

(g) The tenant has without the consent in writing of the landlord, at any time after the prescribed date, assigned, sublet or parted with the possession of the premises or any part thereof. Provided that—

    (i) a landlord who has obtained or is entitled to obtain an ejectment order on the grounds contained in this paragraph may, at his option, either obtain a similar order against the occupier or treat such occupier as his tenant;

    (ii) for the purposes of this paragraph, if the tenant is a private limited Company the transfer at any one time without the consent of the landlord of more than fifty per centum of the total nominal value of the issued shares of the company shall be deemed to be an assignment of the premises; or

(h) The landlord is the owner of a dwelling house which he has previously occupied as a residence for himself and reasonably requires such house for occupation as a residence for himself or for his wife or minor children, and has complied with the terms relating to the giving of notice contained in any lease into which he has entered with the tenant in respect of such house or, in the absence of any such lease, has given the tenant three months' notice to quit:

Provided that if within twelve months next after the date upon which the landlord was, by virtue of the provisions of this paragraph, entitled to vacant possession of such dwelling house, he wished again to let such house (whether for a consideration or without consideration) he shall give to the tenant who, by virtue of the provisions of this paragraph, was required to give up possession of such house, the first option to take a tenancy and possession thereof; or

(i) The landlord requires possession of the premises to enable the reconstruction or rebuilding thereof to be carried out, and has given to the tenant not less than six months notice in writing of such requirement; the Court making an order for possession on this ground shall include in the order a condition that the reconstruction or rebuilding shall be completed within such specified time as the court may consider reasonable; or

(j) The landlord has, in obedience to an order of the Court, let the premises for a definite period, and the landlord requires the premises at the expiry of such period for his own occupation or for the occupation of his wife or minor children or for some person in his whole-time employment; or

(k) The premises are occupied by a larger number of persons than can reasonably be accommodated so that, in the opinion of the Court, the premises are overcrowded or constitute for any reason a danger to the occupiers of the adjoining premises; or

(l) The application for recovery of possession of the premises is made by a person who, having been the tenant of the premises, has been unlawfully dispossessed thereof; and, any order made in such circumstances may include an order for compensation to be paid by the landlord to any tenant of the premises dispossessed thereof by such order.

Within the act there are several punitive provisions for the contravention of the Act. For instance it is an offence for a landlord to obtain an order for possession by misrepresentation (s. 13(17)). It is also an offence for a landlord to obtain an order for possession by concealment of material facts.

Where a landlord has furnished certain premises he cannot remove such furniture except on application to court (s. 21).

S. 25 restricts the right to assign or sublet premises. It provides:

> Notwithstanding the absence of any covenant against the assignment or subletting of the premises, no tenant shall have the right to assign, sublet or part with the possession of any premises or any part thereof except with the consent in writing of the landlord or, where such consent is unreasonably withheld, the consent of the court.

The Act in s. 30(1) creates the office of Rent Controller. Rent Controllers are Public officers and have power in respect of any premises to which this Act applies, for the purposes of making any valuation, assessment or examination or carrying out any function or duty under the rent Act—

(a) to enter at all reasonable times into and upon such premises;
(b) to serve a written notice on the landlord of such premises requiring him to make a return containing such particulars as may be required in such notice;
(c) to elicit from the landlord or the tenant such information as he may require for the purpose.

MISCELLANEOUS

DEVELOPMENT BANK

The government decided to establish a Development Bank of Zambia to assist in the economic development of Zambia. The Act establishing the bank is cited as the Development Bank of Zambia Act.

The Business of the Bank is defined in s. 12 as

(a) to make available long and medium term finance for economic development.
(b) to provide technical assistance and advisory services for the purpose of promoting economic development and at the discretion of the Board to charge fees for such services.
(c) to assist in obtaining and placing foreign investment for the purpose of promoting economic development.
(d) to administer on such terms and conditions as may be approved by the Board such special funds as may from time to time be placed at the disposal of the Bank.
(e) to borrow funds in Zambia and elsewhere.
(f) to buy and sell securities, including securities which the Bank has issued or guaranteed.
(g) to study and promote investment opportunities and
(h) to do all other matters and things incidental to or connected with the foregoing.

The Bank itself is not allowed to engage in any business on its own account in the wholesale or retail trade including the import or export trade except as may be necessary in the course of satisfaction of debts due to it and then only as may be necessary for the purpose (s. 13(1)).

The procedure and requirements for financing by the bank are stipulated in s. 18(1) of the Act which provides that long and medium term finance may be provided only after the Board has given its approval in each case. Provided, however, that the board shall not accord its approval unless it has duly considered the written proposal submitted to the Bank by the applicant for the purpose, together with the comments thereon by the Managing Director.

RADIATION

The government passed legislation relating to the protection of the Public
and Workers from dangers arising from the use of devices or materials
capable of producing Ionizing radiation.

The Act cited as the Ionizing Radiation Act, No. 19 of 1972 provides in
s. 5 for the establishment of the Radiation Protection Board. The Board
makes recommendations to government on the following matters: (a) the
assurance that all activities involving the use of devices or materials
capable of producing dangerous amounts of Ionizing Radiation are
carried out in such a manner as to avoid dangers to the public or to
workers concerned or limit risks to those acceptable as a matter of public
policy; (b) Allocation of priorities and co-ordination of activities in
connection with maintenance of safety in the use of devices or materials
producing Ionizing Radiation and associated matter to make the best use
of available resources taking into account the needs of the country and
alternative methods of achieving equivalent results.

A licence is required for the use of radioactive material or other sources
of dangerous Ionizing Radiation by virtue of s. 210. The licence holder is
responsible for ensuring that any operation, condition of storage,
transport or disposal shall not result, directly or indirectly in exposure to
Ionizing Radiation in such an amount as likely to cause harmful effects to
the public, to his employees, other workers or other users or to property
owned either by the government or private persons.

EDUCATION

The Education Act[8] was amended by the Education (Amendment) Act,
No. 40 of 1972. S. 14 of the Act provides that any person desirous of
establishing a private school shall first make an application for its
registration to the Minister of Education. If the Minister is satisfied that
(a) the school is necessary to meet the educational requirement of the area
in which it is or is proposed to be situated; and (b) that the premises of the
school, including any hostel or other buildings to be used in connection
with the instruction or accommodation of the pupils attending, are or will
be suitable and adequate for the purpose and (c) that adequate financial
provision has been or will be made for the maintenance of the school; and
(d) that the proprietor of School is a fit and proper person or body of
persons to be the proprietors; and (e) that a fit and proper person or body
of persons will be responsible for the management of the school; and (f)
that efficient and suitable instruction of a nature or level approved by the
Minister will be provided at the school in accordance with a syllabus
approved by the Minister; and (g) that the teaching staff to be employed at
the school will be sufficiently qualified for the purpose; and (h) that
proper compliance will be made with the provisions of this Act applicable
to this school, he shall cause the private school to be registered for a
period not exceeding one year.

S. 18 makes it an offence for any person to conduct a private school
which is not registered or whose registration has lapsed or in respect of
which the proprietor has been notified in writing that the registration of
the private school has been cancelled.

ENGINEERING

The Engineering institution of Zambia (private) Act[9] was repealed and replaced by the Engineering Institution of Zambia Act, No. 12 of 1972. The New Act specifies the objects of the Institution and the qualifications for membership, defines the Constitution of the Council of the Institution and provides for other matters connected with Engineering.

CITIZENSHIP COLLEGE

The government established the president's citizenship college by Act No. 21 of 1972. The College, by s. 3 of the Act, is a body corporate with perpetual succession and a common seal and is capable of suing and being sued and of purchasing or otherwise acquiring, holding and alienating property, real or personal and of doing and performing all such acts or things as a body corporate may be law do and perform.

The College is run by a council consisting of sixteen members appointed by the minister of Home Affairs. It will carry out courses aimed at helping the intended leaders to understand and appreciate fully their respective roles in the Zambian society. It is supposed to be a combination of Kivukoni College for TANU leaders in Dar es Salaam and Moshi co-operative college, both in Tanzania and the former labour college in the Ugandan capital, Kampala.

The College is largely financed by the Fredrich Ebert Foundation of the Federal Republic of Germany.

NOTES

1. Court of Appeal, Case No. 6 of 1972
2. Cap. 50 of the laws of Zambia
3. Cap. 45 of the laws of Zambia
4. Cap. 48 of the laws of Zambia
5. HP No. 11 of 1971
6. 1939 11CB 687
7. Cap. 546 of the laws of Zambia
8. Cap. 234 of the laws of Zambia
9. Cap. 826 of the laws of Zambia

CHAPTER TEN

RHODESIA

Harry Silberberg

CONSTITUTIONAL AND OTHER PUBLIC AND ADMINISTRATIVE LAW

There have been no fundamental developments in this field during 1972. But it would be a mistake to describe the various new and amending statutes enacted (59 in all) as being of minor importance only, in so far as they all indicate the general trend towards the establishment of a firm and centrally controlled policy.

LAND TENURE

The Land Tenure Amendment Act, No. 53 of 1972, was passed to reverse the effect of a High Court judgement which had declared the Land Tenure (Licensed Premiss) (Prescription of Occupation) Regulations (GN 717) of 1972 as being *ultra vires* the Lane Tenure Act, No. 55 of 1969, in its original form. The Regulations were intended to prevent Africans from using the bar facilities of hotels and restaurants in the European Area after 7 p.m. and on weekends and public holidays. The Minister, in passing the regulations, had contended that s. 3 of the Land Tenure Act which empowered him to prescribe that *attendance* for a *specified purpose* at a specified class of places or premises to which members of the public are admitted *shall constitute occupation* for the purposes of the Land Tenure Act, authorized him to declare bars in hotels and restaurants in the European Area as a class of premises within the meaning of s. 3 of the Act. This meant that owners of such establishments required a permit to admit Africans and such permits would normally restrict the times during which they could allow Africans to make use of their bar facilities. In a test case—*Queen's Hotel and Others* v. *van Heerden and Others NNO*[1]—Goldin, J., held that a person who had a drink or a meal at a bar or a restaurant could not be said to *attend* or be in attendance at such an establishment. In addition the learned judge pointed out that the regulations were inconsistent with the Liquor Act (Cap. 234) and that the Land Tenure Act did not permit the derogation from rights granted by any other statute. S. 3 of the Land Tenure Act was, therefore, amended so as to authorize the application of this Act '(n)otwithstanding the provisions of any other law' and by substituting the words *presence* and *is present* for the original expressions *attendance* and *attends,* and in order to avoid possible arguments about the meaning of these new words, s. 3 was further amended so as to make it clear that a person will be present at a particular place *irrespective of the period for which he is so present.* Although the occasion for the introduction of the amendment was the use of bar facilities, the wording of the amendment makes it clear that it relates to all other establishments mentioned in sub-section 2 of s. 3, i.e. schools, hospitals, hotels in general, and to the employment on any land, and that it refers conversely to Europeans in the African Area. In view of difficulties which had been found to exist in establishing the race of the controlling interest in companies or associations, s. 68 of the principal Act was amended so as to enable the issue of a deeming certificate in terms of which the company or association may be regarded as European, although the majority of the members are Africans, if the actual control of of the affairs of that company or association is exercised by Europeans, and conversely, such a company or association may be deemed to be African, if the actual control is exercised by Africans, despite the fact that the majority of members consists of Europeans. An appeal against the issue of such a certificate by the Minister lies direct to the President.[2] Finally, it should be mentioned that the occupation of Tribal Trust Land by non-tribesmen and for various other purposes (such as the installation of power lines, pipelines and the construction of dams) will henceforth be controlled by permit.[3]

CONTROL OF IMMIGRATION AND DEPARTURE FROM RHODESIA
In *Barros* v. *Chief Immigration Officer*[4] Lewis, J.A., decided in a special case stated for the opinion of the Appellate Division on a point of law reserved by a magistrate in terms of s. 9(4) of the Immigration Act, No. 43 of 1966, that the holder of a residence or visitor's permit granted to him in terms of the Immigration (Selection) Regulations (GN 811 of 1966) has a right of appeal to the courts, if such permit is cancelled by the Chief Immigration Officer and that, in any event, the date specified in the notice of cancellation by which the permit holder is required to leave Rhodesia cannot be a date prior to the date of the issue of the notice itself, but must always be a date subsequent to that of the notice, however short a time that may be. In this case the appellant was served on 29 June 1971 with a notice informing him that his residence permit had been cancelled with effect from 3 June 1971 on the grounds that in his application for the permit he had failed to declare a conviction elsewhere. Together with that notice he was also served with a *notice to visitor* authorizing a *visit* to Rhodesia for the period 29 June 1971 to 13 July 1971, on which date he was required to leave the country. As the learned judge pointed out, when a person's residence permit is cancelled, he becomes a prohibited immigrant and his right to remain in Rhodesia has been limited to a fixed period, *then such person has been 'restricted as a prohibited immigrant' within the ordinary meaning of the words* and because appeals by prohibited immigrants who have become such by reason of a decision of the Immigrants' Selection Board have not been excluded by s. 10(1) of the Immigration Act, such a person has a right of appeal against the cancellation of his permit.

Subsequent to this decision, the Immigration Act was amended by the

Immigration Amendment Act, No. 32 of 1972. The right of appeal which Lewis, J.A., had held to exist was preserved (although it appears to have been somewhat restricted by an amendment to s. 10 of the principal Act and the extent of this amendment may require clarification either by further legislation or a decision of the courts). But a new s. 14A spells out what was so far assumed to have been implicit in the Act, namely that an immigration officer may refuse to permit a person to enter Rhodesia if he believes on reasonable grounds that consideration is being, or is about to be, given by the Minister to declare that person a prohibited immigrant and a person who has been refused permission to enter Rhodesia in terms of this section has no right to appeal or to make representations. It appears that the section does not apply to persons who were born in Rhodesia, irrespective of whether they have retained their Rhodesian citizenship. In addition, the penalties for certain contraventions of the principal Act have been increased and a person charged with having entered Rhodesia illegally shall be presumed to have entered Rhodesia at a place other than a regular point of entry until the contrary has been proved. A corresponding provision has been introduced by the Departure from Rhodesia (Control) Amendment Act, No. 15 of 1972, which provides that if a person is charged with having left the country otherwise than at an authorized point of exit, the onus of proof will lie on him to rebut such charge. It also introduces a new s. 3A into the principal Act in terms of which the Minister may declare any travel document issued to any person by any government not to be a valid travel document so that it will be possible to prevent the legal departure from Rhodesia of any person if it is considered not to be in the national interest that he should be allowed to leave Rhodesia. If such a person is a citizen of Rhodesia, holding a Rhodesian passport, it may, of course, be impounded but a travel document issued by the government of another state shall not be invalidated or impounded.

The Africans (Registration and Identification) Amendment Act, No. 48 of 1972, repeals s. 16 of the principal Act (Cap. 109) and substitutes a new section therefor in terms of which no African shall leave Rhodesia to proceed to a foreign state without a special permit (which is required in addition to any passport) and which shall be issued by a registration officer who has a discretion as to whether he will grant or refuse such a permit, provided that it shall not be refused to an African foreigner who has been refused registration or re-registration and is, therefore, bound to leave Rhodesia or to an African who is the holder of a valid passport or other travel document. An appeal against a refusal to issue an exit permit lies to a provincial commissioner whose decision shall be final.[5]

SECURITY AND DEFENCE

The State of Emergency was extended for another year until the end of June 1973. A Defence Procurement Act, No. 8 of 1972, was introduced to provide for the supply of equipment to the defence forces and the construction of buildings and other 'structures' required by them. It establishes a Defence Procurement Board and a Defence Procurement Fund. The Board has power to enter into agreements and to raise money for defence purposes which is, however, subject to the approval of the

Minister of Defence and that of the Treasury. It is intended to permit greater flexibility in the planning and execution of defence expenditure than previously existed and to ensure co-ordination in the production and supply of defence equipment.

The Defence Act, No. 27 of 1972, is intended to replace and consolidate the existing legislation based on the Federal Defence Act of 1955 which has been amended and adapted from time to time. In addition, the new Act introduces new features. Whilst it retains the requirement that in every calendar year residents who attain the age of seventeen years and persons taking up residence in Rhodesia between the ages of seventeen and fifty years shall register themselves with the Registrar of Defence Manpower, it makes, in addition, provision for the re-registration of all persons in the aforementioned age group. It also enables the Minister to call upon employers to supply the Registrar with information in respect of their employees who are required to register themselves. A resident is defined as any male inhabitant of Rhodesia who has resided in Rhodesia for a continuous period of not less than six months and is not already serving in any military force, or in the service of a foreign government, unless he is a citizen of Rhodesia. On the other hand, a resident need not be a citizen of Rhodesia in order to be liable for service in terms of the Act. Africans are not liable to serve, but s. 30 of the Act provides specifically that nothing therein contained shall preclude the engagement of any African who volunteers for service in the defence forces. In terms of s. 27 the Minister may from time to time by notice in the Gazette fix the age groups of residents liable for service training and he may fix different age groups for different residents or classes of residents. S. 40 transfers the power to order the employment within and outside Rhodesia of the whole or any part of the territorial force or reserve where it is deemed necessary or desirable in the interests of defence or public safety from the President to the Minister of Defence. The initial period of continuous training for the territorial force remains at 245 days and the total liability for such service likewise remains at four years, but the Minister of Defence is authorized, should the need arise, to increase the initial period of continuous training from 245 to 365 days and the total liability for service from four to six years and any member of a reserve force who is employed on active service in border control operations may be required in terms of s. 36 to undergo an additional continuous period of reserve training not exceeding forty-eight hours in addition to the fourteen days which he is ordinarily required to undergo in any period of twenty-four months. Parts V to VII of the Act deal with military offences, the jurisdiction of military and civil courts and legal procedures in general. Here it should be noted that the law to be observed by courts-martial shall be the law in force in criminal proceedings in the civil courts, which means that Roman-Dutch law will govern such proceedings. Exemptions from service in terms of the Act are provided for judicial officers, members of the Senate or House of Assembly, ministers of religion, as defined by the Minister in consultation with such interdenominational body as may be determined by the Minister for this purpose, and certain classes of public servants. Conscientious objectors, i.e. persons 'whose *bona fide* religious beliefs inhibit participation in military service for the maintenance of peace or public safety in the defence of Rhodesia' may apply to an exemption board for exemption from service or training whose decision shall be final and not subject to any appeal.

CITIZENSHIP

The Citizenship of Rhodesia Amendment Act, No. 49 of 1972, provides that a child born in Rhodesia of parents who are neither Rhodesian citizens nor *ordinarily resident* in Rhodesia shall not, as was hitherto the case, acquire the right of Rhodesian citizenship by virtue of such birth. Conversely, children born outside Rhodesia of parents who are Rhodesian public servants shall be regarded as citizens of Rhodesia by birth. An amendment to s. 15 of the principal Act, No. 11 of 1970, provides that a person who has shown himself to be disloyal or disaffected towards Rhodesia or has acted in a manner likely to be prejudicial to public safety or order or likely to promote feelings of hostility, contempt, ridicule or disesteem towards any group, section or class of the Rhodesian community may be deprived of his citizenship, if he is a citizen by registration.[6]

AFRICAN AFFAIRS

The African Affairs Amendment Act, No. 40 of 1972, introduces a number of provisions designed to streamline the administration of the principal Act (Cap. 92). It amends the definition of 'district commissioner' so that it includes an 'assistant district commissioner' and thus allows for the appointment of officers who will be able to exercise the same powers as district commissioners so that decisions can be made without delay whenever a district commissioner is not immediately available because he may be absent from his office on other duties. In a similar vein, provincial commissioners may appoint an acting chief in order to avoid a legal hiatus resulting from the death of a chief or his removal from office. In this connection it should be mentioned that s. 17 of the principal Act is repealed and replaced by a new section in terms of which the chief in charge of a tribe who is appointed in terms of s. 4, shall hold office during the pleasure of the President; and may be paid such allowances as may from time to time be prescribed. To prevent serious disputes within a tribe, another new s. 29A gives a chief the categorical power to declare any African to be the senior member of a kraal and by such declaration to appoint him as the head of that kraal, if there is any dispute as to who is the senior member of a kraal. In addition, a chief may at any time remove a kraal head by declaring another African to be the senior member of a kraal in his place. S. 44 of the principal Act which deals with the undermining of authority of officials, chiefs, headmen and certain employees, but does not apply to government employees and in any event covers only certain forms of contempt, has been re-drafted so that now any African 'who makes any statement or does any act or thing whatsoever which is likely to undermine the authority of or bring into disrepute or cotempt any officer or prescribed employee of the Government; or Government Ministry or department; or chief' will be guilty of an offence and liable to a fine up to $400 or to imprisonment up to two years, or both, whilst a similar action which brings into disrepute or contempt a headman or a chief's or a headman's messenger is also an offence, though in such cases only the standard penalties prescribed by the Act will apply.

A further African Affairs Amendment (No. 2) Act, No. 59 of 1972, introduces a new definition into s. 2 of the principal Act, viz. 'African Area' has the same meaning as in the Land Tenure Act, No. 55 of 1969. It amends s. 45 of the principal Act by the deletion of sub-sections 6, 7 and 8 and of paragraph (d) in sub-section (2) and the repeal of sub-section (4) for which a provision is substituted that enables the Secretary for Internal Affairs to prohibit any person from entering or remaining in any Tribal Trust Land or other tribal area if he is of the opinion that the presence of such person there is undesirable in the public interests of Africans living there. S. 46 of the principal Act is repealed and a new section substituted therefore which prohibits the holding of any meeting or gathering of twleve, or more, Africans 'in the African Area, or a tribal area outside the African Area', without the written permission of the district commissioner concerned, provided that no such permission shall be required for meetings held by chiefs in the areas for which they are responsible, members of parliament, duly ordained ministers of religion for bona fide religious purposes and public servants. S. 47 of the principal Act is also repealed and for it a provision is substituted which confers on district commissioners the power to prohibit any person from holding or addressing any meeting at which Africans are present, provided that such a prohibition shall not be imposed, unless the district commissioner has first consulted the chief of the area to which the prohibition relates. The reasons for and the effects of these amendments were explained by the Minister of Internal Affairs on the basis that the previous provisions placed district commissioners and chiefs in the invidious position of being able to exercise control over meetings in Tribal Trust Land or other tribal areas, but not over the whole of the African Area in the district concerned so that it was possible for a convener of a meeting to ignore the prohibition of a meeting in the Tribal Trust Land by holding that meeting in an adjacent Purchase Land Area.[7]

The Africans (Registration and Identification) Amendment Act, No. 48 of 1972, amends s. 5 of the principal Act (Cap. 109) and introduces a new s. 5A to it, the combined effect of which is that African foreigners—i.e. Africans who are not members of tribes ordinarily resident in Rhodesia or who were not born in Rhodesia or who are not Rhodesian citizens—will no longer have the automatic right to be registered and to remain in Rhodesia as they have had in the past, inso far as registration officers may refuse to register or to re-register African foreigners. The new Act further makes provision for the introduction of registration books or identity cards in place of the registration certificates provided for under the previous law. An amendment of s. 21 of the principal Act removes doubts which have hitherto existed as to whether African are compelled to carry their registration certificates on their person and now makes it clear that any African who has not been relieved from the obligation of registering under Part I of the principal Act, or otherwise exempted from the requirement to carry a certificate, book, identity card or permit on his person, must carry such a document with him at all times.

The Vagrancy Amendment Act, No. 51 of 1972, adds to the existing definitions of 'vagrant' in the principal Act (Cap. 49) certain further categories so that the Act now also covers any person who is idle or disorderly or is found within an urban area in which he has no lawful place of residence and is not lawfully employed or self-employed in that area, as well as any person who lives wholly or in part on the earnings of prostitution or other immoral acts. S. 3 of the principal Act is amended so as to give district commissioners *in certain respects* the same powers as magistrates in regard to the administration of the Act and three new sections (8A, 8B and 8C) enable a district commissioner to order a person who in his opinion is a vagrant to depart from and be prohibited from entering any urban area specified by the district commissioner for a period not exceeding two years, if the district commissioner is satisfied that it is desirable in the public interest or in the interests of persons residing in an urban area to make such an order.

The Regional Authorities Act, No. 50 of 1972, provides the framework for the establishment of regional authorities rather than a detailed structure for their operations, because it represents a new and certainly untried measure which requires considerable flexibility in the enabling legislation in which it will be possible to adjust and to some extent experiment.[8] A regional authority has power *inter alia* to acquire property and interest therein either solely or in conjunction with an African Council and to develop it: s. 6. It may make by-laws to regulate its operations, provided that no by-law shall come into force until it has been approved by the Minister of Internal Affairs who may also publish model by-laws that may be adopted by regional authorities. Funds enabling a regional authority to fulfil its functions will be obtained mainly from appropriations for that purpose by the legislature, rates paid to the regional authority and fees paid to it in respect of services provided by it. During the debate the Bill was described as non-racial, but for the time being it would seem that it is likely to make a greater impact on the development in the African Area than in the European Area.[9]

The Local Government Amendment Act, No. 9 of 1972, introduces a new s. 67A into the principal Act (Cap. 124) which is designed to prevent the increasing proliferation of individual by-laws for African townships. It enables the Minister for Local Government to 'make standard regulations for the good rule, government, control, use and occupation of any African township area' which shall apply to every designated African township area, unless their operation is suspended in certain circumstances.

CENSORSHIP

The Censorship and Entertainments Control Amendment Act, No. 52 of 1972, amends the principal Act, No. 37 of 1967, by authorising the censorship board to declare as prohibited any publication that has previously been or will be declared as undesirable. The reason for this amendment is that possession of an undesirable publication is not a criminal offence and a merely undesirable publication or record cannot be retained by the board, but must be returned to its owner, if so requested.

S. 13(6) now provides that the board shall not approve any public entertainment which it considers likely to be associated with breaches of the peace, disorderly or immoral behaviour or abuses relating to the consumption of alcohol or drugs, so as to prevent 'entertainment, of itself innocuous' which may lead to such abuses. Finally, a new s. 17A is introduced which empowers the Minister of Internal Affairs to direct (by the issue of a certificate) that proceedings before the censorship appeal board or before any court shall be held *in camera* and that no information relating to the decision, order or proceedings concerned other than the actual result thereof shall in any manner be brought to the notice of the public.

PUBLIC INTERNATIONAL LAW

The Privileges and Immunities Act, No. 13 of 1972, repeals the Immunities and Privileges Act, No. 31 of 1956, and all subsidiary legislation made thereunder. Ss. 3-5 provide that Art. 1, 22-24 and 27-40 of the Vienna Convention on Diplomatic Relations and Arts. 1, 31-33, 35, 39, 41, 43-54, 57, 58, 60-62, 66 and 71 of the Vienna Convention on Consular Relations shall have the force of law in Rhodesia. The privileges and immunities of members of international or regional organisations and those of representatives attending international conferences appear from ss. 7-8, whilst s. 9 envisages that the President may confer such privileges, immunities and facilities as appear to be desirable upon judges and officers of any international court and also on the parties and their legal representatives in proceedings before such court. S. 11 provides that no law or condition in a title deed which prohibits the occupation of immovable property by persons belonging to any particular racial group shall be construed to prohibit the occupation of such property by any person and his family on whom diplomatic or other privileges and immunities have been conferred in terms of the Act.

STATE PRIVILEGE

In *Association of Rhodesian Industries and Others* v. *Brookes and Another*[10] the plaintiffs were two associations which had been appointed agents of the Minister of Commerce and Industry and been charged with the duty of distributing and allocating among industrialists and merchants in Rhodesia such foreign exchange entitlements as the Minister might decide to make available to their respective sectors of the economy for the purpose of importing goods. The defendants were the editor and publisher, respectively, of a financial journal in which an article had appeared alleging that the plaintiffs were guilty of corruption or negligence in the distribution and allocation of foreign currency. The defendants had obtained a discovery order against the plaintiffs directing them to disclose all documents having a bearing on their defence. They objected to this order in reliance on an affidavit in which the Minister claimed that the 'giving or production of evidence or documents in respect of all periods after economic sanctions on Rhodesia' would be harmful to the public interest and national security and that it was, therefore, 'vital to avoid the disclosure of even the most minor items of information concerning Rhodesia's trade'. The defendants contended that the Minister had, on a number of occasions, himself divulged certain information on trade matters so that his objection could not be regarded as *bona fide*. Macaulay, J., did not accept this argument as it was possible that the documents in this case might contain information other than that disclosed by the Minister, and the disclosure of which would be prejudicial to the national interest. However, the Minister was not entitled to claim a 'blanket' privilege as he had done, but was obliged to apply his mind to each document in order to arrive at a proper decision as to whether, or not, he was justified in claiming state privilege on the grounds alleged to exist in his affidavit. The plaintiffs were, therefore, ordered to make further and fuller discovery than they had previously made and to produce all documents 'save those for which state privilege . . .may be claimed by the Minister concerned, after he has seen and considered them and deponed to such in an affidavit . . .'

REVENUE LAW

The Finance Act (No. 20 of 1972) adopts the Budget Proposals[11] which contain no fundamental changes in the Rhodesian revenue law, although it should be mentioned that the tax provisions relating to pension and benefit funds were amended to an extent to which the specialist in this field might wish to refer. Converseley, it will be of general interest to point out here that the low rates of taxation remain the same as in previous years.

The attitude of the courts towards fiscal claims is illustrated in a number of cases decided in 1972. In *H.* v. *Commissioner of Taxes*[12] the taxpayer and his wife were virtually the sole shareholders of four trading companies. In order to avoid undistributed profits tax they had formed a (further) parent company and two subsidiary companies. The parent company derived its income solely from its two subsidiary companies whose sole sources of income were the four trading companies. In this manner it was possible for each of the seven companies to retain one-third of their profits without attracting undistributed profits tax. The Commissioner decided to 'cut the pipeline where it left the trading companies' and to treat the dividends declared by the trading companies on the basis that they had been paid directly to the taxpayer who objected to this method of assessment on the grounds that he could have left the undistributed profits intact and declared no dividends, with the result that there would have been no dividends from the parent company which would be liable to tax and that to tax the total profits in the manner it had been done, the Commissioner had in fact taxed certain portions of the taxpayer's income twice over. The court held that the Commissioner was entitled 'to cut the pipeline as he had done' and that there had been no double taxation since 'the dividends had been paid from the undistributed profits standing to the credit of the parent company, and not from the profits coming from the trading companies'.

In *H. Ltd.* v. *Commissioner of Taxes*[13] the Commissioner had disallowed an assessed loss carried forward for several years on the ground that a change of shareholding in the taxpayer-company had been effected mainly for the purpose of taking advantage of the assessed loss. As is always the case in such situations, the decision must depend on the particular facts, because whenever there is a change of shareholding in a company with an assessed loss, those purchasing the shares will normally take the assessed loss into account when determining the value of the shares. In this sense, an assessed loss is invariably an asset of the company concerned. 'But that does not necessarily prove that the change in the shareholding has been effected solely or mainly in connection with a scheme for taking advantage of the assessed loss.' However, the onus which the taxpayer has to discharge in such cases is always a heavy one and in this case he had failed to discharge it.

The vexed question whether profit made on the sale of an asset attracts tax, or not, was considered in *T*. v. *Commissioner of Taxes*[14] where a one-man company had been formed by its sole beneficial owner as an investment company, 'but not so as to become a "dealer" in shares'. The intention of the controlling shareholder was that the shares in the investment company should on his death be transferred to a trust for the benefit of his children. When the investment company sold some of the shares in companies held by it as investments 'in order to obtain a greater spread of investment and a balanced portfolio', the court held that the profit made from such sales was not subject to tax because the mere fact that a profit is made in circumstances such as these does not prove that the dominant intention for a transaction is the making of a profit, or even that the possibility of making a profit induces a sale of the investments.

A different conclusion was reached in *D*. v. *Commissioner of Taxes*[15] where the taxpayer had acquired certain mining claims with a view to selling them at a profit. When he found it impossible to dispose of them, as intended, he decided to develop them over a number of years. Having done so, he received an offer for the claims and sold them at a profit. The court upheld the Commissioner's assessment on the ground that, despite the change in the taxpayer's intention to develop the claims and hold them as a capital asset, their eventual sale was nevertheless 'the culmination of a scheme of profit making'.[16]

The Customs and Excise Amendment Act, No. 19 of 1972, contains various tariff amendments. The Customs and Excise (No. 2) Amendment Act, No. 43 of 1972, deals with the seizure and forfeiture of goods smuggled into Rhodesia and of vehicles or other means of transport used for that purpose. It confirms the attitude of the courts[17] that goods which the Controller of Customs has seized shall be released to their rightful owner if it is established the the owner was unaware of the use of his property in contravention of the law. The new rules governing seizure, forfeiture and penalties for offences under the Act are very strict and have benn justified on the grounds that they are necessary to protect the economy and the public revenue.[18]

COMMUNICATIONS
The Road Motor Transportation Act, No. 1 of 1972, introduces new provisions for the control of vehicles used for the carriage of passengers and haulage of goods for hire or reward. It revises and consolidates the previous law which was hitherto contained in the Roads and Road Traffic Act.[20] It distinguishes between public service vehicles which are defined as motor vehicles or trailers 'for the carriage or haulage of passengers or

goods or both for hire or reward on one or more occasions', including so-called contract goods vehicles which are let for hire to be used for the haulage of goods, and contract cars which are motor cars designed to carry not more than eight persons including the driver. But in any event, no carriage for hire or reward may be undertaken in any vehicle which is not covered by a road service permit and it may be noted here that if a person has been charged with a contravention of the Act in this respect, the onus rests on him to prove that he did not carry the passengers or goods in question for hire or reward, if *prima facie* grounds exist to suspect that the conveyance was for hire or reward. An important change has been introduced in regard to the issue of road service permits which was previously the function of a road service board whose deicisions were subject to the judicial control of the High Court and which was obliged to hold open meetings. The issue of permits now lies in the hands of a Controller of Road Motor Transportation who will have an entirely administrative discretion subject only to the guide lines established by the Act which require him to consider: the possible effect of the issue of a road permit on existing rail services, the interest of the public and whether the service in respect of which application is made, could reasonably be said to constitute an extension of an existing service or whether it could be combined with, or incorporated in, an existing service, provided that the renewal of a permit shall not be refused only because the service already established may have an adverse effect on existing rail services. The Controller is not obliged to hold public meetings, but his decisions are subject to review by a Road Motor Transport Review Authority. The decisions of this Authority, however, are 'final and without appeal'. In addition, th Act makes the acquisition of an existing transport business and the transfer of a permit subject to the approval of the Minister of Transport and Power and provides for the withdrawal of permits in the event of the holder having been convicted of certain offences. A special feature of the Act is the provision for the issue of permits in respect of Farmers' Syndicate Vehicles—i.e. vehicles operated by a group of farmers for the transportation of their produce and the collection of goods required by them in connection with their farming operations.[21]

In terms of the Emergency Powers (Transport of Passengers and Goods) (Amendment) Regulations, 1972 (No. 2) and (No. 3) (GN Nos. 562 and 907 of 1972) the Minister may '(n)otwithstanding anything to the contrary contained in the principal Act or these Regulations', make provisions for the carriage or haulage of goods generally, if it appears to him that services for such carriage or haulage are not available or being provided to meet the needs of a community in any area or in the whole of Rhodesia.

The Rhodesia Railways Act, No. 41 of 1972, was introduced to consolidate and to some extent amend the existing legislation which was contained in more than thirty different statutes, the most important of which was the Rhodesia Railways Act of 1949 (Cap. 287). Such innovations as have been introduced are mainly aimed at greater flexibility in the administration of the railways and the only aspect which is of special interest to the lawyer in the present context is a provision which, whilst it preserves the existing and far-reaching powers to acquire and occupy land if it is needed for railway purposes, requires the railway administration to pay a fair price for the land itself and not as previously merely for the improvements made by the owner on that land.

Attention is also drawn in this context to the Radio Communications Services Act (No. 45 of 1972) and the Postal and Telecommunications Services Act (No. 46 of 1972), but they do not here require detailed consideration.[22]

Although it contains mainly criminal law provisions, it seems appropriate to refer at this stage to the Aircraft (Offences) Act, No. 7 of 1972, which is designed to cover all forms of what is commonly known as air piracy, including acts committed whilst an aircraft is on the ground, if they are likely to jeopardize the safety of passengers or crew of the aircraft when in flight. The Act has extra-territorial force in so far as it applies to every Rhodesian aircraft, wherever it may be, and to all foreign aircraft *en route* to or from Rhodesia. It imposes the death penalty or life imprisonment for any act done with the intention to cause damage or prejudice the safety of an aircraft with intent to kill, up to fourteen years imprisonment in respect of any act designed to prejudice the safety of an aircraft, and for other offences a fine of up to $5 000 or up to five years imprisonment, or both.

MISCELLANEOUS ACTS (PUBLIC LAW)

The Old Age Pensions Amendment Act, No. 11 of 1972, eliminates the differentiation between maximum pensions payable to Europeans and Asian or Coloured persons. However, it confers upon the Director of Social Welfare a discretion to take into account the individual needs and circumstances of an old age pensioner in the determination of the amount of the pension that he should receive. But the intention of the Act is not that a pensioner should receive more than he had normally earned during his working life so that 'the pension to be paid to persons customarily living at low standards will be calculated to equate to these their normal standards, prior to their reaching pensionable age.'[23]

Three Acts deal with the control of professional organizations and standards: the Land Surveyors Registration Amendment Act, No. 5 of 1972, which is concerned particularly with the alleviation of the shortage of qualified persons in this field; the Medical, Dental and Allied Professions Amendment Act, No. 25 of 1972, which extends *inter alia* the financial powers of the Medical Council and its disciplinary powers by enabling it to order a practitioner who has been found guilty of unprofessional conduct to pay the costs of the enquiry into his conduct and of the proceedings against him, in the hope that this provision will discourage vexatious and expensive delaying tactics; the Correspondence Colleges Amendment Act, No. 56 of 1972, enables the Minister of Education to exempt universities which provide correspondence courses from the control of the Act and lays down certain minimum standards of conduct and service with which correspondence colleges will have to comply.

The Education Act, No. 54 of 1972, regulates 'the education of persons who are not Africans' and during its debate it was stressed that it did not intend to introduce fundamental changes, but that it followed 'in all major respects the principles of the existing legislation'.[24] The new Act emphasizes the need for discipline and specifically gives power to heads of schools to enforce standards of dress and appearance. The establishment of independent schools is now subject to the approval of the Secretary for Education. So far an individual or organization which intended to establish an independent school was compelled to notify the Secretary of his intention and to supply him with certain information at least one month before the school was to open, but the Minister of Education had no power to prevent the opening of the school, even if the Secretary was not satisfied that the school would comply with minimum conditions and standards regarded as desirable. Now the period between the notification of intention to establish a school and the opening of that school has been extended to three months and the Secretary has the right to impose conditions with which the school is required to comply, or to veto its opening altogether. Provision is, of course, also made for the closing of independent schools, if the Minister is not satisfied that such a school complies with any of the conditions, subject to which it has been registered. As far as the right of independent schools is concerned to admit pupils irrespective of race or creed, it has been preserved in principle and if the pupils 'are preponderantly persons who are not Africans' the Minister 'shall cause the independent school to be registered', provided, of course, that it complies with the normal requirements as to the existence of satisfactory school premises and hostels, efficient and suitable instruction and appropriate qualifications of its principal and staff. It thus seems that where the majority of pupils are Europeans, the Minister has no discretion in regard to the registration of the school, whereas if this requirement is not fulfilled, he has a discretion as to whether the school should be registered, or not. The Act provides for the establishment of a tribunal to which a person aggrieved by a refusal to permit the conduct of an independent school or the withdrawal of permission which has previously been granted may refer his case for review. The tribunal shall make a full and impartial enquiry in each case and thereafter make recommendations to the Secretary or Minister of Education who shall give effect to such recommendations.[25] Freedom of religious instruction is guaranteed and no pupil will be required to attend religious classes if his parents object.

S. 9 of the General Laws Amendment Act, No. 57 of 1972, amends ss. 256 and 277 of the Municipal Act (Cap. 125) which deal with the provisions of various designated facilities established by a municipal council (such as sports grounds and swimming pools) for the use of separate races or of all races and which are always subject to the proviso that where separate facilities are provided for separate races, they must be established in a manner which caters equitably for the needs of each such race. In order to eliminate difficulties which have been encountered by municipal councils in the interpretation of the provisions as worded, the Act is now amended by the deletion from the proviso in s. 256(7) of Cap. 125 of the word 'equitably' and the substitution therefor of the words 'in a manner authorized by the Minister on such basis as he considers to be equitable', and a similar amendment has been introduced into paragraph 60A of s. 277 of Cap. 125, where the words 'so, however, that such conveniences shall be afforded equitably according to the needs of each such race' are deleted and substituted by the words 'or for particular races: provided that the Minister shall not approve any by-laws . . . unless he is satisfied that the by-laws require the provision of separate facilities on a basis which he considers to be equitable according to the needs of each such race'

JUDICIAL AND LEGAL SYSTEM

COURTS AND TRIBUNALS

The Housing Standards Control Act, No. 29 of 1972, establishes every magistrates court as a housing court for every authority area within the area of its jurisdiction, provided that the jurisdiction of the court shall be exercised only by a senior magistrate or a provincial magistrate[26] and that it shall select from a list of persons nominated by the Minister of Justice one or two assessors who have skill and experience in any matter which may call for consideration in the proceedings brought in such court. Proceedings must be conducted in public and the parties may appear either in person or be represented by a legal practitioner. The court shall have all the usual powers of summoning and examining witnesses on oath, calling for the production of documents and witnesses shall be entitled to the same privileges and immunities as they would be when giving evidence at a civil trial. An appeal from the court's decision lies to the Appellate Division of the High Court. An interesting rule is contained in s. 9 of the Act which prevents the housing court from adjourning its proceedings for a period of more than three weeks. It will be concerned with applications from municipalities, town and rural councils and other local authorities for the issue of repair, demolition or closure orders, relating to buildings within the area of the local authority making the application. The purpose of the Act as a whole is to enable local authorities to deal with housing conditions which could result in slums. A repair order will, therefore, be competent when the court accepts the local authority's contention that a building is of an unsatisfactory standard but can be raised or restored at a reasonable cost to a satisfactory standard. A demolition order will be competent if such a building cannot be raised or restored at a reasonable cost, whilst a closure order would be appropriate if a building should not be occupied in view of its unsatisfactory condition, although it ought not to be immediately demolished. In making any order the court shall have regard *inter alia* to the age, character, value and locality of the building concerned, the cost necessary to raise it to a satisfactory standard in relation to its value after the completion of such work and, in case of a demolition order in particular, the effect which the demolition may have on any adjoining property. In addition to the aforementioned orders, the housing court shall have the power to make an abatement order with a view to prevent overcrowding of dwellings. It would seem that the court can only issue orders in respect of individual buildings, since special provision is made for the establishment of clearance areas, in so far as an authority which considers that there are a number of buildings of an unsatisfactory standard and that the most appropriate method of dealing with them would be the acquisition and clearance of the whole of the land on which such buildings are situate, must make application to the Minister of Local Government and Housing for the appointment of a board of investigation which will be required to report on the desirability of the proposed clearance of a whole area. Such board will consist of three members, with an advocate, attorney or magistrate of not less than ten years' standing as chairman, and two other members, one of whom shall be a medical officer of health or have similar qualifications.

The African Law and Tribal Courts Amendment Act, No. 42 of 1972, amends ss. 19 and 20 of the principal Act, No. 24 of 1969, which enable a tribal chief's court to order the removal of an African from land in the area of the jurisdiction of that court. So far such order could be enforced only after alternative land had been provided for the African in respect of whom the removal order was to be issued and to whom, in addition, compensation had to be paid for any improvements. These requirements had made it virtually impossible to implement a removal order. The amendments now eliminate the requirements of the provisionof alternative land and of the payment of compensation, although they still authorize an order 'if the chief's court deems fit' which will require the person taking over the land to pay such compensation as the court may fixt to the person who has been ordered to leave that land. If such an order is not made or appears to be inadequate, the district commissioner may refer the case back to the chief's court for further consideration.

The Advocates Amendment Act, No. 55 of 1972, amends s. 2 of the principal Act, No. 15 of 1969, in that it recognizes the BL and LLB degrees of the University of Rhodesia as qualifying examinations for admission as an advocate. Two new sections (7A and 7B) provide that a board of examiners shall require an applicant for admission to the Bar to appear before it in order that he may be tested on his proficiency in spoken English and it also may require the applicant to pass a test in written English for that purpose. Notwithstanding the provisions of s. 6 of the principal Act (which lay down the qualifications for admission) rules of court may provide that an applicant who has not *inter alia* obtained the BL and LLB degrees of the University of Rhodesia, shall be required to pass an examination on the ethics of the profession, unless he is a member of a class of persons specified in the rules of court as being exempted therefrom.

JUDICIAL CONTROL OF TRIBUNALS

In *Bulawayo Asian and Coloured Association* v. *Liquor Licensing Board and Another*[27] the Liquor Licensing Board had renewed unconditionally the liquor licence of a country hotel conducted on land leased from the government and administered by the government in terms of the Rhodes Estates Amendment Act (Cap. 305) and the Rhodes' Will Amendment Act (cap. 309). In so doing it had dismissed an objection lodged by the appellant to the effect that the licence should only be renewed on the condition that the licensee of the hotel would in future serve Asian and Coloured persons with liquor whom, in the past, he had arbitrarily refused to serve 'on no other ground, apparently, than that they happen(ed) to be Asian and Coloured'. Before the Board it had been argued 'that, in terms of Rhodes' will, the licensee had no right to refuse to serve Asian and Coloured persons, and if the lease . . . purported to give him that right, then it was *ultra vires* the will, as that will is now reflected in . . . various statutory measures.' Beadle, C.J., (with whom MacDonald, J.P., and Lewis, J.A., concurred) did not think that this argument was justified and that the real consideration in the case was whether it could be said that the public interest was served by permitting the licensee to impose these conditions'. In coming to the conclusion that the licensee was not justified in excluding Asian and Coloured persons from the bar facilities in the hotel, the fact that there was no other hotel in the vicinity at which such persons could obtain liquor was of vital importance and the learned chief justice expressly refrained from deciding whether the same considerations would apply to a town hotel where numerous alternative facilities were provided. However, he stressed that where rights and privileges are granted to the public in a statute there must be no racial discrimination in the administration of that statute, unless such discrimination is authorized either specifically or by implication and, in so far as the public interest must be taken into account in every decision involving the grant or refusal of a liquor licence, it is not sufficient to take into account one section of the public only. Therefore, a liquor licensee does not have an unfettered right to refuse admission to persons or classes of persons on any arbitrary ground which he may choose. In so far as the Board had apparently relied on the provisions of the Land Tenure Act, No. 55 of 1969, when it referred to the fact that '(t)he multi-racial aspect of the hotel are (sic!) controlled under another statute', it did not appreciate that the Land Tenure Act does not distinguish between Asians, Coloureds and Whites, since in s. 2 it defines Europeans as persons who are not Africans. Whilst the learned chief justice made it perfectly plain that his remarks were confined to the facts of this case and must not be extended beyond these facts, he concluded his judgement by saying saying that the 'arbitrary and capricious action' by which the licensee deprived the Asian and Coloured people of their right to obtain liquor on his premises 'on purely racial grounds' amounted to 'racial discrimination of the worst type and (that) the Board, in the circumstances of this case, should have set its face against it.' The appeal was accordingly allowed to the extent that the licence was renewed on condition that in serving liquor the licensee will not discriminate against Asian or Coloured persons purely on the grounds of their race or colour.

That the application for membership to a club is governed by different considerations from those which may influence the grant of licences, even if that club controls their issue, was made clear by the Appellate Division when it reversed the decision of Goldin, J., in *Troake* v. *Salisbury Bookmakers' Licensing Committee and Another.*[28] The appellant had applied for membership to the Salisbury Tattersalls Club which was a condition precedent for an application for a bookmaker's licence. In practice, the Salisbury Bookmakers' Licensing Committee controlled the membership of the club, as well as the issue of such licences.[29] The Committee had turned down the appellant's application for membership to the club on the ground that the number of bookmakers in Salisbury was adequate and that an increase in their number might even have an adverse effect. Goldin, J., had refused to interfere with this decision. On appeal it was held that in considering factors which might, or might not, be relevant when the appellant eventually made his application for the issue of a licence, the Committee had 'jumped the gun' when it allowed itself to be influenced by these factors in its decision on the appellant's application for membership of the club.

In *Landmark Construction (Pvt) Ltd* v. *Tselentis*[30] a dispute concerning a building contract had been submitted to arbitration. The parties were at daggers drawn and to conduct the proceedings in the presence of both of them was, to say the least, extremely difficult. In addition, one of the parties displayed 'extraordinary laxity' and the arbitrator was compelled to put him on terms in order to submit certain essential information. Eventually it was agreed that the arbitrator should obtain such further evidence as he might require only in the presence of the party from whom he would require additional information. He acted in terms of this agreement, but failed to give the absent party an opportunity of leading further evidence or to comment by way of argument thereon. An award made on this basis was set aside by Beck, J., as being contrary to natural justice, even though the integrity and impartiality of the arbitrator was beyond question.

An interesting illustration of a court's power to control administrative actions through the criminal law is provided by *S.* v. *Mtoko Hotel (Pvt) Ltd*[31] where the appellant-company had been convicted of failing to comply with a demolition order made under s. 17(1)(a) of the by-laws of Rural Councils (Model) (Building) By-laws (published in GN 965 of 1969) which authorizes a council to require the owner of a building 'to repair, alter, remove or demolish a building . . . or part thereof' if such building, in the opinion of the council, is 'insanitary, dangerous, unhealthy, objectionable or unsuitable'. In this case the council had ordered the demolition or removal of certain buildings because they were in a 'dilapidated and unsightly condition' and thus clearly did not refer to one of the grounds which justified the making of such an order. Consequently, it was not at all clear that the members of the council had applied their minds to the requirements of the by-laws. Therefore, a general reference to s. 17(1)(a) thereof was not sufficient and the conviction and sentence were accordingly set aside.

CRIMINAL LAW

Only one new statutory provision was enacted during the period here surveyed which requires specific consideration under this heading. The Miscellaneous Offences Amendment Act, No. 24 of 1972, introduces a new s. 13A into the principal Act (No. 18 of 1964) and amends ss. 247, 255 and 255A of the Criminal Procedure and Evidence Act (Cap. 231). The practical effect of these amendments is that a person who is found in possession of any goods of any description in regard to which there is a reasonable suspicion that they have been stolen and is unable to give a satisfactory account of such possesion, shall be guilty of an offence and liable to the penalties which may be imposed on a conviction for theft. Similarly, a person who acquires or receives (otherwise than at a public sale) stolen goods without having reasonable cause for believing that the goods are the property of the person from whom he acquires them, shall likewise be guilty of an offence and liable to the penalties which may be imposed on a conviction for receiving stolen property, knowing it to have been stolen.

MURDER

The elements of the crime of murder were considered in *S. v. Howard*.[32] The accused had killed the deceased by stabbing him in the heart with a knife in a manner which indicated that he had not been content with simply driving the knife into the deceased's chest once and either let it go or simply withdrawn it. It was argued that he was under the influence of liquor and that he had been 'provoked by the deceased's fisticuffs and sneers'. The court found that the liquor consumed by the accused 'played no more than a very minor role' so that he was capable of forming an intention to kill and that he did in fact form such intention. However, Beck, J., pointed out that according to the trend of Rhodesian decisions and unlike the South African decisions 'a further question must be posed, despite the finding that the accused had, subjectively considered, the intention to kill. This further question is whether, objectively considered, the provocation was such that the hypothetical reasonable man, placed in the same circumstances as the accused, would have lost his self-control' to such an extent that he would 'have yielded to a purposeful desire to kill his provoker.' This would only be rarely the case, whilst an impulsive and instinctive reaction could probably be more easily assumed. But a reasonable man would not draw a knife and deliberately plunge it into the chest of a man (whom he had first overpowered) with the intention of killing him. Therefore, the accused was found guilty of murder, but with extenuating circumstances.

In *S. v. Misheck*[33] the accused was charged with being an accessory after the fact to the crime of murder. The State established that he had assisted the alleged murderer to hide the body of the deceased. However, the principal criminal had not yet been brought to trial and the evidence against the accused in this case did not disclose that the death of the person whose body he had helped to conceal was the result of an unlawful act (let alone murder) or that the accused believed that death had been caused as a result of such act. In these circumstances, he could not be convicted as an accessory after the fact, but only of despoiling or violating a dead body which is itself an offence.

FRAUD AND EXTORTION

In *S. v. Reggis*[34] the accused had told his employer that his child had been killed and his wife been injured in a riot and asked his employer for a loan of $40 and a day's leave in order to bury the child. The employer had believed the accused and granted his requests. In fact, there was no truth whatsoever in the accused's representations. It was held that he was guilty of fraud as the employer had suffered prejudice and that in such circumstances it 'begs the question to reflect upon whether or not the (employer's) rights *as a creditor* (which is what the fraud induced him to become) would have been any better had the stated purpose for which the loan was allegedly required not been false.' This decision may be compared with the judgement in *S. v. Munyani*[35] which dealt with the elements of a crime of extortion in Roman-Dutch law in which the advantage of the extortioner is emphasized as against the prejudice of his victim which is the essential consideration in fraud. The accused had appealed against a conviction for extortion on the following facts: he had assisted a friend (who was also convicted, but apparently did not appeal) in threatening a woman with serious assaults if she did not provide the friend with a letter to the effect that the friend's wife had committed adultery. The friend wanted to use the letter as evidence in divorce proceedings against his wife. The letter which was couched in clumsy terms, had in fact been filed with the clerk of the court when the whole matter came to light. The case against the appellant was, of course, that he was a *socius criminis* and depended on whether the actions of the friend amounted to extortion. It was argued that extortion requires the intention of obtaining a *patrimonial* advantage, such as 'money, property, or some valuable thing'.

After an extensive examination of the Roman-Dutch authorities and of recent South African case law Beadle, C.J., concluded that all that could be said with certainty was that the extortioner 'must intend to obtain some advantage or benefit from the intimidation' (so that intimidation simply to satisfy some sadistic whim would not be sufficient), but there was no clear statement as to 'the nature of that advantage or benefit' on which the authorities differed. Taking into account that extortion has two principal ingredients, i.e. the intimidation and the advantage, the learned chief justice thought that 'the advantage extorted need not necessarily be a proprietary one, or one measurable in terms of money' and that the extortioner's belief that he will secure an advantage for himself is sufficient, even if he is mistaken in this belief or if the anticipated advantage proves to be valueless to anybody else. In other words, the test must be subjective—it is the assumed value to the extortioner which is decisive and 'not the objective value of the advantage extorted'. He accordingly dismissed the appeal and MacDonald, J.P., agreed with him. Lewis, J.A., dissented and preferred the authorities which emphasized that extortion is associated with 'greed of gain' and also felt that a court 'must be careful not to extend this crime beyond its limits according to the Roman-Dutch law'. Admittedly, it is sufficient that the thing extorted need only have a potential value, but if one accepts as sufficient the extortion of something which is 'clearly worthless to the knowledge of the victim . . . one goes beyond the limits of the crime as defined by the weight of authority in Roman-Dutch law'. The learned judge of appeal would, therefore, have quashed the conviction and on this basis he was prepared to accept that e.g. 'threatening to expose a woman's adultery, but without obtaining any material benefit from the threats', would not be punishable as extortion so that 'there would appear to be a lacuna in the law'

TRAFFIC OFFENCES

In *S.* v. *Manzira*[36] the appellant had been convicted of unlawfully carrying passengers in a vehicle not constructed for the carriage of passengers in contravention of s. 235(1) of the Roads and Road Traffic Act (Cap. 289) and the trial court had ordered suspension of his licence for eighteen months. On appeal it was held that the offence committed by the appellant was not related to the manner of driving and, therefore, it was not 'an offence in connection with the driving of a motor vehicle' within the meaning of s. 190(1) of the Act (which authorizes the suspension of driving licences) so that the order of suspension was incompetent.

In *S.* v. *Munks*[37] it was held that a driver is guilty of the offence colloquially referred to as 'failing to stop' if he knows that he has been involved in an accident, even if he believes that no damage has been caused as a result thereof. Once it has become apparent to him that other persons have been in danger of injury or death, then such persons have been 'involved' in his accident and '(a)lthough he may not know he has, in fact, struck such . . . persons, . . . at the same time, without stopping to investigate, he cannot be sure that he has not', and it is then that the duty to stop and investigate the position arises.

ASPECTS OF SENTENCING

In *S.* v. *Gadzi*[38] the Appellate Division thought that since it was held in *R.* v. *Thompson*[39] only in 1969 that a first offender should not be sent to prison for drunken driving if no great injury had been caused to person or property, conditions had changed sufficiently to justify a departure from that decision so that in bad cases of drunken driving and in the absence of special circumstances, sentences of imprisonment without the option of a fine will henceforth be confirmed on appeal or review, 'notwithstanding the fact that the offender may have a clear record and . . . that no serious injury is caused to persons or property'. Another case in which a sentence of imprisonment was imposed upon a first offender 'of hitherto good character and reputation' is *S.* v. *Beach*[40] where the appellant had told the receptionist of an hotel on the telephone that there was a bomb in the hotel. The message was a hoax and the reason for it was that the accused and his friends who were 'running short of beer money (had thought that it) would be funny if we rang up and said there was a bomb . . . and when everybody left, we drank their beers'. The accused had pleaded guilty to a charge under the appropriate section of the Posts and Telegraph Act, No. 20 of 1954 (Fed), and been sentenced to four months' imprisonment with hard labour of which three months were suspended for three years on certain conditions, without the option of a fine. This sentence was confirmed on appeal because if such conduct would not be suppressed, it could lead to warnings of the existence of real bombs being ignored.

When, however, the imposition of a fine as an alternative to imprisonment is justified, then the amount of the fine imposed must be such as to 'constitute a real option' and the accused must be in a position to pay it, although this 'does not mean that it must be within the immediate means of an offender, although this will usually be the case where the offence is not a serious one.' In *S.* v. *Manwere*[41] the appellant had been convicted of contraventions of the Gold Trade Act (Cap. 202) and been sentenced to a fine of $100 or, in default of payment, to six months' imprisonment with hard labour. It was clear that the accused could not afford to pay the fine, even in the long run. By the time the appeal was heard, the accused had already served 101 days' imprisonment so that it was no longer possible to offer him a real option of a fine and the Appellate Division, therefore, altered the sentence to the period of imprisonment which the appellant had already undergone. It emphasized, however, that the trial court had erred when it suggested 'that a fine which is related to the offender's capacity to pay may in certain circumstances make "a mockery of the sentence". A fine of $10 will punish a poor man no less severey than a fine of $100 will punish a person of moderate means. Inability to grasp this point and to have the courage to give effect to it can only result in grave injustice to poorer sections of the community . . .'

In *S. v. S. Sibanda* the accused had been convicted of being in possession of twelve ounces of dagga and cultivating nineteen dagga plants, and sentenced to two and a half years' imprisonment with hard labour. In *S. v. O. Sibanda* the accused had been convicted of cultivating fifty-seven plants (which would yield three pounds) of dagga and been sentenced to three years' imprisonment with hard labour. In *S. v. Yotamu* the accused had been sentenced to two years' imprisonment with hard labour, of which six months were supsended, after he had been convicted of two counts of procuring aproximately one pound of dagga for other persons.[42] Reviewing these sentences, the Court pointed out that the cultivation of dagga was a more serious offence than the possession of dagga and should attract more severe punishment than the latter, despite the fact that it was far easier to detect the cultivation of dagga than its possession. Having regard to sentences imposed in the past, the Court then suspended one-half of the prison sentences in the two *Sibanda* cases for three years, but confirmed the sentence in *Yotamu's* case, thus holding by implication that procuring a drug is more serious than either its cultivation or possession.

In *S. v. Ngwenya*[43] the appellant had been convicted of being in possession of offensive weapons in contravention of s. 36(1)(*a*) of the Law and Order (Maintenance) Act (Cap. 39) and sentenced to ten years' imprisonment with hard labour. He had been living abroad and connected with armed incursions into Rhodesia, but apparently returned of his own free will to Rhodesia where 'he frankly admitted all he had done'. Against this background the Appellate Division reduced the trial court's sentence to six years' imprisonment with hard labour, of which three years were suspended on certain conditions. In the judgement the following general observations were made: although the offence with which the appellant had been charged was an extremely serious one, the fact that he had a complete change of heart and wished to reform was important. Moreover, it must be borne in mind 'that people in the position in which the appellant found himself might genuinely wish to reform . . . and it is in the interests of the State that they should be encouraged to do so, but heavy deterrent sentences, whilst they might deter others from committing the particular offence, are also extremely likely to deter other persons in a position like the one in which the appellant found himself from having a change of heart and from surrendering themselves to the authorities in the manner in which the appellant did.'

In *S. v. Abraham*[44] the appellant had been convicted of making a false declaration in contravention of the Immigration Act, No. 43 of 1966, when he entered Rhodesia. Subsequently, and whilst in Rhodesia, he had been convicted of contravening the Dangerous Drugs Regulations and sentenced to three months' imprisonment, suspended conditionally. He appealed against the severity of the sentence imposed upon him under the Immigration Act: two months' imprisonment wih hard labour. The Appellate Division agreed that this was a severe sentence, but refused to interfere with it, taking into account the appellant's conviction under the Dangerous Drugs Regulations subsequent to his arrival in Rhodesia. The question of principle to be considered was whether a conviction for an offence which had been committed *after* the offence for which the appellant had now been brought to trial could properly be taken into consideration for the purpose of assessing the sentence which was appropriate for the earlier offence. The Court thought that it could do so because the subsequent offence 'had a direct bearing on his character and upon the *bona fides* of the excuse he had tendered in mitigation for making a false declaration, i.e. that he desired to turn over a new leaf and start a new life in Rhodesia'.

The serious view which the courts take of stock theft appears from the observations in *S. v. Farirepi*[45] where it was pointed out that a sentence of twelve months' imprisonment with hard labour imposed on a first offender for the theft of one beast is not excessive, unless there are special mitigating factors which might justify a lesser sentence.

In *S. v. Langton*[46] the Appellate Division confirmed that it was permissible to impose upon an accused a determinate sentence of imprisonment and to pronounce at the same time the indeterminate sentence declaring the accused an habitual criminal, provided that these sentences are imposed for separate offences. However, an accused who has already been sentenced to reduced diet and solitary confinement should not be sentenced to a second period of dietary punishment at the same time, unless there are special circumstances which may justify this course in a particular case and, especially, dietary punishment should certainly not be imposed for the commission of an offence which has led to the declaration of the accused as an habitual criminal.

CONTRACT

MISTAKE

In *Landsbergen v. Van der Walt*[47] the plaintiff claimed that he had been granted and exercised an option to purchase a certain property which he alleged to have leased from the defendant. The defendant refused to transfer the property to the plaintiff on the ground that the contract of lease which contained the option had been concluded between him and the plaintiff's wife who had been given the option on certain conditions with which she had failed to comply. The Court found that the agreement of lease had been concluded with the plaintiff and that the option had also been granted to him. *In any event,* this was a case in which the identity of the party to whom the lease, and in particular the option, had been granted was of no significance or relevance and consideration of the person with whom the contract had been concluded formed no ingredient in the contract as the defendant 'would equally have made the contract with either or both of them', i.e. the plaintiff and his wife.

In *National and Grindlays Bank Ltd* v. *Yelverton*[48] the plaintiff claimed from the defendant payment of certain monies under two standard forms of suretyship in terms of which the defendant had guaranteed (under renunciation of the benefits of excussion and division) to pay to the plaintiff 'all such sums of money as were then or might in the future become due or payable to the plaintiff by (her husband)'. The defendant admitted that she had signed the two forms, but claimed that they contained blank spaces when she did so and that these spaces had been filled in without her authority or consent and that the plaintiff bank could not be said to be her agent for the purpose of completing the forms. It was on this basis that the defendant sought to escape from the trite rule that it is no defence to a written contract signed by a person to say that at the time of signing it he or she did not appreciate its meaning or contents. Davies, J., (before whom this matter came on an exception taken by the plaintiff alleging that the defendant's plea did not disclose a defence in law) thought that the allegations made by the defendant were insufficient and that where a person signs what is on the face of it an inchoate agreement, he or she must be taken to have intended that it should be made choate by filling in the blank spaces. In order to establish her defence, the defendant would, therefore, have to plead (if she could) either fraud or misrepresentation or coercion or *justus error*. The plaintiff's exception to the plea was, therefore, upheld and it is interesting to note that the learned judge equated the doctrine of *justus error* in Roman-Dutch law with that of the doctrine of *non est factum* in English law.

STANDARD CONTRACTS AND EXCEPTION CLAUSES

It is a well known fact that standard contracts deviate from the common law by imposing as many obligations which would normally fall on the 'standard contractor', as possible on the party to whom that contract is presented on a take-it-or-leave-it basis. The only question is how far the courts will enforce them. In *UDC Rhodesia Ltd* v. *Usewokunze*[49] the plaintiff sued the defendant on an agreement of lease in respect of a motor car and claimed from the defendant an amount of $6118 due by way of rentals, less certain credits, after the motor car had been repossessed and sold by the plaintiff. There was no doubt that this claim was justified in terms of the agreement. In addition, however, the plaintiff claimed (apart from costs of suit) judgement for ten per cent collection charges on such instalments as the defendant would offer to pay off the capital amount of the debt and certain other costs, e.g. tracing charges. In *Dan Perkins and Co Ltd* v. *Mather*[50] such collection charges and other costs had been disallowed as penalties. The plaintiff sought to distinguish that case from the present in so far as he did not claim a fixed percentage commission for collection, irrespective of whether, or not, such collection charges were incurred, but only the payment of the collection charges which would actually be incurred. Although this appeared to be a valid distinction, the claim was rejected because collection charges levied on instalments received in satisfaction of a judgement debt are not only essentially attorney-and-client charges, but cannot in any event be regarded as due and payable when the judgement is obtained. On this basis, judgement for the ten per cent collection charges was refused. On the other hand, the Court pointed out that if in the present case the defendant should be unable to satisfy the judgement debt at once and offer to make payment by instalments and the plaintiff accepted that offer 'then of course there is nothing whatsoever to stop the plaintiff agreeing or insisting that the defendant should make such instalment payments of the judgement debt through his attorneys, and in such event there would be nothing at all to prevent the plaintiff from insisting that the defendant should pay the collection charge in respect of such judgement debt.' But this would be an entirely new arrangement and the plaintiff was not entitled to recover from the defendant at this stage commission charges which he had not in fact incurred. One may respectfully ask whether this dictum is not in fact inconsistent with the judgement in the *Dan Perkins* case.

In *Glenburn Hotels (Pvt) Ltd* v. *England*[51] the Appellate Division held that a plaintiff who claimed damages in respect of articles stolen from the room which he had occupied as resident in the defendant's hotel, was bound by his signature in the hotel register next to the statement printed in bold type 'I hereby agree to the abovementioned conditions', when the conditions (although not printed in bold type and appearing in comparatively small print at the top of the register) contained an unequivocal exception clause relieving the hotel owner from responsibility for all loss or damage in regard to guests' property. It was not sufficient for the plaintiff to allege that he had not seen this condition. Only if he could allege and prove that he had signed the register as a result of fraud or misrepresentation would he be able to escape from it.

ENRICHMENT AND RESTITUTION

In *Grizell* v. *P & W Erection Co (Pvt) Ltd*[52] the plaintiff had sued the defendant for payment due to him in respect of work done, claiming an alleged contract price of $720. The defendant alleged that the agreed price was $290 from which it was entitled to deduct $150 being the cost of remedying certain defects. Neither party succeeded in establishing its version of the contract price on a balance of probabilities. In these circumstances, the plaintiff contended that he was entitled at least to a *quantum meruit,* i.e. the 'objective' value of the work done by him. This submission was rejected on the ground that, in effect, it amounted to a claim for payment of a 'reasonable' price. But as each party had alleged a definite contract price there was no room for an implied term to pay a reasonable price. Therefore, 'the court had to start with the contract price and deduct from that the cost of remedying the defects' in so far as the defendant had substantiated their existence. No doubt, the defendant should not be unjustly enriched, but the plaintiff had to prove that the former had in fact been *unjustly* enriched so that even on that basis 'the onus remained on him of proving what the stipulated price was'. As he failed to establish his version of the contract price, the plaintiff had to rely on what was virtually a concession made by the defendant and which established a minimum contract price of $290. Consequently, the plaintiff was entitled to that amount less the cost of remedying the defects, i.e. $140 in the final event.

DELICT

Smith N. O. and Lardner-Burke N. O. v. *Wonesayi*[54] is a case with distinct public law undertones, but the Court resolved the issues it raised by the application of delictual principles and it is, therefore, dealt with in this field. It was decided on exception and thus concerned only with certain points of law raised in the pleadings, the following facts and allegations being accepted as correct for that purpose. The respondent, Wonesayi, was a tribesman and *semble* a kraal head who had been served with an order issued in terms of Proclamation 4 of 1969 under s. 86(1) of the Land Apportionment Act (Cap. 257) requiring him to vacate, together with every member of his family and all other persons living with him, a ranch in the European Area, part of which he had occupied as a 'squatter'. When he did not comply with this order, the appellants, who were the Minister of Internal Affairs and the Minister of Law and Order respectively, acting through their police force, assaulted and removed the respondent forcibly, together with certain other persons, his property (which was not returned to him) and destroyed eleven of his huts. During this operation he was assaulted and subsequently lodged in prison. Thereupon the respondent instituted an action against the appellants for return of his property or payment of its value, monetary compensation for the huts destroyed and damages for the wrongful impairment of his personal dignity, as well as for pain and suffering which he had suffered by the alleged unlawful assault. The appellants denied that their actions were unlawful because they were authorized by Proclamation 4 of 1969 and, in the event of the Proclamation not authorizing their acts, they pleaded in the laternative that their and their officials' acts were performed in the course of their duty and in the *bona fide* belief that they were lawfully authorized to do what they had done. In addition, they specifically denied that they or their officers had any *animus injuriandi* towards the respondent. The latter excepted to this plea as being bad in law and his exception was upheld by the General Division of the High Court. The two Ministers appealed against this decision to the Appellate Division which confirmed the decision of the Court *a quo*. Having disposed of various points (such as the contention that the order was void for vagueness because the term 'persons living with (the respondent)' was too indefinite to permit determination of the circle of persons who was required to comply with it), Beadle, C.J., (with whom MacDonald, J.P., and Lewis, J.A., concurred) thought that the decision depended upon whether the 'purist school of the Roman-Dutch law', or the 'old school of the English law' was aplicable to the law of defamation and of *injuria* in Southern Africa. The former holds that it is a sufficient defence for a person to rebut an allegation of defamation or *injuria* (and thus to avoid liability for damages) if he proves subjectively that the words or acts complained of were uttered or done by him *bona fide* and that he had no intention to injure the complainant when he uttered or performed them. The old school maintains that a defendant has to prove objectively that the words or acts complained of were uttered or performed in circumstances which the law considers justify his uttering or performing them. Reviewing the trend of cases in South Africa, the learned chief justice thought that there had been a swing from the old school to the purist school in recent years, but that it was impossible to say which of the two schools prevailed at the present stage of development. As they were quite irreconcilable with each other, one had to decide which one should be adopted and in the absence of 'a full bench decision of the Appellate Division of South Africa directly in point', Beadle, C.J., preferred to follow the old school. In the result he held that 'the circumstances under which the defendants in this case removed the plaintiff's property and destroyed his huts, if not sanctioned by the Proclamation, would be circumstances not approved by law, becaue what they did, if not sanctioned by the Proclamation, was prohibited by law, and this being so, the *bona fide* belief by the defendants that the Proclamation did sanction their actions would be irrelevant. Consequently the exception to this defence was rightly allowed by the Judge in the Court *a quo* and the appeal must be dismissed.'[55]

In *Association of Rhodesian Industries and Associated Chambers of Commerce of Rhodesia and Others* v. *Brooks and Another*[56] the factors to be taken into account when assessing the *quantum* of damages to be awarded in an action for defamation which consisted of serious imputations in an article levelled at top executives of associations responsible for allocating foreign exchange currency on behalf of the Government were considered. Once the defence of privilege and fair comment on matters of public interest had been dismissed, such imputations were extremely serious and having been published in a specialist journal widely read by industrialists and commercial men, the publication had been focussed on 'the very quarter where it was calculated to do most harm' to the organizations concerned and their top executives. In addition, it was essential that public confidence in the fair administration of their responsibilities should not be undermined and was of the greatest importance to them. On the other hand, an apology had been published and, whilst the contents of that apology did not unreservedly or unequivocally withdraw the aspersions which had been cast upon the conduct of the plaintiffs, the fact that it had been published ought to be given some weight. Another factor to be considered was that the defamatory imputations were, as the evidence had shown 'unlikely to have been believed, as distinct from being understood', and it did not appear that the esteem in which the plaintiffs were held had 'in fact been lowered in the minds of right-thinking people'. In the result, damages were awarded to the two organizations in the sum of $700 each and to the executives in the sum of $900 each.

The perennial problem of whether a wrongdoer must take his victim and the circumstances in which he commits a wrong as he finds them or whether he is entitled to say that he could not reasonably foresee the consequences of his act, was considered in *Manual* v. *Holland,*[57] where Beadle, C.J., held that a person 'who strikes another on the back of his neck . . . with sufficient violence to knock him firmly to the ground, ought to foresee that some fairly serious injury might result' and it is not necessary that he should foresee the precise character of that injury, e.g. that his victim 'should break a leg in falling'.

Finally, in the field of delict, Beadle, C.J., held in *de Jong* v. *Industrial Merchandising Co (Pvt) Ltd*[58] that a 'mere breach of a regulation controlling speed limits is not *per se* negligence', but only one of a number of factors to be taken into account in determining 'whether or not it was negligent to drive at the speed driven.'[59]

FAMILY LAW

ADOPTION AND CHILDREN'S PROTECTION

In re McLeod[60] raised several interesting issues. The appellant, a European, wanted to adopt two minor Coloured girls of whom he was the natural father. When he first submitted his application to the Department of Social Welfare in 1969, he had agreed to make an irrevocable donation of some £2000 to each child in order to provide for their education. He had not done so when the application came before the Court, but it was clear that he had always provided adequate means for the children's needs and that he had no intention to avoid his obligations to them. Nevertheless, a provincial magistrate refused to make an adoption order mainly, it seemed, on the following grounds which appeared from his reasons for judgement: first, there was 'no getting away from the fact that society in Rhodesia is stratified and that the Coloureds are a distinct stratum in that society' so that 'a mass of consequences must follow from what the appellant has done, is doing, and will do to these girls.' Secondly, the magistrate felt that it was, in these circumstances, essential for the appellant to make 'proper financial provisions for these children so that regardless of his ups and downs what he has started will be finished'. The Appellate Division commented on the first consideration in this vein: 'whatever view is taken of the conduct of the appellant in procreating the (se) children . . ., he is to be commended for assuming the responsibility for their maintenance and education and for taking them into his home and devoting his personal care and attention to them', as it was unfortunately 'all too common for White parents of Coloured children to shirk their moral and legal responsibilities'. As for the requirement that the appellant should make independent provision for the children's education and maintenance, it seemed that this was not essential, the more so as an adoption order would strengthen the children's claims for support.

The new Children's Protection and Adoption Act, No. 22 of 1972, repeals the previous legislation and, in particular, Cap. 172, which was introduced in 1950 and based on the South African legislation of 1937. The tendency of the new Act is twofold, first, to exercise a greater degree of control over parents and secondly, the introduction of more efficient procedures and measures to care for children who are not sufficiently cared for by their parents. Thus a parent will be deemed to have neglected or *abandoned* a child not only if he has failed to pay for the child's maintenance, which would include payments for dental care, but also when such parent has shown inadequate interest in the child for more than a year after the child has been placed in an institution or in the care of some other person, because the parent has initially been found wanting in giving the child that degree of care and protection that is expected from him or her. Abandonment in general terms and 'being in possession of drugs' have been added to the conditions in which a child may be found to be 'in need of care' by the Juvenile Court. The power to take action to safeguard the health of a child has been considerably extended in so far as now every magistrate may take such action as he deems necessary to safeguard *all* aspects of a child's health, whereas under previous law such authority was conferred only on the chief magistrate, and even he could act only if he had reasonable grounds for assuming that the child would suffer serious and lasting physical injury. In proceedings under the old Act—as distinguished from divorce proceedings in the High Court—a father could not be deprived of the custody of his child if the mother was guilty of adultery or desertion. This has now been changed and such a mother may still be awarded the custody of a child when the parents have been separated, but no divorce proceedings are pending, because it was felt that such matrimonial misconduct does not necessarily make the wife a bad mother.

CUSTODY OF AFRICAN CHILDREN

In *Kusikwenyu* v. *Parsons NO and Others*[61] the applicant was the mother of eight children. Her husband had died and relatives demanded that the widow and her children should return to the tribal area. When she refused, the head of the family, accompanied by a brother of the deceased husband, came to fetch the children on the ground that the deceased husband had not paid full *lobolo* for his wife and that they were, therefore, entitled to claim the children in accordance with African customary law. The district commissioner (the first respondent) assisted them in removing the children and the mother applied to the High Court for their return. Beadle, C.J., declined to deal with this application on the merits as it was governed by African customary law and ruled that it should be dealt with in a proper manner by a court that was charged with the administration of that law. However, he ordered that 'the children should remain with the applicant until a court of competent jurisdiction had adjudicated in the matter'.

BREACH OF PROMISE

In *Steyn* v. *Smith*[62] it was held that when the conduct of both parties to an engagement was such as to render any hope of a successful marriage remote because of their complete incompatibility, there was no need to apportion blame between the parties so that each of them is entitled to the return of the presents they have given each other.

In *Pietzsch* v. *Thompson*[63] the plaintiff claimed the return of a ring and various other gifts from the defendant to whom he had given them 'in pursuance of their agreement to marry each other after (the defendant) had obtained a divorce from her husband'. The plaintiff alleged that he had not known that the agreement to marry was *contra bonos mores* and urged that for this reason the *pari delicto* rule should not be applied against him. However, the Court held that in the absence of special circumstances, public policy would not be served if an order for the return of these presents were made, although it seems that the Court may have been influenced by the fact that the defendant was justified in breaking off her relations with the plaintiff and that there was considerable doubt as to whether the presents (except for the ring) were intended to be returned if the marriage did not take place.

PROPERTY LAW
VINDICATION AND ESTOPPEL
The almost absolute protection of the owner's *dominium* of Roman law is still a characteristic feature of the Roman-Dutch property law and is evidenced by the fact that there are very few cases in which an owner will be estopped from vindicating his property wherever he finds it. In South Africa, the Appellate Division recently held that, even where an owner had confirmed to a third party that certain property might be disposed of by another person who claimed that he had acquired ownership in such property, could still vindicate his property from the third party if the wrong information was given *bona fide* and without negligence.[64] That the Rhodesian courts adopt the same attitude appears from the decision in *Scottish Rhodesian Finance Ltd* v. *Taylor*.[65] In that case the plaintiff was the owner of a motor car (under a hire-purchase agreement) which it sought to vindicate from the defendant who had bought it from the hirer in good faith and only after he had obtained certain information which satisfied him that the car was not subject to a hire-purchase agreement. This information was elicited in the following manner: there exists in Salisbury a commercial organization, known as the Hire-Purchase Institute, which maintains a register of motor cars sold on hire-purchase terms according to information supplied by dealers who enter into hire-purchase agreements. Details of this register are made available to interested parties, in particular other dealers who buy second-hand cars. It was from this institute that the defendant enquired whether the motor car which he intended to buy was registered and he was informed that this was not the case. Eventually, it transpired that the dealer who had sold the motor car under a hire-purchase agreement (which was then ceded to the plaintiff) had supplied an incorrect registration number to the institute. In dismissing the defendant's plea of estoppel, the Court pointed out that there was no duty on the seller to supply the information to the institute and that, in the absence of such a duty, it could not be said that he had been negligent in the sense of breaching a duty of care that was not owed to the defendant and, apparently, the same decision would have been reached if the hire-purchase agreement had not been ceded to a finance company, but if the dealer himself had claimed the return of the motor car as owner. On this basis the court did not even consider the rule that a person who is not under a duty to perform a certain act must nevertheless act with reasonable care if he chooses, after all, to perform that act.

LANDLORD AND TENANT
In *Smith N. O.* v. *Singandi*[66] the defendant had entered into an agreement of lease with the Minister of Agriculture in respect of certain rural State Land which contained an option to purchase the land on the expiration of the lease, provided that he had complied with all terms and conditions of

the lease. He exercised this option, but the Minister claimed his ejection on the ground that the defendant's occupation was unlawful and that he was not entitled to exercise the option because he had failed to comply with the terms and conditions of the lease. The report does not indicate whether the plaintiff gave any particulars of the alleged breaches, but in any event, the Court held that the onus was upon the defendant 'to establish the fulfilment of the condition precedent entitling him to an accrual of the option to purchase the property' so that it seems as though he was compelled to prove a negative—a contention which Lord Goddard, C.J., had categorically rejected in *Bond Air Services Ltd* v. *Hill*[67] where an insurance company sought to avoid liability by the simply expedient of claiming that the insured was obliged to prove that he had at all times complied with the terms and conditions of the policy, and not only in respect of the accident to which this claim related.

INSOLVENCY LAW

Two decisions should be mentioned briefly under this heading. In *ex parte Berman*[68] the Court held that the surrender of an estate as insolvent should be accepted if it was in the interests of creditors that the applicant's estate is sequestrated, even though he has failed to disclose all relevant facts relating to his financial affairs, provided *semble* that the applicant had not been guilty of dishonesty or deliberate falsifications. In *S.* v. *Malachias,*[69] on the other hand, it was held that the accused—a bankrupt—was rightly convicted of having failed to disclose to his trustee to the best of his knowledge all his property of any kind, even though he had not done so fraudulently.[70] In this case the accused had failed to disclose certain debts due to him because he regarded them as bad debts and, therefore, not as property which he had to declare. The accused could escape conviction only if he satisfied the Court that he had some lawful excuse for such failure.

TRADE MARKS

How far is it possible to decide in regard to two words of a language with which one is not as familiar as one is with one's own mother tongue whether the two words in question are so similar as to be likely to lead to confusion or whether one or both of them are invented words or mere mutilations of proper words? Although they were not clearly spelt out, these questions arose in *Seeco (Pvt) Ltd* v. *Zambezia Furnishers (Pvt) Ltd. and Another*[71] where the appellant, a furniture trading company, had for some time used the *Shona* words 'nyore, nyore' in conjunction with its trade name 'Zimbabwe Furnishers' and now claimed to be entitled to an interdict restraining the first respondent, a rival company trading under Shona word '*zinyore*', together with its trade name. The literal meaning of *nyore* was alleged to be 'an action that is easy to perform' and in connection with the purchase of goods on credit it was supposed to have acquired a secondary meaning so as to convey the concept of credit facilities and, used in repetition, it was further said that this mean 'very easy terms'. The word *zinyore* was said to be an abbreviation of the word '*ziirinyore*' which means 'these things are easy' or 'we are easy' and, by implication, 'these things are cheap' or 'we are cheap'. Both companies catered almost exclusively for trade among Africans and it was on this ground that the applicant was concerned about possible confusion arising between its business and that of the respondent. The Court approached the problem on the basis that, although the applicant had not shown that the use of the word *zinyore* led to actual deception or confusion, it would nevertheless be entitled to succeed if it could establish that the use of that word was likely to attract business to the respondent which would otherwise have gone to the applicant—that is to say, if the use of the word *zinyore* was calculated to make the public think that the respondent was carrying on the business of the applicant and was concerned with it. The matter was decided on affidavit so that there was, e.g., no evidence on how the words in dispute were actually pronounced by the customers or the meaning which they conveyed to *them*, and on this basis the application for an interdict was dismissed, whilst the applicant was given leave to proceed by way of action with the notice of motion to stand as a summons and the affidavits as pleadings.

RESTRICTIVE COVENANTS AND REGISTRATION OF CONTRACTUAL RIGHTS
The General Laws Amendment Act, No. 57 of 1972, introduces two new sections (Nos. 57A and 57B) into the Deeds Registry Act (Cap. 253). The first of these deals with the registration of restrictive covenants in regard to the ownership, ocupation or use of land. It elaborates on the existing law and, in particular, gives the Minister responsible for the administration of the Act authority to prohibit the registration of any restrictive covenant which he considers 'for any reason' should not be registered. The second section provides for the registration of contracts for the sale of land against the title deeds of the land. This is particularly important in cases in which land is purchased by instalments and the purchaser is given occupation thereof before transfer into his name is effected, as is generally the case when a new township is being developed. The effect of the registration of the contract in such cases is to give the purchaser protection in respect of the deposit and instalments he has paid, not only against the seller, but also against any successor in title of the seller. In so far as such purchaser is entitled to enforce the contract against the original owner's successors in title, it is clear that a contractual right is here being converted into a real right.

SUCCESSION

It is sometimes said that it is easy to establish a claim against a deceased estate because the alleged debtor is no longer in a position to dispute it. *Johnston* v. *Johnston and Another NNO*[72] proves that this is certainly not always the case. Here the appellant had claimed to have an option to purchase for £5000 a certain property (from a deceased estate) which at the time he made his claim was valued at several times this amount. The strength of his case rested upon his own sworn evidence and also upon that of his former wife, although the value of the latter's evidence was somewhat weakened by the fact that as a result of certain obligations, she and her children would be likely to gain 'if the appellant were to purchase this very valuable property for the sum of £5000'. The main weakness of the appellant's case was, however, that he was unable to produce a letter allegedly written by the deceased extending the option and no other person who had seen it. In *Thomas* v. *The Times Book Co Ltd*[73] Plowman, J., had said that he was 'enjoined by authority to approach (a claim against a deceased estate) with suspicion having regard to the fact that the other actor in this story . . . is dead and cannot therefore give his own version of what took place'. MacDonald, A.C.J., took the view in the instant case that 'no special *onus* rests on a person making a claim against a deceased estate', although sight must not be lost of the universal rule that a court will in all cases exercise care in coming to its decision. 'A claim against a deceased estate differs only in the need for more than ordinary care, a need which arises from the fact that the other party to the alleged transaction is no longer alive to give his or her version. If in the exercise of special care in examining the claim made against a deceased estate suspicious circumstances emerge, it is the Court's duty to pursue its investigation, sifting and delving into the evidence, until it is satisfied, applying the normal test in civil cases, either that the claim is good or bad.' In addition to the factors already mentioned, the Appellate Division took into account that the trial judge had found the applicant's demeanour unimpressive and described his former wife as 'more adroit than frank'. Applying the principles outlined above, there appeared to be no doubt at all that the applicant had failed to discharge the onus which rested upon him on a preponderance of probabilities.

COMMERCIAL AND INDUSTRIAL LAW

NEGOTIABLE INSTRUMENTS

Rhostar (Pvt) Ltd v. *Netherlands Bank of Rhodesia Ltd*[74] is yet another version of the old tale of a trusted employee who is given a duly signed blank cheque which he fraudulently completes and then deposits in his own private account at a bank different from the one on which the cheque has been drawn. Here the cheque was made out in the name of a fictitious person, the employee apparently having inserted any ordinary name which came to his mind. When the fraud was discovered, the employers tried to recover the amount of the cheque from their own bankers since the employee had already used the proceeds thereof he had received. The employers relied specifically on the fact that the cheque had been marked 'not negotiable—account payee only', with the words 'or bearer' following the name of the payee having been crossed out. They contended that their bankers had been negligent, in so far as they had ignored the instructions prohibiting the transfer of the cheque which meant that the cheque was valid as between the parties, but not negotiable. The defendant bank, in turn, claimed that the payee was 'a fictitious or non-existing person' and that it was, therefore, entitled to treat the cheque as payable to bearer. The Court drew attention to the difficulties of finding a satisfactory definition for the words 'fictitious or non-existing' in this context and pointed out that it seems as though a banker has the right to treat a cheque as payable to bearer whether, or not, he was aware when he accepted the cheque that the named payee was in fact a fictitious or non-existing person. But this would mean that when a cheque which is payable to a named payee only is presented, 'the ridiculous situation could arise that a banker could negligently or deliberately ignore the prohibition against transfer which such cheque contained and be excused from liability by discovering much later that the payee was in fact a fictitious person'. The decided cases in England, as well as in South Africa, do not appear to provide a clear guide, but it would seem that in each of them there were special circumstances which justified the fact that the decision went one way in one case and another way in a different case. The factor which the Court regarded as decisive in this case was that the defendant bank failed to ascertain why a cheque made out in the name of one person was paid into and collected through the account of a different person, when that cheque contained a clear prohibition against the transfer of the cheque by the person named as the payee thereon to any other person. On this basis, the bank was held liable to the plaintiff.

MOTOR VEHICLE INSURANCE

In *Graham and Another* v. *General Accident Fire and Life Assurance Corporation and Another*[75] the rights of a passenger for compensation in respect of injuries received in a collision were discussed. The first plaintiff was the driver of a motor car and the second plaintiff a passenger therein. The collision took place between that car and a motor car driven by the second defendant who was insured with the first defendant in terms of Part XIV of the Roads and Road Traffic Act (Cap. 289). The trial judge found as a fact that the accident occurred as the result of the negligence of both drivers (each bearing the same degree of responsibility as the other), but he held that this finding could not affect the passenger's claim. The matter was complicated by the fact that both plaintiffs had elected to sue the defendant-driver's insurance company direct for the amount to which its liability was restricted under the Act and the driver only for the excess, and further by various counter-claims, in particular by a claim on the part of the insurance company against the plaintiff-driver for a contribution to the damages which were awarded to his passenger, on the basis that the passenger's claim held good despite the accident having been caused as the result of the combined negligence of both drivers. The Court pointed out that the obligations to contribute to the payment of the damages due to the plaintiff's passenger arose from different causes: 'the insurer's from the contract of indemnity and the statutory obligation to discharge that indemnity by paying the creditor direct. (The plaintiff-driver's) cause of debt is his concurrent wrongdoing. The *quantum* of the liability in the latter instance is unlimited; in the former it is restricted (in terms of the Act) to $10 000'. For this reason, the insurer should not have a claim towards contribution against the plaintiff-driver. Moreover, although the insurance company and the plaintiff-driver may be regarded as co-debtors *vis-a-vis* the plaintiff-passenger, the different causes of their respective liability cannot be overlooked. This means that the right of contribution between the two wrongdoers remains undistrubed, but the insurer of one of the wrongdoers 'cannot claim any such right save by subrogation or cession of action from the insured'. In the result, the plaintiff-passenger was awarded damages against the first defendant.

DOUBLE OPTIONS

In *Lindsay* v. *Matthews and Another*[76] the first defendant had granted the plaintiff an option to purchase immovable property owned by the first defendant and leased by him to the plaintiff. During the currency of the lease and before the plaintiff was required to exercise his option, the first defendant sold the property to the second defendant because—strange though it may sound—he had genuinely forgotten about the option which he had previously granted to the plaintiff, his lessee, who now asked for an order setting aside the sale of the property to the second defendant and a declaratory order that he was still entitled to exercise his option. The Court held that there was no reason why the rights of an option holder should 'be considered in any way as being of lesser value than the rights of an actual purchaser to whom delivery has not been given' and accordingly, judgement was entered for the plaintiff.

MASTER AND SERVANT—INDUSTRIAL CONCILIATION

The decision in *S.* v. *Dennis*[77] turned ostensibly on the wording of certain industrial agreements. In essence, it concerned the question whether the Court would permit an employer to escape his liability from paying a gratuity to employees who had completed ten, or more, years continuous service with the same employer, by relying on a technical interpretation rather than to give effect to the intention of the regulation. The Appellate Division had no doubt that the latter course must be adopted and held that an employee who was discharged and re-engaged by the same employer within a short period of such discharge, did not lose his right to claim that he had been in continuous service, as defined by the industrial agreement and was thus entitled to his gratuity if he remained in continuous service for ten years, or more.

Attention might be drawn here to the Workmen's Compensation Amendment Act, No. 35 of 1972, which raises the ceiling of the earnings of workmen to whom the principal Act (Cap. 248) shall apply, from $4,000 to $6,000 per year and also introduces increased benefits to keep pace with the increase in wages and the rising cost of living. The position of workmen under the age of twenty-one years is also improved to ensure that compensation will not automatically be based on the earnings which an apprentice or learner was likely to receive on his twenty-first birthday, as was hitherto the case, but at the end of three years after the accident, if he would have completed his apprenticeship or learnership only after that period, even though he might have attained the age of twenty-one years at an earlier date.

COMPANY LAW

The Companies Amendment Act, No. 33 of 1972, amends s. 8 of the principal Act (Cap. 223) which limits the number of members of a partnership formed for the purposes of acquisition of gain to twenty and allows for larger partnerships if such partnership 'consists solely of persons who are members of a designated profession or calling', i.e. a profession or calling which is controlled and regulated by a council or other body established by a statute in force in Rhodesia. S. 21 of the principal Act which deals *inter alia* with the power of the Registrar of Companies to order a company to change its name if it is in his opinion likely to mislead the public or to cause offence, or if he considers it as undesirable for any other reason, is amended so as to require the registrar to exercise such powers not more than twelve months after the company has been first registered or subsequently changed its name. An appeal against any order made by the registrar in regard to a company's name after it has first been registered, lies direct to the Appellate Division of the High Court. If the registrar or any other person considers it necessary or desirable that a company should change its name after the lapse of the twelve months' period during which the registrar may act, application must be made to the General Division of the High Court which shall then have power to make such order as it may deem fit. With effect from 1 January 1973 all foreign banking and insurance companies are required to register themselves under the Companies Act and will be subject to the provisions of that Act, except in so far as their organization and business activities are regulated, respectively, by the Banking and Insurance Acts.

MISCELLANEOUS

The Industrial Development Corporation Amendment Act, No. 18 of 1972 (amending Act No. 51 of 1963) introduces certain organizational and administrative changes and defines the powers of the shareholders of the Corporation to make regulations concerning its administration.

The African Cattle Marketing Amendment Act, No. 23 of 1972, repeals s. 4 of the principal Act (Cap. 94) and substitutes a provision according to which no person shall purchase African cattle, except at a departmental sale or in terms of a permit issue *to the seller* by a district commissioner, or sell African cattle to any person except at such departmental sale or in terms of a permit, provided that these provisions shall not apply to the sale of African cattle to an 'African who is ordinarily resident in the marketing area in which the cattle are ordinarily depastured'.[78]

The Tobacco Marketing and Levy Amendment Act, No. 28 of 1972, amends ss. 81ff of the principal Act (No. 30 of 1960) and authorizes the Marketing Board, subject to the approval of the Minister, to make arrangements for the pooling of tobacco which which has remained unsold after the close of a selling season and for the disposal of such surplus tobacco by way of auction sales.

EVIDENCE AND PROCEDURE

CIVIL PRACTICE AND PROCEDURE

In *Umtali Farmers' Co-op Ltd* v. *Sunnyside Coffee Estate (Pvt) Ltd*[79] the Court confirmed that it was permissible for a defendant to plead a counterclaim for damages equal to or in excess of the plaintiff's claim for the purchase price of goods sold and delivered, even when the defendant admits the validity of the plaintiff's claim. Although this means that a liquidated claim may be countered by an unliquidated claim, this practice 'was a salutary one to which effect should continue to be given.' However, the defendant in such cases must allege facts which, if proved, would establish that he had in fact suffered patrimonial loss and that, in the absence of such allegations, the unliquidated counterclaim must be dismissed as disclosing no defence.

It seems that in *Belingwe Stores (Pvt) Ltd* v. *Munyembe*[80] the Court went even further when it held that a claim for a certain sum of money based on an undertaking, whereby the defendant, who was the manager of the plaintiff's store, had accepted 'liability for the value of any stock (under his control) found missing or unaccounted for', was a claim for a debt or liquidated amount for which default judgement might be granted without the need to establish the correctness of the amount claimed by leading evidence.

CRIMINAL PRACTICE AND PROCEDURE

In *S.* v. *Millar*[81] the Court pointed out that in a case in which 'a witness has had his evidence impeached because it is obvious that the witness is favourably inclined towards the accused, it is quite illogical to say that because the witness is trying to help the accused to the utmost extent, he must not be believed when he gives evidence which does not help the accused, but which tends to incriminate him'.

That a Court must apply the law as it finds it because serious consequences might follow if it took upon itself the function of amending a statute, if in its opinion the effect of that statute might be to produce undesirable results, was emphasized by the Appellate Division in *S.* v. *Takaendesa.*[82] There a conviction for a failure to comply with a soil conservation order given to the accused under the Natural Resources Act (Cap. 264) was set aside because the order containing details of the measures which the accused was supposed to take, did not comply strictly with the provisions of the Act. S. 77A of the Natural Resources Act lays down that no such order may be made in respect of an area in the Tribal Trust Land 'except after consultation with the chief appointed in terms of the African Affairs Act (Cap. 92) in whose area of jurisdiction the land is situated'. In this case, no chief had been appointed in terms of the African Affairs Act when the order was made. However, the inspector who issued the order had consulted the customary tribal head of the area in which the accused lived. It was held that the inspector's failure to consult *a chief appointed in terms of the African Affairs Act* invalidated the order because the provision of s. 77A (*supra*) was obligatory and not merely directory. The Court also emphasized that there was 'a heavy onus on public officials that, when they state in an official document that they have done something, they have in fact done it, and if circumstances have arisen which might have prevented their carrying out the letter of the law, they should be meticulous in drawing the Court's attention to this fact'.

CONFLICT OF LAWS

Two important cases—both in the field of matrimonial law—should be mentioned under this heading. In *Kader* v. *Kader*[83] the Appellate Division had to decide the extent to which a foreign polygamous—or potentially polygamous—marriage ought to be recognized for civil purposes in

Rhodesia. The parties had entered into a marriage according to Muslim rites in Malawi in 1961. The marriage was valid according to Malawi law. In 1962 they settled in Rhodesia, where they lived together until 1967, when the husband deserted the wife and two minor children and the wife obtained an order in a magistrates court against the husband for payment of maintenance for herself and the children in terms of s. 4 of the Deserted Wives and Children Protection Act (Cap. 173). The husband then made application for rescission of that order, contending that it was void *ab initio* 'because the marriage, being a potentially polygamous one, was not a marriage for the purposes of the Deserted Wives and Children Protection Act'. He relied mainly on *Seedat's Executors* v. *The Master (Natal),* [84] where the Full Bench of the Appellate Division of South Africa had held that a foreign polygamous marriage will not be recognized as valid. Obviously, this argument was countered on behalf of the wife by reference to the decision of the Federal Supreme Court in *Estate Mehta* v. *Acting Master, High Court,* [85] where it was held that 'the strict rule of total non-recognition laid down in *Seedat's* case . . . should not be followed in this country more than forty years later' and that recognition of a polygamous union for some legal purposes had become necessary. Since it has been held that decisions of the Federal Supreme Court have now only persuasive authority, the question was whether the Rhodesian Appellate Division in 1972 should follow *Seedat's* case or *Mehta's* case. In the final event, the answer to this question must involve considerations of public policy and, in this regard, the court accepted the statement of Tredgold, C.J., in *Mehta's* case that it would be 'quite unrealistic to affirm that it is contrary to the policy of our law to recognize polygamous marriages for the purposes of succession when the majority of marriages of this country are under a polygamous system recognized for all purposes'. All the indigenous peoples of this country are living under a system of polygamy and as their marriages are recognized for all civil purposes, it would be 'entirely illogical to withhold similar recognition to polygamous marriages validly contracted by non-Africans in the countries of their domicile particularly where the marriages, though potentially polygamous, are in fact monogamous'. The history of the relevant legislation confirmed this view and there is no indication in either Cap. 173 (which had been revised in 1959) or in the Maintenance Act now in force (No. 51 of 1971)[86] that the legislature had at any time intended to depart from it. It was, therefore, not surprising that the Appellate Division adopted the same attitude as the English Court of Appeal did in *Imam Din* v. *National Assistance Board,* [87] where Salmond, J., had said (at p. 218) that the recognition of a foreign marriage or the construction of the word 'wife' in a statute must depend on 'the purpose for which the marriage is to be recognized and upon the object of the statute'. In that case, a Pakistani husband who had contracted a polygamous marriage in Pakistan, tried to resist a claim by the National Assistance Board to recover from him the sums which it had paid to the Pakistan's second wife and their children who had immigrated with their husband and father into England and whom he had subsequently deserted. Clearly, an analogous situation existed in *Kader* v. *Kader* and there was no good reason why the wife and the children should not be recognized as such for the purposes of the Deserted Wives and

Children Act, but, on the contrary, 'every reason in commonsense and justice why they should be so recognized'.

The reluctance of the Rhodesian courts to deprive a party of his right to institute proceedings of divorce in Rhodesia 'which stems from the fact of domicile' is illustrated by the decision in *Moresby-White* v. *Moresby-White*.[88] In that case the parties were married in Zambia which was the husband's domicile of origin. They lived there until 1965, when the husband settled in Rhodesia, whilst the wife remained in Zambia. At the time of these proceedings it was obvious that the marriage had irretrievably broken down, although the report does not disclose at what point of time this had happened. Within a matter of one day in 1970 the husband instituted proceedings of divorce against the wife by edictal citation in the High Court of Rhodesia, alleging of course, that he had established a domicile of choice within its jurisdiction, whilst the wife issued a summons in the High Court of Zambia claiming a decree of divorce and alleging that she and her husband were still domiciled in Zambia. It appears that the husband allowed the wife's action to go by default, with the result that the High Court of Zambia issued a decree of divorce which the husband claimed should not be recognized in Rhodesia because the Zambian High Court had no jurisdiction, after he had acquired a domicile of choice in Rhodesia. The wife entered a special plea *in limine* claiming that the Rhodesian Court should dismiss the plaintiff's claim on the ground that it was *res judicata,* in so far as the High Court of Zambia had already given a final judgement of divorce in favour of the defendant. This special plea was dismissed on the ground that a person domiciled in Rhodesia had a fundamental right to come before the Rhodesian Courts for matrimonial relief. The case is a glaring example of problems which the amendment of the domicile principle has created in private international law in favour of the deserted wife who has almost universally been given the right to institute proceedings against a deserting husband in the jurisdiction in which she was living with the husband when the latter deserted her.

NOTES

1. Unreported. The decision was upheld on appeal: 1973 (2) SA 14 (RAD) The judgement of the Appellate Division will be discussed in *Annual Survey of African Law,* Vol. VII, 1973
2. When the Minister introduced the Bill he indicated that this provision was intended 'to open the way for *bona fide* religious, educational and charitable organizations to own or lease property anywhere without any question as to race', but that he intended 'to retain control of the situation by making occupation of these properties (i.e. land owned by such organizations) subject to the granting of a permit'. (Parliamentary Debates (Senate), Vol. 3, p. 1239)
3. Instead of by regulation. See e.g. s 6 of Act No. 53 of 1972 amending s. 38 of the principal Act
4. 1972 (1) SA 53 (RAD)
5. Africans always required a special travel document if they left Rhodesia for more than three months. Under the new law they are required to obtain a travel permit, irrespective of the period they are absent from Rhodesia, and their ordinary identity documents are retained by the district commissioner in exchange for the travel permit. See also *infra*: African (Registration and Identification) Act No. 48 of 1972
6. See also Births and Deaths Registration Amendment Act No. 39 of 1972, which amends the principal Act, No. 35 of 1962, to make provision for the keeping of the necessary records to indicate whether, or not, a child has a claim to Rhodesian citizenship by reason of his or her birth

7. Parliamentary Debates, Senate, Vol. 3, pp. 1223-4; House of Assembly, Vol. 83, pp. 250-1
8. *Ibid.* Senate, Vol. 3, p. 1174
9. *Ibid.* 1176; House of Assembly, Vol. 83, at pp. 633 ff
10. 1972 (2) SA 680
11. See Parliamentary Debates (House of Assembly), Vol. 83, pp. 961 ff
12. 1972 (2) SA 719 (RAD)
13. 1972 (3) SA 123
14. 1972 (2) SA 584
15. 1972 (4) SA 268 (RAD)
16. For an excellent discussion of the attitude of the Rhodesian courts towards tax avoidance and double taxation see J. R. Dewhurst in (1972) 12 Rhod. L. J., 15 ff. and 33 ff. Cf. also *G.* v. *Commissioner of Taxes,* 1972 (3) SA 121, where the Court equated an amount accrued to the taxpayer in a particular year, but omitted from the taxpayer's income during that year, because it was recoverable, with a bad debt, so that the amount was taxable in a subsequent year, when a substantial portion thereof was recovered
17. Cp. *Scottish Rhodesian Finance Ltd.* v. *Provincial Magistrate Umtali,* 1971 (3) SA 234, and *S.* v. *Chandivana*, 1971 (3) SA 262, reported in *Annual Survey of African Law,* Vol. V, 1971
18. Parliamentary Debates (Senate), Vol. 3, p. 1069
19. In addition the Act contains certain minor and technical amendments to the Insurance Act, No. 19 of 1967, and the Decimal Currency Act, No. 20 of 1967
20. Cap. 289 Parts IX to XI
21. This provision has obviously been introduced to deal with the situation which arose from the decision in *R.* v. *Bowen N. O.,* 1967 (3) SA 236
22. On the whole, both statutes re-enact existing legislation and a discussion of such technical innovations as have been introduced goes beyond the ambit of this Survey. As for two important issues of principle relating to the Postal and Telecommunications Act—the power of the Postal and Telecommunications Corporation which was established in 1970 to expropriate, with the consent of the President, the whole or part of a telecommunication service and the exclusive privilege of that Corporation of establishing, maintaining and working telecommunication services within, into and from Rhodesia—see Parliamentary Debates (House of Assembly), Vol. 83, pp. 517 ff
23. Parliamentary Debates (House of Assembly), Vol. 81, p. 2147
24. Parliamentary Debates (House of Assembly), Vol. 83, p. 95. When the Bill was first published, fears were expressed that it was intended to prevent Africans from attending European private schools. State controlled schools are, and have been, always subject to segregation, but private schools and in particular mission and religious schools, have invariably accepted pupils on a non-racial basis
25. See ss. 11 to 18
26. S. 4 Housing Standards Control Act (No. 29 of 1972), as amended by s. 28 of the General Laws Amendment Act (No. 57 of 1972)
27. 1972 (2) SA 46 (RAD)
28. 1972 (2) SA 40 (RAD) reversing 1971 (3) SA 555. See *Annual Survey of African Law,* Vol. V, 1971
29. This statement is to some extent an over-simplification, but sufficient for the purposes of this decision. For a more detailed explanation see *Annual Survey of African Law,* Vol. V, 1971, *supra*
30. 1972 (1) SA 435
31. 1972 (1) SA 50 (RAD)
32. 1972 (3) SA 227
33. 1972 (3) SA 131
34. 1971 (2) SA 670
35. 1972 (1) SA 411 (RAD)
36. 1972 (4) SA 418 (RAD)
37. 1972 (2) SA 651 (RAD)
38. 1972 (1) SA 432 (RAD)
39. RAD 182/69, not reported
40. 1972 (3) SA 108 (RAD)
41. 1972 (4) SA 425 (RAD) per MacDonald, A.C.J., and Lewis, J.A., Davies, A.J.A., dissenting
42. These three cases were dealt with together on automatic review by the High Court: 1972 (2) SA 678
43. 1972 (2) SA 665 (RAD)
44. 1972 (3) SA 100 (RAD)
45. 1972 (3) SA 118 (RAD)
46. 1972 (4) SA 279 (RAD)
47. 1972 (2) SA 667

48. 1972 (4) SA 114. See also *infra* n. 53 for a case of *justus error* inconnection with restitution
49. 1972 (4) SA 446
50. 1968 (1) RLR 60
51. 1972 (2) SA 660 (RAD)
52. 1972 (4) SA 449
53. See also *Calder* v. *South African Mutual Life Assurance Society,* 1972 (4) SA 285, which dealt with the right of an assurance company to reclaim over-payments made when refunding contributions to a pensions fund made by a member on his resignation as an employee from the organization for which the company had effected and underwritten a pension scheme. The decision was concerned with the question as to what allegations of fact were required to defeat the company's claim for refund of overpayments made in error—i.e. in what circumstances the society's error in overpaying the employee could be regarded as *justus error* entitling it to demand such refund on the basis of unjust enrichment
57. 1972 (4) SA 454
58. 1972 (4) SA 441
59. See also *Roeloffze* v. *Ranchod*, 1972 (4) SA 80 (RAD), where it was held that the operator of an unwieldy loading vehicle who can only with difficulty see what is going on behind him, is under no duty to persons who walk past the back ff his vehicle without keeping a proper lookout so that they have only themselves to blame when they are injured by the loader. However, this applies only if, and as long as, the operator keeps within a defined loading zone
60. 1972 (2) SA 383 (RAD)
61. 1972 (4) SA 119
62. 1972 (2) SA 656 (RAD)
63. 1972 (4) SA 122
64. *Johaadien* v. *Stanley Porter (Paarl) (Pty) Ltd*, 1970 (1) SA 394 (AD)
65. 1972 (4) SA 434
66. 1972 (4) SA 439
67. (1955) 2 QB 417
68. 1972 (3) SA 128
69. 1972 (1) SA 61 (RAD)
70. Cp. s. 139(b) of the Insolvency Act (Cap. 53)
71. 1972 (4) SA 95
72. 1972 (3) SA 105 (RAD)
73. (1966) 2 All ER 241, 244
74. 1972 (2) SA 703. The relevant provisions of the Rhodesian Bills of Exchange Act (Cap. 218) are either exactly or substantially the same as the corresponding provisions of the English and South African Bills of Exchange Acts. Therefore, it was thought unnecessary to burden the report following this note with references to the details of the sections in the Rhodesian Act
75. 1972 (2) SA 671
76. 1972 (3) SA 133
77. 1972 (2) SA 37 (RAD)
78. Cf. Parliamentary Debates (House of Assembly), Vol. 82, pp. 992 ff
79. 1972 (1) SA 449
80. 1972 (4) SA 460
81. 1972 (1) SA 427 (RAD)
82. 1972 (4) SA 72 (RAD)
83. 1972 (3) SA 203 (RAD)
84. 1917 AD 302 (South Africa).
85. 1958 (4) SA 252 (FC)
86. The maintenance order in this case was made under Cap. 173 before the Maintenance Act of 1971 had been introduced.
87. (1967) 2 QB 213
88. 1972 (3) SA 222 (RAD)

CHAPTER ELEVEN

BOTSWANA

N. N. Rubin

The year under review was not one in which major developments took place in the legal field, though a number of changes were set in motion, including a significant alteration in the law of divorce[1] which only came into the statute book in 1973, and some changes in the criminal law.[2] The same is true of the minor constitutional alterations which were instituted, and, economically, 1972 was a year in which serious preparation began to be made for the major boom which was to follow as the various mining enterprises began large-scale production.

The Court of Appeal Act[3] made specific provision for the composition and functioning of the Court of Appeal, which was previously regulated by the relevant sections of the Constitution which had created it. The Court will ordinarily consist of three members, although where it is constituted to consider an appeal relating to a constitutional matter, it will require a quorum of five judges.

The Legal Practicioners (Amendment) Act[4] was concerned to bring up to date the position regarding the academic qualifications necessary for, and the nationality of practicioners. In this respect, it was similar to the amending legislation introduced in Swaziland.[5]

A comprehensive Police Act[6] was passed, although it was only brought into effect in 1973. The Act is concerned with the administration of the police force and conditions of service for its members.

By the Customary Courts (Amendment) Act,[6] Customary courts were given power to try certain criminal offences, though they may only deal with crimes specified in the penal code or some other written law.[7] The Act prescribes the observance of the customary courts' criminal procedure rules in relation to any trial, but provides for sentences to include corporal punishment as well as fines and imprisonment. In the case of corporal punishment exceeding four strokes, the sentence must in all instances be confirmed by an administrative officer, and, where an appeal has been lodged (against conviction or sentence) a sentence of corporal punishment is automatically suspended pending the outcome of the appeal.

A new Societies Act[8] provided for a comprehensive system of registration of societies, which are required to have a constitution and must be registered within twenty-eight days of their formation or the adoption of a constitution. It is worth noting that a Society is deemed by the Act to have been established in Botswana if any of its officers or members reside in Botswana.

NOTES

1. See the Matrimonial Causes Bill of 1972, which became Act No. 1 of 1973, and which will accordingly be described fully in the *Annual Survey of African Law*, Vol. VI, 1973
2. Matters concerning powers of arrest and bail were dealt with in the Penal Code (Amendment Bill), No. 29 of 1972
3. No. 44 of 1972
4. No. 17 of 1972, which should be read together with the Local Police Act, No. 13 of 1972
5. See above, chapter 13, pp. 233 to 234
6. Act No. 6 of 1972
7. For a discussion of some of the implications of this phrase see Act No. 6 of 1972 in [1973] JAL pp. 24 to 36
8. Act No. 19 of 1972

CHAPTER TWELVE

LESOTHO

C.M.G. Himsworth

CONSTITUTIONAL AND ADMINISTRATIVE LAW

The year under review was for Lesotho the second year of comparatively slight constitutional activity sandwiched between two years of more significant change (1970 and 1973). The Country continued to be governed by Prime Minister Leabua Jonathan with legislative and executive power vested firmly in the Council of Ministers under the Lesotho Order of 1970.

As part of a legislative spring clean the Law (General Amendments) Order, No. 6 of 1972, made a large number of small amendments to existing statutes, many of the amendments have the specific aim of removing anomalous references to the 1966 Independence Constitution swept away in 1970. The Ministers of State (Amendment) Order No. 15 of 1972 amended the 1971 Order to authorize the appointment of three rather than only two Ministers of State.

Of more substance was the creation by Order 19 of a Public Accounts Committee to be appointed by the Prime Minister and with the task of ensuring adequate control over the collection of revenue and spending. S. 3(4) of the order provides that for the avoidance of doubt

'(a) the Committee is required to examine the facts as disclosed by the accounts of Ministries and departments and not the policy of the Government; and
(b) the Committee's examination is directed towards the officials of Government and not towards the political heads of Ministries and departments.'

Also of significance was Order 46, the Limitation of Legal Proceedings Order, which provides that no action is to be instituted against any person in respect of acts performed whether in good faith or otherwise from 30 January 1970 (the date of the suspension of the 1966 Constitution) to the date of the Order pursuant to the subsisting state of emergency.

In addition to the case of *Matime* v. *R* (noted below), 1972 saw legislative activity also affecting aliens. The Consular Powers and Privileges Order, No. 27 of 1972, replaced Proclamation No. 67 of 1950 and incorporated into the Law of Lesotho the 1963 Vienna Convention on Consular Relations. Legal Notice 19 containing the International

Organizations (Privileges and Immunities of the Organization of African Unity) Regulations extended to the OAU the privileges granted under the International Organisations Act of 1969 whilst Legal Notices 9, 10 and 18 under powers contained in the Aliens Control Act of 1966 extended to citizens of the United Kingdom, the United States and the Commonwealth exemptions and benefits corresponding to the benefits accorded to citizens of Lesotho in those countries.

Of more practical effect within the country itself was an amendment to Act 22 of 1967 effected by the Employment (Amendment) Order, No. 30 of 1972, which for the first time required all non-citizens to obtain a certificate of employment before taking up employment in Lesotho.

Also worth noting but this time in the field of local administration was the promulgation of regulations under the Local Administration Act of 1969 which indicate the advent of the complications of urbanization (still fairly new to Lesotho) into the government of the country. Legal Notice No. 35 introduced a new rate on immovable property in Urban Areas whilst Legal Notice No. 36 contained regulations relating to the provision of sanitary services and refuse removal.

CRIMINAL LAW

Matime v. *R* (CR/A/55/72) was a case interesting as the second stage of a continuing legal saga (see also the case of the same name (CR/A/45/71) noted in the 1971 *Annual Survey of African Law*.

On this occasion the appellant had been charged under the Aliens Control Act (No. 16 of 1966) with the contravention of an order made under s. 25 of the Act directing him to remain out of Lesotho. In the court below he had been found guilty and sentenced to the payment of a fine of R100 or five months' imprisonment.

In the High Court, however, the conviction and sentence were set aside and the case remitted to the magistrate on the grounds that the latter had, in the original trial, concerned himself solely with the appellant's entry into Lesotho and had ignored his evidence to the effect that he was not an alien at all but rather a citizen of Lesotho to whom the Act was not applicable. The magistrate was directed to call further evidence on the question of whether or not the appellant was at the time of his expulsion an alien.

PROCEDURE AND EVIDENCE

An amendment to the Criminal Procedure Proclamation, No. 59 of 1938, effected by Order No. 7 of 1972 is worth noting. A new subsection (8) to section 315 is inserted the first paragraph of which provides:

'(8)(i) Whenever any person has been convicted by any court of an offence involving damage or loss of Government property, that conviction shall, in respect of the loss or damage sustained by the Government, have the effect of a Civil judgement for the payment of money and shall be enforced in the same manner as any other judgement for the payment of money in a Civil Court.'

CONTRACT

In *Stevenson* v. *Pitso* (CIV/T/8/71) the defendant was unsuccessful in an ingenious attempt to resist the plaintiff's claim for payment of R2,106 plus interest and costs in respect of liquor supplied by the plaintiff to the defendant. The plaintiff was a South African trader and the defendant a Mosotho who was making a business of illegally importing the liquor to Lesotho and then selling it—again illegally because of his lack of a licence. It was on these circumstances of illegality that Pitso based his defence. This was that the whole series of transactions were *in fraudem legis* and that they could not, therefore, give rise to an action. Following a consideration of *dicta* of Watermeyer, J.A., in *Commissioner of Customs and Excise* v. *Randles Bros. and Hudson Ltd* 1941 AD 369 at 395, Evans, J., held that despite the illegality of the defendant's activities there was not sufficient evidence of complicity on the part of the plaintiff to constitute a transaction *in fraudem legis*.

REVENUE LAW

In the interests of some measure of completeness in this survey, it should simply be noted that the Income Tax Order, No. 32 of 1972, has completely replaced existing laws in this field (particularly Proclamation 30 of 1959) whilst Proclamation 16 of 1907 has been repealed and replaced by the Stamp Duties Order, No. 5 of 1972.

FAMILY LAW

There were no statutory developments in this field during the year nor were there any cases notable for their introduction or development of a new legal principle. The more interesting cases decided were related to the question of internal conflict and are noted separately. One or two others are, however, worth a mention.

In *Thulo* v. *Thulo* (CIV/T/10/70), the plaintiff's action for divorce on the grounds of his wife's adultery relied entirely upon the fact that a child had been born to his wife 310 days after the last occasion on which he could have had intercourse with her. However, just as in *Makhetha* v. *Motsoto* (CIV/A/12/69), reported in the *Annual Survey of African Law*, Vol. V., 1971, seven months was not accepted as impossibly short for a period of gestation, so here a period of ten months was not held to be impossibly long.

Per Jacobs, C.J :

'Now it may be that judicial notice may be taken of the fact that the normal period of gestation is approximately nine months but it is a far cry from that to say that a period of ten months is so lengthy as to be impossible or even improbable.'

The Chief Justice made reference to even longer periods held not to be impossibly long in *Mitchell* v. *Mitchell* 1963 (2) SA 505 and *Williams* v. *Williams* 1925 TPD 538.

The action for damages against a third party adulterer remains part of the Roman-Dutch law operating in Lesotho. This was affirmed by the case of *Thabane* v. *Thabane and Ntsukunyane* (CIV/T/48/71), although here the claim for loss of *consortium* failed altogether and the damages in respect of *contumelia* were assessed at a mere R20.

Sengoai v. *Sengoai* (CIV/A/10/70) raised a couple of interesting jurisdictional points. The High Court had previously awarded a divorce with an order for forfeiture of benefits. There had been no order at this stage, however, regarding maintenance and the custody of minor children. The present case arose in the form of an appeal against the award by a Subordinate (Magistrate's) Court of both an order of custody and of maintenance. Both orders were challenged on the ground that the Magistrate had no jurisdiction to issue them.

It was held that so far as the custody order was concerned the court below had erred. It had 'no inherent jurisdiction' and was a 'creature of statute' (Proclamation 58 of 1938). Regarding the maintenance order, however, it was held that despite the fact that there had been no express reference to it in the application, the Deserted Wives and Children Proclamation, No. 60 of 1959, conferred sufficient jurisdiction upon a subordinate court. The maintenance order was, therefore, saved.

INTERNAL CONFLICT

Several interesting cases were decided during the year which may be loosely grouped together as all related in one way or another to the parallel existence in Lesotho of both the Roman Dutch law and the customary law.

In *Ramalapi* v. *Ramalapi* (CRI/A/21/71) the tough nut of repugnancy came to be considered. The magistrate in the court below had held that a rule of customary law which failed to recognise legitimation *per subsequens matrimonium* (such as is recognised by the Roman-Dutch Law) must necessarily be repugnant to justice and morality and, therefore, void. Evans, J., held that he could see no reason for finding the custom repugnant and affirmed that a custom was not invalidated merely because it was contrary to the provisions of the Roman-Dutch Law.

The case of *Sethathi* v. *Sethathi* (CIV/T/58/72) was another case decided by Evans, J., during 1972 and is interesting in its similarity to *Rakhoabe* v. *Rakhoabe* (CIV/T/11/68) noted in the *Annual Survey of African Law*, Vol. III, 1969. As in the earlier case the action arose out of a marriage contracted by civil rites in South Africa but following *Rakhoabe* it was held that since the parties' domicile had been Lesotho and not South Africa the law governing property rights within the marriage was that of Lesotho which contrary to the position over the border meant that community of property resulted. (No mention was made of *Khatala*'s case (1963–66) HCTLR 97 which might have suggested a different result.) Evans, J., went on to say that once this civil marriage had been contracted no customary polygamous associations with other women were permissible:

'A party cannot, therefore, have the benefits of community of property and as many customary marriages as he feels inclined to enter into as well.'

Finally, in this section, there should be considered a case decided by Acting Chief Justice de Villiers concerning the proof of the existence of a rule of customary law—*Tjabane* v. *Motsoane* (CIV/A/23/71). Lesotho remains without any statutory guidance in this area and any indication of high judicial attitudes is, therefore, most interesting. This particular case arose out of an action originating in the customary courts for the value of certain crops. The customary law rule relied upon in the courts below as stated by the Judicial Commissioner (from whose court the case came most immediately) was:

'As a general customary rule a land that is ploughed and sown *bona fide* is reaped by the person who planted it even though the land may be awarded to another party after it has been planted.'

The appellant in this case alleged *inter alia* that:

(a) in the Judicial Commissioner's court the custom had not been proved to exist; and therefore,
(b) appropriate rules of the common law (Roman-Dutch) should have been applied.

Both points were rejected by the High Court. In the first place, it was held that, since the case had arisen first in a customary court and concerned customary tenure of land, customary law had clearly to be applied. It was further held, deriving support from *dicta* of Wessels, J.A., in *Ngcobo* v. *Ngcobo,* 1929 AD 233 at 236, that it was not necessary for the custom to be proved in evidence.

Per de Villiers, Ag. C.J :

'The Judicial Commissioner, who deals and has for many years dealt with customary law, supported by an assessor, has declared that the customary law applicable in Lesotho is as stated by him and since the law so stated cannot be said to clash with public policy, it was correctly applied in the present case in preference to the Common Law.'

It is interesting, if also a little distressing, to note the contrast between this comparatively lenient approach to the proof of custom by the Judicial Commissioner as compared with that of Evans, J., in *Moonyane* v. *Maqoacha* (CIV/A/5/71) noted in the *Annual Survey of African Law*, Vol. V, 1971. In that case it was held that the Judicial Commissioner ought to have satisfied himself of the existence of a custom by the application of the rigorous (and, it is respectfully submitted, inappropriate) tests formulated in the case of *Van Breda* v. *Jacobs,* 1921 AS 330.

This situation is clearly unsatisfactory and one in which legislation should be employed to prevent further swinging of the judicial pendulum.

CHAPTER THIRTEEN

SWAZILAND

N N Rubin

The year under review was the last full one in which the independence constitution[1] survived. Although the constitution was only set aside by the King early in the following year, and the reasons given at that time were vague and referred only to its alleged unsuitability to the conditions of the country there can be little doubt that some of the legal issues which arose during 1972 were, in part, contributory to the unrest which preceded the Royal coup: specifically, the matters relating to immigrants and their status, and the legislation relating to 'land speculation control', and to some of the King's powers.

CONSTITUTIONAL AND ADMINISTRATIVE LAW

It is worth noting that, although a Bill which curtailed the King's influence over the composition of the Senate was passed in July[2] by both houses of the legislature, it did not receive the Royal assent during the year under review and thus did not become law. The measure reduced from ten to two (of a total of thirty) the number of Senators to be nominated by the King, and provided that a further ten were to be elected by the lower house. The number of members of that house to be appointed by the King was to be increased from ten to sixteen.[3]

Elections were held during the year, and, although the national movement known as *Imbokodvo* (in effect, the King's party) was returned with an overwhelming majority, one of the opposition members was alleged to be disqualified by reason of his non-citizenship of Swaziland—or, as the Immigration Act[4] puts it rather quaintly, by virtue of the fact that he did not 'belong to Swaziland'. An amending Act was passed,[5] creating a special tribunal of five persons appointed by the Deputy Prime Minister to adjudicate on the question of whether or not a person 'belongs to Swaziland', at the instance of the person so affected or of the Chief Immigration Officer or of the Permanent Secretary to the Deputy Prime Minister. Although the procedure to be followed required that the tribunal follow the relevant provisions of the commissions of Enquiry Act[6]—thus providing the essential elements of natural justice—the tribunal was given sole jurisdiction by the new statute on this question, subject to the right of appeal to the Prime Minister whose decision was said to be final. The decision of the Prime Minister was declared not to be subject to appeal in any court, and the burden of proving that a person belongs to Swaziland is placed by the amending statute on the person whose citizenship is in doubt.

In a contemporaneous note on the legislation[7] the Attorney General of Swaziland was bold enough to suggest that, notwithstanding the purported exclusion of the powers of the courts in respect of a decision by the Prime Minister, 'in terms of the constitution, and it is submitted in terms of the common law, this does not exclude the revisionary powers of the High Court'. This indeed proved to be the case, as the proceedings in *B. T. Ngwenya* v. *The Deputy Prime Minister*[8] showed. The applicant had been declared a prohibited immigrant by the Deputy Prime Minister and sought to set aside this order and a declaration that he was a citizen of Swaziland—it being clear from s. 10 of the Immigration Act that a person who 'belongs to Swaziland' may not be declared a prohibited immigrant. Although the full court of two judges (Pike, C.J., and Johnston, A.J.) accepted that the onus of proof of citizenship lay on the applicant, it declined to consider the matter solely on the basis of affidavits and took the unusual step of hearing *viva voce* evidence; as a result, it came to the conclusion that, on a balance of probabilities, the applicant was a citizen. It is worth noting that the court took the view that the action was one which challenged the Deputy Prime Minister's jurisdiction, and that it was not based on an administrative law claim that the Minister had acted *mala fide*.

An amendment to the Interpretation Act[9] was designed to facilitate ministerial functions by providing that a minister named in a particular statute is not necessarily the one charged with its administration but that this is to be determined separately by designation of the appropriate minister in a government notice.

It is of some significance that, during the course of the year, Botswana and Lesotho were designated as 'countries' to which the Fugitive Offenders (Commonwealth) Act applied.[10]

JUDICIAL AND LEGAL SYSTEM

Legislation enacted during the year made the retiring age for the Chief Justice and the judges of the Court of Appeal seventy-five years.[11]

Minor, but not insignificant, changes were made in the regulations affecting the legal profession, by means of subsidiary legislation proclaimed in terms of the Legal Practitioners Act.[12] The first of these raised the fee for enrolment or admission as an advocate or attorney from R10 to R50 (or R40 in the case of a person resident in Swaziland). This was said to presage legislation designed to limit the right of non-Swaziland citizen practitioners to appear before the courts.[13] It is, of course, a notorious fact that the overwhelming majority of advocates and a substantial number of attorneys admitted to practice in Swaziland are not resident, and are from the Republic of South Africa. Other changes made during the year concerned the degrees and examinations recognized as sufficient to qualify an applicant for admission or enrollment.[14] These took into account a number of new law degrees which are being conferred by South African universities, and the law degrees now being given by the ethnically restricted universities set up in terms of the South African 'Extension of University Education' Act.

The power of the Court of Appeal and of the High Court to increase the severity of a sentence imposed by a lower court were considered in *R. T. Johns* v. *R.*[15] Maisels, J.A., took the view that the High Court had powers *mero motu* in an appropriate case to increase the sentence of a lower court, and in choosing not to deal with the allegation by the appellant that such action had been irregular in that he had not been afforded an opportunity of addressing the court on the question of the increase, pointed out that the Court of Appeal had powers to substitute a sentence, whether more or less severe, for that of a lower court.[16] The case was also interesting in that the learned Judge of Appeal cited case law not only from South African Courts (*Union Government* v. *Lee,* 1927 AD 202 and *R.* v. *Horwitz,* 1922 CPD 406), but also English law (*Admiralty Commissioners* v. *Lee,* 1922 1 AC 1929) and—significantly in view of the fact that Swaziland does not recognize the Smith regime in Rhodesia—the Rhodesian decision of McDonald, J.A., in *R.* v. *John,* reported in South Africa in 1962 2 SA 500. (See below, Criminal Law). It is interesting to consider whether, if the latter is thought to be the *ratio* of the case, it may have been misapplied, particularly if Swaziland chooses to follow the Privy Council, rather than the Rhodesian courts' views, in the *Madzimbamuto* cases.

CRIMINAL LAW

One of the issues in *R. T. Johns* v. *R.* was whether the fact that the deceased in a culpable homicide case had been negligent was sufficient to remove the basis of the conviction. It was in this respect that the cases cited above were followed by Maisels, J.A.; and, in particular, the Rhodesian case was used as a basis for dismissing the appeal, as McDonald, J.A., had taken the view (at p. 568) that the notion of a *causa sine qua non* was not the cause required in the law of culpable homicide.

Aspects of the law relating to accessories were considered by the Court of Appeal in *Philemon Mdluli* v. *R*[17] Maisels, J.A., with whom Schreiner, P.J., and Milner, J.A., concurred, dealt with the question of whether one of the chief crown witnesses was an accessory after the fact, and, if so, whether his evidence had to be treated on the same basis as if he had been an accomplice. The court is reported as adopting what was said by the Privy Council in *Majara* v. *The Queen,* 1954 AC 235, at 242, to the effect that it is sufficient that the assistance rendered by the accessory is such that the accessory associated himself, in the broad sense of the word, with the offence which was committed. The court went on to follow the statement in *R.* v. *Jongani,* 1937 AD 400, at 401, that it was a prerequisite that the person had knowledge that the crime had been committed before he could be said to be associating himself with it. In the instant case, the court found that there was no evidence that the witness had any such knowledge, and the appeal was dismissed.

PROCEDURE AND EVIDENCE

Two lacunae in the procedural law were dealt with during the year: the provision, in legislation for limiting proceedings against the government; and the creation, through an additional set of rules for the subordinate courts, of small claims proceedings. Both sets of innovations are worth noting, though neither is exactly worthy of acclaim.

The Limitation of Legal Proceedings Against the Government Act[18] is a far-reaching measure, which gives a good deal more protection to the government than other such laws in related jurisdictions. Although it is only concerned with actions against the government as such, and not against its officers; and although it excludes counterclaims by the government and claims arising under either the Motor Vehicle Insurance Act,[19] and the Workmen's Compensation Act,[20] its scope is not confined to delictual actions but includes contractual ones as well. In respect of both types of claim, it is laid down that, before instituting proceedings, a written demand must be served on the Attorney-General claiming payment of the debt and setting out the reasons and particulars thereof; but in the case of a debt arising from a delict, the demand must be served within ninety days from the date on which the debt became due. No legal proceedings against the government may be commenced within ninety days of the serving of the demand, nor after 24 months from the date on which the debt became due. S. 4(1) of the Act provides that the High Court may grant special leave to a claimant who might otherwise have been debarred, if it is satisfied that

(a) he has a reasonable prospect of succeeding in such proceedings;
(b) the Government will in no way be prejudiced by reason of the failure to receive the demand within the stipulated period; and
(c) having regard to any special circumstances he could not reasonably have expected to have served the demand within such period;
Provided that the Court in granting such leave may impose such conditions as it deems fit (including the payment of any costs) and . . . stipulate the day by which such proceedings may be instituted.

The second of the conditions gives an indication of the extent to which the statute is government-oriented, as does the second sub-section, which allows the Court to grant an extension to the Government beyond the ninety-day period 'if it is satisfied that Government has a reasonable prospect of succeeding', and subject only to a proviso which is, *mutatis mutandis,* the same as that in the first sub-section. A far more worrying provision, from a policy point of view, is contained in the succeeding section. Here, the Act lays down that a court cannot of its own accord raise the failure of a claimant to comply with the act's provisions as regards notice or time, or with any conditions laid down by the court itself; but it is open to the Government to raise this defence if the court is satisfied, first, that it could not have raised the matter earlier and, secondly, that no prejudice will be suffered by the claimant which cannot be cured by an order of costs.

The Subordinate Courts (Amendment) Rules[21] provide a simplified procedure for the recovery of R50 or less (excluding costs) in respect of rent due, loans or advances, services performed or good sold and delivered. There is, basically, a fairly straightforward attempt to accelerate the proceedings, but they still look complicated enough to require an attorney; and there does not appear to be provision for arbitration or adjudication by someone other than a magistrate prior to trial. In addition to these rather disappointing aspects of the Rules, there is also the severe limitation placed upon their application by the small class of matters to which they are confined. It is difficult to see why actions in delict were ommitted, for instance.

In *Mavimbela* v. *R.*[22] Schreiner, P., made the following remarks concerning the role of assessors in a criminal trial, after drawing attention to the fact that the relevant provision (s. 6) of the High Court Act merely provided that the assessors had to give 'such assistance and advice as the judge may require':

> 'While it is provided, for reasons that are not clear to me, that the agreement or disagreement with the decision of the Judge shall be noted on the record, this does not mean that the views of the assessors on the various issues that fall to be decided should be stated in the judgement or that the Judge's decision on such issues should be recorded in the form of concurrence with the views of the assessors.'

Mr Justice Schreiner was said in another case, *B. M. Zwane* v. *The King,*[23] to be the source of a provision in the Swaziland criminal procedure code. The question before the court concerned evidence relating to the identification of the accused's/appellant's voice and whether the trial judge had erred in accepting certain evidence on the matter, Milne, J.A., referred to s. 224(2) of the Code[24] which reads:

> 'It shall be lawful to admit evidence that any fact or thing was discovered in consequence of the pointing out of anything by the accused person or in consequence of information given by him notwithstanding that such pointing out or information forms part of a confession or satement which by law is not admissible against him.'

and expressed the view that the section was worded as it is in the light of *R.* v. *Tebetha,* 1959 2 SA 337 AD, 'as if to ensure that in Swaziland the law should be as stated by Schreiner, J.A., in his dissenting judgement' which was, of course delivered in respect of a South African provision similar, but not identical, to the one quoted above. As Milne, J.A., pointed out, the Swaziland provision did not provide, as the South African one does, that it would be lawful to admit evidence that anything was pointed out by the accused; but only that 'it shall be lawful to admit evidence that any fact or thing was *discovered* in consequence of the pointing out of anything.'[25] by the accused.

CONTRACT

In *Swaziland Dairies (Pty) Ltd* v. *R. J. Meyer,*[26] Pike, C.J., in considering an application for an interim interdict restraining the respondent from selling milk to anyone other than the applicant and for an interim order for specific performance of an alleged existing contract for the sale of his entire milk production to the applicant, stated the requirements for the exercise of the court's discretion. An applicant was required to show:

(a) that the right which is the subject matter of the main action and which he seeks to protect is clear, or if not clear is *prima facie* established;
(b) that if the right is only *prima facie* established, there is a well-grounded apprehension of irreparable harm to the applicant if the interim relief is not granted and he ultimately succeeds in establishing his rights;
(c) that the balance of convenience favours the grant of an interim relief;
(d) that the applicant has no other satisfactory remedy.[27]

FAMILY LAW

The effect of the provisions of the Swaziland Marriage Act of 1964 was considered in *Joseph Jabulani Duba* v. *Regem,*[28] an appeal against a conviction for bigamy, where the first marriage of the appellant had been under the Roman-Dutch common law in South Africa and he had purported to marry a second time by Swazi customary law. While it is clear that a different result would have been obtained in South Africa, the appellant failed in his argument that the Roman-Dutch common criminal law had not been modified by the passage of the Marriage Act. The relevant provision of that Act, s. 7(1) reads:

'No person already legally married may marry in terms of the Act may marry during the subsistence of the marriage, irrespective of whether that previous marriage was in accordance with Swazi law and custom or civil rites and any person who purports to enter into such a marriage shall be deemed to have committed the offence of bigamy.'

It thus leaves no room for doubt, though one is bound to remark that it is fortunate that in this case the draftsman addressed himself with such clarity to the criminal as well as the civil effects of second and subsequent marriages. How many complications have been caused by the bland reference to these as being null and void, while bigamy charges elsewhere in Africa seem to have become a dead letter.[29]

PROPERTY AND ENVIRONMENT LAW

Two important measures in the field of environmental control were the Water (Amendment) Act[30] and the Control of Tree Planting Act.[31] The first is explicitly designed to prevent pollution by penal provisions. It replaces s. 20 of the Water Act[32] with new sections which make it an offence to pollute or cause to be polluted any public or private water (as defined in the original Act), including underground water in such a way as to render it less fit for (1) the purpose for which it is ordinarily used, or (2) for the propagation of fish or other aquatic life, or (3) for recreation, or (4) for other legitimate purposes. In addition to this sweeping definition, there is a presumption of guilt by an owner or lessee or occupier of land or his agent or servant unless he establishes that he has taken all reasonable steps to prevent the pollution. And, what is more, the penalty for a first conviction is a fine of R5,000 or two years imprisonment or both, and double in each case for a second and subsequent conviction. Finally, the Minister is authorized by the Act to take any steps he considers necessary to prevent pollution and, for this purpose, he may authorize the entry onto private land, and on top of this, may recover the costs of his anti-pollution measures from the pollutant.

The Control of Tree Planting Act is more general in its scope, and is designed to enforce a distinction between the use of land for agricultural development and the growing of trees for timber. To this end, the Natural Resources Board[33] in empowered to make recommendations to the Minister for a tree control areas plan, based on a classification of land in the country into 'agricultural', 'intermediate' and 'marginal' (in roughly descending order as to the ease with which it can be used for agricultural production)—all three terms being fully defined in the Act, as are the terms 'commercial tree' and 'agricultural production'. The Act forbids the planting of commerical trees on agricultural land except under license granted by the Board, and the planting of such trees on intermediate land except by permit of the Permanent Secretary to the Ministry of Agriculture. S. 7(2) provides that, in

'deciding whether to grant or refuse a license to plant commercial trees on agricultural land, the Board shall act on the principle that such land ought generally to be utilized for agricultural production and that commercial trees should displace agricultural production on such land only for exceptional reasons consonant with efficient land management and the rational use of land in relation to the surrounding area'

while s. 8(2) establishes that, in relation to intermediate land, the principle to be applied is that

'a permit ought generally to be issued unless it appears that the planting of commercial trees on such land would inhibit or interfere with the agricultural land use capability of the area in which such land is situated.'

The effect of the provisions in the Act, which appear wholly worthy in themselves, is somewhat weakened by the exclusion from its ambit of three categories of land, namely (a) any land so designated by the Minister by notice in the Gazette, (b) land held by the King in trust for the Swazi nation, and (c) land listed in a schedule to the Act, which last category appears to include most (if not all) of the substantial commercial afforested areas of Swaziland.

But this exercise in the watering down of the apparently swingeing provisions of a statute is comparatively insubstantial as compared with that which was applied to the Land Speculation Control Act[34]—by the same method, i.e. the exclusion of so much land from its sphere of operation that is is difficult to see what practical effect the measure can have, except in rhetorical, political terms. The principal mechanism of the Act is the establishment of a Land Control Board (and an Appeal Board), whose composition and powers are specified in the Act, and whose purpose is to control the disposal of land through what are called 'controlled transactions' to persons who are not citizens of Swaziland. The definition of a controlled transaction in the Act is:

(a) the sale, transfer, lease, mortgage, exchange or other disposal of land to a person who is not—
    (i) a citizen of Swaziland;
    (ii) a private company or co-operative society all of whose members are citizens of Swaziland;
    (iii) a person listed in the Schedule to this Act;
(b) the issue, sale, transfer, mortgage or any other disposal of or dealing with any share in a private company or co-operative society which for the time being owns land in Swaziland, to or with a person who is not a Swaziland citizen.

but does not include—

(a) the transmission of land or shares by virtue of the will or intestacy of a deceased person;
(b) a donation by a parent to his descendants;
(c) a sale in execution of a judgement of any court;
(d) a sale by a trustee of an insolvent estate or the liquidator of a company or co-operative society in liquidation.

In addition to these exclusions, land is defined in the Act to include

'any right, title or interest in immovable property, but shall not include—
(a) any land, including minerals and mineral oils, which is vested in the Ngwenyama[35] in trust for the Swazi nation;
(b) the rental or lease of a room or cottage by a hotel, inn or boarding house;
(c) the rental or lease of residential or business premises to a resident of Swaziland or a company which is registered in Swaziland for a period not exceeding three years or a renewal of the period of such rental or lease for a period not exceeding three years.

In addition blanket power is given to the Minister in s. 20 to exempt (by publication of an appropriate notice in the Gazette)

(a) any land or share, or any class of land or share; or
(b) any controlled transaction, or any class of controlled transaction; or
(c) any person, in respect of controlled transactions or a class of controlled transaction
from any of the provisions of this Act, on such conditions as he may deem fit to impose.

When the Land Speculation Control Regulations[36] were issued the Minister added considerably to the exemptions already contained in the definitions and specified in the Schedule, by exempting from the provisions of the Act: (1) the registration of any transfer, lease, mortgage or dealing with any share, pursuant to a written agreement entered into on or before the date of commencement of the Act (1 December 1972), notwithstanding that such was a controlled transaction; (2) any land, share, controlled transaction or person described in the first schedule to the Act (which includes the Matsapha Industrial Estate or any other industrial area or township), approved of by the Minister in writing for the purpose of the Regulations, as well as (3) land on which any hotel duty licensed by any lawful authority is erected or is to be erected; (4) any hiring or letting of any room, cottage or plot by a caravan park, holiday camp or similar enterprise; (5) any disposal of or dealing with shares in a private company or co-operative society if the value of the land (excluding buildings) owned by it is less than fifteen per cent of its total assets.

MINING CONCESSIONS AND ROYALTIES

Ever since talks concerning Swaziland's independence were first contemplated, the King has made it clear that regarded his claim to minerals as superior to that of any other person or body, including the government; and that he wished to have this position acknowledged as part of the law of Swaziland. Reference was made to the question at the constitutional conference which preceded independence, and the Constitution contained a formula relating to the King's and the Swazi people's rights which was regarded as a satisfactory compromise between the competing claims. Two pieces of legislation which came into force during the year under review serve to re-state the position as the King would have it, and to eliminate any doubt concerning the various kinds of royalties and rentals which may be due from concession-holders. The Concessions and Mining (Amendment) Act[37] add the following new section to the original Act:

'Concession rental to accrue to Ngwenyama in trust for the Swazi nation.
19 bis. Notwithstanding anything in this Chapter, any concession rental payable in respect of any concession relating to any grant of land or the use thereof for mining purposes or to any grant of minerals or mineral products and any interest due on such concession rental shall accrue to the Ngwenyama in trust for the Swazi nation.'

The Mining (Amendment) Regulations[38] replace the words 'Government' and 'Government of Swaziland' in certain key regulations with the words 'The Ngwenyama in trust for the Swazi Nation' and add the following new sentence in replacement of the first sentence of Regulation 4:

'A mineral royalty at the rate prescribed in the Sixth Schedule to these regulations shall be paid to the Ngwenyama in trust for the Swazi Nation by every holder of a mining right in respect of precious metals and non-precious minerals won from land held under such mining right, which mineral royalty shall be in addition to any other mineral royalties being paid to the Ngwenyama.'

COMMERCIAL AND INDUSTRIAL LAW

There were three amending Acts relating to the Liquor Licenses Act[39], two of which were of relatively little significance (one providing for exemption to be granted from the Liquor Licensing laws to certain categories of hotels and bottle stores, the other for the convening of special meetings the Liquor Licensing Board at the discretion of its Chairman). Of slightly more interest was the other Liquor Licenses (Amendment) Act[40] which authorized the Minister for Local Administration to issue licenses to manufacturers of spirits on such conditions as he thinks fit. The Act contains a long—and fascinating—set of definitions of the various kinds of spirits, the reproduction of which here is unnecessary, though there can be little doubt of its educational value.

The Factories, Machinery and Construction Works Act[41] is a comprehensive piece of legislation which seeks to regulate the establishment of factories and their registration and inspection; and also deals with the notification and investigation of accidents and industrial diseases. It repeals, and replaces, the Factories Law[42] and it repeals the

Mines, Works and Machinery Act[43] to the extent that it deals with any matter falling under the new Act.

Subsidiary legislation brought into operation during 1972[44] amends a schedule of the Industrial Conciliation and Settlement Act[45] so as to bring civil servants within the scope of its Part IV, which provides for compulsory arbitration of disputes and prohibits strikes and lockouts.

NOTES

1. See *Annual Survey of African Law,* Vols. I and II
2. *Africa Contemporary Record,* 1972-3, p. B429
3. Africa Research Bulletin, p. 3534C
4. S. 10 of Act No. 32 of 1964
5. No. 22 of 1972
6. Ss. 10(8)-11 of Act No. 35 of 1963
7. Comparative and International Law Journal of Southern Africa (hereinafter referred to as CILSA), Vol. VI, p. 136
8. CILSA, Vol. V, pp. 371-2
9. The Interpretation (Amendment) Act, No. 20 of 1972
10. By Legal notices (hereafter referred to as LN) Nos. 37 and 62 of 1972
11. The Court of Appeal Judges (Age of Retirement) Act, No. 1 of 1972
12. No. 15 of 1964
13. See the remarks of the Attorney-General in CILSA, Vol. V, at p. 368, and the Legal Practitioners (Fees) (Amendment) Regulations, LN No. 49 of 1972
14. The Legal Practitioners (Examinations) (Amendment) Regulations, LN No. 50 of 1972
15. CILSA, Vol. V, pp. 369-70
16. S. 5(3) of the Court of Appeal Act, No. 74 of 1954 as amended by Act No. 5 of 1967
17. CILSA, Vol. V, p. 368
18. No. 21 of 1972
19. Cap. 210 of The Laws of Swaziland
20. No. 4 of 1963
21. LN No. 39 of 1972
22. CILSA, Vol. V, p. 369
23. Idem., p. 368
24. As amended and introduced by Act No. 20 of 1968
25. Italics added
26. CILSA, Vol. VI, p. 138
27. The decision followed that in *L. F. Boshoff Investments v. Cape Town Municipality,* 1969 2 SA at p. 267
28. CILSA, Vol. VI, p. 138
29. See generally, Phillips and Morris, *Marriage Laws in Africa*
30. No. 5 of 1972
31. No. 7 of 1972
32. No. 25 of 1967
33. Established in terms of the Natural Resources Act, Cap. 139 of The Laws of Swaziland
34. No. 8 of 1972
35. i.e. The King of Swaziland
36. LN No. 67 of 1972
37. No. 14 of 1972
38. LN No. 19 of 1972, issued in terms of the Mining Act, Cap. 145 of The Laws of Swaziland
39. Acts Nos. 2, 4 and 6 of 1972
40. Act No. 4 of 1972
41. No. 17 of 1972
42. No. 15 of 1965
43. No. 61 of 1960
44. LN No. 61 of 1972
45. No. 12 of 1963

PART II

L'Afrique Francophone
(Francophone African Countries)

CHAPTER FOURTEEN

LA REPUBLIQUE ISLAMIQUE DE MAURITANIE

Michel L. Martin

La poursuite des objectifs du développement économique et social de l'Etat marque de ses exigences la vie nationale de la Mauritanie.

La vie politique, dominée par le leadership du président Mokhar Ould Daddah, ne sê signale par aucune modification particulière.

La vie sociale cependant fut à plusieurs reprises agitée. On note quelques manifestations estudiantines au cours du premier trimestre. Au mois de mai c'est l'organisation des travailleurs de Mauritanie qui manifeste son mécontentement à Nouakchott.

Sur plan général, signalons que l'année 1972 est marquée par la contestation par le gouvernement des accords de coopération avec la France.

DROIT ADMINISTRATIF

Un comité de tutelle des Régions et du district de Nouakchott est créé par le décret n° 71-21 du 6 août 1971, (JORIM, du 22 mars 1972, p. 63). Ce comité a des attributions consultatives. Il donne son avis sur les projets de budget des régions et du district de Nouakchott. Il est, en outre, chargé de la gestion du Fonds Interrégional de Solidarité.

La loi du 18 juillet 1972, (JORIM, 25 juillet 1972, p. 226) fixe le statut des sous-officiers de carrière. Cette loi, destinée, à stabiliser leur situation est applicable non seulement aux sous-officiers de l'Armée, mais aussi à ceux de la gendarmerie nationale.

Les principales nesures concernant le recrutement et le grade, les soldes et les indemnités (fixées par décret), les positions (activité, non-activité, réforme et retraite), la hiérarchie et l'avancement, les limites d'âge fixées par décret), la discipline (les sous-officiers ont droit à la communication de leur dossier avant de faire l'objet d'une mesure disciplinaire) et la démission.

Le décret n° 71.157 du 27 juillet 1972, (JORIM du 30 août 1972, p. 264 crée et organise la Société Nationale Industrielle et Minière.

La SNIM est un établissement public. Elle a pour objet de promouvoir la recherche et l'exploitation des ressources minérales. Des représentants des travailleurs, de l'Assemblée Nationale et du Gouvernement siègent au Conseil d'Administration. la tutelle de la SNIM est assurée par le ministère chargé des Mines. la compatibilité est tenue selon les règles de la comptabilité commerciale.

DROIT DU TRAVAIL

Il convient de noter que le décret n° 72.036 du 26 janvier 1972 (JORIM 23 février 1972, p. 50) procéde à une augmentation du SMIG (le taux en est désormais à 44,50 Frs dans la zone I et de 38,50 dans la zone II), pour les travailleurs relevant des professions soumises au régime de la durée hebdomadaire de travail de quarante heures. par contre les salaires des travailleurs relevant des entreprises agricoles subissent un abattement de 10%.

Le Décret n° 72.126 du 21 juin 1972, (JORIM, 21 juin 1972 p. 192) détermine les salaires des domestiques des exploitations agricoles et industrielles.

Dans le cadre des deux zones préalablement déterminées, l'ensemble des salaires des différentes catégories de travailleurs (des exploitations agricoles, personnel domestique, chauffeurs et travailleurs des entreprises industrielles non visées par les conventions collectives) fait l'objet d'une augmentation d'environ 10%.

La loi n° 12.146 du 18 juillet 1972, (JORIM du 26 juillet 1972, p. 222) apporte d'importantes modifications au Code du Travail (loi du 23 juin 1963).

Ces modifications affectent notamment la question de travail de nuit pour les enfant de mois de 16 ans, le repos nocturne pour les femmes et les enfants de moins de 16 ans et le droit de jouissance au congé acquis après la période dite de 'préférence egale à douze mois.

PROCÉDURE CIVILE

En 1965, le tribunal de première instance comprenait deux juges: l'un de droit musulman et le second de droit moderne.

Désormais, le tribunal est composé de deux chambres: chambre de droit moderne et la chambre de droit musulman, chacune étant composée d'un président et de deux juges. Le président et l'un des juges de la chambre de droit moderne sont choisis par les magistrats de droit moderne, le deuxième juge est un magistrat de droit musulman. Le processus est le même (président et un juge de droit musulman et l'autre juge de droit moderne) en ce qui concerne la composition de la chambre de droit musulman.

DROIT PÉNAL

La loi n° 72.158 dy 31 juillet 1972 (JORIM, 15 août 1972, p. 1) institue un

Code Pénal.

Quatre livres et 449 articles forment le grille de ce document. La partie la plus importante du nouveau code pénal est le livre trois (art. 67 à 437). Le titre premier traite essentiellement des crimes et délits contre la chose publique (c'est-à-dire la Sûreté de l'Etat, la constitution, la paix publique). Le titre second concerne les crimes et les délits contre les personnes et la propriété.

CHAPTER FIFTEEN

SENEGAL

Birame N'Diaye

1972, la République du Sénégal aura enregistré bien des textes législatifs et réglementaires dont certains sont importants entre tous; de ceux-ci sont le code de la famille, le code des investissements, la loi portant réorganisation de l'armée et celle portant autorisation de ratifier la convention instituant l'organisation pour la mise en valeur du Fleuve Sénégal (OMVS).

Le code de la famille institué pour répondre aux exigences de l'intégration et du développement nationaux, permet de rompre avec les incertitudes de coutumes multiples dont de nombreuses prescriptions sont perçues comme inadaptées à la société sénégalaise contemporaine.

Un nouveau code des investissements s'est substitué à l'ancien. Il tente d'attirer l'investisseur à l'étranger, mais, plus que le premier, il vise à créer des effets utiles quant au développement national.

L'armée nationale, au moment du départ de son chef d'Etat-major général de division, Jean Alfred Dialb, est réorganisée au sommet. Dans le domaine international enfin, l'assemblée nationale a autorisé le Président de la République à ratifier la convention instituant l'OMVS.

DROIT CONSTITUTIONNEL

La loi organique n° 72-88 abrogeant et remplaçant l'article 1er de l'ordonnance n° 63-04 du 6 juin 1963 portant loi organique fixant le nombre des membres de l'Assemblée Nationale, leurs indemnités, les conditions d'éligibilités, le régime des inéligibilités et des incompatibilités (JO N° 4257 du 28 octobre 1972 p. 1781) porte le nombre des députés de 80 à 100.

Cette messure a été rendue nécessaire, de l'avis des autorités sénégalaises, par le dépeuplement de l'Assemblée Nationale (députés appelés à exercer d'autres fonctions) et la volonté de renforcer la représentation de certains groupements (Organisations socio-professionnelles, mouvement des femmes du parti, mouvement des jeunes du parti).

DROIT ADMINISTRATIF

Les lois 72-25 et 72-26 du 19 avril 1972 (JO 42.24 du 13 mai 1972 p. 755 et suivantes, p. 763 et suivantes) sont relatives aux communautés rurales et au régime municipal de Dakar.

La communauté rurale est une personne morale de droit public, dotée de l'autonomie financière. Elle est 'constituée par un certain nombre de villages appartenant au même terroir, unis par une solidarité résultant notamment du voisinage, possédant des intérêts communs et capables de trouver les ressources nécessaires à leur développement'. (art. 1er al. 1.) Créées par décret après avis du comité départemental de développement, elles ont pour organes le Conseil rural et le Président du Conseil rural dont les attributions sont définies au chapitre III.

Selon la loi nouvelle portant régime municipal de Dakar, le territoire de la commune de Dakar qui s'étend sur toute la région du Cap-Vert, est subdivisé en circonscription urbaine par décret. A la tête de chaque circonscription urbaine est placé un préfet chargé, sous la direction du gouverneur, de l'administration de la circonscription. La loi prévoit également la section rurale et la section urbaine comme organes de participation.

La loi n° 72-27 du 26 mai 1972 (JO 42.28 du 3 juin 1972 p. 903) organise les conseils régionaux, les conseils départementaux et les conseils d'arrondissement et détermine leurs attributions et leurs modalités de fonctionnement.

La loi n° 72-42 (JO 4231 du 24 juin 1972, p. 995) réorganise l'armée nationale sénégalaise. Le Président de la République assure le haut commandement des Forces armées. Il est assisté d'un Etat-Major particulier et de l'inspection générale des Forces armées. Le Premier Ministre est responsable devant le Président de la République de l'application de la politique militaire définie en Conseil Supérieur de la Défense Nationale. Sous son autorité le Ministre des Forces armées est chargé de la mise en condition des Forces armées et de l'exécution des décisions du Président de la République. Pour ce faire, le Ministre dispose de la Direction de la gendarmerie et de l'Etat-Major de l'armée nationale.

Les décrets n° 72-687 du 12 juin 1972 (JO n° 4231 du 24 juin 1972 p. 999) et n° 72688 paru dans le même JO, à la p. 1001, fixent respectivement les attributions et l'organisation du Ministère des Forces Armées, et celles du Chef d'Etat-Major de l'Armée nationale et du commandant des Forces de gendarmerie.

L'économie de ces trois textes semble être l'abandon de la forte centralisation qui avait prévalu pendant que le général de division Jean Alfred Diallo était Chef d'Etat-Major général, commandant en chef des Forces Armées et Haut commandant de la Gendarmerie.

La loi n° 71-48 du 12 juin 1972 (JO n° 41-32 du 24 juin 1972 p. 1035) définit, d'une part, les établissements publics à caractère administratif, industriel et commercial ou professionnel et, d'autre part, les sociétés d'économie mixte, les associations reconnues d'utilité publique et les fondations. Elle établit dans son titre deuxième les modalités de contrôle des Etablissements publics, des sociétés d'économie mixte, des personnes

morales de droit privé bénéficiant du concours financier de l'Etat. le titre
III de la loi institue une commission de vérification des comptes et de
contrôle des établissements publics. Dans son annexe, il est dressé une
liste des Etablissements publics existant actuellement au Sénégal.

Le code des investissements, défini par la loi n° 72-43 (JO 42-31 du 24
juin 1972, p. 995) témoigne de la grande sollicitude du législateur
sénégalais pour les investisseurs étrangers.

Le nouveau code donne aux investisseurs étrangers la possibilité
d'acquérir, sous réserve de disposition en vigueur, tous droits de toute
nature en matière de propriété, de concessions et d'autorisations
administratives. Il leur est permis de participer aux marchés publics et
surtout, il leur est garanti le droit de transfert des capitaux et de leurs
revenus dès lors que l'investissement a été financé par un apport de
devises convertibles. Dans le même acte, le Sénégal s'interdit, d'ailleurs,
de prendre des mesures discriminatoires en matière d'obligations sociales
ou de mesures fiscales entre les investisseurs éventuels et ceux exerçant
déjà la même activité. Les seules discriminations que le Sénégal s'autorise
de prendre s'analysent comme des avantages consentis à des entreprises
classées prioritaires (ch. II, Titre II) ou conventionnées (Ch. III, Titre II)
pour favoriser l'exportation, la création d'emplois nouveaux, l'implication
d'entreprises en dehors du Cap-Vert. Elles sont conformes à l'esprit du
nouveau code dont les égards vis-à-vis des investisseurs sont à la mesure
du souffle qu'ils apportent au développement national.

DROIT CIVIL

La loi n° 72-61 du 12 juin 1972 (JO 41-42 du 12 août p. 1295) a institué au
Sénégal, un code de la famille.

Pour deux raisons, un tel travail méritait d'être fait. L'intégration
nationale l'exigeait, tout comme le postulait le développement de l'Etat
sénégalais. '

La République laïque du Sénégal compte plusieurs ethnies, à majorité
musulmane, avec néanmoins une forte minorité de chrétiens et quelques
animistes. Les différentes coutumes ayant survécu à l'adoption de l'Islam
(droit écrit) ou de droit canonique, le droit de la famille variait d'une
ethnie et d'une religion aux autres. Or il est bien entendu que
l'application d'un droit de la famille in différem-ment, sinon de la
confession, tout au moins de l'ethnie, est un des conditions préalables à
l'intégration nationale.

Par ailleurs, le Sénégal d'aujourd'hi ne pouvait pas négliger de rompre
avec les incertitudes de coutumes multiples. Il lui fallait un droit, au plan
familial surtout, apte à promouvoir son développement. C'était d'autant
plus urgent que des regroupements sociaux d'inspiration variable avaient,
depuis longtemps, manifesté leur volonté de favoriser la suppression de
certaines règles perçues par eux comme injustes et inadaptées. Parmi les
règles contestées, on pourrait citer la dot, la polygamie, le divorce par
répudiation, certaines pratiques en matière de succession.

Les travaux préparatoires du code de la famille auront mobilisé,
pendant longtemps, de nombreuses personnes, notoriétés de toute sorte,
cadis, hommes du clergé, notables, professeurs, magistrats, etc . . . Les

résultats sont à la mesure des efforts déployés. 874 articles, répartis en 8 livres traitent: des personnes, du bien matrimonial, de la parenté et de l'alliance, des incapacités, des régimes matrimoniaux, des successions, des intestat et des donations entre vifs et les testaments.

Ils offrent tantôt un statut unique aux nationaux sénégalais, tantôt plusieurs options. En règle générale, les dispositions du code sénégalais s'inspirent soit du code civil français, soit du droit musulman, soit d'une sorte de compromis entre ce qui est et ce qui est souhaité. Nous nous trouvons hors du radicalisme des mesures prises ailleurs. Rien de semblable à la loi guinéene (N° 4-68 du 5/2/68) portant interdiction de la polygamie et réglementation du divorce. Et l'on pourrait peut-être regretter, de la part du législateur senégalais, un certain manque d'audace. mais n'était-ce pas donner applicabilité à la loi nouvelle, et en tout cas, respecter les convictions des uns et des autres, car finalement on pourrait se demander au nom de quel principe supérieur imposer la monogamie à des adeptes de Mahomet.

Le code de la famille sénégalais, oeuvre législative hautement appréciable, aura été le produit d'un compromis entre les exigences d'une société qui se voudrait intégrée, moderne et développée et ses mentalités peu ouvertes aux changements, tout au moins en ce qui concerne le droit de la famille. La publicité faite autour du code, le dynamisme novateur des associations socio-professionnelles, dans l'esprit du législateur sénégalais, devraient achever de convaincre les Sénégalais de choisir les voies du siècle. D'ores et déjà, le facteur ethnique n'est guère plus actif, même si le facteur confessionnel reste encore puissant.

DROIT COMMERCIAL

La loi n° 72-46 du 12 juin 1972 (JO n° 42.31 du 24 juin 1972, p. 998) tente d'encourager les personnes physiques ou morales de nationalité sénégalaise à créer ou étendre la petite et moyenne entreprise dans le domaine de la pêche, de l'agriculture, de l'élevage, de l'industrie et du tourisme.

Cette loi quailfie de sénégalaises les sociétés dont la majorité du capital est détenue par les nationaux sénégalais ayant exclusivement la nationalité sénégalaise. Elle assimile les sociétés de gestion des domaines industriels créées dans les régions pour faciliter le développement industriel, aux personnes morales de nationalité sénégalaise, si l'Etat participe à leur capital.

DROIT PÉNAL

A l'occasion de l'adoption de la loi n° 72-21 du 19 avril 1972 (JO 4224, 13 mai 1972, p. 649), la République du Sénégal définit une zone de pêche de 100 Milles marins au-delà des eaux territoriales et fixe l'échelle des sanctions relativement sévères qu'encourent les contrevenants. Toutefois, l'article 8 prévoit la possibilité de transactions. De toute façon, on se demande comment, dans l'état actuel des choses, le Sénégal pourra faire respecter cette législation qui, dans ses défintions, s'inspire de la Convention de Genève de 1958 sur le Plateau Continental.

CHAPTER SIXTEEN

NIGER

Birame N'Diaye

L'examen des textes législatifs et règlementaires de la République du Niger, pour l'année 1972, révèle le souci qu'ont les autorités de ce pays de le doter d'une administration sûre et efficace.

DROIT ADMINISTRATIF

Les conflits plus ou moins ouverts qui se produisaient entre les différents services de la Présidence de la République devraient être résolus par l'affirmation de la prééminence du Secrétariat d'Etat à la Présidence de la République par les décrets 72.1 PRN/DIR/CAB du 3 janv. 1972 (JO 15 janvier, 1972, n° 2 p. 30) et 72.66 PRN/SEP du 15 juillet 1972 (JO 1er Août, 1972, n° 15, p. 367).

Un institut national de gestion, établissement public à caractère industriel et commercial, est créé par la loi n° 72-16 du 18 avril 1972 (JO 1er mai 1972, n° 9, p. 251. Agissant en qualité de gérant unique et permanent, l'institut national de gestion (ING) exerce les droits d'actionnaire de l'Etat, dans toutes les sociétés où celui-ci détient une participation, à l'exception des sociétés de statut international. L'ING doit aider sociétés d'économie mixte énumérées par la loi n° 72-16 à coordonner leurs activités, veiller à ce qu'elles réalisent les missions d'intérêt général que leur a confiées l'Etat. L'ING doit apporter assistance à ces sociétés sous forme de conseils et d'aides pour la tenue des compatibilités, le recrutement des cadres et techniciens et l'étude des réorganisations utiles. Si les établissements publics en font la demande, l'ING peut gérer leurs participations dans les sociétés et procéder à toute étude de gestion. L'institut national de gestion n'est pas habilité à prendre des intérêts dans une société. Les statuts et règles de fonctionnements de l'ING sont fixés par le décret n° 72-51 du 19 mai, 1972 (JO 1er Juin 1972, n° 11, p. 285).

Un Comité national pour la promotion humaine est créé par le décret n° 72-52 PRN/DEP du 19 mai 1972 (JP 1er Juin 1972, N° 11, p. 288). Parmi les membres du comité, il faut citer les Ministres et Secrétaires d'Etat, les deux représentants à l'Assemblée Nationale, le président du PPN-RDA. Le Secrétariat d'Etat à la Présidence de la République assure le secrétariat du comité.

Le décret n° 72-64 PRN du 15 Juillet 1972 (JO 1er août 1972, p. 366) modifiant le décret n° 68-97 PRN/DIR/CAB du 23 juillet 1968 portant création et organisation du comité technique interministériel de l'uranium, établit la nouvelle liste des membres de droit du comité.

PROCÉDURE CIVILE

D'après la loi n° 72-2 du 17 Février 1972 portant modification de la loi n° 68-28 du 15 juillet 1961, déterminant la composition, l'organisation, les attributions et le fonctionnement de la Cour Sumprême (JO du 1er mars, 1972, n° 5 p. 109), ne peuvent être investis de fonctions de conseiller au sein des chambres judiciaire ou administrative que les titulaires de la licence en droit.

Le Vice-Président, les conseillers et le procureur général, aux termes de cette loi, sont nommés pour une période de cinq ans renouvelable par décret du Président de la République.

La Chambre judiciaire (art. 40) est composée du Vice-président de la Cour Suprême et de deux conseillers. Les deux conseillers doivent appartenir à l'ordre judiciaire.

DROIT PÉNAL

La loi n° 72-9 du 5 avril 1972 (JO 15 avril 1972, n° 8, p. 182) a autorisé le Président de la République à ratifier la convention pour la répression d'actes illicites dirigés contre la sécurité de l'aviation civile.

La loi n° 72-19 du 19 septembre (JO 1er Octobre 1972 n° 19 p. 489) a donné au Président de la République l'autorisation de ratifier la convention concernant les mesures à prendre pour interdire et empêcher l'importation, l'exportation et le transfert de propriété illicites de biens culturels. La dite convention avait été adoptée par la Conférence générale de l'UNESCO le 14 novembre 1970 en vue de rendre efficace la protection du patrimoine culturel.

CHAPTER SEVENTEEN

LA GUINEE

Birame N'Diaye

Des textes législatifs et réglementaires de la République de Guinée, pour l'année 1972, ressortent deux préoccupations majeures du gouvernement de M. Sekou Touré: la survie du régime, la volonté d'exploiter les ressources culturelles nationales.

La réservation de l'idéologie à la compétence exclusive du Responsable suprême de la Révolution, la Répartition des compêtences entre quelques super-ministres, tous membres du BPN, la création du Bureau de gestion des hauts fonctionnaires et les Experts étrangers et enfin la qualification de crime de la fuite des établissements scolaires, attestent que la base du régime de M. Sékou Touré se restreint de jour en jour et que la préoccupation majeure de son gouvernement est de subsister, s'il le faut, au mépris des règles les plus élémentaires du centralisme démocratique et des libertés fondamentales.

D'un autre côté, le texte portant création d'une direction chargée des langues nationales démontre la volonté mordante du gouvernement de Conakry d'exprimer et d'exploiter les valeurs culturelles nationales en vue d'accélérer le processus de développement et de favoriser l'éclosion d'une civilisation.

Dans le domaine international, le fait saillant, pour la République de Guinée, est son absence de la nouvelle organisation pour la mise en valeur du Fleuve Sénégal.

DROIT CONSTITUTIONNEL

Le décret n° 113.PRG du 26 avril (JO n° 12 du 15 juin 1972, p. 110), a une importance particulière. Dans son article premier il réserve l'idéologie à la compétence exclusive du Responsable suprême de la Révolution et marque ainsi une nouvelle étape dans la personnalisation du régime guinéen.

L'article deuxième fixe les six domaine ministériels quo composent désormais le Gouvernement de la République de Guinée.

Autour du Premier Ministre (fonction nouvelle), on trouve désormais un Ministère de l'Economie et des Finances, un Ministère du Commerce, un Ministère des Affaires sociales, un Ministère de l'Education Nationale et un Ministère de l'Intérieur et de la Sécurité.

Le décret n° 114 PRG du 26 avril 1972 (JO n° 12 du 15 juin 1972, p. 111) article 1er interdit à toutes les fédérations du parti de créer de nouvelles sections et réserve un tel pouvoir aux instances nationales. Selon l'article deuxième du dit décret la mesure est justifiée par le fait que la création des sections nouvelles modifie les bases structurelles du parti.

DROIT ADMINISTRATIF

Le décret n° 65 PRG du 3 mars 1972 (JO n° 6 du 15 mars 1972, p. 51) crée au sein du Secrétariat d'Etat à l'Idéologie, au Télé-enseignement et à l'alphabétisation, une Direction générale de l'enseignement des langues nationalies.

La nouvelle direction est chargée de promouvoir 'tant dans les CER que chez les travailleurs des entreprises agricoles, industrielles ou commerciales et au sein des militants des Pouvoirs Révolutionnaires locaux, l'acquisition de la pratique écrite des langues nationales (guinéennes) utilisées comme instrument de diffusion de la science, de la technologie et de la philosophie et de recherche dans ces divers domaines'.

La direction générale de l'enseignement des langues nationales doit également assurer la mise au point d'une 'pédagogie efficiente', l'élaboration de manuels scolaires portant sur tous les domaines, principalement les manuels scolaires destinés aux CER (1er, 2ème, et 3ème cycles), les manuels techniques de formation et de surformation professionnelles destinés à la formation des spécialistes de langues nationales'; 'la direction ' doit de ce fait promouvoir une politique de qualification des langues nationales laur permettant de remplir pleinement leur office de langue de civilisation écrite, de culture, de philosophie, de science et de technique à tous les niveaux'.

Le décret du 15 Mars organise en même temps l'ensemble des services qui constituent la direction des langues:

(1) Le service pédagogique d'élaboration des manuels scolaires de langues nationales
(2) Le service national d'alphabetisation
(3) Le service du Bureau de Recherche, Presse et Documentation.

DROIT DU TRAVAIL

Le décret n° 2P2 PRG du 31 juillet 1972 (JO n° 19 du 1er Octobre 1972, p. 166) donne droit à tout travailleur guinéen, à l'exception du personnel enseignant, à un mois de congé payé par an. Ce droit au congé annuel est accordé indifféremment du statut dont relève le travailleur guinéen.

Le décret n° 232 PRG du 14 septembre 1972 (JO n° 20 du 15 octobre 1972, p. 174) crée un Bureau de la Fonction Publique des hauts cadres, appelé Bureau de gestion des Hauts Cadres et rattaché au Secrétariat général du Gouvernement. Le Bureau de gestion des hauts cadres est 'chargé de constituer et de tenir à jour en vue de suivre leur vie administrative, les dossiers personnels et tous les documents de gestion administrative des hauts cadres de l'Etat, des experts étrangers'.

Relèvent du Bureau:

Les Membres du Governement, les Ambassades de la République de Guinée, les Officiers Supérieurs de l'Armée, les Directeurs et Chefs des Cabinets ministériels, les Gouverneurs de Région et les Inspecteurs des Affaires administratives et financières et les Secrétaires généraux de Région, les Chefs de Service, les Directeurs des Sociétés et Entreprises publiques ou semi-publiques, les experts étrangers.

Ce texte témoigne de la méfiance du régime de M. Sékou Touré à l'égard des hauts fonctionnaires guinéens et experts étrangers.

DROIT PÉNAL

Le décret n° 226 PRG du 1er Septembre 1972 (JO n° 20 du 15 octobre 1972, p. 174) portant modification des articles 3 et 6 du décret n° 224 du 3 juin 1964 relatif à la limitation des eaux territoriales de la République de Guinée fixe les sanctions en cas de violence de ces dispositions:

(a) une amende de 1 à 500.000 francs guinéens.
(b) une peine d'emprisonnement allant de 6 mois à 2 ans.
(c) les peines peuvent être portées jusqu'au double en cas de récidive.

Il y a récidive, lorsque dans une délai de 5 ans, l'auteur de l'infraction a fait de la fuite des établissements scolaires par les élèves ou étudiants gui-précitées.

Indépendamment des peines prévues à l'article 3, le tribumal compétent peut ordonner la confiscation au profit de l'Etat tant des engins de pêche dont l'emploi a permis l'infraction, que du navire lui-même, ainsi que du produit de la pêche.

Le décret n° 261 PRG du 3 octobre 1972 (JO 1er décembre 1972, p. 199) fait de la guite des établissements scolaires par les élèves ou étudiants gui néens un crime contre la sûreté extérieure de l'Etat. D'après le même acte, toute personne qui 'aura par aide ou assistance contribué à faciliter cette fuite' sera considérée comme complice. Les parents des élèves ou étudiants déserteurs sont tenus de rembourser les frais de scolarité et peuvent être contraints par tous 'les moyens tels que , par exemple, arrestation, détention, saisie et vente publique de tous leurs biens, etc . . .' la constatation de crime de désertion des établissements scolaires entraîne, ipso facto, la suppression de la bourse aux frères et soeurs et le rejet des demandes de bourse présentées par eux.

Ce texte revêt une importance singulière et témoigne de la profondeur du malaise guinéen. C'est un fait que les Etats du Tiers-Monde consacrent des sommes importantes à l'éducation et que de l'évasion des élèves et étudiants résulte une perte énorme pour l'économie de la nation toute entière. Mais est-il pour autant permis de qualifier de tels actes d'atteinte à la sûreté extérieure de l'Etat? Il est regrettable, nous semble-t-il, que le gouvernement de Conakry ait recouru au système des otages et à la notion de solidarité familiale pour décourager les éventuels déserteurs. Ces méthodes médiévales comportent des injustices aussi insupportables que celles reprochées aux élèves et étudiants déserteurs.

CHAPTER EIGHTEEN

LA REPUBLIQUE DE COTE D'IVOIRE

Michel L. Martin

Vedette africaine du développement et de la modernisation, la Côte d'Ivoire poursuit ses objectifs économiques avec sérénité. Diverses mesures d'ordre social (cf. les mesures d'austérité prises fin janvier) sont venues calmer les tensions engendrées par ce 'boom économique' qui creuse davantage, convient-il de faire remarquer, le fossé entre une élite socio-économique et les couches sociales plus défavorisées.

D'autre part, les disparités économiques et sociales entre le nord et le sud du pays représentent toujours le problème le plus complexe et le plus urgent à résoudre.

Quant à l'activité législative, elle témoigne surtout de réformes et de modifications dans le cadre des structures politiques actuelles.

DROIT ADMINISTRATIF

Le décret n° 72-86 du 28 janvier 1972 fixe le statut du personnel des établissements publics à caractère industriel et commercial et des sociétés d'Etat. Il unifie ainsi des dispositions diverses qui résultaient notamment de la loi du 1er août 1964 portant Code du Travail, de la loi du 5 novembre 1970 fixant le régime des sociétés à participation financière publique et le décret du 11 janvier 1972 fixant les règles de gestion et de contrôle des sociétés à participation financière publique.

Le décret n° 72-141 du 16 février 1972 fixe le nouveau régime des déplacements des fonctionnaires et agents en service dans les Administrations et établissements publics administratifs de l'Etat. Il ne modifie le précédent décret, qui datait du 26 avril 1966, que sur des détails concernant le montant des frais de mission alloués aux divers corps de fonctionnaires.

Le décret n° 72.07 du 11 janvier 1972 crée un Fonds d'emploi des bénéfices réalisés par les Sociétés d'Etat et les sociétés d'Economie Mixte, et fixe ses modalités de fonctionnement.

Le décret n° 72-08 du 11 janvier 1972 fixe les règles de gestion et de contrôle des Sociétés à participation financière publique. Il annule le décret n° 63-277 du 12 juin 1963 règlementant le contrôle des Sociétés d'Etat, modifie le décret n° 64-116 du 6 mars 1964 portant organisation du contrôle économique et financier et complète la loi n° 70-633 du 5 novembre 1970 fixant le régime des Sociétés à participation financière publique.

DROIT COMMERCIAL

Le décret n° 72-06 du 11 janvier 1972 constate le droit électoral et l'éligibilité des ressortissants libanais aux assemblées consulaires ivoiriennes. Il complète sur ce point les décrets du 17 mai 1963 portant organisation des Chambres de Commerce et des Chambres d'Industrie et le décret du 9 janvier 1964 portant organisation des Chambres d'Agriculture.

La loi n° 72-513 du 27 juillet 1972 règlemente la location-gérance des fonds de commerce. Elle stipule notamment que le locataire-gérant a la qualité de commerçant et que les personnes physiques ou morales qui concèdent une location-gérance doivent avoir été commerçantes ou avoir exercé les fonctions de gérant ou de directeur commercial et technique pendant 5 ans. Ces personnes doivent également avoir exploité pendant 2 années au moins en qualité de commerçant le fonds mis en gérance. Ces dispositions n'ont cependant pas d'effet rétroactif et ne s'appliquent donc pas aux contrats en cours.

CHAPTER NINETEEN

REPUBLIQUE DU DAHOMEY

François Constantin

Ayant instauré une forme de gouvernement originale pour réaliser au sommet la synthèse de forces régionales qui se disputaient la direction du Dahomey, le 'Conseil présidentiel' paraissait fonctionner de manière satisfaisante. Pourtant une première alerte est intervenue en février, où une 'mutinerie' animée par quelques officiers et sous-officiers échoua. Quelques mois plus tard, le Conseil Présidentiel et ses Ministres se retrouvaient enfermés au 'Palais de l'Entente' où avait lieu le Conseil des Ministres, par d'autres officiers, qui installaient au pouvoir le Commandant Kerekou (26 octobre). Reprenant un thème familier aux auteurs de coups d'Etat le nouveau chef du Dahomey dénonçait la corruption et l'incompétence du Conseil présidentiel et annonçait des réformes sérieuses afin de moraliser la vie politique, administrative ou économique du pays. Au niveau de l'activité législative, le changement n'est guère perceptible, d'autant que l'oeuvre du Conseil Présidentiel, entre janvier et octobre 1972, était restée mince.

Tout au plus peut-on souligner l'apparente volonté qui s'était manifestée d'un retour à la 'normale', c'est-à-dire l'atténuation des lois d'exception qui s'étaient succédées au cours des années précédentes. L'essentiel demeure encore dans des mesures qui n'interviennent guère que dans les domaines que peut prétendre contrôler le gouvernement, c'est-à-dire la règlementation administrative.

DROIT CONSTITUTIONNEL

L'ordonnance n° 72.39 du 26 octobre abroge l'ordonnance n° 70.34 qui instituait le Conseil présidentiel. Un Conseil Militaire de la Révolution, composé de 15 officiers et Sous-Officiers, est institué par l'Ordonnance n° 72.47 du 11 novembre 1972. Il est chargé de 'soutenir' l'action du 'Gouvernement Militaire Révolutionnaire' et de contrôler l'application des décisions prises par le Gouvernement.

DROIT ADMINISTRATIF

Il faut noter pour mémoire l'intervention de nombreux décrets, complétant non sans hésitations et contradictions la carte administrative du Dahomey, par la création de nouveaux arrondissements (Voir par exemple les Décrets 72.117 à 126 du 3 mai 1972, JORD n° 12, p. 465 à 473, ou les Décrets 72.263 et 264 du 29 septembre 1972, JORD n° 22, p. 830-831).

Si ces mesures témoignent de la volonté d'améliorer l'encadrement des populations, leur portée concrète demeure sans doute limitée. Plus opérationnelles sont les décisions qui interviennent en matière de droit public économique.

La première ordonnance de l'année (Ordonnance n° 72.1 du 8 janvier, JORD, n° 5, p. 162) définit le nouveau Code des Investissements, qui remplace les dispositions antérieures (Lois n° 60.18 du 13 juillet 1960 et 61-53 du 31 décembre 1961). Ce nouveau Code définit deux régimes différents: Un régime de droit commun applicable à toutes les entreprises, pose le principe de la liberté d'établissement et apporte la garantie de l'Etat pour l'indemnisation en cas d'expropriation et le transfert des bénéfices. Un régime 'privilégié' est réservé aux entreprises qui, par la localisation des Investissements, leur volume, leur impact sur le marché de l'emploi ou sur la balance du commerce international. présentent un intérêt particulier pour le Dahomey. Le bénéfice de ce régime 'privilégié' est accordé par le Conseil des Ministres, après consultation d'une 'Commission Technique des Investissements'. Selon le cas, trois formules de 'privilèges' sont prévues: les régimes A, B et C fixent les avantages et obligations des investisseurs (Voir art. 30 à 42). Un régime spécial (D) est prévu pour les entreprises privées dahoméennes.

Complétant ce réaménagement de l'activité économique privée, l'Ordonnance n° 72.11 du 8 avril 1972 (JORD n° 9, 310) précise la place de l'Etat dans les Sociétés d'Etat, les Sociétés d'Economie Mixte et les autres sociétés où l'Etat a une participation, ainsi que les principales modalités de gestion de ces entreprises. Le premier mérite de cette ordonnance est de donner une définition précise des 'Sociétés d'Etat' et des critères distinctifs de la 'Société d'Economie Mixte', critères qui ne tiennent pas seulement à la part de L'Etat dans le capital de la société. Par contre, la notion d'Etablissement Public à caractère industriel ou commercial reste floue. L'ordonnance prévoit en outre les règles de la gestion de ces entreprises publiques, les modalités de contrôle, par le biais notamment d'un Conseil Supérieur d'Animation et de Contrôle, dont la composition et les règles de fonctionnement font l'objet du Décret 72-77 du 8 avril (JORD n° 9, p. 316).

En ce qui concerne la fonction publique, un nouveau statut général est publié avec l'Ordonnance n° 72-23 du 24 juillet (JORD n° 15 p. 559) qui remplace le statut antérieur datant de 1959. Ce statut s'applique à tous les agents de l'Administration, des services extérieurs et des établissements publics de l'Etat (en sont toutefois exclus les magistrats judiciaires, les militaires, les forces de police et le personnel des services industriels ou commerciaux). Ce statut réserve en principe les emplois publics aux nationaux dahoméens. L'exposé des devoirs et droits des fonctionnaires demeure fort proche du régime appliqué en France (obligation de discrétion, incompatibilités, droit syndical, droit de grève), tout comme l'exposé des positions du fonctionnaire. On retrouve dans la procédure disciplinaire des garanties classiques telles que la comparution devant un Conseil de discipline et le droit à communication du dossier. En définitive, ce statut, complété par le Décret 72.196 du 24 juillet (JORD n° 15 p. 565), doit accorder au fonctionnaire dahoméen la sécurité qui caractérise la fonction publique en droit administratif français.

Curieusement, le lendemain de la publication de ce nouveau statut, un statut particulier est publié, qui repose sur le système antérieur de 1959 puisqu'il s'agit d'un Décret n° 71-103 adopté le 22 avril (JORD, n° 16, p. 594) concernant les modalités techniques du déroulement de la carrière du personnel des Postes et Télécommunications.

DROIT COMMERCIAL

Une brève ordonnace n° 78-19 du 8 juin (JORD n° 14 p. 328) définit les entreprises de leasing ou de crédit-bail et les situe dans le cadre juridique antérieurement mis au point pour les établissements financiers (Loi du 8 juin 1965, Décrets du 26 février 1966, du 30 juin 1966 et arrêté du 6 juillet 1966). Elle interdit en outre à ces entreprises de procéder à des activités de vente à crédit.

DROIT PÉNAL

Dans une perspective d'apaisement, le Conseil Présidentiel avait décidé, par l'Ordonnance n° 72-15 du 3 mai (JORD n° 12 p. 464), l'abrogation d'une ordonnance antérieure (N° 69-33 PR) qui élargissait la définition des crimes et délits contre la sûreté de l'Etat et apportait au Code Pénal des modifications quant à leur répression (Art. 98 à 108 du Code Pénal).

Une autre mesure à caractère pénal est intervenue. Malgré sa portée générale, elle parait liée aux circonstances, à savoir le développement de la peste bovine au Dahomey. En effet, l'Ordonnance n° 72-31 du 27 septembre (JORD) n° 22 p. 828) règlemente de façon très stricte le contrôle sanitaire des animaux et l'inspection des denrées alimentaires (Déclaration des animaux atteints, isolement obligatoire, conditions d'abattage des bêtes contaminées, sanctions contre ceux qui ne respectent pas les dispositions de l'ordonnance).

CHAPTER TWENTY

REPUBLIQUE DU CAMEROUN UNI

Michel L. Martin

L'année 1971, en commençant par l'éxécution du leader de l'Union des Populations du Cameroun, Ernest Ouandié, symbolisait, semble-t-il, la fin de la rébellion Bamileké.

Le gouvernement s'était alors attelé à de nouvelles tâches de caractère national dont it devrait poursuivre l'éxécution en 1972.

L'une d'entre elles a particulièrement marqué l'activité politique du Cameroun. Il s'agit de la transformation de la République fédérale en un Etat unitaire. La vieille constitution fédérale de 1961, qui avait permis de garantir les institutions du Cameroun Occidentale (ex-possession britannique) ne répondait plus aux besoins actuels d'intégration nationale, à l'évolution politico-institutionnelle du pays et, convient-il d'ajouter, exigeait pour son application des coûts financiers fort élevés.

Mais cette évolution s'inscrit aussi dans le cadre d'un phénomène politique plus large que celui du renforcement de l'éxécutif des systèmes politiques africains.

DROIT CONSTITUTIONNEL

Toute l'activité législative est animée par le mouvement vers l'unité. La réforme législative centrale s'est articulée autour d'une nouvelle constitution et du référendum.

Les modalités référendaires ayant été fixées par le décret n° 72.DF 236 du 8 mai 1972 (JO RFC du 8 mai), c'est le Décret n° 72 DF 239 du 9 mai 1972 (JO RFC, 9 mai, n° supplémentaire) qui porte publication du projet de constitution et décide de le soumettre au référendum. Le référendum est fixé pour le 20 mai.

Le décret 72-270 du 2 juin 1972 (JO RUC, 2 juin 1972, p. 33) porte promulgation de la nouvelle constitution de la République Unie du Cameroun. Le texte de cette constitution exige quelques remarques.

Cette orientation consacrait sur le plan législatif un certain nombre de mutations institutionnelles implicites.

Les principes fondamentaux portent essentiellement sur l'Unité (mais sauvegardent aussi une certaine diversité culturelle puisque le français et l'anglais sont les deux langues officielles) et sur la Démocratie (attachement à la Déclaration universelle des Droits de l'homme).

Quant aux structures, la nouvelle constitution témoigne d'un renforcement sensible de l'éxécutif et d'un recul parallèle du rôle de l'Assemblée. Le Chef de l'Etat tient ses pouvoirs de l'élection au suffrage universel (art. 2). Il est à la fois Président de la République et chef unique du gouvernement. En temps normal, il dispose des pouvoirs traditionnels vis-à-vis de l'Administration, de l'Assemblée et de la Cour Suprême. En ce qui concerne les attributions extraordinaires, il faut noter l'art. 11 qui lui permet, si les circonstances l'exigent, de proclamer l'état d'urgence, lui confiant une série de pouvoirs spéciaux. La procédure l'oblige simplement à informer la Nation par voie de message. (C'est une sorte d'art. 16 renforcé). L'assemblée n'exerce aucun contrôle, elle ne siège même pas. Si le rôle de l'assemblée, en cas d'urgence, est extrêmement réduit, il reste en période normale indiscutablement faible. Elle est élue au suffrage universel; elle est composée de 120 membres. Le domaine de la loi est fixé et délimité par l'art. 20 D'autre part, diverses restrictions (art. 42, par exemple et l'art. 36 concernant recours au référendum) permettent à l'éxécutif d'empiéter sur le domaine législatif de l'Assemblée.

A côté de ces deux principaux organes, la constitution crée une Cour suprême, une Haute Cour de justice et le Conseil économique et social.

Par conséquent, cette nouvelle constitution établit un régime présidentiel solide que vient renforcer l'existence d'un parti dominant sinon unique. Dès lors le train des mesures de réorganisation allait suivre:

Le décret 72-282 du 8 juin 1972 (JO RUC, 15 juin 1972, p. 20) organise la Présidence de la République.

Le décret 72 LF 6 du 26 juin 1972 (JO RUC, 1er juillet 1972, p. 48) fixe les conditions d'élection des membres de l'Assemblée nationale, en application de l'article 17 de la Constitution promulguée le 2 juin 1972.

Ces membres sont élus pour une durée de 5 ans, au suffrage universel direct et secret. 120 sièges sont à pourvoir. Le scrutin est à un tour, sans vote préférentiel, panachage ou liste incomplète. La majorité électorale est de 21 ans. Pour être éligible il faut avoir 23 ans au minimum.

L'ordonnance 72-7 du 26 août 1972 (JO RUC 1er septembre 1972, p. 70) organise la Haute Cour de Justice en vertu de l'art. 34 de la Constitution (Rappelons que la Haute Cour est chargée de juger les membres du gouvernement et le Président de la République).

L'ordonnance 72-10 du 26 août, 1972 (JO RUC 1er septembre 1972, p. 79) fixe la procédure de référendum. Le Président de la République peut désormais soumettre à référendum tout projet de loi ayant des répercussions profondes sur l'avenir du pays.

L'ordonnance 72-13 du 26 août 1972 (JO RUC, 1er septembre 1972, p. 82) est relative à l'état d'urgence (au cas d'évènements considérés comme étant calamités publiques, ou tous troubles susceptibles de porter atteinte à l'ordre public).

DROIT ADMINISTRATIF

Peu d'éléments sont à signaler sous cette rubrique; une exception peut être faite pour ce qui concerne l'organisation du statut du personnel militaire.

La loi 72 FL du 23 mai 1972 (JO RFC, 27 mai 1972, p. 19) organise la profession d'Avocat (ses conditions d'accès, les stages et tableaux, l'exercice de la profession, l'Ordre des avocats et la discipline).

Ajoutons que l'ordonnance 72-8 du 26 août 1972 (JO RUC, 1er septembre 1972, p. 74) fixe l'organisation et les fonctions du Conseil Supérieur de la Magistrature.

Le Décret 72-349 du 24 juillet 1972 (JO RUC 1er Août 1972, p. 143) porte sur l'organisation administrative de la République Unie du Cameroun.

En ce qui concerne les Forces armées, il convient de noter le Décret 72-303 du 27 juin 1972 (JO RUC 1er août 1972, p. 130) qui organise le Cabinet militaire.

Le Décret 72-126 du 11 juillet 1972 (JO RUC, 1er août 1972, p. 131) modifie le décret 72-DF 93 du 23 février 1972, précisant les modalités d'application du statut des officiers d'active des Forces Armées.

Le Décret 72-319 du 11 juillet 1972 (JO RUC, 1er août 1972, p. 131) porte modificatif et additif au décret 68-DF 270 du 15 juillet 1968, portant règlement général du régime des rémunérations applicables aux personnels militaires des Forces Armées.

Le Décret 72-356 du 25 juillet 1972 porte organisation du ministère des Forces armées.

Enfin l'ordonnance 72-5 du 26 août 1972 (JO RUC, 1er octobre 1972, p. 90) organise le système de justice militaire.

En matière économique, signalons que l'ordonnance 72-18 du 17 octobre 1972, (JO RUC, 1er novembre 1972, p. 131) institue un régime générale des prix. Ce texte permet notamment au gouvernement d'intervenir sur le prix. Ce texte permet notamment au gouvernement d'intervenir sur le prix, la vente et la circulation de certains produits afin d'éviter des hausses d'origine spéculative. Il fixe les modalités décisionnelles de contrôle et de fixation des prix. Il prévoit les infractions à ce régime, leurs constatations, la procédure (avec possibilité pour le contrevenant de bénéficier d'une transaction pécunière) et les sanctions (elles sont judiciaires et administratives).

DROIT PRIVÉ ET PROCÉDURE CIVILE

Notons l'ordonnance 72-6 du 26 août 1972 (JO RUC 1er octobre 1972, p. 97) qui fixe l'organisation de la Cour suprême. On sait que la Cour est chargée notamment de statuer sur les recours en cassation admis par loi contre les décisions rendues en cour d'appel.

L'ordonnance 72-16 du 28 septembre 1972 (JO RUC, 1er octobre 1972, p. 108) porte simplification de la procédure pénale en matière de répression du banditisme. En fait, on s'efforce ici de favoriser la rapidité de l'opération judiciaire.

L'ordonnance 72-4 du 26 août 1972 (JO RUC, 1er Novembre 1972, p. 126) porte organisation judiciaire, en vertu de l'art. 42 de la nouvelle constitution.

Cette ordonnance fixe les dispositions générales relatives à cette organisation. Les diverses mesures portent sur l'organisation (compétence, composition) des tribunaux de première instance, de grande instance (crimes et délits au pénal, différends au civil pour demande excédent 5000.000 Frs CFA), des cours d'appel et du Parquet. Toutefois, les compétences des *Customary Courts,* des polices de paix et juridictions traditionnelles sont provisoirement maintenues; le *Chief Justice* de la Cour Suprême de l'ancien Cameroun Occidental exerce les attributions de président de cour d'appel.

CHAPTER TWENTY-ONE

GABON

Jean-Louis Balans

DROIT CONSTITUTIONNEL

L'ordonnance n° 22.72 du 8 mars (JORG du 15 mars, p. 242) transforme l'Union Nationale des femmes gabonaises créée par l'ordonnance n° 12.7 du 26 février 1971, en Union des Femmes du parti démocratique gabonais chargée de promouvoir l'amélioration de la condition sociale de la femme au Gabon et placée sous la tutelle du Ministre chargé des Affaires sociales.

DROIT ADMINISTRATIF

Le décret n° 00205/PR du 25 janvier (JORG du 15 Février p. 115) porte réorganisation partielle des armées en plaçant l'armée de l'air sous l'autorité directe du Chef de l'Etat.

L'ordonnance n° 2972 du 7 avril (JORG spécial du 15 mai) porte création et statuts de l'office du chemin de fer 'Transgabonais' daté du statuts d'établissement public industriel et commercial.

L'ordonnance n° 31.72 du 17 avril (JORG du 1er Mai p. 392) institue un Conseil Supérieur des Transports auprès du Ministre des transports habilité à donner un avis sur toutes les questions de transports. Ce Conseil comporte une Assemblée où siègent des représentants de l'Administration et des personnalités compétentes, trois commissions spécialisées dans les transports terrestres, maritimes et fluviaux et aériens. Un comité des contestations est eompétent pour donner des avis sur les sanctions administratives et les recours dont est saisi le Ministre contre des décisions d'ordre individuel.

DROIT CIVIL

L'ordonnance n° 40.72 du 17 avril (JORG spécial du 3 juillet) institue le barreau du Gabon organisé sur le modèle du barreau français.

Le décret n° 00229/PR du 4 mars (JORG du 15 mars, p. 115) porte création d'une Inspection des services judiciaires auprès du Ministère de la Justice. Cette inspection est chargée de la vérification et du contrôle de la gestion administrative des greffiers, des parquets et des services dépendant totalement ou partiellement du Ministère de la Justice.

DROIT COMMERCIAL

L'ordonnance n° 41.72 du 10 juin (JORG spécial du 5 juillet rend obligatoire la cession à l'Etat de 10% des parts du capital des sociétés anonymes qui s'installent au Gabon.

DROIT PÉNAL

L'ordonnance n° 25.72 du 27 mars (JORG 1er avril p. 297) complète la loi n° 6.70 du 12 juin 1970 sur la libération conditionnelle: la demande de libération conditionnelle peut être renouvelée deux fois. la décision de rejet qui intervient à la suite de la troisième demande est définitive.

CHAPTER TWENTY-TWO

REPUBLIQUE POPULAIRE DU CONGO

François Constantin

L'étude des livraisons 1972 du Journal Officiel de la République Populaire du Congo est plus révélatrice des vicissitudes de l'appartenance à la 'classe' politique que de l'état du droit positif congolais.

On sait que le régime du Commandant M. Ngouabi cherche à réaliser un équilibre délicat entre certaines factions qualifiées de 'gauchistes' qui n'ont pas été étrangères à son arrivée au pouvoir, et d'autres forces internes ou externes qu'il peut difficilement contrôler. Il en découle des difficultés certaines pour adapter la vie nationale aux principes marxistes-léninistes invoqués par les gouvernants du moment. Les rivaux ou les adversaires du Commandant Ngouabi tirent profit des décalages évidents entre le verbe et la réalité pour contester l'autorité du Chef de l'Etat. Cette autorité demeure cependant suffisante pour lui permettre de transformer en simples soldats d'anciens officiers supérieurs ou obtenir la condamnation à la peine capitale d'anciens leaders politiques ou militaires; promotion, rétrogradation, commutation des peines occupent donc une part significative du Journal officiel.

Dans ce contexte, il est difficile d'envisager la mise au point de changements fondamantaux dans les règles de droit positif. Suivant la nouvelle tradition, une part importante des mesures prises touche les activités administratives. A celles-ci s'ajoutent diverses mesures à caractère répressif, témoignant du souci de contrôl 1er l'activité des particuliers, sinon de l'orienter dans le sens souhaité par les gouvernants. Ces textes essentiels ont donc en commun le souci d'améliorer l'emprise de l'Etat, dans tous ses aspects.

DROIT ADMINISTRATIF

Parmi diverses mesures de réorganisation des administrations centrales, la plus remarquable est sans doute l'Ordonnance nº 2.72 du 19 janvier´

(JORPC n° 3, p. 43) qui décide l'intégration des forces de police dans l'Armée Populaire Nationale. Autrement dit, toutes les forces de maintien de l'ordre sont placées sous l'autorité du Ministre de la Défense Nationale. En application de cette ordonnance, le décret n° 72-180 du 18 mai (JORPC n° 11 p. 358) détermine les conditions de reciassement des fonctionnaires de police dans la hiérar chie militaire.

En matière économique, deux mesures importantes interviennent. Le Décret n° 72-168 du 15 Mai (JORPC n° 11 p. 352) institue auprès de la Présidence du Conseil d'Etat un Commissariat Général au Plan chargé de mettre au point des plans pluriannuels de développement. Pour ce faire, le Commissariat comporte sept divisions (Etudes, Statistique et comptabilité économique, ressources humaines, documentation économique, contrôle, planification régionale, investissements). Complétant cette organisation, le Décret 72.248 du 17 juillet (JORPC n° 15 p. 495) oblige chaque Ministère à créer une 'cellule' autonome permanente chargée de la prévision des activités annuelles de chacun.

L'ordonnance n° 7.72 du 1er février (JORPC n° 4 p. 73) fixe les grandes lignes du statut général des entreprises d'Etat, qui constituent des établissements publics à caractère industriel, agricole ou commercial. Ces entreprises sont soumises aux règles du droit commercial sauf disposition spéciale prévue par l'Ordonnance (art. 2). Les biens constituent les biens de l'Etat; les pouvoirs des autorités de tutelle (Ministre, organe du Parti ou collectivité publique) sont précisés par les Art. 6 à 8: les choix idéologiques du régime apparaissent dans l'organisation de ces Entreprises, où intervient un 'Comité révolutionnaire' de entreprise qui participe, avec les représentants du 'Syndicat de base ou d'entreprise', au Comité de Direction, organe supérieur. Le Directeur est nommé par le 'Conseil d'Etat' (c'est-à-dire le gouvernement). Le statut général prévoit ι en outre mécanismes du fonctionnement sur le plan financier.

DROIT COMMERCIAL

Deux ordonnances n° 24.72 et 25.72 du 12 juin (JORPC n° 13 p. 421) règlementent l'exercice du commerce et le régime des prix en République populaire du Congo. Après avoir posé le principe d'après lequel le commerce se définit par 'l'ensemble des transactions effectuées en vue de favoriser le développement économique et social de la Nation Congolaise' (par opposition à 'l'exploitation'), l'ordonnance définit les différentes formes de commerce (selon l'objet des échanges, selon 'l'importance' (ou plutôt la place dans le circuit économique), selon la cause, selon le lieu). Elle précise que seuls les Congolais peuvent être commerçants sauf exception (art. 4 et 5). Le reste des dispositions demure imprécis et renvoit à des décrets d'application.

La seconde Ordonnance, plus détaillée, précise les différentes modalités possibles de règlementation des prix (art. 2). Elle définit les conditions de constitution de l'infraction de 'majoration illicite des prix' (art. 8, 9, 10 et 12). La publicité des prix est obligatoire, les conditions de la détention de stocks est strictement règlementée et la procédure de répression de toutes les infractions à l'Ordonnance fait l'objet des art. 18 à 46 de l'Ordonnance. La possibilité de transaction pécuniaire est prévue par l'article 28 sans que les conditions précises soint explicitées. Les peines le s plus lourdes menacent ceux qui s'opposeraient au contrôle des agents des services des Prix. La part de responsabilité incombant au commettant, à l'employé, ou à la société fait l'objet des dispositions de l'article 45 de cette Ordonnance.

DROIT INTERNATIONAL PRIVÉ

L'Ordonnance n° 15.72 du 10 avril (JORPC n° 8 p. 213) a pour objet de fixer les règles concernant l'entrée et le séjour des étrangers sur le territoire de la République Populaire du Congo. Elle institue le principe d'un carnet de séjour ou de résident sauf convention de libre circulation avec certains Etats (OCAM, UDEAC, etc . . .). L'Ordonnance distingue sept catégories d'étrangers: les touristes (soumis à un 'visa de court séjour', valable trois mois), les résidents temporaires (soumis à la possession d'un 'carnet bleu' valable un an et renouvelable), les résidents ordinaires ('carnet jaune', valable trois ans et renouvelable. Le titulaire de ce carnet ne peut exercer d'activité professionnelle salariée qu'avec l'autorisation du Ministre du Travail), les résidents privilégiés ('carnet rose' pour celui qui justifie de cinq ans de résidence ininterrompue au Congo (sauf exception), valable cinq ans, renouvelable de plein droit), les ressortissants français et des Etats membres de l'OCAM ('carnet violet', valable trois ans), enfin les diplomates accrédités en République Populaire du Congo et consuls honoraires sont exonérés des obligations de l'ordonnance mais leurs déplacements en République Populaire sont soumis à autorisation du Ministre des Affaires étrangères. Les articles 18 à 23 fixent les peines auxquelles s'exposent les contrevenants. Notons que l'article 22 oblige toute personne logeant un étranger à faire une déclaration à la police dans les 24 heures.

Divers décrets viennent compléter ces règles générales: le décret 72.113 étrangers; le décret 72.115 du 10 avril (JORPC n° 8 p. 216) fixe la procédure de demande de carnet et de son renouvellement; le Décret 72.116 (JORPC, n° 8, p. 218) précise les points obligatoires d'entrée en territoire congolais, les mesures sanitaires, les modalités de versement (ou d'exonération) du cautionnement et les mesures spéciales applicables aux ressortissants de l'UDEAC ou des Etats frontaliers (Zaïre, Angola, Cabinda).

DROIT PÉNAL ET PROCÉDURE PÉNALE

Outre les dispositions mentionnées ci-dessus, il convient de signaler l'adoption de l'Ordonnance n° 6.72 du 26 janvier (JORPC n° 3, p/44) qui précise certains aspects de la réparation des dommages causés par les véhicules appartenant au Corps Diplomatique. Ces véhicules à moteur, qu'ils soient terrestres, maritimes ou fluviaux, doivent être désormais assurés aux tiers, les compagnies d'assurance étant alors appelées directement devant la juridiction civile ou pénale en cas de dommage. Le procureur de la République pourra saisir la juridiction pénale pour statuer sur les intérêts civils.

Enfin l'ordonnance n⁰ 12.72 du 27 février (JORPC n⁰ 6 p. 139) institue une nouvelle cour spéciale, la Cour Martiale, composée d'un président et de deux juges militaires, chargée de juger 'certains crimes' intéressant·la sûreté de l'Etat (art. 1). Cette cour se situe en dehors de l'ordre judiciaire et de l'ordre administratif. L'article 2 définit de façon particulièrement large la nature des crimes et délits qui lui sont soumis. Si celle-ci est appelée à appliquer les peines 'ordinaires', ses décisions ne sont susceptibles d'aucun recours.

CHAPTER TWENTY-THREE

REPUBLIQUE CENTRAFRICAINE

François Constantin

Sous la conduite du Général Bokassa, la République Centrafricaine subit les aléas d'un pouvoir politique incontrôlé. L'activité 'législative' se manifeste par une abondance de mesures à caractère individuel, de rectificatifs aux ordonnances fixant le budget de l'Etat, ou d'annulation de mesures légales ou règlementaires prises quelques semaines ou quelques mois auparavant, alors que des textes fondamentaux demeurent non publiés, du moins pour la période que nous avons pu étudier.

Dans l'ensemble, l'année 1972 n'a été marquée en République Centrafricaine par aucun incident politique remarquable. Les changements dans l'équipe gouvernementale sont pratique courante et les relations extérieures sont davantage marquées par le souci du spectaculaire sans lendemain que par des tentatives profondes de réorientation qu'il serait d'ailleurs difficile de réaliser; le Général Bokassa s'est surtout fai remarquer par l'opinion publique internationale par la méthode mise au point pour mettre un terme aux activités des voleurs sur le territoire de la République Centrafricaine.

DROIT CONSTITUTIONNEL

Le 2 mars, le Congrès du parti unique centrafricain, le MESAN (Mouvement pour l'Evolution Sociale en Afrique Noire) décidait de nommer le Général Bokassa 'Président à vie' de la République Centrafricaine (Voir Bulletin Quotidien d'Afrique—(AFP) n° 7735 du 3 mars 1972). Cette décision, qui modifie en fait les actes constitutionnels des 4 et 8 janvier 1966, n'a pas fait l'objet d'une publication au Journal Officiel de la République Centrafricaine.

DROIT ADMINISTRATIF

L'un des thèmes d'indignation du Général Bokassa étant le mauvais fonctionnement des services administratifs, on comprend que l'activité legislative en République centrafricaine, plus encore que dans les autres Etats africains francophones, soit marquée par de multiples textes réorganisant les Ministères ou les différentes sociétés étatiques ou para-étatiques d'interventionnisme économique. Dans le même esprit-et plus précisément pour lutter contre l'incompétence et la corruption—divers décrets et ordonnances s'efforcent de faire respecter la hiérarchie de la fonction publique (comme par exemple le Décret 72.015 du 4 janvier 1972, JORCA n° 10, p. 261) et l'intégrité des responsables politiques et administratifs (comme l'Ordonnance n° 72.014 du 17 février 1972, JORCA n° 7 p. 171 interdisant aux Ministres de recevoir des dont ou subventions de la part des organismes publics ou para-publics placés sous leur tutelle, et l'ordonnance 72.033 du 7 mars 1972, JORCA n° 7. p. 174 concernant les prises de participation dans les Sociétés d'exploitation ou de commercialisation des diamants et autres métaux précieux).

En matière de responsabilité administrative, l'arrêté n° 0037 MET PHTR du 8 février (JORCA n° 5 p. 145) détermine les sanctions applicables au fonctionnaire responsable d'un accident de la circulation avec un véhicule administratif. Outre les sanctions administratives, la responsabilité pénale du fonctionnaire peut être engagée, l'administration demeurant civilement responsable.

De façon plus générale, le souci du Chef d'État d'améliorer son emprise sur l'appareil administratif et sur la moralité publique se traduit par la création d'un 'Contrôle Général de l'Etat' avec l'Ordonnance 71.140 et le Décret 71.471 du 25 novembre 1971 (JORCA 1972, n° 1 p. 8 et 27). La mise en place de cette nouvelle structure a pour corollaire la suppression des Inspections particulières (Administration et Finances) que confirmeront les Décrets 72.091 et 72.108 (JORCA n° 10, p. 265 et 269). Le nouveau service est placé sous l'autorité directe du Président de la République. Sa compétence s'étend à tous organismes public, nationaux ou locaux, para-publics et privés, lorsque ceux-ci reçoivent une aide du gouvernement (Décret 71-471 a. 9). Ce contrôle est non seulement un contrôle financier, mais aussi un contrôle de la gestion, entendu dans son sens le plus large (Ibid. a. 10).

En matière fiscale, le changement le plus remarquable est apporté par l'Ordonnance 71-147 du 22 décembre (JORCA 1972, n° 1, p. 54). Il modifie le mode de perception de l'Impôt Général sur le Revenu. L'Impôt est soit prélevé à la source (retenue mensuelle) ou versé par accompte mensuel (calculé par le contribuable). Chaque versement doit être égal au 1/5ème du montant de l'impôt; autrement dit à la fin du mois de mai, l'Etat devrait avoir perçu l'essentiel de l'Impôt sur le Reveu. Ce souci d'accélérer les rentrées fiscales est confirmé par d'autres mesures plus particulières qui réduisent les délais des versements libératoires.

Signalons enfin dans le domaine des libertés publiques que l'Ordonnance 72-040 du 12 mai 1972 (JORCA n° 12, p. 326) autorise la création d'Etablissement privés d'enseignement laïc, dont le fonctionnement doit faire l'objet d'un contrôle ministériel très strict.

DROIT SOCIAL

Le Décret n° 71-431 du 15 octobre 1971 (JORCA, 1972 n° 1, p. 11) fixe par le détail l'organisation nouvelle de l'Office Centrafricain de Sécurité Sociale. Il reprend l'ensemble de la règlementation antérieure (Décret n° 64387 du 24.12.64) dont la portée était générale, puisqu'elle recouvrait, non seulement les structures de l'Office, mais aussi les règles de fonctionnement (gestion, comtpabilité, cotisations, contrôle). Cependant, dans ce domaine, les réformes sont mineures (voir les articles 60 à 102). Par contre, les structures sont assez nettement modifiées dans le sens d'un renforcement de la représentation gouvernementale dans les différents organes, notamment au sein du Conseil Supérieur de Sécurité Sociale (qui succède au Comité de Gestion), dont les compétences sont élargies (ainsi entrent dans ses compétences les discussions sur les tarifs des honoraires médicaux ou sur les prix de journée dans les établissements de soins publics et privés; art. 4). Le Directeur Général est désormais 'secondé' par un Secrétaire Général, qui est plus spécialement 'chargé d'assurer la discipline' (a. 29). Le nouveau décret détaille l'organisation des différentes Directions (art. 30 à 44).

Enfin, la représentation du gouvernement est désormais prévue dans les organismes de contrôle de l'Office (commission de contrôle des comptes, art. 103 et commission de recours gracieux, art. 108), ce qui fait perdre aux représentants des employeurs et des salariés la majorité qu'ils détenaient jusqu'alors.

DROIT PÉNAL ET PROCÉDURE PÉNALE

L'initiative la plus spectaculaire du Général Bokassa est intervenue dans ce domaine.

Une ordonnance n° 72.058 complétée par le Décret n° 72.241, datés du 29 juillet 1972 (JORCA n° 16, p. 425 et 433) fixent les peines applicables à toutes personnes prises en flagrant délit de vol et la procédure d'éxécution de ces peines.

Les personnes ainsi appréhendées pour la première fois auront une oreille coupée, le récidiviste aura la deuxième oreille coupée, et celui qui récidivera une nouvelle fois aura la main droite coupée. Dans tous les cas, une peine de 5 ans de prison est prévue. Aucune circonstance atténuante ne peut être invoquée. La personne arrêtée est déférée immédiatement au Parquet, et après condamnation, le Président du Tribunal commet d'office un praticien pour procéder, dans les 24 heures, à l'amputation.

On sait que, passant outre aux 'règles' ainsi proclamées, le Chef de l'Etat a présidé à une bastonnade publique de tous les détenus qui s'est traduit par un certain nombre de fractures et de décès.

NOTES
1. Novembre 1971—Août 1972

CHAPTER TWENTY-FOUR

ZAIRE

Johan M. Pauwels

INTRODUCTION

L'examen de la législation zaïroise promulguée en 1972 a été rendue possible par la régularité retrouvée de la publication du Journal Officiel. Si la publication de l'édition définitive (imprimée) du Journal Officiel a continué à accuser des retards très considérables, une édition provisoire (stencilée) bi-mensuelle par contre a paru régulièrement.[1]

Ce qui frappe, lors de l'examen de la législation intervenue au cours de l'année 1972, est le volume grandissant des textes d'une part, d'autre part la prépondérance des mesures prises dans le domaine du droit public.

Ainsi, la législation dans le domaine des établissements publics a été abondante et importante (p.ex. création de l'Institut de Gestion du Portefeuille).

Signalons par ailleurs la Création d'un Code de Justice Militaire; la réforme de la police (qui s'intḡre à la gendarmerie); la création d'une sections judiciare et administrative), une troisième, la section de personnes que d'institutions, révélatrice du désir d''authenticité'.

DROIT CONSTITUTIONNEL

MODIFICATIONS DE LA CONSTITUTION
La Constitution fut modifiée deux fois.

(a) Loi 72-003 portant révision de la Constitution (*JO*, éd déf., 1972, n° 2, p. 49; éd. prov., 1972, n° 2, p. 12).

Cette loi prévoit que la province du Katanga s'appellera désormais 'Shaba'.

(b) La Loi n° 72-008 du 3 juillet 1972 (*JO*, éd. déf., 1972, n° 15, p. 453; éd. prov., 1972, n° 14, p. 4 avec l'exposé des motifs).

Celle-ci revise l'art. 60 de la Constitution, en prévoyant que la Cour Suprême de Justice comportera, à côté des deux sections existantes (les dections judiciaire et administrative), une troisième, la section de législation.

La section de législation est compétente, pour donner, dans le délai fixé par la loi, à la demande soit du Président de la République ou de ses délégues, soit du Bureau de l'Assemblée Nationale—chacun en ce qui le concerne—des avis consultatifs portant sur les projets ou propositions de lois, les projets d'ordonnances—lois , d'ordonnances et d'arrêtés à caractère réglementaire.' (nouvel alinéa 4 de l'art. 60 de la Constitution).

La même loi églargit également la compétence de la Cour Suprême quant au fond, ratione personae. Les dispositions procédurales nécessitées par ce changement sont contenues dans la loi n° 72-009 du 3 juillet 1972 (*JO*, 1972, éd. déf., n° 15, p. 454; éd. prov., 1972, n° 14, p. 8).

RÉFORME DU POUVOIR EXÉCUTIF
L'ord. n° 72-411 du 18 octobre 1972 relative à l'organisation du pouvoir exécutif (*JO*, éd. prov., 1972, n° 22, p. 9; éd. déf., 1973, n° 1, p. 49) introduit certaines innovations en ce qui concerne le gouvernement:

—les ministres portent désormais le titre de commissaire d'Etat;
—les vice-ministres portent désormais le titre de commissaire d'Etat adjoint;
—les ministères sont désormais appelés 'départements'.
—la réunion des commissaires d'Etat et des commissaires d'Etat adjoints est désignée sous le nom de 'Conseil éxécutif national'.

Cette ordonnance reprend pour le reste les dispositions de l'Ord. n° 69-147 du 1er août 1969 qu'elle abroge.

Par ailleurs, le ministère de la fonction publique est remplacé, en vertu de l'ord. n° 72-413 du 18 octobre 1972 (*JO*, 1973, éd. déf., n° 1, p. 51; éd. prov., 1972, n° 22, p. 3) par une 'Commission permanente de l'administration publique' dont le président a rang de commissaire d'Etat et assiste aux réunions du Conseil exécutif national.

LÉGISLATION PAR VOIE D'ORDONNANCES-LOIS
Habilitent le Président de la République à prendre des mesures qui sont du domaine de la loi en dehors des sessions du Conseil Législatif National, conformément à l'art. 52 de la Constitution:

—la loi n° 72-001 du 5 janvier 1972 (*JO*, ed. déf.. 1972, n° 2, p. 42; éd. prov., 1972, n° 2, p. 4);
—la loi n° 72-007 du 3 juillet 1972 (*JO*, 1972, éd. déf., n° 15, p. 453).

PUBLICATION DES LOIS
La loi n° 72-004 du 5 janvier (*JO*, éd. prov., 1972, n° 2, p. 12) modifie le titre du 'Moniteur Zaïrois (Congolais)': s'alignant à la terminologie usitée dans les Etats ex-français d'Afrique, il devient 'Journal Officiel de la République du Zaïre'.

LIBERTÉ D'ASSOCIATION
L'ord. n° 72-223 du 26 avril 1972 (*JO*, éd. prov., n° 12, p. 8) supprime la franc-maçonnerie de la liste des associations dissoutes en vertu de l'ord. n° 72-207 su 28 juillet 1971.

LIBERTÉ RELIGIEUSE—EXERCICE DES CULTES
L'AM n° 002 du 7 janvier 1972 (*JO*, éd., prov., 1972, n° 3, p. 7) porte mesures d'exécution de la loi réglementant l'exercice des cultes. Il prévoit comment les associations religieuses non reconnues par la loi doivent introduire leur demande de reconnaissance.

L'ord. n° 72-195 du 28 mars 1972 accorde à 79 associations protestantes l'agrégation prévue par la loi du 31 décembre 1971 sur l'exercice des cultes, et décide qu'elles 'sont groupées d'office au sein de l'Eglise du Christ au Zaïre, tout en conservant leur propre personnalité juridique' (art. 1).

De même, la personnalité civile a été accordée à 'l'Assemblée spirituelle nationale des Baha'is de la République du Zaïre' par l'ord. n° 72-248 du 9 juin 1972 (*JO*, éd. prov., 1972, n° 18, p. 14).

DROIT ADMINISTRATIF

FINANCES PUBLIQUES

Le budget de 1972, établi par la loi n° 71-04 du 31 décembre 1971, a été modifié à plusieurs reprises: O-L n° 72-026 du 28 mars 1972 (*JO* éd. déf., 1973, n° 4, p. 197); ord. n° 72-256 du 6 juillet 1972 (*JO*, éd. prov., 1972, n° 18, p. 15); ord. n° 71 (sic)-434 du 14 novembre 1972 (*JO*, éd. prov., 1972, n° 22, p. 6).

La loi financière du 5 décembre 1969 fut modifiée par la loi n° 72-005 du 5 janvier 1972 (*JO*, éd. déf., 1972, n° 2, p. 49).

L'ord. n° 72-230 du 27 avril 1972 (*JO*, éd. prov., 1972, n° 11, p. 8) porte organisation de la procédure disciplinaire applicable aux fonctionnaires en service dans les administrations financières.

Elle est différente de celle applicable aux fonctionnaires en général (décret-loi de 20 mars 1965, art. 64 à 71).

Une 'Ecole nationale des finances' été créée. Elle a 'pour objet la formation professionnelle et le perfectionnement du personnel du Département des finances ainsi que les candidats à l'exercice de fonctions dans ce Départment' (art. 2). OL n° 72-045 du 14 septembre 1972, *JO*, éd. déf., 1973, n° 1, p. 26; éd. prov., 1972, n° 18, p. 3.

ORGANISATION TERRITORIALE

L'ord. n° 72-462 du 8 décembre 1972 (*JO*, éd. prov., 1972, n° 24, p. 5) porte création de la 'zone' de Badolite. Ce texte devance ainsi la réforme des structures territoriales de la République, intervenue par les lois de 5 janvier 1973 en vertu de laquelle les anciens territoires ansi que les communes deviennent des 'zones'.

RÉFORME DE LA GENDARMERIE ET DE LA POLICE

L'OL n° 72-031 du 31 juillet 1972 porte institution d'une gendarmerie nationale (*JO*, 1972, éd. déf., n° 15, p. 460; prov., n° 16, p. 3). Cf. aussi l'OL n° 72-041 du 30 août 1972 portant organisation de la Gendarmerie nationale (*JO*, 1973, éd. déf., n° 1, p. 9).

Celle-ci remplace la gendarmerie qui existait antérieurement et la police nationale. Ces deux corps sont dissous (OL n° 72-032 du 31 juillet 1972—*JO*, 1972 éd. déf., n° 15, p. 461; éd. prov., n° 16, p. 4—intégrant la gendarmerie des Forces Armées Zairoises dans la gendarmerie nationale et OL n° 72-033 du 31 juillet 1972—*JO* 1972, éd. déf., n° 15, p. 461; éd. prov., n° 16, p. 5—portant dissolution de la police nationale; Ord. n° 72-303 du 31 juillet 1972 portant mesure collective de mise à la retraite des agents de la police—*JO*, 1972, éd. déf., n° 15, p. 462—).

La gendarmerie nationale fait partie des forces armées zaïroises (art. 2).

MILITAIRES INVALIDES

L'ord. n° 72-429 du 7 novembre 1972 (*JO*, 1973, éd. déf., n° 2, p. 111) attribue à 200 militaires, infirmes à cause de faits survenus dans le service, le payement jusqu'à leur mort, de leur solde pleine majorée des allocations familiales.

ENSEIGNEMENT UNIVERSITAIRE

La loi organique de l'Université Nationale du Zaïre (UNAZA) du 6 août 1971 fut légèrement modifiée par l'O-L n° 72-002 du 12 janvier 1972 (*JO*, éd déf., 1972, n° 3, p. 69), qui introduit notamment la fonction de pro recteur de l'université).

L'ord. n° 72-383 du 22 septembre 1972 dispose que désormais le commissaire d'Etat à l'éducation établit les affections des vice-recteurs de l'Université (*JO*, 1973, éd. déf., n° 2, p. 103).

RÉQUISITION DES DIPLÔMES UNIVERSITAIRES

L'OL n° 72/058 du 22 septembre 1972 portant réquisition des diplômes zaïrois (*JO*, éd. prov., 1972, n° 21, p. 7; éd. déf., 1973, n° 1, p. 44) ressuscite sous une forme nouvelle le 'service civique', supprimé en 1971.

Le nouveau système ne concerne pas les médecins, dont la réquisition continue à être régie par l'OL n° 68-071 du 1er mars 1968 (art. 10).

'Sont soumis à la réquisition tous les diplômés zaïrois qui ont obtenu après le 1er juillet 1972 un diplôme de fin d'études soit du niveau de l'enseignement secondaire, soit du niveau de l'enseignement supérieur ou universitaire.

'La réquisition est de deux ans pour les diplômés de l'enseignement secondaire; les diplômés de l'enseignement supérieur ou universitaire sont réquisitionnés pendant le nombre d'années correspondant à la durée normale de leurs études supérieures ou universitaires.' (art. 1).

'La remise des diplômes de fin d'études n'aura lieu qu'après la période normale de réquisition; toutefois à la fin de leurs études les étudiants diplômés auront chacun une attestation de fin d'études . . .'' (art. 3). Des sanctions pénales visent ceux qui se soustrayent à la réquisition ainsi que ceux qui engagent un diplômé requis (art. 8-9).

ENSEIGNEMENT SECONDAIRE

L'ord. n° 72-069 du 21 février 1972 (*JO*, éd. prov., 1972, n° 5) concerne l'inspection de l'enseignement secondaire.

L'ord. n° 72-223 du 26 avril 1972 (*JO*, éd. prov., n° 12, p. 8) réorganise l'examen d'Etat en vue de l'obtention du diplôme sanctionnant les études secondaires du cycle long.

EXERCICE DE LA PHARMACIE

L'OL n° 72-046 du 14 septembre 1972 règle l'exercice de la pharmacie (*JO*, éd. prov., 1972, n° 18, p. 6; éd. déf., 1973, n° 1, p. 27). Ce texte prévoit notamment que les pharmaciens doivent être des diplômés universitaires; il prévoit en outre les professions de 'gradué en pharmacie' et de 'préparateur en pharmacie'.

Les mesures d'exécution sont contenues dans l'Ord. n° 72-359 du 14 septembre 1972 (*JO*, éd. prov., 1972, n° 19, p. 7).

ETABLISSEMENTS PUBLICS

INSTITUT DE GESTION DU PORTEFEUILLE

L'O-L n° 72-034 du 10 août 1972 (*JO*, éd. prov., n° 16, p. 6) porte statuts de l'Institut de Gestion du Portefeuille.

Cette 'société d'Etat à caractère financier dotée de la personnalité juridique et soumise au pouvoir de tutelle du président de la République' (art. 1) a pour objet d'administrer le portefeuille de la République; de prendre et de gérer des participations dans les sociétés contribuant au développement économique du pays et d'exercer les droits qui y sont attachés; d'assurer le contrôle des organismes de droit public de la République , à l'exception de ceux qui seront déterminés par une ordonnance du président de la République; de gérer les immeubles bâtis de l'Etat.' (art. 3).

'Lorsque sa participation dans une société est au moins égale à 10% du capital social, l'Institut a droit, au sein du Conseil d'administration et du Collège des commissaires de cette société, à nombre de sièges proportionnel à sa participation avec un minimum d'un siège.

'Les administrateurs et les commissaires représentant l'Institut dans les sociétés dans lesquelles celui-ci a une participation financière sont nommés et, le cas échéant, relevés de leurs fonctions par le président de la République.' (art. 3).

'L'Etat octroie à l'Institut de gestion du portèfeuille, lors de sa création, une dotation de 500.000.000.-de zaïres. Cette somme sera inscrite au passif du bilan de l'Institut à un compte intitulé "Capital".' (art. 4)

'L'Institut est soumis au droit commun en matière fiscale, mais échappe à l'application des législations relatives à la contribution réelle et aux contributions cédulaires sur les revenus.' (art. 34)

'Il est ouvert, au sein de l'Institut, un compte spécial institué 'compte de l'Etat'.

'Au crédit de ce compte figuremt les recettes provenant de la location et de la vente des immeubles bâtis appartenant à l'Etat et dont l'Institut a la gestion, ainsi que les sommes versées par l'Etat en vue de l'alimentation de ce compte.

'Au débit figurent les dépenses effectuées par l'Institut pour la gestion des immeubles susvisés, ainsi que les sommes versées à l'Etat sur ordre de celui-ci.' (art. 35)

'Le Conseil d'administration de l'IGP approuve les bilans, les comptes de profits et pertes et les rapports annuels des organismes de droit public précités sont nommés et, le cas échéant, relevés de leurs fonctions par le président de la République. (. . .).' (art. 39)

L'O-L n° 72-035 du 14 août 1972 (*JO*, éd. prov., 1972, n° 16, p. 16) porte dissolution de la Société de Gestion et de Financement (Sogefi); cette mesure intervient suite à la création de l'IGP qui reprend les biens et droits de la société dissoute.

FONDS MOBUTU SESE SEKO EN FAVEUR DES ARTISTES ET ÉCRIVAINS

L'O-L n° 72-022 du 28 mars 1972 (*JO*, éd. prov., 1972, n° 12, p. 4) porte création du Fonds Mobutu Sese Seko en faveur des artistes et écrivains.

Ce fonds, un établissement public doté de la personnalité juridique (art. 1), a pour objet 'd'apporter son aide matériel (sic) aux artistes et écrivains zaïrois qui ont leur domicile au Zaïre et qui sont inscrits à la matricule générale des artistes et écrivains zaïrois tenue par le fonds' (art. 3). Le fonds accordera des allocations de secours en cas de maladie ou d'infirmité, une rente de viellesse et les frais de funérailles aux artistes se trouvant dans le besoin (art. 3).

Les ressources du fonds sont constitués notamment par une dotation initiale du Président de la République de 100.000 Zaïres (200.000 $US) (art. 6).

Le Fonds dépend du Ministère (Département) de la Culture et des Arts (art. 7).

Les mesures d'exécution ont été déterminées par l'ord. n° 72-358 du 14 septembre 1972 (*JO*, éd. prov., 1972, n° 18, p. 17).

OFFICE NATIONAL DES FIBRES TEXTILES

L'ord. n° 72-235 du 8 mai 1972 (*JO*, éd. prov., 1972, n° 11, p. 10) porte réquisition au profit de l'Office National des fibres textiles, des installations d'usinage du cotton brut et des approvisionnements ainsi que du personnel du neuf sociétés cotonnières.

Cette ordonnance a été prise en application de la loi n° 72-006 du 8 mai 1972 (*JO*, éd. prov., 1972. n° 10, p. 20) invitant le Président de la République à réquisitionner les installations et le personnel des établissements d'usinage du coton et de ses sous-produits et de confection des balles de coton-fibres, ceci pour la campagne de 1972 (avec possibilité de prorogation).

OFFICE NATIONAL DU CAFÉ

La culture et le commerce du café sont réglementés par l'O-L n° 72-030 du 27 juillet 1972 (*JO*, éd. déf., 1972, n° 15, p. 457; éd. prov., 1972, n° 15, p. 6), qui crée notamment l'Office National du café, lequel remplace les offices antérieurs ayant un but semblable.

Cet office, établissement public à caractère commercial et industriel, obtient le monopole de l'achat, de transport, de vente et d'exportation du café.

Les statuts de cet office sont contenus dans l'O-L n° 72-040 du 30 août 1972 (*JO*, éd. déf., 1973, n° 1, p. 5).

CRÉATION OU RÉORGANISATION D'AUTRES ÉTABLISSEMENTS PUBLICS

De nombreux établissements publics ont été créés ou réorganisés. Voici ceux dont les statuts ont été publiés:

—l'Office Zaïrois des Chemins de Fer des Grands Lacs: OL n° 72-014 du 21 février 1972 (*JO*, éd. déf., 1972, n° 6, p. 165; éd. prov., 1972, n° 10, p. 10);
—le Fonds Mobutu Sese Seko en faveur des artistes et écrivains, voy. plus haut;
—l'Office National des Fibres Textiles, voy. Plus haut;
—l'Office National des Fibres Textiles, voy. plus haut;
—l'Institut de Gestion du Portefeuille, voy. plus haut;

—l'Office des transports en commun du Zaïre (OTCZ), OL n° 72-042 du 14 septembre 1972, *(JO*, éd. prov., 1972, n° 17, p. 8;
—l'Office National des transports (ONATRA): OL n° 72-043 du 14 septembre 1972, *JO*, éd. déf., 1973, n° 1, p. 20; éd. prov., 1972, n° 17, p. 13;
—la Régie des voies maritimes (RVM): OL n° 72-047 du 14 septembre 1972, *JO*, éd. déf., 1973, n° 1, p. 30; éd. prov., 1972, n° 17, p. 21;
—la Régie des voies fluviales (RVF): OL n° 72-048 du 14 septembre 1972, *JO* éd. déf., 1973, n° 1, p. 33; éd. prov., 1972, n° 18, p. 9.
—la Société Nationale des Assurances (SONAS): OL n° 72-049 du 14 septembre 1972, *JO*, éd. prov., 1972, n° 19, p. 3; éd. déf., 1973, n° 1, p. 37.
—la Générale des Carrières et des Mines (GECAMINES), OL n° 72-050 du 14 septembre 1972, *JO*, éd. prov., 1972, n° 21, p. 3; éd. déf., 1973, n° 1, p. 41.

Des modifications furent apportées aux statuts de:

—la Foire internationale de Kinshasa (FIKIN) (ord. n° 72-031 du 21 février 1972, *JO*, éd. prov., 1972, n° 7, p. 4;
—l'Institut National pour la Conservation de la Nature (O-L n° 72-012 du 21 février 1972, *JO*, éd., prov., 1972, n° 10, p. 10);
—l'Office des Routes (O-L n° 72-016 du 21 février 1972, *JO*, éd. prov., 1972, n° 10, p. 19);
—la Caisse Générale d'Epargne du Zaïre (ord. n° 72-205 du 19 avril 1972, *JO*, éd. prov., 1972, n° 11, p. 11);
—Air Zaïre (ord. n° 72-222 du 26 avril 1972, *JO*, éd. prov., 1972, n° 11, p. 3).

DIVERS
L'ord. n° 72-076 du 21 février 1972 (*JO*, éd. prov., 1972, n° 8, p. 7) déclare d'utilité publique l'établissement des lignes électriques reliant la Centrale d'Inga à divers postes d'alimentation.

L'ord. n° 72-114 du 21 février 1972 (*JO*, éd. prov., 1972, n° 9, p. 16) permet l'établissement de barrières de pluie, interdisant le passage des véhicules lorsqu'il pleut.

L'ord. n° 72-224 du 26 avril 1972 (*JO*, éd. prov., n° 11, p. 4) fixe les conditions d'utilisation des aérodromes par mauvaise visibilité.

DROIT FISCAL

Nous n'avons pas relevé de mesures fondamentales.

Une commission tarifaire chargée d'adapter régulièrement les tarifs des droits d'entrée et de sortie a été créée par l'ord. n° 72-101 du 21 février 1972 (*JO*, éd. prov., 1972, n° 10, 3).

De multiples mesures concernent l'imposition ou la modification de taxes et de droits divers:

—droits de sortie: AM n° 72-002 du 25 janvier 1972 (*JO*, éd. prov., n° 6, p. 21); O-L n° 72-009 du 16 février 1972 (*JO*, éd. prov., 1972, n° 8, p. 4 et 5).
—droits d'entrée: AM n° 72-003 CAB-FIN-GC du 25 janvier 1972 (*JO*, éd. prov., 1972, n° 6, p. 21); O-L n° 72-011 du 21 février 1972, (*JO*, éd. prov., 1972, n° 8, p. 7),
—télégrammes: ord. n° 72-172 du 20 mars 1972 (*JO*, éd. prov., 1972, n° 8, p. 15).
—installations radioélectriques: ord. n° 72-173 du 20 mars 1972 (*JO*, éd. prov., 1972, n° 8, p. 12).
—taxe rémunératiore pour fourniture de renseignements par le service de météorologie: ord. n° 72-098 (*JO*, éd. prov., 1972, n° 7, p. 7).
—redevances en matière de navigation aérienne: ord. n° 72-096 du 21 février 1972 (*JO*, éd. prov., 1972, n° 5, p. 18).

—taxes en matière de navigation maritime et fluviale: ord. n° 72–095 du 21 février 1972 (*JO*, éd. prov., 1972, n° 7, p. 6). L'ord. n° 72–225 du 26 avril 1972 (*JO*, éd. prov. 1972, n° 10, p. 6) institue une taxe de navigation à charge des armateurs et propriétaires de bâtiments destinés à faire des opérations lucratives de navigation sur les voies de navigation intérieure. Cette taxe est perçue au profit des régies des voies maritimes et fluviales.

L'ord. n° 72–0421 du 3 novembre 1972 (*JO*, éd. prov., 1972, n° 22, p. 3) fixe les taxes de navigation et de pilotage pour les navires faisant escale dans un des ports du Bas-Zaïre.

DROIT PENAL ET PROCEDURE PENALE

CODE DE JUSTICE MILITAIRE

L'O-L n° 72–060 du 25 septembre 1972[2] porte Code de Justice Militaire.

Ce Code le 'Code Provisoire de Justice militaire' (Décret—loi du. 18 décembre 1964) (art. 541) qu'il remplace, et achève ainsi, par une codification impressionnante (543 articles), l'oeuvre de la réforme de la justice militaire entamée en 1964 par la promulgation du Code provisoire précité qui se caractérisait par sa brièveté (18 articles).[3]

Le Code comprend trois livres, consacrés respectivement à l'organisation et à la compétence des tribunaux militaires, à la procédure pénale militaire et aux infractions et peines spécifiquement militaires.

ORGANISATION ET COMPÉTENCE

Le substituant aux anciens cour militaire, conseils de guerre et tribunaux militaires de police, les nouvelles juridictions des forces armées sont: 1° Le Conseil de Guerre Général, qui juge les amiraux et officiers généraux ainsi que les magistrats militaires poursuivis pour infractions commises dans l'exercice de leurs fonctions, et qui connaît de l'annulation et de la révision des jugements rendus par les juridictions militaires inférieures.

Il est composé 'autant que possible' de cinq membres officiers généraux (art. 6). L'un d'eux doit être magistrat de carrière en cas d'annulation et de révision, ou lorsque l'un des justiciables est un magistrat de carrière (art. 7).

2° Les Conseils de Guerre de Région, dont il existe un dans chaque région militaire (art. 12), et qui juge les militaires d'un rang inférieur à celui de Général de Brigade, les justiciables non-militaires et, en temps de guerre, les militaires ennemis et insurgés (art. 14).

Ces conseils sont composés 'autant que possible' de cinq membres, dont l'un doit être magistrat de carrière, nommé par le Président de la République (art. 15).

3° Les Conseils de Guerre de Police, dont il existe un dans chaque région militaire et qui sont constitués par un seul membre, substitut de l'auditeur militaire de région (art. 20). Ils sont compétents pour connaître d'infractions punissables au maximum d'un an de servitude pénale ou dont on estime qu'ils ne doivent pas, en fait, être punies d'une servitude pénale dépassant un an (art. 22).

4° Les Conseils de Guerre opérationnels, qui 'connaissent sans limite de compétence territoriale de toutes les infractions justiciables de la juridiction militaire qui leur sont déférées.' (art. 28).[4]

Le corps de justice militaire est composé de magistrats militaires et d'auxiliaires de la justice (art. 41-103).

Les fonctions du ministère public près les juridictions des forces armées sont remplies par:

(a) l'auditeur général des forces armées, chef de corps de justice militaire (art. 44), qui remplit les fonctions près le Conseil de Guerre général et exerce la plénitude de l'action publique devant toutes les juridictions militaires (art. 46), 'sous le contrôle exclusif et direct' du Commissaire d'Etat chargé de la défense, en temps de paix (art. 50; en temps de guerre: sous celui du président du Conseil Exécutif National, art. 51), dont il est le conseiller juridique (art. 56).

(b) les premiers substituts et substituts de l'auditeur général (art. 53);

(c) les auditeurs militaires de région, qui dirigent les parquets près des conseils de guerre de région (art. 57);

(d) les premiers substituts de l'auditeur militaire de région (art. 58).

Le magistrats da carrière membres des conseils de guerre ont le statut des magistrats civils (art. 39 et 102) mais ils ne sont pas inamovibles (art. 40).

Les juridictions militaires connaissent:

1° des infractions de toute nature, commises par des militaires;

2° des infractions spécifiquement militaires, prévues par le Code de justice militaire et commises par des militaires ou des non-militaires (art. 106 et 109);

3° des infractions pour lesquelles les juridictions militaires sont rendues compétentes par d'autres lois (il s'agit notamment du vol de substances précieuses);

4° des infractions pour lesquelles elles sont rendues compétentes par le Président de la République, en cas d'état de siège ou d'urgence (art. 58 de la Constitution).

PROCÉDURE

'Autant que possible, la procédure devant les juridictions militaires sera celle en vigueur devant les juridictions de droit commun conformément aux dispositions du Code de Procédure Pénale ordinaire qui ne sont pas incompatibles avec celles du présent Code.' (art. 137). Deux cent cinquante articles (art. 138 à 387) sont consacrés à ces dispositions particulières, très détaillées et ouvrant de multiples domaines.

Limitons-nous à signaler que les voies de recours ordinaires ne sont normalement pas disponibles. Art. 270:

'Les jugements et arrêts des juridictions militaires ne sont susceptibles ni d'opposition ni d'appel.
'Ils sont immédiatement exécutoires.
'Toutefois, lorsque, conformément à l'article 58 alinéa 2 de la Constitution, l'action des juridictions des forces armées est substituée à celle des cours et tribunaux de droit commun, un droit d'opposition et d'appel est ouvert aux personnes qui ne sont justiciables des juridictions militaires que pendant la substitution.
'L'appel est ouvert devant le Conseil de Guerre Général.'

Par contre, le Code introduit l'annulation et la révision.

L'annulation est une variante de la cassation. Art. 272:

'En tous temps, les jugements rendus par les juridictions des forces armées peuvent être annulés en cas de violation de la loi sur recours en annulation formé par le ministère public ou par la partie à laquelle il est fait grief, dans les conditions prévues par le présent Code.

'Le recours est porté devant le Conseil de Guerre Général.'

Art. 273—'La violation de la loi comprend:

(1°) l'incompétence;
(2°) l'excès de pouvoirs des juridictions militaires;
(3°) la fausse application ou la fausse interprétation de la loi;
(4°) la non-conformité aux lois;
(5°) la violation des formes prescrites à peine de nullité.'

La révision (art. 303 à 310) peut être demandée, quelle que soit la juridiction judiciaire qui a statué, au bénéfice de toute personne reconnue auteur d'une infraction relevant de la compétence des juridictions militaires, lorsque l'innocence du condamné résulte de faits nouveaux, de pièces inconnues qui sont révélées, d'une nouvelle décision condamnant un autre individu, de la preuve de la vie de la prétendue victime, ou encore de la condamnation d'un témoin pour faux témoignage (art. 303).

PEINES ET INFRACTIONS MILITAIRES

Les peines et infractions militaires font l'objet du Livre III du Code (art. 388 à 530).

Le Code distingue les infractions purement militaires (qui ne peuvent être commises que par des militaires) et les infractions mixtes (prévues à la fois par le Code pénal ordinaire et le Code de Justice militaire) (art. 405).

Les infractions prévues par le Code de Justice militaire sont l'insoumission, l'absence irrégulière, la désertion, la provocation à la désertion et le récel de déserteur (art. 406–428); la capitulation, la trahison et le complot militaire, les pillages, les destructions, le faux, corruptions, etc., l'usurpation d'uniformes etc., l'outrage au drapeau, au parti ou à l'armée, l'incitation à commettre des actes contraires au devoir et à la discipline (art. 429–457); la révolte militaire, la rébellion, le refus d'obéissance, les violences envers différentes catégories de personnes, le refus d'un service dû légalement, les abus d'autorité (art. 458–479); les infractions contre le secret de la défense militaire (art. 492–500); les crimes de guerre et contre humanité (art. 501–505); les évasions de détenus ou de prisonniers de guerre (art. 506–517); des infractions diverses dont le génocide (art. 518–530).

L'organisation pénitentiaire fait l'objet des articles 531 à 538.

PRIVILÈGE DE JURIDICTION

Des règles spéciales de compétence en ce qui concerne le jugement d'infractions commises parr des membres du Bureau Politique, des hauts fonctionnaires ou dirigeants du Parti ont été introduites par les lois n° 72-008 et 72-009 du 3 juillet 1972, mentionnées plus haut (voy. V° Droit Constitutionnel).

VOL DE SUBSTANCES PRÉCIEUSES

L'O-L n° 72-005 du 14 janvier 1972 'tendant à renforcer la protection de certaines substances contre les vols' (*JO*, 1972, éd. déf., n° 3, p. 71) punit 'le trafic et la détention sans titre légal de l'uranium, du mercure, du cadium, de la cassérite, du cuivre, de l'étain, du soufre, de la cocaine' (art. 1).

La confiscation générale des biens des condamnés est prévue (art. 3). Ces infractions ainsi que les infractions connexes sont de la seule compétence des juridictions militaires (art. 4-5).

MESURES PARTICULIÈRES

Les ord. n° 72-245 du 25 mai 1972 (*JO*, éd. prov., n° 12, p. 15) et n° 72-439 du 22 novembre 1972 (*JO*, éd. prov., 1972, n° 23, p. 4; éd. déf., 1973, n° 2, p. 116) portent mesure collective de grâce.

L'O-L n° 72-006 du 14 janvier 1972 (*JO*, 1972, éd. déf., n° 3, p. 72) assure à l'Etat la propriété de tous les biens présents de cinq citoyens zaïrois, vraisemblablement à la suite de condamnations pour infractions en matière de vol de substances précieuses.

Séquelle de l'affaire Socobanque, les biens et droits de deux sociétés (Solidus et Interimmo) ont été transférés à l'Etat par l'O-L n° 72-037 du 21 août 1972 (*JO*, éd. prov., 1972, n° 18, p. 3).

DROIT SOCIAL

SYNDICAT UNIQUE DES EMPLOYEURS

L'O-L précise maints détails quant au contenu et à l'approbation des prov., n° 15, p. 3) autorise la création d'un syndicat des employeurs, 'l'Association Nationale des Entreprises Zaïroises', dotée de la personnalité civile (art. 5).

'L'association sera seule admise à représenter auprès des pouvoirs publics les activités commerciales, industrielles, artisanales et agricoles ainsi que les employeurs.' (art. 6).

L'O-L précise maits détails quant au contenu et à l'approbation des statuts.

L'association est appelée à remplacer toutes autres chambres de commerce et syndicats d'employeurs, lesquels sont dissous (art. 13).

HYGIÈNE ET SÉCURITÉ DES LIEUX DE TRAVAIL

En vertu de l'Ord. n° 72-112 du 21 février 1972 (*JO*, éd. prov., 1972, n° 8, p. 11), 'tout employeur qui n'a pas satisfait, dans le délai imparti, à la mise en demeure prévue par les articles 141 et 142 du code de travail (qui concernent l'hygiène et la sécurité des lieux de travail) est passible d'une majoration de 50% du taux de cotisation afférant à la branche des risques professionnels' (art. 1).

JOURS FÉRIÉS LÉGAUX

Les jours fériés légaux ont été de nouveau fixés par l'ord. n° 72-363 du 14 septembre 1972 (*JO*, éd. prov., 1972, n° 18, p. 21). Ils ne sous plus qu'au nombre de huit.

SÉCURITÉ SOCIALE

Ont été soumis à la branche des risques professionnels de la sécurité sociale, les élèves des écoles professionnelles et artisanales, ainsi que les stagiaires et les apprentis (Ord. n° 72-111 du 21 février 1972, (*JO*, éd. prov., 1972, n° 8, p. 9). 'Les cotisations et les prestations sont calculees sur le salaire minimum légal de l'emploi auquel l'assuré se prépare, ou sur la rémunération réelle si elle est supérieure.' (art. 6).

DROIT PRIVE

NATIONALITÉ

La loi n° 72-002 du 5 janvier 1972 relative à la nationalité zaïroise (*JO*, éd. prov., 1972, n° 2, p. 4; éd. déf., 1973, n° 2, p. 43) abroge et remplace le décret—loi du 18 septembre 1965 sur la nationalité (art. 48).

En fait, ce texte ne fait en bonne partie que reproduire, avec certaines modifications terminologiques, celui du décret—loi de 1965. Ainsi, Il réaffirme les grands principes du *jus sanguinis* (art. 1, 5, 6) et de l'unité de la nationalité (art. 2 et 18 sv.); il reprend les règles édictées en 1965 sur l'acquisition de la nationalité zaïroise par naturalisation (art. 8 à 11) ou par option (art. 12 à 14); les dispositions relatives à la perte et au recouvrement de la nationalité zaïroise (art. 18 à 24), les dispositions procédurales (art. 25 à 34), celles concernant la preuve (art. 35 à 42) et les dispositions fiscales (art. 43 à 45) sont reprises textuellement du décret—loi de 1965.

Quelles sont alors les modifications intervenues? Voici les principales:

(a) Le sort des habitants du Zaïre originaires du Rwanda-Burundi a été fixé; la nationalité zaïroise leur a été attribuée de façon plus restrictive que ne le prévoyait l'O-L n° 71-020 du 25 mars 1971 (celle-ci est déclarée 'nulle et non avenue' par l'art. 47 de la loi sous examen):
'Art. 15—Les personnes originaires du Rwanda-Urundi qui étaient établies dans la province du Kivu avant le 1er janvier 1950 et qui ont continué à résider depuis lors dans la République du Zaïre jusqu'à l'entrée en vigueur de la présente loi ont acquis la nationalité zaïroise à la date du 30 juin 1960.'
(b) Les droits des étrangers devenus Zaïrois par naturalisation ou par option sont restreints de façon plus sévère que par le décret—loi de 1965:

'Art. 17—L'étranger, tout comme ses descendants, qui devient Zaïrois par l'effet de la naturalisation ou par l'effet de l'option est soumis aux incapacités suivantes:

(1) il ne peut être investi de fonctions politiques ou de mandats électifs;
(2) il ne peut être électeur pendant un délai de 15 ans à partir de la date à laquelle il a acquis la nationalité zaïroise;
(3) il ne peut être nommé à la Fonction publique à un grade équivalent ou supérieur à celui de chef de bureau pendant un délai de 15 ans à partir de la date à laquelle il a acquis la nationalité zaïroise;
(4) il ne peut faire partie de l'armée ni de la police nationales zaïroises.'

Notons que le décret—loi de 1965 (art. 13) n'appliquait pas ces restrictions aux descendants des étrangers devenus Zaïrois, et qu'il les limitait à une période de 5 ans.[5] La disposition de l'article 17 de la loi du 5 janvier 1972 risque de susciter la création de deux catégories de citoyens, et ne constitue certainement pas un encouragement aux demandes de naturalisation ou d'option.

L'article 46 de la loi sur la nationalité, concernant les noms étrangers, sera examiné ci-après (n° 3).

RÉFORME DU DROIT CIVIL

Les membres de la Commission de Réforme et d'Unification du Droit Civil Zaïrois, instituée par la loi n° 71-002 du 12 juin 1971, ont été nommés par l'ord. n° 72-062 du 21 février 1972 (*JO*, éd. déf., 1972, n° 5, p. 134; cf. aussi l'ord. n° 72-063 du 21 février 1972, *JO*, éd. déf., 1972, n° 5, p. 135, fixant leurs indemnités).

Jusqu'à ce jour, les résultats des travaux de la Commission n'ont pas été rendus publics.

Alors qu'on aurait pu croire que dans le domaine du droit familial, certains problèmes relatifs au mariage (la dot, le consentement des époux ou des parents) seraient les premiers à appeler une réforme, les premières préoccupations des autorités zaïroises ont pöutôt concern la filiation.

Lors de l'ouverture du premier congrès ordinaire du Mouvement Populaire de la Révolution, le 21 mai 1972, le général Mobutu, président de la République du Zaïre, évoqua le problème des enfants naturels et énonça de façon non équivoque les principes qui devront désormais régir leur statut. A la suite de ces paroles, le Congrès prit une résolution invitant la Commission de Réforme et d'Unification du Droit Civil Zaïroise à préparer un avant-projet de loi dans ce domaine.

Voici le passage du discours du Chef de l'Etat, relatif aux enfants naturels:

'Nous devons toujours avoir à l'esprit que tous les citoyens de la République du Zaïre sont égaux devant la loi; cette égalité commence dès la naissance.

'Aussi, nous ne pouvons plus tolérer dans la société zaïroise les appellations importées de l'Occident, comme celles de bâtard ou d'enfant naturel.

'L'enfant constitue une richesse pour la famille africaine. La notion d'enfant de père inconnu date de la colonisation et est donc contraire à l'authenticité zaïroise.

'Si un père honnête, un bon citoyen, doit être responsable de tous ses actes, il va sans dire qu'il doit i'être encore plus pour cet acte, le plus noble de tous, qu'est la procréation. Nous invitons le congrès à décider qu'à partir de maintenant, tout enfant né dans la République du Zaïre, ait un père et que nul Zaïrois n'ait plus le droit d'ignorer son enfant, qu'il soit conçu de façon régulière ou pas.

'En même temps, nous attirons l'attention des citoyennes qu'un enfant n'a qu'un seul père.'

Dans son discours du 21 mai 1972, le Chef de l'Etat s'est prononcé également sur le sort de la polygamie au Zaïre:

'D'aucuns peuvent s'imaginer qu'en parlant de la reconnaissance de ce qu'on appelle 'enfant naturel', nous ouvrons une porte à la polygamie. Certains pourraient même fonder leur justification sur le recours à l'authenticité. Il ne peut en être question, car, dans la société traditionnelle, la polygamie, quoique tolérée, n'était pas généralisée. Jadis, elle était basée sur une justification économique, la thésaurisation des biens sous forme de placement s'opérant au moyen de la dot. Elle permettait ainsi au polygame de disposer d'une main-d'oeuvre presque gratuite.

'Dans notre société zaïroise d'aujourd'hui, la polygamie ne peut plus trouver un pareil fondement, d'une part parce que la thésaurisation se practique au moyen des structures financières modernes, telles les banques et les caisses d'épargne, d'autre part à cause de la politique d'émancipation de la femme, que nous avons amorcée dès l'aube de notre révolution. Contrairement à la situation que connaissent les pays industrialisés, où la citoyenne se sent colonisée par l'homme, et organise des mouvements de libération féminine, nous sommes fiers d'avoir réalisé dans notre pays, l'égalité totale entre l'homme et la femme. Celle-ci connaît un épanouissement de sa personnalité par l'accès aux responsabilités profesionnelles, sociales et politiques.

'Nous avons aboli, chez nous, autant l'exploitation de la femme par l'homme que celle de l'homme par la femme.'

NOM

La matière des noms fut le terrain où, en 1972, se concentrèrent les efforts rn vue vue de recouvrer l' 'authenticité zaïroise'.

C'est au cours de la seconde moitié de 1971 et au début de 1972 que la doctrine de l'authenticité vint s'installer au centre de la vie politique zaïroise. Le 27 octobre 1971, la République Démocratique du Congo devint la République du Zaïre. Le thème de l'authenticité fut développé par le Chef de l'Etat au cours du périple qu'il effectua à travers la République au mois de décembre 1971. Alors fut annoncé que tous les noms et monuments de l'époque coloniale devaient disparaître avant le 1er janvier 1972. Les Zaïrois portant des noms étrangers (il s'agit du nom principal, l'équivalent du nom de famille occidental) furent obligés à porter des noms à résonnance zaïroise, en vertu de l'article 46 de la nouvelle loi sur la nationalité, du 5 janvier 1972, commentée plus haut.

Avec ses mesures d'exécution,[6] ce fut le seul texte promulgué en matière de noms, mais en fait les Zaïrois furent amenés à rejeter même leurs prénoms à origine étrangère. En effet, l'authenticité atteignait le centre de l'actualité lorsque le Chef de l'Etat annonça, le 9 janvier 1972, qu'il remplaçait ses prénoms chrétiens par ses noms ancestraux. L'affaire des prénoms devint rapidement 'l'affaire Malula' (20 janvier 1972), lorsque le cardinal-archevêque de Kinshasa fut rendu responsable de la parution d'un article critiquant le rejet des prénoms chrétiens, publié par le la revue 'Afrique Chrétienne' de Kinshasa, ce qui amena son exil temporaire à Rome.

L'exemple du Président, optant pour une série de noms africains, fut suivi par bon nombre de Zaïrois, dont tous ceux occupant une situation politique ou sociale en vue.[7]

Une loi, concrétisant les idées nouvelles lancées en matière de noms et de prénoms, fut approuvée par le Conseil Législatif National (alors Assemblée Nationale) le 6 mai 1972 et publiée par les journaux locaux. Mais elle ne fut pas promulguée et il est peu probable qu'elle ne le soit, sans que des modifications importantes n'y soient apportées.[8]

DROIT FONCIER

Dans l'aperçu législatif relatif à l'année précédente, nous avons commenté la loi n° 71-009 du 31 décembre 1971 assurant à la République la plénitude de ses droits sur le sol et le sous-sol non mis en valeur (la loi dite 'renforçant la loi Bakajika').

L'ord. n° 72-003 du 7 janvier 1972 (*JO*, éd. prov., 1972, n° 2, p. 21) porte mesures exécutoires de cette loi. Voy. aussi l'arrêté interministériel n° 72-001 minurbaf du 8 janvier 1972 (*JO*, éd. prov., n° 3, p. 6); et AM n° 72-0004 du 12 janvier 1972 (*JO*, éd. prov., 1972, n° 3, p. 9). En application de la même loi, l'ord. n° 72-232 du 2 mai 1972 (*JO*, éd. prov., 1972, n° 11, p. 9) crée une commission ayant pour mission d'examiner les déclarations des droits fonciers, miniers et forestiers.

L'ord. n° 72-003 du 7 janvier 1972 fut déjà abrogée par l'O-L n° 72-365 du 14 septembre 1972 (*JO*, éd. prov., 1972, n° 17, p. 4) qui porte de nouvelles mesures d'exécution de la loi n° 71-009 du 31 décembre 1971 renforçant la loi Bakajika. Elle prévoit l'obligation de déclaration, au plus tard le 31 décembre 1971, des droits fonciers acquis avant le 1er janvier 1972 par toute personne physique ou morale de droit privé.

Les déclarations seront examinées par la commission instituée par l'ord. n° 72-232 du 2 mai 1972.

Nous n'examinerons pas ces nouvelles mesures en détail, puisqu'une nouvelle réforme foncière, constituant un nouveau 'renforcement de la loi Bakajika' est annoncée, et sera sans doute mise en oeuvre au cours de l'année 1973.

DROIT COMMERCIAL—INVESTISSEMENTS

En application du Code des investissements (O-L du 26 juin 1969), plusieurs conventions d'investissement ont été approuvées (ord. n° 72-093 du 21 février 1972, *JO*, éd. prov., 1972, n° 9, p. 3: Ford Motor Cy.; ord. n° 72-094 du 21 février 1972, *JO*, éd. prov., 1972, n° 9, p. 10: General Motors Corp; ord. n° 72-375 du 14 septembre 1972, *JO*, éd. déf., 1973, n° 3, p. 176; éd. prov., 1972, n° 20, p. 10: Cimenterie Nationale; ord. n° 72-367 du 14 septembre 1972, *JO*, éd. prov., 1972, n° 19, p. 3: K. Danzer).

NOTES

1. Signalons que le CEDIOM (Centre d'études et de documentation pour les investissements outre-mer), 34, rue de Stassart, 1050 Bruxelles, publie, sur feuilles volantes, une table analytique de la législation zaïroise, ainsi que des recueils couvrant respectivement le droit fiscal, le droit du travail et la sécurité sociale zaïrois. Le Centre publie en outre un bulletin bi-mensuel qui reproduit parfois des textes avant leur publication officielle.

x. Abréviations utilisées: AM = arrêté ministériel; éd. déf. = édition définitive; éd. prov. = édition provisoire; *JO* = Journal Officiel de la République du Zaire; OL = ordonnance-loi; ord. = ordonnance.
    Ont été dépouillés en vue de l'élaboration du présent aperçu: Journal Officiel, édition provisoire, 1972, n°s 1 à 24; 1973, n°s 1 à 5; edition définitive, 1972, n°s 1 à 6, 8, 15; 1973, n°s 1 à 4.

1. Signalons que le CEDIOM (Centre d'études et de documentation pour les investissements outre-mer), 34, rue de Stassart, 1050 Bruxelles, publie, sur feuilles volantes, une table analytique de la législation zaïroise, ainsi que des recueils couvrant respectivement le droit fiscal, le droit du travail et la sécurité sociale zaïrois. Le Centre publie en outre un bulletin bi-mensuel qui reproduit parfois des textes avant leur publication officielle.

2. Non publiée au Journal Officiel. Nous avons consulté le texte publié par le Départment de la Défense Nationale, sous forme d'ouvrage, contenant outre le Code de Justice Militaire diverses mesures législatives intéressant les Forces Armées et les juridictions militaires: République du Zaïre, Département de la Défense Nationale, *Code de Justice Militaire*, [Kinshasa], 1972, Imprimerie de l'Etat, [4]—163—[12] pp.

3. Sur le Code provisoire, voy. A Rubbens, La Justice militaire, *Revue Juridique du Congo*, XLII (1966), n° 1, pp. 3-12; ce commentaire demeure intéressant pour éclairer certains principes de la nouvelle législation

4. Un Conseil de guerre opérationnel a été créé pour la sous-région du Tanganyika par l'ord. n° 72-425 du 7 novembre 1972 (*JO*, éd. prov., 1972, n° 21, p. 10; éd. déf., n° 1, p. 53).

5.   Nous avouons que le texte de l'article 17 ne nous paraît pas tout à fait clair: d'une part il soumet les descendants aux diverses restrictions, d'autre part il limite dans deux cas l'application des restrictions à une période de 15 ans
6.   A-M n° 001-72 du 6 janvier 1972 (*JO*, éd. prov., 1972, n° 3, p. 3; éd. déf., 1972, n° 2, p. 61)
7.   Notons que le 15 février 1972, le Bureau Politique du Mouvement Populaire de la Révolution proclama la doctrine selon laquelle les paroles du Président ont force de loi
8.   Entremps, la Commission de Réforme et d'Unification du Droit Civil Zaïrois a préparé un avant-projet sur le droit du nom

CHAPTER TWENTY-FIVE

BURUNDI

J. Vanderlinden

Comme les années précédentes, le droit public domine la législation du Burundi en 1972. Tandis que le statut constitutionnel du pays demeure inchangé (le Chef de l'Etat, le Colonel Micombero, a eu cependant l'occasion de rappeler que les travaux d'élaboration de la nouvelle Constitution étaient en cours) non seulement des textes importants en matière administrative, fiscale et sociale ont été promulgués, mais également quelques textes de droit privé qui méritent de retenir l'attention.

DROIT ADMINISTRATIF

Le décret-loi du 10 décembre 1971 (BOB , 1972, p. 5) organise la compatibilité publique de l'Etat en trois articles fort longs remplaçant des dispositions de la loi du 19 mars 1964 relative à cette matière. Le texte nouveau précise de manière détaillée les compétences du Ministre des Finances qui se retrouve seul ordonnateur des budgets nationaux, assurant à la fois leur élaboration, leur exécution et leur contrôle; il est assisté dans cette tâche par un département du Budget et du Contrôle, tandis qu'à l'échelon inférieur fonctionnent des gestionnaires et sous-gestionnaires de crédits; le contrôle du Ministre s'étend notamment à toute opération pouvant engager l'Etat au delà de 500.000 francs, lesquelles requièrent son approbation préalable pour être valables.

Conscient de l'importance que pourrait jouer le tourisme dans son développement économique, le Burundi s'est doté ·d'un parastatal dénommé 'Office national du Tourisme' par décret-loi du 26 janvier 1972 (BOB, 1972, p. 171). Placé sous la tutelle du Ministre de l'Economie, le nouvel organisme, dirigé par un Conseil, géré par un Comité et administré par un Directeur, a dans ses attributions tous les problèmes du tourisme dans le pays. Le Conseil est entièrement composé de ministres et de fonctionnaires désignés sur base de leurs fonctions dans l'administration, à l'exception de trois personnes représentant le Chambre de Commerce et d'Industrie, les agences de voyage et les hôteliers; ceux-ci disparaissent totalement du comité de gestion.

Signalons enfin un décret présidentiel du 15 novembre 1972 (BOB, 1972, p. 499) qui rend obligatoire l'instruction militaire à l'Université et dans toutes les écoles supérieures.

DROIT FISCAL

Trois textes on été promulgués en cette matière et ils sont importants car ils remplacent complèment la législation organique existante en matière douanière; il s'agit du décret-loi du 12 novembre 1971 et des ses textes d'application du 30 décembre 1971 (BOB, 1972, pp. 41, 56 et 63); ils remplacent des textes datant de la colonisation dont le caractère caduc n'était plus à démontrer puisqu'ils avaient été conçus dans le cadre de l'union administrative et douanière avec le Rwanda et le Zaïre. La nouvelle législation conserve cependant la structure du texte colonial et toutes les procédures et institutions dont l'efficacité a été éprouvée par l'expérience tandis qu'elle en introduit de nouvelles parmi lesquelles on peut citer: l'alignement de la définition de la valeur en douane sur celle admise internationalement sur base des principes du GATT, la primauté de la notion d'origine sur celle de provenance dans les tarifs de droits d'importation à double colonne, un chapitre spécial consacré aux exonérations. Le texte principal, qui compte 113 articles, est accompagné de deux textes d'application; le premier compte 31 articles et règle les privilèges divers octroyés aux diplomates, fonctionnaires internationaux, coopérants techniques, etc. . . . tandis que le second, qui compte 276 articles, met en oeuvre dans tous ses détails le texte principal.

DROIT SOCIAL

Le texte le plus important dans le domaine social est sans aucun doute le décret-loi du 5 avril 1972 (BOB, 1972, p. 323) portant en 155 articles institution d'un régime général de sécurité sociale; il concerne essentiellement la couverture des accidents de travail et maladies professionnelles et l'organisation de pensions ou allocations de retraite, d'invalidité ou de survie. Il y assuiettit tous les travailleurs du Burundi (c'est-à-dire toutes les personnes liées par un contrat de travail conclu pour être exécuté en ordre principal dans le pays), les Barundi travaillant dans leurs missions diplomatiques ou consulaires à l'étranger et tous les membres du personnel de l'Etat ou des parastataux non-assujettis à un régime spécial. La couverture des risques professionnels est en outre accordée à diverses catégories de personnes dont les apprentis et les travailleurs à l'essai. Pour administrer ce nouveau régime, un Institut national de Sécurité sociale, établissement public doté de la personnalité juridique et de l'autonomie financière sous le contrôle et la garantie de l'Etat, est créé. Il tire ses ressources essentielles de cotisations, le travailleur et l'employeur cotisant en matière de pensions, tandis que seul l'employeur cotise pour les risques professionnels. Ceux-ci sont couverts aussi bien en ce qui concerne les soins de santé que l'indemnisation des incapacités temporaires ou permanentes de travail. Quant aux pensions, elles sont acquises à 65 ans pour les hommes et à 60 ans pour les femmes, si on excepte les pensions d'invalidité et les allocations de survie.

Indépendamment de ce texte fondamental, diverses dispositions ont complété ou organisé le régime d'allocations familiales au bénéfice des travailleurs et apprentis (ordonnance ministérielle du 18 novembre 1971, BOB, 1972, p. 12), celui des congés payés et de circonstance (décret-loi du 10 novembre 1971 et ordonnance ministérielle du 18 novembre 1971, BOB, 1972, p. 1 et p. 14) et celui de la prime d'ancienneté (ordonnance ministérielle du 23 novembre 1971, BOB, 1972, p. 14).

DROIT CIVIL

Le premier des trois textes pris en cette matière concerne les mesures d'èxécution du décret-loi du 10 août 1971 sur la notionalité; il s'agit en fait de l'organisation du certificat de nationalité et du registre-répertoire des actes modificatifs ou déclaratifs de nationalité (ordonnance ministérielle du 19 novembre 1971, BOB, 1972, p. 291).

Plus important, du moins pour les étrangers, est le décret-loi du 16 novembre 1972, relatif à l'administration et à la liquidation des successions d'étrangers abandonnées (BOB, 1972, p. 493). Ce texte modifie les textes existants dont certains remontaient à l'Etat indépendant du Congo. Sont ainsi réputés abandonnés les biens délaissés au Burundi suite à un décès sans qu'il n'existe dans le pays d'héritier, de conjoint ou d'exécution du décret-loi du 10 août 1971 sur la nationalité; il s'agit en fait d'héritier se fait conformément à la loi nationale du défunt, mais il faut remarquer la nécessité, en cas de succession testamentaire, d'un exécuteur résidant au Burundi. L'exécution du décret est confiée au Curateur aux Successions informé de l'existence de successions abandonnées par lesfonctionnaires communaux, d'arrondissement ou provinciaux; le Curateur administre ces successions avec le concours, à divers stades de la procédure, soit des représentants diplomatiques ou consulaires, soit de compatriotes du défunt. Le décret règle en outre les modalités d'inventaire, d'ouverture, d'administration, et de liquidation de la succession. Quant aux actions en cette matière, elles sont confiées par le décret à la compétence exclusive du tribunal de première instance de Bujumbura. Enfin il faut souligner une exception *ratione personae* aux règles du décret: l'administration des successions abandonnées de menbres de congrégations religieuses est confiée aux supérieurs de ces congrégations et échappe entièrement au Curateur.

Enfin, le dernier texte concerne aussi presqu' exclusivement des étrangers; il s'agit du décret-loi du 29 février 1972 (BOB, 1972, p. 178). Il tient en un article qui résilie tous les contrats de bail emphytéotiques passés entre l'Administration et des particuliers avant l'indépendance. Il est difficile de mesurer la portée exacte de cette disposition sans de longues recherches dans les recueils législatifs antérieurs à l'indépendance, mais le texte a en tout cas été suivi d'exécution, puisque 200 hectares environ ont été récupérés par l'administration en 1972 sur base du décret-loi du 29 février.

CHAPTER TWENTY-SIX

RWANDA

J. P. Vanderlinden

L'année 1972 a été plus pauvre encore que les précédentes sur le plan de l'activité législative au Rwanda. En tout, quatre textes, en l'occurrence des arrêtés présidentiels, méritent de retenir l'attention; aucune loi de portée générale n'a donc été promulgée.

DROIT ECONOMIQUE ET SOCIAL

Les deux premiers arrêtés présidentiels, datés respectivement du 13 janvier et du 10 février 1972 (JORR, 1972, pp. 8 et 25), établissent des institutions administratives de coordination et de consultation auprès du Secrétariat d'Etat au Plan. La première, le Conseil général de l'Orientation économique et sociale a pour objet général d'assister le Secrétaire d'Etat au Plan, d'apprécier le bilan annuel des divers secteurs économiques et sociaux et de proposer des lignes de politique ou des réformes dans ces mêmes secteurs. Le Conseil est composé de personnes nommées par le Secrétaire d'Etat au Plan. les secondes, les Commissions de Planification, ont pour objet d'associer étroitement les divers secteurs de l'activité économique et sociale à l'élaboration du plan; neuf Commissions de planification et une Commission de synthèse sont ainsi créées. Leurs membres sont nommés par le Secrétaire d'Etat au sein des fonctionnaires des départements ministériels intéressés, des personnalités particulièrement qualifiées du secteur privé, des représentants du parti national majoritaire, des représentants du parti national majoritaire, des représentants des confessions religieuses ou autres et des représentants d'autres organisations socio-économiques.

Le troisième arrêté, daté du 29 février 1972 (JORR, 1972, p. 38), crée établissement industriel public doté de la personnalité civile et d'une certaine autonomie administrative et financière, en l'occurrence l'Usine d'extraction de la pyréthrine, dont l'objet est l'ensemble des activités en rapport avec l'extraction du pyrèthre.

Enfin le dernier texte, daté du 15 juin 1972 (JORR, 1972, p. 85) a seulement pour objet de préciser la composition et les modalités de fonctionnement du conseil d'administration de la Caisse sociale du Rwanda.

PART III

Other African Countries

CHAPTER TWENTY-SEVEN

LIBERIA

Robert Chasen

In furtherance of the continuing revision of the *Liberian Code of Laws of 1956*, which will culminate in a six-volume work entitled *Liberian Code of Laws Revised*, the Forty-Seventh Legislature at its 1971-2 Session enacted into law those titles succinctly summarized herein.

The Transportation and Communications Law has been significantly expanded to include comprehensive regulation of civil aeronautics, radio broadcasting and television transmission. Jurisdiction over the former is vested in a Bureau of Civil Aviation in the Ministry of Commerce, Industry and Transportation (ch. 1). The provisions of the law are designed to secure the safe and efficient operation of civil aircraft and to limit the number of air carriers to those sufficient for public convenience and necessity. Control over aircraft is further assured by the requirement that all Liberian-owned civil aircraft must be registered. Foreign civil aircraft may be operated in Liberia only on permit issued by the Ministry of Commerce, Industry and Transportation. For operation of a foreign air carrier engaged in scheduled air transportation, special authorization is necessary. Procedures are prescribed and powers granted to the Minister of Commerce, Industry and Transportation or to a specially appointed Board of Special Inquiry to conduct investigations of accidents involving civil aircraft. Finally, provision is made authorizing fees for the use of air navigation facilities by airports maintained by the Government and for annual operating licenses for aircraft.

The revised title develops more fully than the former law the power of the government through the Commissioner of Telecommunications to establish an effective system of radio and television communication (ch. 21). Among his powers are the following: to license and classify radio and television stations, prescribe the nature of the service to be rendered by them, assign frequencies, license operators for all transmitting apparatus, and grant permits for construction of stations. Procedures either with or without a hearing are established for issuance of station licenses and construction permits, and for enforcement of orders to carry out the provisions of the statute and regulations issued thereunder.

Another important addition to the Transportation and communications Law is the chapter (ch. 4) providing for creation of a commission empowered to fix reasonable rates to be charged by common carriers and to prescribe routes to be followed and territories to be serviced by such carriers.

For the first time under the new law railroads in Liberia are subject to criminal liability for failure to take measures prescribed in detail to prevent accidents, as sounding a bell or whistle at crossings, posting warning signs at crossings, equipping locomotives with power brakes, and using headlights on locomotives after dark (ch. 5).

The limitations imposed on aliens with regard to engaging in the business of transporting passengers or property are continued under the new statute, but the applicability of the provisions has been broadened to include transportation by air and water as well as overland transportation, and to cover private as well as common carriers (§6.1). As formerly, aliens are restricted in transporting property for use even in their own businesses.

The revised National Defense Law is a restatement and clarification of the provisions of the title by the same name in the 1956 Code. It integrates into the organization of the armed services the Coast Guard and National Guard, the latter a successor to the Frontier Force, which for many decades formed the first line of defense.

Restrictions on importation of firearms and ammunition and requirements for registration of privately owned firearms are reenacted in the new law with minor changes.

The revised Executive Law reflects the changes in the top levels of the executive branch of the Government made in the interval since the 1956 Code. Most notable is the shift of nomenclature with reference to the divisions of the executive branch of government from department to ministries. The members of the Cabinet heading those divisions are accordingly entitled Ministers rather than 'Secretaries' as formerly, and the titles of their principal assistants are changed to conform. The ministries now composing the executive branch, apart from a number of autonomous agencies, are the following: Ministry of Foreign Affairs; Ministry of Finance; Ministry of Justice; Ministry of Postal Affairs; Ministry of National Defense; Ministry of Local Government, Rural Development, and Urban Reconstruction; Ministry of Education; Ministry of Public Works; Ministry of Agriculture; Ministry of Health and Social Welfare; Ministry of Commerce, Industry and Transportation; Ministry of Information, Tourism and Cultural Affairs; Ministry of Planning and Economic Affairs; Ministry of Lands and Mines; and Ministry of Labour and Youth (§10.1). The President is also authorized to appoint Ministers of State without Portfolio to serve as members of the Cabinet (§10.3).

The new title expands the law relating to presidential succession by providing that the Speaker of the House of Representatives or the President pro tempore of the Senate shall succeed to the office in case of vacancy in the offices of both the President and Vice President (§4.3). Also included is provision for the mechanics for assumption of powers of the Presidency by the Vice President in case the President is disabled from performing his duties (§4.4).

Included in the new Executive Law is a complete Administrative

Procedure Act which sets forth the minimum requirements for hearings
and determinations by administrative agencies (ch. 82). The procedure for
review of administrative orders and for their enforcement is also provided.
The Act will govern the conduct of all administrative proceedings for
which conflicting provisions are not included in other statutes with
reference to proceedings before a particular agency.

A chapter has been added to the title relating to preservation, storage,
reproductions and disposal of Government records (ch. 81).

A revised Decedents Estates Law was passed. It consists of two parts:
(1) the Law of Wills and Intestate Succession, and (II) a Probate Court
Procedure Code.

The major contribution of the revision with respect to the law of wills is
a comprehensive Liberian statute of wills. For the first time all aspects of
wills are covered by statutory provisions: who may make and receive
testamentary dispositions of property, what property may be disposed of
by will, formal requirements concerning the execution, revocation and
alteration of wills and rules of construction.

With respect to the law of intestate succession, the modifications were
considerable. Apart from eliminating ambiguities concerning persons
entitled to distribution of an intestate estate and their respective priorities,
a surviving spouse was for the first time included in the scheme of
distribution and given a priority. Coupled with this, in lieu of any intestate
or testamentary share due him, a widower was given a statutory right of
election to accept a modified form of common law courtesy in his deceased
wife's estate to the same extent as the constitutional right given to a widow
to take a modified form of common law dower. By virtue of these rights, a
surviving spouse may elect to take one-third of the deceased spouse's
personal property outright and a life state in one-third of the deceased
spouse's real estate. Inchoate dower problems are avoided since the
statute provides that only the real and personal estate of which the
deceased died seized is applicable to the surviving spouse's elective share.

The Probate Court Procedure Code is entirely new and corresponds in
its scope to the new Civil Procedure Law. It provides in great detail for
every kind of probate court procedure.

A new Judiciary Law provides for a unified judicial system vested in one
Supreme Court and four subordinate courts of record: a court of general
jurisdiction, known as the Circuit Court; a court whose original
jurisdiction is limited to civil actions to obtain payment of a debt, known
as the Debt Court; a court whose jurisdiction is limited to probate and
related matters, known as the Monthly and Probate Court; a court whose
jurisdiction is limited to minor civil and criminal matters, known as the
Magistrates' Court; another court whose jurisdiction is similarly limited
to minor civil and criminal matters, known as the Magistrates' Court;
another court whose jurisdiction is similarly limited to minor civil and
criminal matters, known as the Justices of the Peace Court; a court whose
jurisdiction is limited to cases involving infractions of the Vehicle and
Traffic Law (Title 38 of the *Liberian Code of Laws Revised*), known as the
Traffic Court; and a court whose jurisdiction is limited to special
proceedings involving children under the age of eighteen years, known as
the Juvenile Court. It expressly excludes tribal courts, whose organization

and exclusive jurisdiction over tribal matters, except for matrimonial causes arising under tribal customary law within the territorial jurisdiction of seven of the magisterial courts, is set forth in the Local Government Law (title 21 of the *Liberian Code of Laws Revised*).

All of the courts in the new court system, except the Tax Court, the Debt Court and the Juvenile Court had been heretofore established under provisions codified in title 18 of the *Liberian Code of Laws of 1956*, and the cumulative supplement thereto through the laws of 1957-8.

The Tax Court, the provisions for which were approved on Jauary 22 1959, is an extension of the prior Revenue Courts and reflects their increased functions. The Debt Court, which was established by an enactment approved 10 April 1967, initially had exclusive jurisdiction of all debt cases in which the alleged debt was $2000.00 or more. The present re-enactment provides that it has jurisdiction in debt cases in which the amount is $500 or more.

The Juvenile Court was first projected in an enactment approved February 21, 1959. It was given exclusive jurisdiction of juvenile offenders under nineteen years of age but was not to be established until the President so authorized. The current provisions, incorporated in chapter 10 of the new Judiciary Law, establishes a court in and for the Commonwealth District of Monrovia in Montserrado County and, until regularly constituted juvenile courts are established in other areas of the Republic, the magisterial courts in those areas are to assume jurisdiction as juvenile courts. Supplementing the provisions for the court, in chapter 11 of the new Judiciary Law, is a detailed Juvenile Court Procedural Code setting forth the proceedings concerning the court's jurisdiction over juvenile delinquents, juveniles in need of care and protection necessary for their well being, and neglected children.

A new revised Patent, Copyright and Trademark Law was enacted as title 24 of the *Liberian Code of Laws Revised*. A significant addition has been made in the revision in each field. In Patent Law, so long as reciprocal rights are granted to Liberian citizens, a foreign patent has been granted a right of priority, as of the date of filing the application therefore in the foreign country, provided the application for patent rights in Liberia is made within twelve months from the earliest date on which the foreign application was first filed in the foreign country. In Copyright Law, unpublished as well as published works are given copyright protection. In the Trademark field, service marks are given equal protection with trademarks.

CHAPTER TWENTY-EIGHT

SUDAN

Natale Olwak Akolawin

The year 1972 witnessed major political and constitutional developments which had and would continue to have direct impact on the law. The first of these developments was the holding from 2 to 8 January 1972 of the National Founding Conference of the Sudanese Socialist Union, the only legal political organization sanctioned by the Republican Order No. 5. The second development and perhaps the most important in the troubled political history of the independent Sudan was the signing on 27 February and ratification on 27 March 1972, of *'The Addis Ababa Agreement on the Southern Problem'* between the Sudàn Government and the Southern Sudan Liberation Movement (SSLM) which granted Regional self-Government to the Southern Sudan and brought to an end the civil war which had plagued the Sudan since 1955.

The third development of major importance was the convening on 12 October 1972 of the First People's Assembly constituted in accordance with Presidential Order No. 104, issued by the President under Art. 37 of the Republican Order No. 5. Besides these major developments 1972 is also rich in legislation.

CONSTITUTIONAL LAW

THE SUDANESE SOCIALIST UNION.
The founding National Conference of the Sudanese Socialist Union took place in Khartoum on 2 to 8 January 1972. The Conference approved the constitution, standing Orders and the National charter of Union. The conference also approved twenty-four basic principles of the Sudan Permanent Constitution.

Most of the basic principles are already embodied in the Republican Order No. 5, which serves as the transitional Constitution of the Sudan. The first nine principles deal with the nature of the state. The first principle declares the Sudan a sovereign socialist Democratic state built on the alliance of the popular working forces and is an inseparable part of the Arab and African Nations.

Sovereignty in the state shall be vested in the people represented by the popular working forces (defined as Farmers, Workers, members of the Armed forces, Elites and National Capitalists) which shall be exercised by them through constitutional institutions and organizations. The Sudanese Socialist Union is to be the only authorized political organization in the Sudan. The Democratic Republic of the Sudan is to be a presidential Republic with Arabic as its official language. Legislative power is to be vested in the people's Assembly.

The Conference affirmed the 9th of June Declaration which recognized the right of the Southern Sudan to regional autonomy and the right of its people to develop their cultures and languages.

Basic principles 10 to 22 deal with the economic policy, the family and fundamental rights and freedoms. The economy of the Sudan is to be based on the Socialist system which aims at creating a community of sufficiency and justice and which prevents any form of exploitation. The economic policy recognizes four sectors of economy; the Public Sector, the Joint Government and Private enterprises Sector, the Co-operative Sector and the Private Sector.

Self-help and reliance is to be the basic instrument in the socio-economic development. The last two basic principles deal with foreign policy. In the realization of its being inseparable part of Arab and African Nations, the Sudan is to pursue a foreign policy which preserves its sovereignty and freedom. It is to adopt a policy which stands against imperialism and colonialism and shall establish its foreign relations with other states on the footing of equality, mutual respect, protection of joint interests and preservation of sovereignty.

Though the principles on foreign policy allow for establishment of defence alliances, they have definitely ruled out future union of the Sudan with any other state or states which involves the loss of sovereignty.

THE ADDIS ABABA AGREEMENT ON THE SOUTHERN PROBLEM AND THE SOUTHERN PROVINCES SELF-GOVERNMENT ACT, 1972.

The Addis Ababa Agreement on the Southern Problem which granted self-government to the three southern Provinces consists of six documents:

1. The basic Law for the organization of regional autonomy in the three Southern Provinces.
2. The Amnesty Law for those who participated in Anya-Nya—the Southern Sudan Resistance Movement and political leaders in exile,
3. The Administrative arrangements for the interim period until the establishment of the institutions of regional autonomy organized by the basic law mentioned above.
4. The cease fire.
5. The temporary arrangements concerning the Armed Forces in the Southern Sudan.
6. The organization of the immigration of the refugees and the resettlement of those dwelling in towns and who were originally forced by insecurity to leave the countryside.

The basic law on regional autonomy which is the cornerstone of the Agreement was enacted as 'The Southern Provinces Regional Self-Government Act, 1971'[1] on 3 March 1972. Other provisions of the

Agreement were implemented by the Amnesty Act, 1972[2] and Presidential Orders Nos. 39-45.

Under the Southern Provinces Regional Self-Government Act, 1972, the Southern Provinces of the Sudan are to constitute a self-governing Region with an elected Regional Assembly and Executive Council. The Southern Provinces are defined by the Act, as the Provinces of Bahr El Ghazal, Equatoria and Upper Nile as they stood on 1 January 1956 and any other areas that are 'culturally and geographically a part of the Southern complex as may be decided by a referendum'.[3] Juba is designated as the capital of the Southern Region.

Except for national defence, external affairs, currency and coinage, air and inter-regional river transport, communications and tele-communications, customs and foreign trade (except border trade and certain commodities which the Regional Government may specify with the approval of the central Government) nationality and immigration, planning for economic and social development, educational planning and public audit, the Regional Assembly and Executive Council may legislate and exercise powers for the preservation of public order, internal security, efficient administration and the development of the Southern Region in the cultural, economic and social fields.

The President of the Regional Executive Council is appointed and relieved of office by the President of the Republic on the recommendation of the Regional Assembly. The members of the Regional Executive Council are appointed and removed by the President on the recommendation of the President of the Executive Council. The President and members of the Executive Council are responsible to the President of the Republic and the Regional Assembly for the efficient and good administration in the Southern Region.

The Act guarantees that the citizens of the Southern Region shall constitute a sizeable proportion of the Sudan Armed Forces in such reasonable numbers as will correspond to the population of the Region. The Act imposes a duty on the Regional Assembly to consolidate the unity of the Sudan and to respect its constitution. The President of the Republic is given a right to veto any legislation passed by the Regional Assembly which he deems contrary to the provisions of the Constitution.

Although Arabic is to be the official language of the Sudan, English is to be the principal language of the Southern Region without prejudice to the use of any other language or languages which may serve as a practical necessity for the efficient and expeditious discharge of the executive and administrative functions of the Region.

The Southern Provinces Regional self-government Act, 1972, can only be amended by a three-quarters majority of the National Assembly and with the approval of a majority of two-thirds of the electorate of the Southern Region in a referendum held for that purpose in the Region.

INTERIM ARRANGEMENT.

The Agreement has been implemented in its entirety by Presidential Orders Number 39-45, dealing respectively with (i) revenue of taxes, duties and other financial aid and revenues, (ii) provisional measures preceding the election of the Regional Assembly, (iii) ending military operation in the Southern Provinces and the joint ceasefire commission of officers of the Sudan Armed Forces and the Anya-Nya National Organization, (iv) provisional arrangements for the Armed Forces in the Southern Region and (v) establishment of a Commission for repatriation of the Southern Sudan Refugees in the neighbouring countries.

A provisional High Executive Council under Presidency of Sayed Abel Alier, Vice-President of the Republic was set up with eleven members, seven of whom are politicans returned from exile. The Provisional Regional Executive Council is to remain in office for a period not exceeding eighteen months and is entrusted with the task of taking all the necessary measures for holding the elections for the Regional Assembly.

Besides the Southern Provinces Regional self-Government Act, 1972, two other statues were enacted dealing with Provisional Arrangements pending the Election of the Regional People's Assembly[4] and the Revenue of Taxes and Duties (Financial Aid and other Revenues) for the Southern Region of the Sudan[5].

THE FIRST PEOPLE'S ASSEMBLY.
The First People's Assembly constituted in accordance with the provisions of the Presidential Order No. 104 was convened on 12 October 1972 charged by the Republican Order No. 5 with the responsibility of making and passing a permanent constitution for the Sudan. It was composed of ministers as ex officio members and 208 elected and appointed members. The seats of the Assembly were divided as follows:-

1. 90 Seats for regional constituencies,
2. 44 seats for popular organizations,
3. 73 national seats.

Every attempt was made under Presidential Order No. 104 to represent all the people in different walks of life in the Assembly. The elected members were elected in accordance with the provisions of Presidential Order No. 104 and the Regulations for the Election of the People's Assembly, 1972.[6]

The quorum for meetings of the Assembly is half of its members and, subject to Article 41 of Republican Order No. 5, resolutions of the Assembly are to be passed by absolute majority. Deliberations of the Assembly are to be in Arabic but English and other languages may be allowed by the Speaker.

Though the Assembly may deliberate on any matter, its primary task is to discuss the Draft Constitution as prepared by the Sudan Socialist Union.

AMNESTY LAW
The Indemnity Act, 1966, was extended for another year by the Indemnity (Continuation) Act, 1972,[7] but was repealed by the Amnesty Act, 1972,[8] which enacted into law the Amnesty provisions for those who participated in Anya-Nya, the Southern Sudan Ressistance Movement and political leaders in exile.

NATIONALITY.
The Sudanese Nationality Act, 1958, was amended twice during the year.

The first Amendment[9] substituted the words '31 December 1897' in s. 5(i) and (ii) with the words '1 January 1924'. The effect of this Amendment is that any person born in the Sudan or whose father was born in the Sudan and has been domiciled in the Sudan since 1 January 1924 shall be considered Sudanese by descent.

The second Amendment[10] amended s. 9(6) by adding the following clause:

'Provided the Council of Ministers on the recommendation of the Minister may exempt her from the provisions of the this subsection if she lived in the Sudan with her Sudanese husband continuously for at least two years directly before the date of her application.'

SEQUESTRATION OF PROPERTY.

S. 4(4) of the Sequestration Act, 1970, was amended[11] in order to empower the Sequestrator General to sell with the approval of the Sequestration Supervisor General the immovable and movable property of the debtor.

RENUMERATION OF THE VICE-PRESIDENTS.

The renumeration and privileges of the Vice-Presidents were laid down by the Renumeration of the Vice-Presidents Act, 1972[12] which is deemed to have come into force on 12 October 1971.

REPUBLICAN ORDER NO. II

The Republican Order No. II (Amendment) 1972 deleted the words 'with death' in Art. 6, thus removing death as a punishment for offences committed under Art. 5 of that Order.

ADMINISTRATIVE LAW

ADMINISTRATION

The People's Local Government Act, 1971, ss. 6(1) and (2) were amended by the People's Local Government (Amendment) Act, 1972.[13] Under ss. 6(1) and (2) as amended the President of the Republic appoints as Commissioner of a Province any person with ability, experience, high administrative capability and who is politically committed to the aims of Revolution.

The Commissioner is responsible to the President through the Minister of Local Government for the good administration and the execution of government policy in the Province.

GOVERNMENT CARS

Under s. 2 of the Supervision of Government Cars Act, 1971, as amended in 1972[14] cars belonging to public corporations and companies in which the Government owns shares are now excluded from the operation of the provisions of this Act.

THE DIPLOMATIC AND CONSULAR CORPS

The Diplomatic and Consular Corps Act, 1970, was amended during the year but the Amendment[15] is of no legal importance.

PASSPORTS AND IMMIGRATION

The Passports and Immigration Act, 1960, s. 27 was amended by the Passports and Immigration (Amendment) Act, 1972.[16] Under the 1960 Act as amended all foreign visitors are required to present themselves to the nearest Immigration Authorities within three days of arrival in the country or of moving from one part to another within the country.

The Act imposes a duty on managers of hotels to obtain all the necessary information about the foreign visitor, the purposes of the visit and duration of stay in the hotel and to communicate it to the competent authority. The managers of the hotels have to inform the Immigration authorities of the departure of foreign visitors within twenty-four hours.

The foreign visitor who wants to visit another District in the Sudan is required to obtain permission from the Alien Registration Office or Office established for the purpose in the District and should present himself within twenty-four hours to the competent authority in the District. S. 34 is repealed. The Passports and Immigration Act, 1960 was amended a second time[17] but the amendment is of no legal importance.

PENSIONS

The Civil Service Pensions Act, 1962, was amended three times during the year. The first Amendment[18] affected s. 2 and is of no legal significance. The second Amendment[19] incorporated the Academic Staff, the sub-Academic Staff and officials of the University of Khartoum appointed directly by the University into the Civil Service Pensions Scheme laid down under 1962 Act.

In assimilating the University Staff and officials into the Pensions Scheme, the salary of the Professor is to be treated as being equivalent to that of Group 1. The third Amendment[20] affected s. 91. In that section, the words 'or any post with the rank of Minister or rank of Deputy Minister' were to be added. Similar amendment was effected in s. 59 of the Armed Forces (Officers) Pensions Act, 1963 by the Armed Forces (Officers) Pensions (Amendment) Act, 1972.[21]

STATISTICS

The Statistics Act, 1970, was amended by the Statistics (Amendment) Act, 1972.[22] A new section, s. 21, was added which gives the President special power to order the compiling of statistics at any time and in the manner he thinks suitable.

REGISTRATION OF BIRTHS AND DEATHS

The Registration of Births and Death Ordinance, 1939, was repealed and replaced by the Registration of Births and Deaths Act, 1972.[23] All the registers of Births and Deaths and other documents established under the 1939 Ordinance are to be handed to the Department of Statistics. The new Act provides for the registration of all births and deaths throughout the Sudan. It imposes a duty on all local Councils to appoint an official responsible for the registration of births and deaths. Fourteen cities and towns are declared under the Act to be centres for the registration of births and deaths. Other centres may be established by the Council of Ministers on the request of the Ministers of Local Government and

Health. The Director of Statistics is the Registrar General of Births and Deaths under the Act.

SOCIETIES

The Registration of Societies Act, 1957, was amended by Registration of Societies (Amendment) Act, 1972.[24] The Amendment gives the Minister power with the approval of the Prime Minister to amend the constitution or internal regulations of any societies if he thinks it is in the public interest to do so. Such amendment or alteration shall be binding on the societies and its members from the date determined by the Minister.

LEGAL SYSTEM

THE JUDICIARY

Major changes in this field of law were introduced by the Judicial Authority Act, 1972,[25] and the Exercise of Judicial Powers Act, 1972,[26] which came into force in June 1972. The first Act merged the Civil and the Sharia courts into one system of state courts responsible for the administration of Justice in all fields of law including personal matters of Muslims and non-Muslims. It repealed the Judiciary Act, 1969, the Sharia Courts Act, 1967, ss. 1 to 10 of the Sudan Mohammedan Law Courts Organization and Procedure Regulations, 1916, and all sections of the Civil Justice Ordinance, 1929, and the Code of Criminal Procedure, 1925, which deal with the constitution of Civil and Criminal Courts. The provisions of the Judicial Authority Act, 1972, prevail over the provisions of any other Act in case of conflict or inconsistency and the provisions of such Act are to be deemed amended to the extent necessary to remove such conflict or inconsistency.

The Act consists of 126 sections in addition to Regulations on Judges' Conduct[27] issued by the Minister of Justice under it.

The Act has introduced a major reorganization in the structure, hierarchy and the internal administration of the Sudan Judiciary. It establishes four types of courts: (1) The Supreme Court, (2) the Court of Appeal, (3) the Province Courts and (4) the District Courts, although any other courts may be established by law. These courts are competent to hear and determine all disputes, suits and offences except what has been excluded from their competence by special provision of the law and they have jurisdiction to determine all matters brought before them in accordance with the law. The courts may not however entertain directly or indirectly any matter or suit involving sovereignty or Act of State. They exercise their jurisdiction in specialized panels or divisions.

The jurisdiction and the powers of the Courts remain as laid down in the Civil Justice Ordinance, 1929, and the Code of Criminal Procedure, 1925, or any other enactment replacing any or all of them. The Courts, in settling disputes or suits involving personal matters, are to follow the procedure laid down in the Civil Justice Ordinance, 1929, or any other enactment replacing it.

The exercise of Judicial Powers Act, 1972, deals with the transfer and of distribution of the judicial and administrative powers of the Chief Justice and transitional arrangements in respect of cases pending before courts when the Judicial Authority Act, 1972, came into force.

Under this Act all the judicial powers of the Chief Justice under any enactment in force are transferred to the Supreme Court and all the administrative powers to the Minister of Justice. The powers of the Chief Justice in respect of the constitution of Benches of Magistrates, Chiefs' Courts, Native Courts and any other courts are transferred to the Minister of Justice.

The Major Courts and Courts of Magistrate of the First and Second Class are to continue disposing of criminal cases before them. The Minister of Justice is authorized under this Act to appoint temporarily any public servant or officer of the Armed Forces who is qualified to sit on Courts-Martial or any other suitable person as a Magistrate of First, Second or Third Class and to sit as a member of any Criminal Penal of the Province Court and such public servant, officer or other person shall be considered as if appointed under s. 11(1) of the Code of Criminal Procedure.

The Minister of Justice, in consultation with the Council of the Supreme Court, may redistribute when necessary the powers distributed under this Act.

ADVOCATES

The Advocates Act, 1970, was amended twice[28] during the year. The first Amendment which affected s. 7(4), deals with applications to practise as Advocates by members of the Judiciary and Law Officers who have been removed or dismissed. The second Amendment which affected s. 40(2) gives the Minister of Justice power, after consultation with the Committee of the Sudan Bar Association, to amend any agreement concluded by an advocate and his client as regards fees payable to him if he is convinced in the light of circumstances surrounding such agreement that such fees is high and does not suit the volume, the type and the nature of legal services rendered. The Minister of Justice exercises his power under s. 40(2) upon complaint from the Advocate's client.

THE ATTORNEY GENERAL

The Reorganization of the Ministry of Justice Act, 1969, was repealed by the Reorganization of the Ministry of Justice Act, 1972,[29] except that the regulations and orders made or issued under the repealed Act are to remain in force until they are repealed or amended in accordance with 1972 Act.

Under this Act, the Ministry of Justice shall be headed by person known as 'The Attorney General' who shall have the status of the President of the Supreme Court. He shall be responsible to the Minister of Justice. Any reference in any law to the Under-Secretary, Ministry of Justice should be construed as referring to the Attorney General. The Attorney General has three Deputies; the Prosecutor General, the Advocate General and Solicitor General.

The Attorney General, his Deputies and Senior Legal Counsellors are appointed by the President on the nomination of the Minister of Justice.

The Attorney General may, by order published in the Gazette, delegate any or all of the powers given to him by this Act to any of his Deputies or any other person holding their posts.

The Minister of Justice may issue regulations dealing with the organization of the Ministry of Justice including the terms of service of the Law Officers, their promotion and discipline; the formation of different departments or sections of the Ministry; the appointment, promotion and discipline of the officials of the Ministry as well as the responsibilities of the officials in charge of departments or sections within the Ministry.

SALARIES OF THE JUDICIARY, THE ATTORNEY GENERAL AND THE LEGAL COUNSELLORS

New and better terms of service for the members of the Judiciary, the Attorney General and the Legal Counsellors were introduced by the Judiciary Salaries Act, 1972,[30] and the Attorney General's and Legal Counsellors' Salaries Act, 1972,[31] respectively. The former Act repealed the Judiciary Salaries Ordinance, 1953. Besides the new and better salary scales, the two Acts deal with pensions, free housing, free transport and holidays.

CRIMINAL LAW, PROCEDURE AND EVIDENCE

Though there is no direct amendment to the Penal Code important legislation was enacted during the year dealing with the protection of Public property. There have also been minor amendments of no major legal significance to the Unjust Enrichment Act, 1966,[32] the Punishment of Corruption Act,[33] and the Road Traffic Ordinance.[34]

THE PROTECTION OF PUBLIC PROPERTY ACT, 1972[35]

This Act provides for special trials and enhanced punishments from those provided for under the Penal Code, for Theft, Robbery or Criminal Misappropriation of public property, Criminal breach of Trust involving public property, Receiving Stolen public property, Cheating and Falsification of accounts in connection with public property and receiving bribes. This Act is to be considered complementary to the Penal Code and its provisions are to prevail in case of conflict with the Code. The provisions of the Penal Code (chapters 5, 6, 7 and 8 dealing with Joint Acts, Abetment, Attempt and Conspiracy) are to apply in determining offences committed under this Act.

Public property is defined as immovable or movable property which he Government owns or possesses. The Government is defined to include Central Government, People's Executive Councils, People's Local Councils, and the Companies of the Public sector and corporations and the incorporated bodies established in accordance with special law or the Corporations of Public Sector Act, 1971, and those companies and partnerships or any other business in which the Government owns more than fifty per cent of the capital.

The words and expressions used in this Act are to have the same meaning as that used under the Sudan Penal Code. The burden of proof in cases involving offences under this Act lies on the accused. This is a deliberate departure from general provision of the Sudan Criminal Law and Procedure which places the burden of proof in criminal trials on the prosecution. The Act also lays down minimum sentences for offences committed under it, including death or life imprisonment for Theft or Criminal Breach of Trust or any offences against public property, the value of which is £S.5000.

The offences committed under this Act are tried by special courts set up by the Minister of Justice. Appeals from the decisions of these courts lie to the president whose decision is final.

CRIMINAL PROCEDURE

Wide powers of investigation were conferred on the Under-Secretary, Ministry of Justice or any person nominated by him under s. 122 of the Code of Criminal Procedure, as amended by the code of Criminal Procedure (Amendment) Act, 1972.[36]

The Under-Secretary, Ministry of Justice, upon iformation from any person or on his own initiative, if he has sufficient reason to believe an offence has been committed, may under s. 122(h) of the Code of Criminal Procedure, investigate the offence personally or through any other person nominated by him except a Judge. Once an investigation has commenced under s. 122(h), no Magistrate or policeman shall begin a fresh investigation or continue the investigation without obtaining the permission of the Under-Secretary, Ministry of Justice.

Anyone carrying out investigation under this Section has the same powers conferred by law on any policeman. Any police officer in charge of a police station is to render any help to any person carrying out an investigation under this Section.

COMMERCIAL LAW

The Registration of Business Names Ordinance, 1933, and the Registration of Partnership Ordinance, 1933, were amended during the year.[37] The Amendments which affected ss. 6A and 12A of these Ordinance respectively give the Minister of Economics and Trade the power to refuse the registration of any Business Names or Partnership if in his opinion it is in the public inerest to do so. The decision of the Minister refusing the registration of a Business Name or Partnership is binding on the Registrar. The applicant can appeal to a Judge of High Court against the refusal of the Minister within a month from the date he receives the decision of the Minister refusing registration. The Control of Crops Act, 1972,[38] was enacted during the year which gave the Minister of Economics and Trade wide powers of search and control over the export of certain crops appearing in the Schedule to this Act.

CORPORATIONS LAW

Two new public corporations were established during the year, the Fashaqa Development and Construction Corporation and the Rahad Corporation, set up under the Fashaqa Development and Construction Corporation Act, 1972,[39] and the Rahad Corporation Act, 1972.[40] The

Fashaqa Development and Construction Corporation Act, 1972[41] was amended but the amendment of no legal importance.

Ss. 7, 9, 10 and 11 of the Public Sector Corporations Act, 1971, were amended[42] but these amendments are also of no legal significance.

EVIDENCE AND CIVIL PROCEDURE

Two Major Acts were enacted in this field of the law during the year, the Evidence Act, 1972,[43] and the Civil Pleadings Act, 1972,[44] which came into force on 1 July 1972. These two Acts follow the footsteps of the Civil Code Act, 1971. The primary provisions of these Acts are drawn from Egyptian Law and Laws of other Arab Countries.

THE EVIDENCE, (CIVIL PROVISIONS) ACT, 1972

This Act lays down for the first time in one enactment the rules of evidence in civil matters in one enactment. Hitherto the Sudan Courts have relied on some provisions of the Civil Justice Ordinance, 1929, and the Indian Evidence Act. The Act, which consists of ninety-five sections applies in settling civil, commercial, personal and any other matters unles they are excluded by special provision of the laws governing them.

It repealed the following sections of the Civil Justice Ordinance, 1929, and Orders issued under it: ss. 75–85 and 104–107; Orders No. I, II, VII, VIII, IX and s. 4 of Order No. XXI; the following provisions of the Sudan Mohammedan Law Courts Organization and Procedure Regulations 1916: ss. 85–7, 103–5, 114–17, 120–161 and 164–6.

THE CIVIL PLEADINGS ACT, 1972

This consists of 460 sections and applies to judicial proceedings involving civil, commercial and personal matters and any proceedings involving any other matter unless excluded by special provision of the law governing it. If there is no provision of this Act dealing with any matter before the court, it shall act in accordance with the principles of natural justice. This Act has repealed the Civil Justice Ordinance, 1929, except ss. 27, 29, 30, 31, 112-18 and 227, all the Orders issued under that Ordinance, except Orders VI, XVIII, XIX, XXI, XXII and XXIII.

It repealed also the Sudan Mohammedan Law Courts Organization and Procedure Regulations, 1916, except ss. 51, 81(b), 118, 119 and 208–252.

The Civil Pleadings Act, 1972, was amended by the Civil Pleadings (Amendment) Act, 1972.[45] The amendment which affected ss. 89 and 222 are of minor importance.

EDUCATION

Six statutes were enacted in the field of education during the year. The University of Khartoum Act, 1970, was amended twice; the Post-Graduate Medical Education Act, 1970,[46] was repealed, a National Council for Higher Education was set up under the National Council for Education Act, 1972,[47] the Eradication of Illiteracy and Functional Education Act, 1972,[48] and Sudanese Atomic Energy Commission Act, 1972[49] were enacted.

UNIVERSITY OF KHARTOUM

The first Amendment to the University of Khartoum Act, 1970 dealt with the appointment of the Principal, the composition of the University Council and the Executive and Finance Committee. The second Amendment[50] provided for the continuation in force of Statutes and Regulations issued under the 1956 Act, until they are repealed or amended in accordance with the 1970 Act.

NATIONAL COUNCIL FOR HIGHER EDUCATION

The National Council for Higher Education Act, 1972, is a welcome development in the field of Higher Education where there had been not only lack of definite policy but there was also waste of resources and duplication. The Act regulates all Higher Education, whether conducted by Universities, Institutes, colleges, training schools run by Ministeries, or by Private institutions or persons which accept students who have a senior secondary school Certificate or equivalent for a minimum period of two years except the institutions for education and training belonging to or run by the Armed Forces, the Police, prisons and the in-training schools of the Ministries and departments. The National Council for Higher Education is given wide powers by the Act. It is responsible *inter alia* for the organization, co-ordination and planning of Higher Education in the Sudan. The Council is composed of the Minister of Education as chairman, the Vice-Chancellors of the Universities, the Principals of colleges and Under-Secretaries of Ministries and Directors of Government Department concerned with higher Education as well as of six non-officials members nominated by the Minister.

SUDANESE ATOMIC ENERGY COMMISSION

A Sudanese Atomic Energy Commission in charge of peaceful uses of Atomic Energy was set up by the Sudanese Atomic Energy Commission Act, 1972. The Commission is responsible to the Minister of Higher Education and Scientific Research for the discharge of its functions under this Act.

INDUSTRIAL AND LABOUR LAW

Besides the amendments[52] to the Trade Unions Ordinance, 1948, new legislation was enacted in this field of the law dealing with the development and encouragement of industrial investments,[53] petroleum resources,[54] Mines and Quarries,[55] the setting up of an Industrial Consultancies Corporation,[56] and the Industrial Consultancy Agencies,[57] The Petroleum Ordinance, 1931, was amended during the year but the amendment,[58] is of no legal importance. A new law, the Gold and Silver (Jewellery) Engraving Act, 1972,[59] dealing with engravings and plating on gold and silver ornaments and other works, was also enacted.

LAND LAW

The Unregistered Land Act, 1970, was amended by the Unregistered Land (Amendment) Act, 1972.[60] Under this, s. 4 of the 1970 Act becomes subsection 1 of the new s. 4 and the following two subsections are added:

'(2) The Minister of Housing and Public Utilities may by order specify and enumerate lands owned by the Government by virtue of the above subsection and which the government intends to dispose of for the purposes of housing or development and the order shall include, the survey, division into plots, specification and numbering of such lands.
(3) The Chief Justice may on application by the Minister of Housing and Public utilities order the establishment of registers for the lands so enumerated and specified, in the Registry Office within whose jurisdiction such lands are situate and these registers shall be deemed to be/have been established under s. 23 of the Land Settlement and Registration Ordinance.'

FINANCIAL AND REVENUE LAWS

A number of Acts were enacted during the year dealing with fiscal financial and revenue matters none of which is of major legal importance.[61]

PERSONAL LAW.

The Charitable Trusts Act, 1971, was amended by the Charitable Trusts (Amendment) Act, 1972.[62] The Committee entrusted with the implementation of the objectives of the Act, established under s. 3 as amended, consists of the Minister of Religious Affairs and Wakfs as Chairman, and the Ministers of Justice, Treasury and Housing and Public Utilities as members.

The Islamic Charitable Trusts Act, 1970, was also amended[63] during the year. Under the amendment, the Ministry Religious Affairs and Wakfs is entrusted with the responsibility for developing economincally the trusts for the benefit of the Community. The Minister of Religious Affairs and Wakfs is assisted in the exercise of his responsibilities under the Act by the Supreme Council for the Trusts established under his Chairmanship, with the Grand Kadi, Under Secretaries and the Ministries of Planning, Treasury, Justice, Housing and Public Utilities, Local Government and the Director, Department of Trusts as members.

PUBLIC INTERNATIONAL LAW

The Democratic Republic of the Sudan acceded to a number of multilateral Agreements and ratified bilateral Agreements with a number of states in the fields of International Trade and co-operation.

MULTILATERAL AGREEMENTS
The Sudan acceded to the Amendment to Art. 6 of the International Atomic Energy Agency;[64] the Agreement concerning the Settlement of Investment Disputes between a State and a citizen of another State;[65] the Agreement establishing the Arab Organization for Social Defence,[66] the objects of which are the study of the causes of crime, its prevention, treatment of criminals and the strengthening of the machinery for combating traffic in drugs in the Arab States; the Agreement to facilitate transfer of hearing and optical instruments, printed material and

technical equipments of educational, cultural and scientific nature between the Arab States;[67] The Four Parties Agreement between the Sudan Government, the UN High Commissioner for the Refugees, the International Red Cross and the Sudanese Red Crescent regarding the settlement of 20,000 Ethiopian refugees in eastern Sudan;[68] and the Agreement establishing the Arab Company for Ocean Navigation.[69]

BILATERAL AGREEMENTS
The Sudan ratified Border Agreement with Ethiopia;[70] loan Agreements with the African Development Bank to finance the purchase of equipments for Sudan Railways;[71] and for the establishment of three quarantines for the export of livestock from the Sudan;[72] with the Kuwaiti fund for Arab Development[73] and with the United Kingdom.[74]

It ratified Trade Agreements with the People's Republic of Hungary[75] and Romanian Socialist Republic;[76] economic and technical Agreement with People's China[77] and the Romanian Socialist Republic;[78] technical co-operation Agreement in the field of veterinary training and animal husbandry with the Kingdom of the Netherlands;[79] financial co-operation and financial Aid Agreements with the Federal Republic of Germany;[80] a Protocol with the People's China[81] regarding the provision of a Chinese Medical Team to work in the Sudan and a co-operation agreement with the Central African Republic[82] in the field of posts, Telecommunications and Wireless.

NOTES

1. Act No. 4 of 1972
2. Act No. 14 of 1972
3. Section 2 (III).
4. Act No. 23 of 1972
5. Act No. 24 of 1972
6. LRO No. 34
7. Act No. 8 of 1972
8. Act No. 14 of 1972
9. Act No. 47 of 1972
10. Act No. 48 of 1972
11. Act No. 44 of 1972
12. Act No. 10 of 1972
13. Act No. 2 of 1972
14. Act No. 27 of 1972
15. Act No. 12 of 1972
16. Act No. 54 of 1972
17. Act No. 70 of 1972
18. Act No. 9 of 1972
19. Act No. 43 of 1972
20. Act No. 50 of 1972
21. Act No. 53 of 1972
22. Act No. 11 of 1972
23. Act No. 71 of 1972
24. PO No. 1 of 1972
25. Act No. 32 of 1972
26. Act No. 45 of 1972
27. LRO No. 20
28. Acts Nos. 7 and 34 of 1972
29. Act No. 39 of 1972
30. Act No. 72 of 1972
31. Act No. 73 of 1972
32. Act No. 36 of 1972
33. Act No. 51 of 1972

34. Act No. 56 of 1972
35. Act No. 42 of 1972
36. Act No. 33 of 1972
37. Acts Nos. 18 and 19 of 1972
38. Act No. 67 of 1972
39. Act No.   of 1972
40. Act No. 35 of 1972
41. Act No. 21 of 1972
42. Act No. 16 of 1972
43. Act No. 40 of 1972
44. Act No. 41 of 1972
45. Act No. 46 of 1972
46. Act No. 65 of 1972
47. Act No. 63 of 1972
48. Act No. 1 of 1972
49. Act No. 68 of 1972
50. Act No. 3 of 1972
51. Act No. 73 of 1972
52. Acts Nos. 26 and 75 of 1972
53. Act No. 58 of 1972
54. Act No. 59 of 1972
55. Act No. 60 of 1972
56. Act No. 62 of 1972
57. Act No. 61 of 1972
58. Act No. 69 of 1972
59. Act No. 66 of 1972
60. Act No. 30 of 1972
61. 1.   The Treasury (Bills) Bonds (Amendment) Act, Act No. 5 of 1972.
     2.   The Liquor Licence (Amendment) Act, 1972 Act No. 13 of 1972.
     3.   The Additional Duty (Amendment) Acts, 1972 Acts Nos. 15 and 20 of 1972.
     4.   (Amendment Nos. 1 and 2) Acts, Acts Nos. 22 and 37 of 1972.
     5.   The Customs (Amendment) Act, 1972, Act No. 38 of 1972.
     6.   The Land and Dates Taxation (Amendment) Act, 1972, Act No. 13 of 1972.
     7.   The Weights and Measures (Amendment) Act, 1972, Act No. 49 of 1972.
62. Act No. 28 of 1972
63. Act No. 29 of 1972
64. Republican Order (Legislative) No. 101, 1972
65. RO Leg. No. 121, 1972
66. RO Leg. No. 119, 1972
67. RO Leg. No. 112, 1972
68. RO Leg. No. 51, 1972
69. RO Leg. No. 53, 1972
70. RO Leg. No. 96, 1972
71. RO Leg. No. 54, 1972
72. RO Leg. No. 56, 1972
73. RO Leg. No. 52, 1972
74. RO Leg. No. 55, 1972
75. RO Leg. No. 120, 1972
76. RO Leg. No. 81, 1972
77. RO Leg. No. 65, 1972
78. RO Leg. No. 80, 1972
79. RO Leg. No. 7, 1972
80. RO Leg. No. 87, 1972
81. RO Leg. No. 100, 1972
82. RO Leg. No. 104, 1972

CHAPTER TWENTY NINE

ETHIOPIA

Bruno-Otto Bryde

As there is no regular system of case reporting[1] and no doctrine of *stare decisis* in Ethiopia this survey on Ethiopian legal deveopment in 1972 will limit itself to the laws published in the country's official government gazette, the *Nagarit Gazeta,*[2] during this period. This gazette is published in Amharic and English. Amharic, as the official language,[3] prevails in cases of discrepancies. As the Ethiopian year differs from the Gregorian year (Gregorian 1972 ran from 23rd Tahsas 1964, to 22nd Tahsas 1965 Ethiopian Calendar), two years of the *Negarit Gazeta* have been used for this report: it covers Nos. 6–38 of the 31st year (1964 EC) and Nos. 1–6 of the 32nd year (1965EC).

During this period 14 Proclamations (P)[4] Orders (0)[5], 15 Legal Notices (LN)[6] and 14 General Notices[7] have been published.

This chapter concentrates on the Proclamations, Orders and the more important Legal Notices.

ADMINISTRATIVE LAW

A comprehensive statistical system was created in 1972 by the establishment of the Central Statistical Office[8] and a corresponding Proclamation defining the powers of this Authority.[9] The Central Statistical Office, an autonomous Public Authority responsible to the Planning Commission (Art. 5 Central Statistical Office Order) has as its organs a Head and the necessary personnel (Art. 6 Central Statistical Office Order). With the exception of defence and public security the Office is responsible for and empowered to deal with all statistical activities of the government (Arts. 4 and 7 Central Statistical Office Order). This includes advising the government on statistical matters, carrying out designated statistical work and developing statistical policy (Art. 4 Central Office Order).

The necessary powers to fulfill these functions are given to the office by the Central Statistical Office Proclamation. The Office may require information from any person and has corresponding powers of access and of inspection (Art. 5 Central Statistical Office Proclamation), and the citizens have to furnish required information and to allow access and inspections (Art. 6 Central Statistical Office Proclamation), but are protected by the office's obligation to keep secrecy (Art. 7 Central Statistical Office Proclamation). Both the citizens' co-operation and the office's secrecy are enforced by penal sanctions (Arts. 8 and 9 Central Statistical Office Proclamation).

Two public authorities created in 1970 and 1971, the Ethiopian Standards Institution[10] and the Addis Ababa Water and Sewerage Authority[11] were invested with the necessary powers for their functions this year.[12] The Post Office Proclamation[13] was amended to change the rank of the Office's Head from Director General to General Manager.[14]

In the field of public service new rules (based on the system of position classification) have been promulgated for the classification, salary and promotion of public servants.[15]

FISCAL AND TAX LAW

The Ethiopian Budget must be approved by both Houses of Parliament[16] and is published as a Proclamation. The Budget for the fiscal year 1965 (EC)[17] totals Eth. $757,014,282,[18] Six foreign loan agreements[19] and one guarantee agreement[20] have been aproved by Parliament.

In the field of taxation, the Transaction Tax for imported goods has been raised[21] and the 1967/68 assessment made applicable for two more years as the basis for agricultural income tax.[22] The customs tariff has been amended three times during 1972.[23]

ECONOMIC REGULATION

Probably the most important single piece of legislation promulgated in 1972 is the Regulation of Trade and Price Proclamation.[24] The Proclamation is an attempt at a comprehensive law for the regulation of domestic trade. Previously, special laws had dealt with price control of imported goods, of locally produced goods, of locally rendered services, and with unfair trade practices. All these laws have now been repealed and substituted by the new Proclamation (Art. 2). Due to this attempt to deal with the regulation of domestic trade in one single piece of legislation, the Proclamation covers a wide variety of different subjects: it provides sweeping powers for the Ministry of Commerce, Industry and Tourism to control prices (Arts. 5-6)[25] and to control the distribution of goods (Arts 6-8); it obliges traders to indicate goods and prices (Arts. 10-11) and provides for the protection of trade names (Art. 12); in Art. 13 it prohibits agreements restricting competition, subject to exceptions granted by the Ministry; Art. 14 generally forbids unfair trade practices and enumerates certain practices, deemed to be especially unfair. In fighting unfair trade practices the Proclamation partly overlaps with corresponding provisions in the Codes.[26] But while the emphasis of the Code provisions is on the protection of the individual competitor against illegal and immoral acts (fraud, deceit, bribery etc.) which no legal system could tolerate, the Proclamation is more concerned with the protection of the competitive system as a whole against distortions due to abuse of economic power (e.g. imposition of unfair conditions, unequal terms, binding, dumping).

Other developments in economic regulation include regulations for the administration of the Industrial Licence Proclamation[27] and the Foreign Trade Proclamation,[28] promulgated last year,[29] and regulations for meat inspection.[30]

NATURAL RESOURCES

After the start made in 1971 with the Wildlife Conservation Order[31] a further step to improve the protection of wildlife has been taken this year with the issuing of the Wildlife Conservation Regulations.[32] These Regulations restrict human activities in National Parks, Game Reserves, Sanctuaries and Controlled Hunting Areas (Arts. 5–9) and control hunting throughout the Empire by making it subject to licencing (Arts. 10–25) and prohibiting certain hunting methods (Art. 26). These rules are enforced by provisions severely restricting possession of and dealing in game animals and trophies (Arts. 27–35) and by penalties (Art. 47). Ethiopia also ratified the Phyto-Sanitary Convention for Africa[33] of 13 September 1967, intended to control and eliminate plant diseases.

EDUCATION, CULTURE AND RELIGION

For the development of the national language, Amharic, the 'National Academy of the Amharic Language' has been established as an autonomous Public Authority.[34] The Academy is generally charged with developing Amharic language and literature (Art. 3), and is specifically empowered, *inter alia*, to decide authoritatively about correct spelling, vocabulary, grammar and style, and to modernize the language by adopting words from other languages and by creating new Amharic words for modern concepts (Art. 4). Government organizations shall, and private organizations may be requested to follow the rules of the Academy in these matters (Art. 5). The organs of the Academy are a Council, an Executive Committee, and a Permanent Secretariet Art. 6). The Council consists of sixteen to twenty-four 'Academicians who have to be Ethiopians distinguished in the fields of language and literature' (Art. 5). The first Academicians are appointed by the Emperor upon the recommendation of the Minister of Education and Fine Arts; every five years a quarter of the members are to be retired by drawing lots; vacancies thus created and vacancies occurring for other reasons are filled by elections by the Academicians (Arts. 6, 13). In addition to the Academicians as regualr members, the Academy may have honorary and associate members who can also be foreign nationals (Art. 7).

The Ethiopian Orthodox Church, the Established Church of the Empire,[35] created a new body, the Ethiopian Orthodox Church Development Commission, to strengthen its role in education, charity and national development.[36] The administration of the Debre-Libanos monastery, which exerted an enormous influence on the spiritual and political life of the country throughout history,[37] was regulated by Imperial Order.[38]

NOTES

1. Some of the more interesting cases (10-12 a year) are published in the *Journal of Ethiopian Law*
2. Cited: *Neg Gaz*, year/No., page
3. Art. 125 Revised Constitution of 1955 (Constitution)
4. Laws approved by the Emperor and both Houses of Parliament
5. Laws promulgated by the Emperor pursuant to Imperial Prerogative, most important being Art. 27 Constitution (right to organize government and administration)
6. Subsidiary legislation by ministries or government agencies based on authorizations in Proclamations, Orders or Decrees.
7. Announcements, especially of appointments and conferring of titles.
8. Central Statistical Office Order, 1972 0.79, *Neg Gaz*, 31/18, p. 116
9. Central Statistical Office Proclamation, 1972, P. 303, *Neg Gaz*, 31/18, p. 120
10. Ethiopian Standards Institution Order, 1970, O. 64, *Neg Gaz*, 30/1, p. 1 see R. A. Melin, 'Ethiopia', *Annual Survey of African Law*, Vol. IV, 1970
11. Addis Ababa Water and Sewerage Authority Order, 1971, O. 68, *Neg Gaz*, 30/10, p. 52
12. Ethiopian Standards Institution Proclamation, 1972, p. 300, *Neg Gaz*, 31/14 p. 80; Addis Ababa Water and Sewerage Proclamation p. 298, *Neg Gaz*, 31/12, p. 69
13. Post Office Proclamation, 1966, p. 240, *Neg Gaz*, 25/22, p. 117
14. Post Office (Amendment) Proclamation, 1972, p. 296, *Neg Gaz*, 31/9, p. 64
15. Public Service Position Classification and Salary Scale Regulations No. 2, 1972, LN 419, *Neg Gaz*, 31/15, p. 86
16. Constitution Art. 116
17. 8 July 1972 to 7 July 1973
18. Budget Proclamation 1965 EC, p. 308, *Neg Gaz*, 31/23, p. 141
19. P. 295, *Neg Gaz*, 31/9; China, p. 297, *Neg Gaz*, 31/11: IDA; p. 302, *Neg Gaz*, 31/17: Germany; p. 304, *Neg Gaz*, 31/20: IDA; p. 305, *Neg Gaz*, 31/20: IDA; p. 306, *Neg Gaz*, 31/20: International Bank for Reconstruction and Development
20. Bole Housing Project Development Agreement Guarantee, 1972, p. 299, *Neg Gaz*, 31/14, p. 79
21. Transaction Taxes (Amendment) Proclamation, 1972, p. 307, *Neg Gaz*, 31/21, p. 137
22. Agricultural Income Tax Assessment Continuation Regulation, 1972, LN 426, *Neg Gaz*, 32/2 p. 3
23. Customs Tariff (Amendment) Regulations, 1972, LN 420, *Neg Gaz*, 31/22, p. 138; Customs Tariff (Amendment) Regulations, 1972, LN 425, *Neg Gaz*, 32/1, p. 1; Customs Tariff (Amendment) Regulations, 1972, *Neg Gaz*, 32/3, p. 4
24. Regulation of Trade and Price Proclamation, 1972, P. 301, *Neg Gaz*, 31/16, p. 104
25. This power has already been exercised in the case of bread prices
26. Commercial Code, Arts. 133-4, Civil Code, Arts. 2057, 2122; Penal Code, Art. 673
27. Industrial Licence Regulations, 1972, LN 423, *Neg Gaz*, 31/25, p. 182
28. Foreign Trade Regulations, 1972, LN 424, *Neg Gaz*, 31/251, p. 190
29. For the content of the Proclamation see Bryde, 'Ethiopia', *Annual Survey of African Law*, Vol. V, 1971
30. Meat Inspection Regulation, 1972, LN 428, *Neg Gaz*, 32/4, p. 5
31. See R. A. Melin, 'Ethiopia', *Annual Survey of African Law*, Vol. IV, 1970
32. Wildlife Conservation Regulations, 1972, LN 416, *Neg Gaz*, 31/7, p. 35
33. Phyto-Sanitary Convention for Africa order, 1972, O.78, *Neg Gaz*, 31/17, p. 114
34. National Academy of the Amharic Language Establishment Order, 1972, O. 80, *Neg Gaz*, 31/19, p. 126; *cum Neg Gaz*, 31/24, p. 181. By mistake this Order had been numbered Order 79 originally. The corrected numbering as Order 80, however, creates new confusion as now two Orders bear the number 80
35. Constitution Art. 126-7
36. Church Development Commission Regulation, 1972, LN 415, *Neg Gaz*, 31/6, p. 32
37. The head of the monastery, the *itchege*, was the highest ranking Ethiopian priest during the centuries when the Patriarch was an Egyptian, named by the Patriarch of Alexandria.
38. The Debre-Libanos Monastery Administration Order, O. 77, *Neg Gaz*, 31/8, p. 53

CHAPTER THIRTY

SOMALI DEMOCRATIC REPUBLIC

Marco Guadagni

INTRODUCTION

In the early months after the 1969 revolution the aim of legislation was to create new constitutional structures to replace those abolished by the revolution itself. These constitutional changes are essentially reported in the third volume of this series.[1]

In the following three years (1970–1972) the legislature made its most relevant efforts to establish a legal foundation for the new 'socialist' society as it was officially proclaimed in the Second Charter of the Revolution on 21 October, 1970. Therefore, changes in the Somali legal system in this period involve mainly the framing of new social, economic, political and administrative structures designed to implement and accomplish the aims of the 1969 revolution.

The Somali legal system is based on legislative enactments such as: (a) laws promulgated by the President of the Supreme Revolutionary Council (hereafter referred to as the SRC) and approved by the Council itself; (b) decrees issued by the President of the SRC on his own initiative; (c) regulations issued by presidential decree.[2] Legislation is published in the *Bollettino Ufficiale della Repubblica Democratica Somala* (hereafter cited as the BU)[3] in Italian and/or English (occasionally in Arabic as well). In cases of conflict between the two versions, where no preference is expressly given to either of the two, the interpreter should rely upon the version of the act in the language originally used to draft the act. The 'original' version (the other being a more or less accurate translation) is generally apparent in the construction of the act itself.

The role of common law in what was formerly the British Protectorate of Somaliland has been reduced as the new judicial system[4] and most of the legislation adopted after Independence has been based on Italian models. Case law generally, and hence the common law, has now become even less relevant because both the highest legislative and judicial powers have been vested in the same body, the SRC Judicial precedents in Somalia may have only a persuasive effect; actually they are rather unknown since cases are very seldom reported in any published form.[4a] Islamic law has not been greatly affected by revolutionary legislation and still regulates personal, family, succession and waqf law in Muslim

Somalia. It should be noted that the revolutionary government has always proclaimed its great respect for the religion of Islam and recognizes its leading role in the country.

In contrast, the scope of customary law, which regulated mainly land tenure, water usages and grazing rights in the Somali tribal society, has been drastically reduced by the Law for Social Protection enacted in 1970.[5]

CONSTITUTIONAL LAW AND JUDICIAL SYSTEM

Shortly after the revolution, under the ruling of the newly established SRC exclusively composed of members of the Armed Forces, it was authoritatively announced that power was to be given to a civilian government in due time.[6] Meanwhile 'technicians' were appointed as heads of Ministries with the rank of Secretaries of State and without political power.[7] In 1972 a law was passed, to be retroactively effective from 21 October, 1969, giving to the President of the SRC power to convene a 'joint meeting' of the SRC and the Council of Secretaries of State.[8] In a 'joint meeting,' which may adopt measures of legislative and executive character each Secretary of State has the right to express his views and to give his vote. No legislation, however, has yet been passed by the new organ.

On the other hand the pre-eminent positions of the SRC and of its President have been strengthened. Exclusive power had been given to the President to legitimate any arrest, detention or seizure act and to take final decisions in any administrative matter.[9] In order to help the President in discharging his duties a Presidential Advisory Board has been established, composed of three members of the SRC serving by presidential appointment.[9] Power has been given to the SRC to intervene in any judicial matter.[10] In exercising such power, the Council may, on its own initiative or on the petition of an aggrieved party, review any final judgement, civil or criminal, taken by any Court, including the National Security Court. This power of review consists of taking any of the following measures: (a) confirm, vary or set aside any judgement; (b) order a retrial by the competent Court; (c) make any consequential or incidental order that may be just or proper.

The judicial system previously existing in Somalia has been further modified by three other relevant enactments. The first is the establishment of a National Security Court, outside the ordinary Courts system, in order to safeguard the security of the State.[11] The new Court sits in Mogadishu and has Regional and District sections. Its President and Vice-President are appointed from among the members of the Armed Forces, while another two judges are appointed from the judiciary or the Armed Forces. The Court's decisions are final, subject only to the power of the SRC to annul them or to grant a pardon to the convicted person.[12] The Court has exclusive jurisdiction over: (a) offences against the personality of the State or against public order, and offences committed by public officers against public administration; (b) crimes provided for by the Law for Safeguarding National Security; (c) certain crimes provided for by the Law for Social Protection; and (d) any other offences that the SRC may, by decree, declare to be against the security of the State.

A special judge has been appointed,[13] and special regulations have been issued[14] for the execution of the Court's decisions as to the seizure of properties of the convicted person and to the compensation of damages to the State.

The second provision is in the Local Government Reform Act, 1972, under which power is given to newly established Regional and District administrative Councils to appoint special Committees for arbitrating disputes among community members.[15] In accomplishing this conciliatory function, the Committee may impose disciplinary sanctions against the disputing parties.

This conciliatory and disciplinary power outside the judiciary was previously vested only in the *nabaddon* established immediately after the revolution to replace traditional local group-leaders, who under customary law assumed the function of settling disputes arising among group members.

The third provision is the establishment of Juvenile Courts and reformatories.[16] The Presient of the Regional Court sits as the Juvenile Court and has jurisdiction in cases involving children (under the age of fourteen years) and young persons (under the age of eighteen years) accused of any offence except murder. The Juvenile Court's judgement may be brought to the Court of Appeal for final decision. Children and young persons may be committed to a reformatory up to the age of eighteen years; young persons, however, may be sentenced to imprisonment when the reformatory is deemed to be unsuitable.[17]

ADMINISTRATIVE LAW

Temporary provisions on public administration issued immediately after the revolution[18] were replaced in 1972, by a new Local Government Reform Act based on the principle of socialist democratic centralism.[19] Local administrative units are designed there and their administration committed to Regional, District and Village Councils.

Regional and District Councils are composed of the following members: (a) the Chairman, appointed by the President of the SRC; (b) the local heads of Ministerial departments; (c) one representative from each District, in the case of Regional Councils, and from each Community, in the case of District Councils. Community representative are appointed by the Secretary of State for Interior on the recommendation of the Regional Council.

Village Councils, established by the Regional Council, are composed of no more than seven Community representatives selected annually by a general meeting of the permanent residents of the village.

Executive power at the Regional and District levels is exercised by Executive Secretaries appointed respectively by the President of the SRC and by the Secretary of State for Interior.

Regional and District Councils appoint special Committees dealing with economic and social matters, public security, financial control over the Council's finances, political orientation, mediation and conciliation among community members and disciplinary measures. Regional and District Councils under the direction of the Secretary of State for the Interior or of any Secretary of State or head of a public body in matters relating to his° particular area of competence, are responsible for the development of local government institutions and for the performance of their services in accordance with the national policy of the central government. For these purposes they enjoy legal personality, have their own financial budget (which is part of the unified State budget under the control of the Magistrates of Accounts),[20] may collect local fees and taxes as authorized by the laws and decrees of the central government, may run enterprises and public bodies. Provisions regulating Revolutionary Councils established after the revolution,[21] so far as applicable, continue to be in force.

The city of Mogadishu and its district enjoy a special administrative organization.[22] They are governed by a City Council, an independent administrative body having legal personality, but under the direction of the President of the SRC. The Council consists of: (a) the Mayor, as chairman of the Council; (b) representatives from each quarter of the town drawn from the following groups: youths, workers, women and 'the most revolutionary spirited elements'; (c) representatives of the Police, the Public Relations Office, the National Security Service, the Ministries of Health, Education and Labour.

Quarter Councils are appointed by the President of the SRC for each sector ('quarter') of the town and their composition is similar to the composition of City Council, with the addition of the Secretary of the Orientation Centre of the quarter as Secretary of the Council, and representatives of the Revolutionary Youth Volunteers (*guulwadayaal*). The functions and responsibilities of the City and Quarter Councils are not specified in the decree establishing them but reference is made there to the functions and responsibilities provided for the Regional and the District Councils by the Local Government Reform Act, 1972, and this is generally applicable to the city and the district of Mogadishu, unless otherwise expressly provided.

Civil service in Somalia, besides being one of the most expensive and uncontrolled items in the national budget, has for some time been criticized by, and a source of dissatisfaction to, both public servants and the population because of its disorganization, and its widespread corruption and nepotism.

The Civil Service Law enacted in 1970,[23] and its ensuing amendments have attempted to remedy the situation. The principle of appointment on the basis of an open competitive examination has been adopted.[24] Examinations are conducted by the Special Recruiting Board, upon which representatives of the National Security Service, the Public Relations Office and the National Co-ordination Committee for Self-help Schemes now sit, complementing the purely administrative composition of what was formerly the Examination Board Promotion to the Highest grades is made by the President of the SRC Disciplinary matters are thoroughly regulated.

Several other separate provisions complete the new legislation on civil service and cover a number of areas. Pension schemes and gratuities have been provided for;[25] temporary personnel,[26] personnel appointed to the Public Relations Office,[27] and members of the judiciary,[28] have all been absorbed into the permanent establishment of the civil service; new regulations have been provided for the Armed and the Police Forces,[29] and the personnel of public autonomous agencies.[30]

Other measures have been taken to strengthen the probity and efficient functioning of public administration. (a) A Public Administration Inquiry Commission has been established within the Presidency of the SRC to inquire into complaints of civil servants against decisions of their superiors, and into complaints of the people against the public administration.[31] In general the Commission has the function of ensuring that the public administration is run in accordance with the law and the principles of the revolution. The results of the Commission's enquiries, together with its recommendations are submitted to the President of the SRC. (b) Civil servants of the highest grades, members of the SRC, and Secretaries of State, are prohibited from constructing or purchasing (directly or through agents, and the prohibition extends to relatives of the mentioned persons) houses for dwelling or for profit-seeking purposes; other civil servants may do so provided they receive a special authorization from the Ministry of Public Works.[32] (c) To reduce public expenditures, drastic cuts have been made in all civil servants' salaries[33] and, for reasons of equity, equivalent taxes have been levied on private employees' wages.[34]

Autonomous agencies have become of paramount importance in new socialist Somalia and are being developed to take over activities previously neglected by private initiative or carried out for private profit only. The para-administrative nature of their functions and organization may well justify dealing with autonomous agencies here, although many of them operate in industrial, agricultural, financial and commercial fields.

Their organization[35] and personnel[36] have been regulated by general laws, which have—among other effects—strengthened the agency's dependence on the central government. The previously existing offices of 'president' and 'board of auditors' have been abolished and now the agency is under the 'general manager' and the 'board of directors' both appointed by the President of the SRC. On the other hand personnel representatives have been made members of the 'management committee' within the general manager's office. Special legislation provides for the financial regulation of autonomous agencies,[37] where auditing is to be done by the Magistrates of Accounts.[38]

LABOUR LAW

Although a labour code had been issued in 1969, a few months before the revolution,[39] replacing the one enacted in 1958 by the Italian Trust Administration,[40] the revolutionary government felt that the 1969 code, or part of it, was incompatible with its newly adopted socialist views in the matter. As a consequence a new Labour Code was enacted in 1972, expressly recognizing the importance of the workers' role in the development of the national economy and assuring the participation of workers in the planning and management of the means of production.[41]

The 1969 and 1972 codes differ mainly in the regulation of collective associations' rights and activities, while no significant change has been made as to individual rights. The new code, although dealing primarily with private employees, is, unless otherwise provided, applicable to civil servants too.

As the code itself states in Art. 8, auxiliary sources of labour law are: (a) equity (in the sense in which the expression is elsewhere used, for instance, in the 'justice, equity and good conscience' provision); (b) general principles of labour law; (c) ILO conventions and recommendations ratified by the Somali Republic; (d) general principles of law; (e) legal doctrine (to be taken in a wide international sense, as no local dictrine on labour law exists yet in Somalia); (f) case law (as a non-binding but persuasive interpretative element); (g) local custom.

At the time of the revolution labour unions and employers' associations were dissolved, together with all other associations;[42] similarly, lock-out, strike and slow-down at work were prohibited and made subject to severe penal sanctions including death.[43] The new code has no provision as to employers' associations, which, therefore, are deemed still to be prohibited. Lock-out is expressly forbidden. The formation and functioning of free labour unions are, however, thoroughly regulated, although none of them has yet come into existence. Similarly, the right to strike is recognized by the code, but its exercise is made subject to further regulations which have not yet appeared. Collective contracts are subject to public registration and their content should be based on democratic principles and freely discussed and approved by workers' assembly. Moreover, they should take into consideration the revolutionary social policy of the State, the role of labour unions, the workers' duty to increase by every possible means the national production and their participation in the planning and management of the national economy.

It is one of the primary tasks of the Public Relations Office to work towards the gradual establishment of workers' associations.[44] When they do come into existence, the exercise of the right to strike will most probably be regulated and collective contracts will be bargained and signed. In the meantime special legislation has partially regulated matters that in the future will be dealt with in collective contracts, according to the code provisions.

So, the workers' duty to increase national production has led to the prohibition of accumulating annual leave.[45] The principle of workers' participation in the planning and management of national economy has led to the formation of workers' 'management committees', at first spontaneously created by workers in various private and public enterprises, and now generally provided for by the Personnel of Autonomous Agency Act, 1972.[46] The workers' role in political matters and the concern by public authorities for private employment are further strengthened legally by the duty imposed upon holders of school certificates to attend political orientation courses before seeking employment;[47] by the presence of workers' representatives in the local administrative councils in Mogadishu;[48] by the prohibition against employment of foreigners where Somali citizens may perform the same functions; and by the extension to private employment of the principle of recruitment through open competitive examinations held by the Special Recruiting Board.[49] Special legislation, finally, provides for compulsory insurance against accidents at work and professional diseases.[50]

LAW RELATING TO ECONOMIC ACTIVITIES

The most significant legislative measures taken by the new government since the revolution have been directed towards the establishment of new economic structures. Their intention is to improve national development on one hand and turn the State economy gradually from a private—and often foreign—hegemony into a socialist system on the other hand. Such legislative measures may be grouped under four headings:

(a) nationalizations of large private enterprises operating in the fields of banking, industry and commerce;
(b) organization of State commercial monopolies, protected markets and compulsory price ceiling systems for goods of wide consumption or of high social utility;
(c) establishment of fully or partially State-owned agencies and enterprises;
(d) promotion and support of private initiative in co-operative form and of collective voluntary activities.

Under the measures of nationalization[51] four foreign banks operating in the country were absorbed into the Somali National Bank; the shares still in private (foreign) hands (the majority) of the only large industry existing in Somalia at the time of the revolution, i.e. the sugar factory in Jowhar (*SNAI*), were taken over by the State; properties and activities of foreign-owned enterprises monopolizing the production and distribution of electricity and the distribution of oil products were taken over by public agencies; later on[52] insurance was made exclusively an activity of two State-owned insurance companies. The right to compensation has been recognized for private subjects affected by these measures of nationalization.[53] Similarly, professional activities such as notary,[54] the medical profession[55] and hospitalization[56] were made public and their exercise by private persons have been prohibited.

Pastural and agricultural usage of land and water is both a primary economic resource in the country and a determining element in its social life and structures. Nationalization of land and water resources as an economic measure, therefore, has come apparently as a side effect of the Law for Social Protection, 1970,[57] which has as its principal aim the abolition of tribal structures in Somali society. Art. 3 of the law provides that land and water resources that do not belong to any public body or other juridical person or private individual shall belong to the State.

Until now this provision has had a limited application, especially in effecting the reallocation of land by means of State concessions. Its implementation is expected to come by means of a new land law, which has already been announced. State control over private immovable properties, however, is already effective at the time of their transfer, which is made subject to authorization by public authorities.[58]

In the future minerals and sub-soil products in general are expected to become an important source of wealth for Somalia. They already belong to the State and private extractive activity may occur only by concession. The whole matter is now thoroughly regulated by the Mining Code of 1970, and by its subsidiary regulations.[59]

State commercial monopolies are active in the trade of natural products which represent the main assets of export for Somalia, i.e. bananas,[60] aromatic resins[61] and livestock[62] and products for widespread internal consumption, i.e. coffee, tea, sugar, soap, etc.[63] Their activities also extend to products of high social value, i.e. electric batteries,[64] medicines,[65] building materials, etc. Export, import and trade of most of these products are committed to the National Agency for Trade, which also organizes their distribution within the country through local government offices. Some other products are dealt with by *ad hoc* public agencies, e.g. the National Bananas Agency,[66] which has taken over the properties and activities of two foreign commercial companies operating in the field on a monopolistic basis, and now trades bananas produced in Somalia (still primarily by foreign planters).

Great political relevance has been attached by the government to the State monopoly for trading certain cereals which was established in 1970, as a challenging example of direct public intervention in economic matters of general and high social concern.[67] Cereals such as maize and sorghum form the basis of the traditional agriculture in Somalia and are the basic food stuffs consumed by the majority in Somali society. Exploiting the precarious economy of traditional cultivators and their limited mobility and access to local markets, merchants used to gain high profits in trading cereals by speculating on price fluctuations due to periodical or local shortage or abundance of agricultural production. Under the new monopolistic regime any private trading activity in cereals has been prohibited: the entire production must be sold to the State at a statutorily fixed price and the State itself, through the Agricultural Development Corporation, sells it to consumers at a statutorily increased price.

The increase in the selling price in respect to the purchasing price, which now amount to sixty-six per cent of the price which the cultivator receives from the State,[68] is motivated by storage and distribution expenses and by the need to compensate for the decrease of customs duty revenues due to the diminished consumption of imported pastry as a side-effect of the decree on locally produced cereals.

In an effort to reduce the cost of living compulsory price ceilings have been established for other essential commodities such as edible oil, cement, wheat flour, rice, etc.,[69] and, in order to compensate for salary reductions affecting Somali civil servants and private employees,[70] rents have been statutorily reduced for houses for dwelling or other profit-seeking purposes, with the exclusion of foreign tenants.[71]

The State is getting more and more directly involved in the national productive process through public agencies and enterprises and through public participation in private firms. In the field of agriculture, beside the already mentioned autonomous agencies, such as the National Bananas Agency, the Agricultural Development Corporation and others, State farms are now experimenting especially with a view to diversifying crops for export (at present represented almost exclusively by bananas).

In the industrial field, beside the sugar factory in Jowhar, the number of enterprises in which the State has an exclusive or dominant role continues to increase, especially in the sector of processing agricultural, livestock and fishing products (e.g. the Industry for Processing Horticultural and Fruit Products—ITOP—in Afgoi, the Meat Factory in Kisimayo and the Fish Canning Factory in Las Koreh). Medium to small industries, the handicraft and the retailing trade are mainly left to private initiative and are encouraged to take co-operative form.[72] In this case tax exemptions, technical and material assistance are granted by the government and special credit facilities are offered by the Somali Development Bank.[73] Also, the co-operative form is imposed for provision of public utility services such as pharmacies and transportation.[74]

Both economic and social importance has been attached to the 'agricultural crash programmes' in which 'agricultural pioneers' work on a voluntary basis and under strict military discipline in State-owned farms.[75] The programmes have the twofold aim of increasing national agricultural production and of offering a working place to urban unemployed youth. Moreover it is expected that 'crash programmes' will be joined by land-less nomads as an opportunity for them to turn from nomadic pasturalism to settled agriculture.

LAW RELATING TO SOCIAL STRUCTURES AND WELFARE

The social situation inherited by the new government at the time of the revolution was characterized by tribal structures and colonial survivals. Legislation, therefore, has been directed towards eliminating both of them and to substituting egalitarian structures and Somali national culture. Moreover, the socialist choice made in 1970 required that the masses should participate in the direct management of the State.

Tribal structures and privileges were given a death blow by the Law for Social Protection enacted in 1970,[76] which provided for the abolition of all tribal titles and offices; prohibited associations having tribal character; definitely replaced blood-compensation (dya) with the personal responsibility of the offender; made subject to prosecution (imprescriptible in time) and severe punishment tribal favouritism and nepotism as well as crimes stemming from tribal mentality, such as homicide, abduction of a married woman, cattle rustling, retaliation, etc.

The government's struggle against economic privileges based on colonial vestiges has already been discussed above. The colonial heritage, however, was not only in the economic field, but it was affecting also the social and cultural development of the country. The most remarkable example was the use of foreign languages (Italian, English and Arabic) in education and official matters, as a result of the lack of script for the national language.

Now the Somali language, in its new script adopting a latin alphabet, has been declared to be the only official language of the country;[77] its exclusive use has been imposed for all official matters and public servants have been required to take an examination in the new script; 'Xiddigta Oktoobar', the only newspaper now existing in the country, being the official organ of the government, is published in Somali; by October, 1975, the Somali language will be introduced in all schools as the medium for instruction.[78]

When the latter provision was enacted, private schools (all run by foreign governments or institutions) were nationalized and the establishment of new ones has been prohibited and made subject to penalty.[79]

Education in Somalia is now expressly aimed at preparing citizens to participate in the social, political, cultural and economic life of the country according to the principles of socialism. Therefore, beside Islamic religion and Somali language, history and culture, new subjects have been introduced in all schools, such as 'philosophy of the Revolution' and 'principles of socialism'.[80]

The political role of education and of educated people is further strengthened by the principle that students of both sexes, after having obtained their diploma, must follow a one-year course for political orientation and military training and must serve one year in the national service.[81] Scholarships from, and for, study abroad may not be accepted without permission granted by the Ministry of Education, which has the duty, together with the Ministry of Planning and Co-ordination and the Ministry of Labour and Sports, to select fields of study and candidates for scholarships according to the social and economic needs of the country.[82] Students abroad are under the supervision of the Ministry of Education and, as soon as they finish their course, they must return to Somalia for public service for a minimum number of years varying from two to six.

The establishment of courses for popular education for adults is provided for under an *ad hoc* National Co-ordinative Committee within the Ministry of Education, formed by representatives of all the Ministries and social organizations involved.[83]

Literacy, social and political campaignes are held throughout the country under the leadership of Quarter and Village Orientation Centres. These popular and revolutionary units are under the supervision of the Public Relations Office, which has been established under the Presidency of the SRC with the statutory duty to promote and facilitate the establishment of mass organizations; to select trained cadres (*guulwadayaal*) to fulfill the leadership roles of those organizations; to supervise and guide the activities of village, town and regional Orientation Centres; to disseminate and impart to the people the decisions, directives and policies of the SRC.[84]

Within the programmes of mass-mobilization a leading role is also given to the voluntary corp of *guulwadayaal* and to self-help schemes (*iskaa awax u gabso*) which are now organizd under the supervision and co-ordination of the National Committee established for that purpose under the Secretary of State for Interior.[85]

Mass-media are all in the hand of the State. Radio broadcasting was already public before the revolution, while the importing of films was nationalized later together with printing presses and both are now under the Ministry of Information and National Guidance.[86]

As to social services, a substantial reform has taken place in the field of public health, where the following measures have been adopted: (a) nationalization of hospitals and dispensaries, taken over by the Ministry of Health;[87] (b) abolition of fees for treatment in hospitals;[88] (c) interdiction to private exercise of the medical profession;[89] (d) State monopoly in importing medicines and pharmaceutical products through an autonomous agency especially established under the Ministry of Health, also having the duty to fix selling-prices applied by pharmaceutical co-operatives which have the exclusive authorization to sell medicines to the public.[90]

CRIMINAL LAW

The main set of rules in this area are still the Penal Code of 1962[91] and the Criminal Procedure Code of 1963.[92] Scattered legislation, however, has introduced significant innovations in substantive and procedural matters, the most important ones being the following:

(a) Penal sanctions have been provided for enforcing the revolutionary policy and legislation in economic, labour and social matters, such in case of attempted private activity in public monopolized sectors; in case of strikes and employers' associations; and in case of behaviour stemming from tribal mentality.

(b) Similarly, political and constitutional achievements of the revolution are protected by penal sanctions. At first life imprisonment was provided for trying to subvert the new order established by the revolution.[93] Later, the more comprehensive Law for Safeguarding National Security was enacted.[94]

The Law provides life or long term imprisonment and in most cases even the death penalty for: (a) acting against the independence, unity or security of the State; (b) organizing associations or raising money for subversive purposes; (c) conspiring with foreign powers against the State; (d) causing death or physical injury to a member of the Armed Forces or person entrusted with a State mission; (e) carrying weapons or arms; (f) banditism; (g) sabotage; (h) unlawful occupation of public building; (i) exploiting religion for creating national disunity or subversive purposes; (j) committing crimes against public administration or the national economy; (k) anti-State propaganda, including rumour-mongering (afminshar).

Jurisdiction over these crimes is vested in the National Security Court.

(c) The Criminal Procedure Code of 1963 has been modified by a large amendment affecting mainly summary trial, trial in the absence of accused persons, and disposal of an accused's property.[95] The most substantial changes in the area, however, are to be found outside the Code, and refer mainly to arrest and detention before trial.

The power to legitimate such acts, vested at first in the SRC,[96] is now given to the President of the SRC.[97] The right of habeas corpus was suspended[98] and later abolished.[99]

NOTES

1. Haji Noor Muhammad, *Somali Democratic Republic*, in *Annual Survey of African Law, Vol. III, 1969*, Chapter 32
2. The SRC may also issue decrees on its own initiative and actually sometimes it does
3. The *Bollettino Ufficiale* is published monthly in Mogadishu under the Presidency of the SRC by the Chief State Council (see Pres. Decree N. 166/17.9.1972/BU 1972 Supplement 2 Number II). This office resulted from the unification of the offices of the Legal Adviser and the General State Attorney (Law N. 39/22.4.1971)
4. Decreto Leg. VO N. 3/12.6.1962/BU 1962 S. 6 N. 6
4a. After the revolution, however, relevant decisions of the courts (xukun maxkamadeed) are often reported in summarized form in the national newspaper, for political rather than for legal purposes.
5. Changes in the Somali legal system since the revolution are summarily reported in Haji

Noor Muhammad, *The legal system of the Somali Democratic Republic,* Charlottesville 1972, and in Sacco R., *Introduzione al diritto privato somalo,* Torino 1973, which is a more thorough and up-to-date survey.

6. *New Era* (monthly review published in English, Italian and Arabic by the Ministry of Information and National guidance), Mogadishu, February 1970
7. Law N. 1/21.10.1969/BU 1969 N. 1 and Pres. Decree N. 170/27.7.1970/BU 1970 S. 2 N. 8
8. Law N. 45/31.7.1972/BU 1972 S. 1 N. 8
9. Law 64/12.9.1971/BU 1971 S. 3 N. 10
9a. bis. Law N. 4/28.12.1971/BU 1972 S. 1 N. 1
10. Law 38/5.4.1972/BU 1972 S. 2 N. 5
11. Law N. 3/10.1.1970/BU 1970 S. 2 N. 2. This law, which is declared to be retroactively effective from 21 October 1969, has been repeatedly modified.
12. Law N. 7/21.1.1970/BU 1970 S. 2 N. 3
13. Law N. 16/2.3.1972/BU 1972 S. 3 N. 3
14. Pres. Decree N. 54/24.3.1972/BU 1972 S. 4 N. 3
15. Law N. 52/8.6.1972/BU 1972 S. 1 N. 9
16. Law N. 13/8.3.1970/BU 1970 N. 3
17. A new Prison Act has been issued at the end of 1971 (Law N. 7/30.12.1971/BU 1972 S. 2 N. 1) and later amended (Law N. 14/12.2.1972/BU 1972 N. 3)
18. Decree of the SRC N. 1/25.10.1969/BU 1969 N. 1
19. See note 15
20. Magistrates of Accounts are now regulated by the Law N. 34/14.4.1972/BU 1972 S. 2 N. 4
21. See note 19
22. Pres. Decree N. 121/17.9.1972/BU 1972 S. 2 N. 9
23. Law N. 29/1.4.1970/BU 1970 S. 1 N. 6
24. Law N. 66/29.10.1972/BU 1972 S. 4 N. 10
25. Law N. 11/25.2.1970/BU 1970 S. 1 N. 3, and Laws Ns. 5, 6, and 7/31.12.1969/BU 1969 S. 6 N. 3
26. Law N. 26/2.3.1972/BU 1972 N. 4
27. Law N. 20/12.3.1972/BU 1972 S. 3 N. 3
28. Law N. 70/1.11.1972/BU 1972 S. 2 N. 11. Article 1 reads as follows: 'Judges shall be independent while exercising their judicial functions, but for administrative purposes they shall be treated as members of the civil service'
29. Law N. 6/31.12.1969/BU 1969 S. 6 N. 3. Law N. 23/1.3.1970/BU 1970 N. 5. Law N. 2/23.12.1972/BU 1973 S. 3 N. 1
30. Law N. 36/22.4.1972/BU 1972 S. 3, N. 4. Regulations are provided by the Pres. Decree N. 74, same date and BU
31. Law N. 28/14.2.1972/BU 1972 S. 1 N. 4
32. Law N. 50/10.8.1972/BU 1972 N. 9—Pres. Decree N. 185/14.9.1972/BU 1972 S. 3 N. 12
33. Law N. 62/28.9.1970/BU 1970 S. 4 N. 10
34. Law N. 57/27.9.1970/BU 1970 S. 7 N. 9
35. Law N. 16/1.4.1970/BU 1970 S. 2 N. 4, and Law N. 56/14.9.1970/BU 1970 S. 5 N. 9
36. See note 30
37. Law N. 58/31.7.1972/BU 1972 S. 2 N. 8
38. See note 20 bis
39. Decreto Leg. VO N. 5/10.8.1969/BU 1969 S. 2 N. 8
40. Decreto Leg. VO N. 5/15.11.1958
41. Law N. 65/18.10.1972/BU 1972 S. 3 N. 10
42. Law N. 43/16.8.1970/BU 1970 S. 3 N. 8
43. Art. 17, Law N. 54/10.9.1970/BU 1970 S. 4 N. 9
44. See note 84
45. Law N. 44/19.7.1972/BU 1972 N. 8
46. Art. 10 of the Decree cited in note 30
47. Law N. 66/22.10.1972/BU 1972 S. 4 N. 10
48. See note 22
49. See note 24
50. Law N. 76/7.12.1972/BU 1972 S. 1 N. 12
51. Law N. 26/7.5.1970/BU 1970 S. 4 N. 5
52. Law N. 68-9/30.9.1972/BU 1972 S. 2 N. 11
53. Law N. 26/cited in note N. 51 and Law N. 30/30.3.1972/BU 1972 S. 1 N. 4
54. Law N. 19/11.3.1972/BU 1972 S. 3 N. 3 and Law N. 35/16.4.1972/BU 1972 S. 4 N. 4
55. Law N. 23/2.3.1972/BU 1972 S. 4 N. 3
56. Law N. 63/21.10.1972/BU 1972 S. 2 N. 10
57. Law N. 67/1.11.1970/BU 1970 S. 1 N. 11
58. Law N. 67/2.7.1972/BU 1972 S. 2 N. 11

59. Law N. 77/22.11.1970/BU 1970 S. 10 N. 12 and Pres. Decree N. 173/3.4.1971/BU 1971 S. 2 N. 3
60. Law N. 45/13.8.1970/BU 1970 S. 4 N. 8
61. Law N. 17/4.3.1972/BU 1972 S. 3 N. 3
62. Pres. Decree N. 58/31.3.1972/BU 1972 S. 1 N. 4
63. Pres. Decree N. 56/10.3. 1972/BU 1972 N. 4—Pres. Decrees N. 163/5.61971 and N. 33/10.2.1972/BU 1972 N. 3
64. *Ibid.*
65. Law N. 11/10.1.1972/BU 1972 N. 3
66. Law N. 45/13.8.1970/BU 1970 N. 8
67. Law N. 51/22.7.1971/BU 1971 N. 7
68. Decree of the Secretary of State for Agriculture N. 124/15.8.1972/BU 1972 S. 2 N. 9
69. Decree of the Secretary of State for Commerce N. 72/22.1.1972/BU 1972 S. 2 N. 4
70. See notes 33 and 34
71. Law N. 30/12.4.1971 and Law N. 15/12.2.1972/BU 1972 S. 3 N. 3
72. Co-operatives are now regulated by the Law N. 12/14.1.1969/BU 1969 S. 1 N. 3, but a new draft law is under discussion.
73. Law N. 25/30.4.1970/BU 1970 N. 4
74. Law N. 22/13.3.1972/BU 1972 S. 3 N. 3
75. Law N. 64/21.10.1972/BU 1972 S. 2 N. 10
76. See note 57
77. Law N. 60/21.10.1972/BU 1972 S. 2 N. 10
78. *Ibid.*
79. Law N. 61/23.10.1972/BU 1972 S. 2 N. 10
80. Law N. 46/31.7.1972/BU 1872 S. 1 N. 8
81. Law N. 40/19.5.1971 as amended by Law N. 2/20.12.1971/BU 1972 S. 1 N. 1
82. Law N. 27/18.3.1972/BU 1972 N. 4
83. See note 81
84. Law N. 40/26.3.1972/BU 1972 N. 6
85. Law N. 39/11.5.1972/BU 1972 S. 4 N. 5
86. Law N. 62/21.10.1972/BU 1972 S. 2 N. 10
87. See note 56
88. *Ibid.*
89. See note 55
90. Law N. 11/10.1.1972/BU 1972 N. 3 and Law N. 18/11.3.1972/BU 1972 S. 3 N. 3
91. Decreto Leg. VO N. 5/16.12.1962
92. Decreto Leg. VO N. 1/1.1.1963
93. Law N. 2/10.1.1970/BU 1970 N. 1
94. Law N. 54/10.9.1970/BU 1970 S. 4 N. 9
95. Law N. 84/12.12.1972/BU 1972 S. 4 N. 12
96. Decree of the SRC N. 22/21.10.1969/BU 1969 S. 1 N. 3
97. See note 9
98. Law N. 12/3.3.1970/BU 1970 S. 6 N. 3
99. Law N. 64/10.10.1970/BU 1970 S. 7 N. 10

CHAPTER THIRTY-ONE
AFRICAN LAW BIBLIOGRAPHY 1972

The *African Law Bibliography* 1972 includes books and articles dealing with African legal problems and published during the year 1972. Within books and articles are included government reports, but not legislative materials published under one form or another; essays included in collective works are also covered. By African legal problems, one means studies which have a definite legal import. The dividing line between law on the one hand and anthropology, economics, politics and sociology on the other being what it is the compiler has attempted to be restrictive in his choice in order to keep the bibliography within satisfactory limits; thus studies of which the major import is either anthropological, economic, political or sociological have in most cases been omitted. The whole African continent is considered, as the Centre for African Legal Development has been assigned such geographical limits by its promoters. Only published works (and thus no archives or theses) are incorporated in the bibliography.

J. Vanderlinden
Director
Centre for African Legal Development.

AFRICA — AFRIQUE

Agbede , I., 'A Short Critique on the "Governmental-interests" Analysis', *Journal of Ethiopian Law*, 8: 184, 1972.
Agbede, I. O., 'Conflict of Tort under the Received English Law in Common Law Africa: A Review', *Zambia Law Journal*, 3-4: 64, 1971-2.
Akiwumi, A. M., 'The Economic Commission for Africa', *Journal of African Law*, 16: 254, 1972.
Akiwumi, A. M., 'Solucion de conflictos en los procesos de integracion economica de Africa', *Derecho de la Integracion*, (10): 77, 1972.
Alliot, M., 'Le droit des successions dans les Etats africains francophones', *Revue juridique et politique*, 26: 846, 1972.
Andemikael, B., 'UNITAR and its Contribution to the Field of Development Relating to Africa', *Journal of African Law*, 16: 266, 1972.

Austin, D., 'Ex Africa semper eadem?' *The Study of International Law*, 156.

Bainbridge, J., *The Study of Teaching of Law in Africa*, South Hackensack 1972.

Bentsi-Enchill, 'The Lawyer's Calling in Africa', *Zambia Law Journal*, 3-4: 5, 1971-2.

Bibliography on Land Tenure, Roma 1972.

Bipoun-Woum , J.-M., 'Recherches sur les aspects actuels de la réception du droit administratif dans les Etats d'Afrique noire d'expression française', *Revue juridique et politique*, 26: 359, 1972.

Blum, A., 'Continental Shelf Convention and African Ratification', *African Law Studies*, (6): 35, 1972.

Bockel, A., 'Le juge et l'administration en Afrique noire francophone', *Annales africaines*, —: 9, 1971-2.

Bono, S., *Le frontiere in Africa*, Milano 1972.

Borella, F., 'Les résultats de la coopération économique', *Journal of African Law*, 16: 244, 1972.

Bourel, P., 'Revue de jurisprudence africaine en droit interpersonnel et en droit international privé', *Annales africaines*, —: 139, 1971-2.

Delorme, N., *L'association des Etats africains et malgache à la Communauté européenne*, Paris 1972.

Diaite, I., 'Les constitutions africaines et le droit international', *Annales africaines*, —: 33, 1971-2.

Elias, T. O., *Africa and the Development of International Law*, Leiden-Dobbs Ferry 1972.

Filesi, T., 'Rinnovamento e crisi delle istituzioni politico-costituzionali nell'Africa indipendante', *Africa (Roma)*, 27: 569. 1972.

Fortes, M., *Marriage in Tribal Societies*, Cambridge 1972.

Integration of Customary and Modern Legal Systems in Africa: Papers, New York 1972.

Kamanda, J. G., 'L'organisation de l'unité africaine et le développement économique de l'Afrique, *Journal of African Law*, 16: 279, 1972.

Kamara, L. et D'Hauteville, B., 'Aspects juridiques de l'intégration économique en Afrique', *Tiers-Monde*, 13: 531, 1972.

Karlsson, P. H., 'Sources for African Constitutional Studies', *African Law Studies*, (6): 123, 1972.

Koffi-Amega, L., 'Dix ans de droit en Afrique Noire', *Penant*, 82: 485, 1972.

Kraiem, M., 'L'Association des compagnies aériennes africaines', *Journal of African Law*, 16: 295, 1972.

Krause-Ablass, G., 'Der Rechtgrundsatz der afrikanischen Solidarität', *Afrika Spectrum*, —(2): , 1972.

Lampue, P., 'Les conflits de loi d'ordre international en Afrique francophone', *Penant*, 82: 445, 1972.

Lampue, P., 'Les rapports de la coutume et de la loi dans le droit des successions en Afrique francophone, *Revue juridique et politique*, 26: 833, 1972; *Zaïre-Afrique*, (69): 525, 1972.

Le Roy, E., 'Réflexions sur une interprétation anthropologique du droit africain: le laboratoire d'anthropologie juridique', *Revue juridique et politique*, 26: 427, 1972.

Milner, A., 'Hexenwesen, Ehestand und Peitsche-Einige Kulturprobleme in Afrikanischen Strafrecht', *Zeitschrift für die Desante Strafrechtswissenschaft*, 84: 254, 1972.

Mushkat, M., 'Les pays en voie de développement, en Afrique en particulier, et quelques problèmes du droit des gens', *Miscellanea Ganshof van der Meersch*, I, 173.

Niang, M., 'Structures parentales et stratégie juridique du développement en Afrique noire francophone', *Revue sénégalaise de droit*, 6: 59, 1972.

Nwabueze, B. O., *Constitutionalism in the Emergent States*, London 1972.

Ocran, T., 'Law, African Economic Development and Social Engineering: A Theoretical Nexus', *Zambia Law Journal*, 3-4: 16, 1971-2.

Ogundere, J. D., 'The Development of International Environmental Law and Policy in Africa', *Natural Resources Journal*, 12: 255, 1972; *Nigerian Journal of Contemporary Law*, 3: 1, 1972.

Okoye, F. C., *International Law and the New African States*, London 1972.

Opoku, K. T., 'Le mariage africain et ses transformations', *Genève-Afrique*, 11 (1): 3, 1972.

Papers of the Third Annual Conference of the Nigerian Society of International Law, Bengin City 1972.

Payne, R. H., 'Sub-Saharan Africa: The Right of Intervention in the Name of Humanity', *Georgia Journal of International Law*, 2(1): 89, 1972.

Pepper, H. W. T., 'Taxation of Land and Real Property in Developing Countries', *Bulletin for International Fiscal Documentation*, 26: 355, 1972.

Person, Y., 'L'Afrique noire et ses frontières', *Revue francaise d'études politiques africaines*, (80): 18, 1972.

Robertson, A. H., 'African Legal Process and the Individual', *Revue des Droits de l'Homme*, 5: 465, 1972.

Smith, D. N., 'Men and Law in Urban Africa: A Role for Customary Courts in the Urbanization Process', *American Journal of Comparative Law*, 20: 223, 1972.

Sohn, L. B. (ed.), *Basic Documents of African Regional Organizations*, 4 vols., Dobbs Ferry 1971-2.

Sohn, I. B., 'The Organs of Economic Co-operation in Africa', *Journal of African Law*, 16: 212, 1972.

Sundstrom, G. O. Z., 'The Legal Procedures and Techniques of Economic Co-operation', *Journal of African Law*, 16: 228, 1972.

Tall, A. B., 'L'Organisation commune africaine, malgache et mauricienne', *Journal of African Law*, 16: 304, 1972.

Tanner, R. E. S., 'Penal Practice in Africa', *Journal of Modern African Studies*, 10: 447, 1972.

Touval, S., *The Boundary Politics of Independent Africa*, Cambridge (Mass.) 1972.

Umozurike, U. O., 'International Law and Colonialism in Africa', *Zambia Law Journal*, 3-4: 95, 1971-2

Vanderlinden, J., *African Law Bibliography—Bibliographie de Droit africain, 1947-1966*, Bruxelles 1972.

Vanderlinden, J., 'Objectif, objets et degrés de la coopération économique', *Journal of African Law*, 16: 220, 1972.

Woronoff, J., 'Différends frontaliers en Afrique', *Revue française d'études politiques africaines*, (80): 58, 1972.

Zar, W., 'Double Taxation Treaties of African States', *African Law Studies*, (6): 47, 1972.

AFRICA (CENTRAL) — AFRIQUE CENTRALE

Tchanque, P., 'L'Union douanière et économique de l'Afrique centrale', *Journal of African Law*, 16: 339, 1972.

Tonwe, B. O., 'The Lake Chad Basin Commission', *Journal of African Law*, 16: 343, 1972.

AFRICA (EAST) — AFRIQUE ORIENTALE

Akiwumi, A. M., 'East African Community', *Journal of World Trade Law*, 6: 203, 1972.

Akiwumi, A. M., 'Solucion de conflictos en los procesos de integracion economica de Africa', *Derecho de la Integracion*, (10): 77, 1972.

Byamugisha, J., 'Criminal Responsibility under the East African Penal Codes', *Zambia Law Journal*, 3-4: 76, 1971-2; *Uganda law Focus*, 1: 72, 1972.

Eze, O., 'Patents and the Transfer of Technology, with Special Reference to the East African Community', *Eastern Africa Law Review*, 5: 127, 1972.

Ghai, Y. P., 'Constitutions and the Political Order in East Africa', *International and Comparative Law Quarterly*, 21: 403, 1972.

Hodgin, R. W., *Cases and Materials on East African Mercantile Law*, London 1972.

Kanyeihamba, G. W., and Katende, J. W., 'The Supranational Adjudicatory Bodies and the Municipal Governments, Legislatures and Courts', *Public Law*, —: 107, 1972.

Njuba, S. K., 'Security of Employment in East Africa', *East African Law Journal*, 8: 46, 1972.

Ross, S., 'Common Market Tribunal—The Solution to the Conflict between Municipal and International Law in East Africa', *International and Comparative Law Quarterly*, 21: 361, 1972.

Sebalu, P., 'The East African Community', *Journal of African Law*, 16: 345, 1972.

Shivji, L. G., 'Introduction—From the Analysis of Forms to the Exposition of Substance. The Tasks of a Lawyer—Intellectual'. *Eastern Africa Law Review*, 5: 1, 1972.

Veitch, E., *East African Cases on the law of Tort*, London 1972.

AFRICA (NORTH) — AFRIQUE DU NORD

Moustapha, M. M., 'L'indemnisation de la victime de l'infraction pénale dans les législations des Pays Arabes', *Proche-Orient, Etudes Juridiques*, (75): 233, 1972.

AFRICA (WEST) — AFRIQUE OCCIDENTALE

Bornstein, R., 'The Organization of Senegal River States', *Journal of Modern African Studies*, 10: 267, 1972.
Ould Amar, M., 'L'Organisation pour la mise en valeur du fleuve Sénégal', *Journal of African Law*, 16: 299, 1972.
Tamboura, A., 'La Communauté économique de l'Afrique de l'Ouest', *Journal of African Law*, 16: 310, 1972.

ALGERIÊ — ALGERIA

Baumann, H., 'Neugestaltung der staatlichen Leitung auf Bezirksebene in Algerien, *Staat und Recht*, 21: 80, 1972.
Belkacem, K., 'Le code des investissements privés en Algérie, *Revue juridique et politique*, 26: 299, 1972.
Berchiche, A. H., 'La notion d'infraction économique en droit prositif algérien', *Revue algérienne des sciences économiques, juridiques et politiques*, 9: 695, 1972.
David, M., 'La Banque Nationale d'Algérie', *Revue algérienne des sciences économiques, juridiques et politiques*, 9: 7, 1972.
David, C., 'La liberté du commerce en Algérie', *Revue algérienne des sciences économiques, juridiques et politiques*, 9: 633, 1972.
Depuydt G. et Garelick, J., *Fiscalité algérienne*, Alger 1972.
Fenaux, H., 'Eléments de droit judiciaire Algérien', *Revue algérienne des sciences économiques, juridiques et politiques*, 9: 95, 1972.
Fenaux, H., 'Eléments de Droit Judiciaire Algérien. Les Saisies Mobilières', *Revue algérienne des sciences économiques, juridiques et politiques*, 9: 409, 1972.
Heymann, A., *Les libertés publiques et la guerre d'Algérie*, Paris 1972.
Lourdjane, A., 'Le code pénal algérien', *Revue juridique et politique*, 26: 77, 1972.
Mahiou, A., 'Le contentieux administratif en Algérie', *Revue algérienne des sciences économiques, juridiques et politiques*, 9: 571, 1972.
Pomel, B., 'Contribution à l'étude du domaine de l'Etat et de son régime juridique. exemple des exbiens vacants', *Revue algérienne des sciences économiques, juridiques et politiques*, 9: 719, 1972.
Schliephake, K., 'Die algerische Agrar-revolution', *Afrika Spectrum*, —(1): 44, 1972.
Tavernier, P., 'Aspects juridiques des relations économiques entre la CEE et l'Algérie', *Revue trimestrielle de droit européen*, 8: 1, 1972.
Touscoz, J., 'La nationalisation des sociétés pétrolières françaises en Algérie et le droit international', *Revue belge de droit international*, 8: 482, 1972.
Vlachos, G., 'Le régime juridique des entreprises publiques en Algérie', *Revue algérienne des sciences économiques, juridiques et politiques*, 9: 471, 1972.
Zöller, A. C., 'Algerian Nationalizations: The Legal Issues', *Journal of World Trade Law*, 6: 33, 1972.

BOTSWANA

Aguda, A., 'Discriminatory Statutory Provisions and Fundamental Rights Provisions of the Constitutions of Botswana, Lesotho and Swaziland', *South African Law Journal*, 89: 299, 1972.
Himsworth, C. M. G., 'The Botswana Customary Law Act 1969', *Journal of African Law*, 16: 4, 1972.
Roberts, S., *Tswana Family Law*, London 1972.
Roberts, S., 'The Survival of the Traditional Tswana Courts in the National Legal System of Botswana', *Journal of African Law*, 16: 103, 1972.
Rowny, K., 'Independence and International Treaties Valid under protectorate', *Africana Bulletin*, (17): 43, 1972.

Will, D. D., *The Citizenship, Immigration and Allied Laws of Botswana*, Gaborone 1972.

Bellon, R., 'Commentaire technique du code de la nationalité burundaise', *Revue administrative et juridique du Burundi*, 6 (18-19): 47, 1972.

Bukera, J., 'La dévolution successorale en droit burundais', *Revue juridique et politique*, 26: 611, 1972.

Mabushi, C., 'La succession testamentaire en droit coutumier burundais', *Revue juridique et politique*, 26: 625, 1972.

Mpozagara, G., 'Traits généraux des modes d'acquisition de la nationalité burundaise', *Revue administrative et juridique du Burundi*, 6 (18-19): 77, 1972.

Nzohabonayo, C., 'La possession d'état de national', *Revue administrative et juridique du Burundi*, 6 (18-19): 60, 1972.

Pereira, C. C., 'Décentralisation et developpement national au Burundi', *Bulletin de l'IIAP*, (21): 55, 1972.

Verbrugghe, A., 'Introduction historique au problème de la nationalité au Burundi', *Revue administrative et juridique du Burundi*, 6 (18-19): 5, 1972.

CAMEROON — CAMEROUN

Amougou-Akala, J. P., 'Le mariage coutumier chez les Bene', *Revue de droit canonique*, 22: 291, 1972.

Bidias, B., *Les finances publiques et l'économie financière de la République Fédérale du Cameroun*, Yaounde 1971.

Breton, J. M., 'Le contrôle supérieur de l'Etat au Cameroun', *Bulletin de l'IIAP*, (23): 543, 1972.

Dolivet, M., 'La fiscalité des entreprises au Cameroun Oriental', *Revue camerounnaise de Droit*, 1: 110, 1972.

Electa, 'Le contrôle a posteriori des dépenses publiques au Cameroun: l'Inspection Générale de l'Etat', *Revue camerounnaise de Droit*, 1: 118, 1972.

Mbella Mbappe, R., 'La rupture du contrat de travail à durée indéterminée au Cameroun', *Penant*, 82: 41, 1972; 82; 332, 1972.

Melone, S., 'L'article 228 du Code Pénal Camerounais et la répression des activités dangereuses', *Revue camerounaise de Droit*, 1: 125, 1972.

Melone, S., 'Le Code civil contre la Coutume: la fin d'une suprématie (à propos des effets patrimoniaux du mariage)', *Revue camerounaise de droit*, 1: 12, 1972.

Ngongang-Ouandji, A., 'La dévolution successorale au Cameroun', *Revue juridique et politique*, 26: 639, 1972.

Pannier, J., 'Réflexions sur le Code camerounais de la nationalité', *Revue camerounaise de Droit*, 1: 21, 1972.

Prouzet, M., 'L'expropriation pour cause d'utilité publique au Cameroun oriental', *Revue camerounaise de Droit*, 1: 27, 1972.

CONGO

Etudes sur les coutumes (Cour d'Appel de Brazzaville, 1953-1954), Brazzaville 1972.

Mayinguidi, E., 'Le droit fiscal des successions au Congo', *Revue juridique et politique*, 26: 1311, 1972.

Mayinguidi, E., 'Des successions en droits coutumiers du Congo', *Revue juridique et politique*, 26: 663, 1972.

COTE D'IVOIRE — IVORY COAST

Akoi, P. A., 'L'administration du travail en Côte d'Ivoire', *Annales de l'Université d'Abidjan, série A, Droit*, (1): 1, 1972.

Deniel, R., 'Mesures gouvernementales et/ou intérêts divergents des pays exportateurs de main-d'oeuvre et des pays hôtes, Haute Volta et Côte d'Ivoire', *Notes et documents voltaïques*, 5(3): 5, 1972.

Fadika, M., 'Le droit, les sorciers, magiciens, guérisseurs féticheurs et marabouts', *Revue ivoirienne de droit*, —: 45, 1972-3.

Fadika, M., 'Le régime fiscal des successions en Côte d'Ivoire', *Revue juridique et politique*, 26: 313, 1972.

Fadika, M., 'Les successions en Côte d'Ivoire', *Revue juridique et politique*, 26: 675, 1972.
Fouchard, P., 'Les effets successoraux en Côte d'Ivoire d'une légitimation adoptive étrangère', *Revue ivoirienne de droit*, —: 65, 1972-3.
Ley, A., *Le régime domanial et foncier et le développement économique de la Côte d'Ivoire*, Paris 1972.
Talon, J.-F., 'Un cas d'application de la doctrine du capitalisme d'Etat en Côte d'Ivoire: le groupe SODEPALM', *Revue ivoirienne de droit*, —: 11, 1972-3.

DAHOMEY

Beynel, J., 'Réponses dahoméennes à quelques problèmes en matière pénale, civile et sociale', *Revue juridique et politique*, 26: 247, 1972.
Beynel, J., 'Revue des différentes solutions dahoméennes au problème du développement de l'agriculture', *Penant*, 82: 209, 1972.
Toko, M. B., 'La dévolution successorale au Dahomey', *Revue juridique et Politique*, 26: 687, 1972.

ETHIOPIA — ETHIOPIE

Beckstrom, J. H., 'Adoption in Ethiopia ten Years after the Civil Code', *Journal of African Law*, 16: 145, 1972.
Bryde, B. O., 'Rechtstechnik ùnd Gerechtigkeit—Zur Rezeption formaler Rechtsnormen in Äthiopen', *Verfassung und Recht in Ubersee*, 5: 295, 1972.
Bryde, B. O., 'Some Observations on Art. 1922 (3) of the Civil Code', *Journal of Ethiopian Law*, 8: 544, 1972.
Daniel, Haile, 'Penal and Civil Law Aspects of Dismissal Without Cause', *Journal of Ethiopian Law*, 8: 532, 1972.
Fasil, Nahum, 'Ethiopian Nationality Law and Practice', *Journal of Ethiopian Law*, 8: 168, 1972.
Goldberg, E. F., 'An Introduction to the Law of Business Organizations', *Journal of Ethiopian Law*, 8: 495, 1972.
Goldberg, E. F., 'Protection of Trademarks in Ethiopia', *Journal of Ethiopian Law*, 8: 130, 1972.
Guadagni, M., *Ethiopian Labour Law Handbook*, Asmara 1972.
Haile Gabriel Dagne, 'The Gebzenna Charter 1894', *Journal of Ethiopian Studies*, 10(1): 67, 1972.
Krzeczunowicz, G., 'The University College Period of Legal Education in Ethiopia', *Journal of Ethiopian Law*, 8: 89, 1972.
O'Donovan, K., 'A Problem on Family Law', *Journal of Ethiopian Law*, 8: 570, 1972.
O'Donovan, K., 'Void and Voidable Marriages in Ethiopian Law', *Journal of Ethiopian Law*, 8: 439, 1972.
Ross J. and Zemariam, Berhe, *Legal Aspects of Doing Business in Ethiopia*, Addis Ababa 1972.
Selamu Bekele, *Private Commercial Companies Under Ethiopian Law*, Addis Ababa 1972.
Sklar, R., 'Desire', 'Knowledge of Certainty', and 'Dolus Evantualis', *Journal of Ethiopian Law*, 8: 373, 1972.
Zemarian Berhe, 'Compliance with Legal Obligations by Businesses in the Mercato', *Journal of Ethiopian Law*, 8: 560, 1972.

GABON

Minko, H., 'Le régime fiscal des successions en République gabonaise', *Revue juridique et politique*, 26: 1319, 1972.

GAMBIA — GAMBIE

Deschamps, M., 'Les frontières de la Sénégambie', *Revue française d'études politiques africaines*, (80): 44, 1972.

GHANA

Bentsi-Enchill, K., 'Intestate Succession Revisited (A Comment on Dr Kludze's "Problems of Intestate Succession in Ghana")', *University of Ghana Law Journal*, 9: 123, 1972.

Bimpong-Buta, S. Y., 'Caveats in an Application for Grant of Probate', *Review of Ghana Law*, 4: 157, 1972.

Daniels, J., 'Statute Law in Ghana', *Review of Ghana Law*, 4: 113, 1972.

Daniels, W. C. E., 'Judgement Debt—Payment by Instalments, *Review of Ghana Law*, 4: 146, 1972.

Daniels, W. C. E., 'Jurisdiction of the High Court in Chieftaincy Matters', *Review of Ghana Law*, 4: 81, 1972.

Daniels, W. C. E., 'The Legal Position of Women under our Marriage Laws', *University of Ghana Law Journal*, 9: 39, 1972.

Date-Bah, S. K., 'Akrong and Another *v.* Bulley: the Perpetration of Injustice?', *University of Ghana Law Journal*, 9: 64, 1972.

Date Bah, S. K., 'The Limitation Decree, 1972', *Review of Ghana Law*, 4: 150, 1972.

Date-Bah, S. K., 'The Rights of Cuckolds in Dagomba Customary Law', *Review of Ghana Law*, 4; 221, 1972.

Dei-Anang, K., 'The Law as an Instrument of Trade Policy', *Review of Ghana Law*, 4: 22, 1972.

Dickey, W. J., 'Some Reflections on Hire Purchase Law in Ghana', *Review of Ghana Law*, 4: 184, 1972.

Dickey W. and Fui, Tsikata, 'A look at Administrative Law in Ghana', *University of Ghana Law Journal*, 9: 135, 1972.

Fiadjoe, A., 'Conversion—A New Twist', *Review of Ghana Law*, 4: 78, 1972.

Fiadjoe, A., 'The Discretion of a Prosecutor to Call Witnesses', *Review of Ghana Law*, 4: 248, 1972.

Fiadjoe, A., 'Fatal Accidents: Capacity to Sue', *Review of Ghana Law*, 4: 65, 1972.

Fiadjoe, A., 'Fatal Accident Claims', *Review of Ghana Law*, 4: 143, 1972.

Fiadjoe, A., 'The Police Service Act, 1970 (Act 350)', *University of Ghana Law Journal*, 9: 81, 1972.

Kludze, A. K. P., 'Problems of Intestate Succession in Ghana', *University of Ghana Law Journal*, 9: 89, 1972.

Kom, E. D., 'Recovery of Damages and Costs from Insurers', *Review of Ghana Law*, 4: 52, 1972.

Kom, E. D., 'Test for Joinder under Order 16, r. 11', *Review of Ghana Law*, 4: 153, 1972.

Kom, E. D., 'Total Loss of Property and Loss of Use or Earnings', *Review of Ghana Law*, 4: 68, 1972.

Kyerematen, A. A., *Interstate Boundary Litigation in Ashanti*, Cambridge 1972.

MacDonald, G. P., 'Recent Legislation in Nigeria and Ghana Affecting Foreign Private Direct Investment', *International Lawyer*, 6: 548, 1972.

Mettle, M. A., 'Compulsory Acquisition of Land', *Review of Ghana Law*, 4: 129, 1972.

Mettle, M. A., 'On Matrilineal Inheritance in Ga Mashi', *Review of Ghana Law*, 4: 72, 1972.

Mettle, M. A., 'Precedent: Fetish of the Bench', *Review of Ghana Law*, 4: 241, 1972.

Ofori Boateng, J., 'Rules of Evidence under Act 220', *Review of Ghana Law*, 4: 43, 1972.

Opoku, K., 'Divorce in Ghana', *Verfassung und Recht in Ubersee*, 5: 407, 1972.

Pozen, R. C., 'Public Corporations in Ghana', *Wisconsin Law Review*, —: 802, 1972.

Sawyerr, G. F. A., 'The "Choice of Law" Approach and the Application of Law in Ghana', *University of Ghana Law Journal*, 9: 173, 1972.

Sey, K., 'Some Observations on Trade Marks Law and Practice in Ghana', *Review of Ghana Law*, 4: 103, 1972.

Tiewul, S., 'Injunctions against Public Officers', *University of Ghana Law Journal*, 9: 181, 1972.

Tsikata, F. S., 'The Wills Act, 1971 (Act 360)', *Review of Ghana Law*, 4: 1, 1972.

Veitch, E., 'Constitutional Protections of Liberty and the Tort of False Imprisonment', *University of Ghana Law Journal*, 9: 66, 1972.

Woodman, G., 'The Assessment of Compensation under Act 107', *Review of Ghana Law*, 4: 227, 1972.

Woodman, G., 'Giving Teeth to the Land Registry Act, *Review of Ghana Law*, 4: 231, 1972.

Woodman, G., 'Whittaker v. Choiteram: Choice of Law in Cases Concerning the Rights of Children to be Maintained from the Estates of their Deceased Fathers', *University of Ghana Law Journal*, 9: 195, 1972.

GUINEE — GUINEA

Charles, B., *La République de Guinée*, Paris 1972.

HAUTE-VOLTA — UPPER VOLTA

Deniel, R., 'Mesures gouvernementales et/ou intérêts divergents des pays exportateurs de main d'oeuvre et des pays hôtes, Haute Volta et Côte d'Ivoire', *Notes et documents voltaïques*, 5(3): 5, 1972.

Herbert, J., 'Organisation de la société en pays Tussian', *Notes et documents voltaïques*, 5(4): 14, 1972.

Lippens, P., *La République de Haute-Volta*, Paris 1972.

Zorome, M. et Tani, E., 'La dévolution successorale en droit coutumier mossi', *Revue juridique et politique*, 26: 705, 1972.

KENYA

Horrut, C., *La république du Kenya*, Paris 1972.

Kalsi, S. S., 'Encouragement of Private Foreign Investment in the Developing Country: Provisions in the Laws of Kenya', *International Lawyer*, 6: 576, 1972.

Potter, K., Comment: Compensation for Deprivation of property under the Kenya Constitution', *East African Law Journal*, 8: 65, 1972.

Kimani, S. M., 'The Structure of Land Ownership in Nairobi', *Canadian Journal of African Studies*, 6: 379, 1972.

Maini, K. M., *Cooperatives and Law with Emphasis on Kenya*, Nairobi 1972.

Nellis, J. R., *Who Pays Tax in Kenya*, Uppsala 1972.

Nowrojee, P., 'Public Enterprise and Co-operatives in Kenya and Tanzania: Some Comparative Illustrations', *Eastern Africa Law Review*, 5: 141, 1972.

Okoth-Ogendo, M. W. O., 'Constitutional Change in Kenya since Independence', *African Affairs*, 71: 9, 1972.

Pennill, B., *Kamba Customary Law*, (reprint), Nairobi 1972.

Practice note: s. 143 (1) of the Registered Land Act', *East African Law Journal*, 8: 68, 1972.

Slattery, B., *A Handbook on Sentencing* Nairobi 1972.

LESOTHO

Aguda, A., 'Discriminatory Statutory Provisions and Fundamental Rights Provisions of the Constitutions of Botswana, Lesotho and Swaziland', *South African Law Journal*, 89: 299, 1972.

Palmer, V. V. and Poulter, S. M., *The Legal System of Lesotho*, Charlottesville 1972.

Poulter, S., 'The Place of the Laws of Lerotholi in the Legal System of Lesotho'. *African Affairs*, 71: 144, 1972.

Rowny, K., 'Independence and International Treaties Valid under Protectorate', *African Bulletin*, (17), 43, 1972.

Williams, J. C., *Lesotho Land Tenure and Economic Development*, Pretoria 1972.

LIBERIA

Falkman, E. G., 'Liberia's Struggle with Western Land Tenure', *African Law Studies*, (6): 1, 1972.

Fulton, R. M., 'The Political Structures and Functions of Poro in Kpelle Society', *American Anthropologist*, 74: 1218, 1972.

LIBYA — LIBYE

Ansell, M. D. and Al Arif, I. M., *The Libyan Revolution: A Sourcebook of Legal and Historical Documents*, Stoughton 1972.
Haight, G. W., 'Libyan Nationalization of British Petroleum', *International Lawyer*, 6: 541, 1972.

MADAGASCAR

Andrianada, J. et Rakotomanana, H., 'La dévolution successorale. La détermination des héritiers en droit malgache', *Revue juridique et politique*, 26: 713, 1972.
Herbecq, P., 'Les causes de divorce en droit positif malgache', *Penant*, 82: 67, 1972.
Leymarie, P., 'Les accords de coopération franco-malgaches', *Revue française d'études politiques africaines*, (78): 55, 1972.
Randrianarisoa, J., 'Le testament et la protection de la famille légitime contre les libéralités du défunt en droit malgache', *Revue juridique et politique*, 26: 733, 1972.
Razoharinoro-Randriamboavonjy, 'Le Fokonolona comme institution judiciaire (1868–1885)', *Bulletin de Madagascar*, 22: 647, 1972.
'L'union conjugale en Imarina', *Cahiers du Centre d'Etude des coutumes*, 9: 7, 1972.

MALAWI

Brietzke, P., 'Witchcraft and Law in Malawi', *East African Law Journal*, 8: 1, 1972.
Fleming, C. J. W., 'The Peculiar Institution among the Early Tumbuka', *Society of Malawi Journal*, 25(1): 5, 1972.

MALI

Diarra, T. D., 'Les successions au Mali', *Revue juridique et politique*, 26: 741, 1972.

MAROC — MOROCCO

Camau, M., 'Evolution du droit constitutionel au Maroc depuis l'indépendance 1955–71)', *Jahrbuch des öffentlichen Rechts des Gegenwarts*, 21: 383, 1972.
Rousset, M., 'Le pouvoir réglementaire au Maroc: dix années d'évolution', *Revue juridique et politique*, 26: 333, 1972.

MAURITANIE — MAURETANIA

Mohamed Fall, O. A., 'Les successions en droit mauritanien', *Revue juridique et politique*, 26: 757, 1972.
Rowny, K., 'Independence and International Treaties Valid under Protectorate', *Africana Bulletin*, (17: 43, 1972.

NIGERIA

Achike, O., 'Abolition of Customary Courts in East Central State', *Nigeria Lawyers Quarterly*, (6): 122, 1972.
Adeogun, A. A., 'The Industrial Training Fund', *Nigerian Journal of Contemporary Law*, 3: 40, 1972.
Adesanya, J. A., 'Capacity of a Muslim Native of Nigeria to Dispose of Property in Accordance with the English Wills Act', *Journal of Islamic and Comparative Law*, 4: 29, 1972.
Adesanya, M. O. and Oloyede, E. O., *Business Law in Nigeria*, New York 1972.
Adesanya, S. A., 'Financial Relief under the Matrimonial Causes Decree', *Nigeria Lawyers Quarterly*, (6): 70, 1972.
Adesanya, S. A., 'Separation, Non-Objection and Fault under the Matrimonial Causes Decree, 1970 of Nigeria—A Comparative Study with English and Australian Laws', *University of Ghana Law Journal*, 9: 15, 1972.
Agbede, I. O., 'Conflict between Customary and Non-Customary Systems of Law:

Preliminary Observations', *Journal of Islamic and Comparative Law*, 4: 47, 1972; *VerFassung und Recht in Übersee*, 5: 415, 1972.

Agbede, I. O., 'Discretionary Jurisdiction in Nigerian Law', *Nigeria Lawyers' Quarterly*, (6): 23, 1972.

Aguda, A. and Aguda, O., 'Judicial Protection of Some Fundamental Rights in Nigeria and in the Sudan before and During Military Rule', *Journal of African Law*, 16: 130, 1972.

Aihe, D. O., 'Preventive Detention in Nigeria', *Review of the International Commission of Jurists*, (9): 68, 1972.

Ajomo, M. A., 'The Nigerian Territorial Waters (Amendment)', *Nigerian Journal of Contemporary Law*, 3: 68, 1972.

Akinkugbe, O. O., 'Corroborating Complainant of Rape', *Nigerian Journal of Contemporary Law*, 3: 74, 1972.

Akpamgbo, C. O., 'Magistrates' Courts Law (Amendment) in East Central State', *Nigeria Lawyers' Quarterly*, (6): 133, 1972.

Babafemi, E. O. B., 'A Critique of the Quasi—Judicial Treatment of "Unjust Enrichment" in Nigeria', *Nigerian Journal of Contemporary Law*, 3: 27, 1972.

Balogun, H. A., 'Status of Women in Private Law in Nigeria', *Abogada internacional*, 16: 21, 1972.

Carew, B., 'Our Penal Policy and the Prison System', *Nigeria Lawyers' Quarterly*, (4): 60, 1972.

Cotrell, J., 'Ultra Vires Is Alive and Living in Nigeria', *Nigerian Journal of Contemporary Law*, 3: 19, 1972.

Delano, I. B., 'Bail'; *Nigeria Lawyers' Quarterly*, (4): 35, 1972.

Egboh, E. O., 'Labour Relations in Nigeria. The Development of Joint Consultative and Negotiating Machinery (1940-64)', *Genève-Afrique*, II (1): 52, 1972.

Egboh, E. O., 'Polygamy in Iboland', *Civilisations*, 22: 431, 1972.

Ekejiuba, F., 'Igba Ndu: An Igbo Mechanism of Social Control and Adjustment', *African Notes*, 7 (1): 9, 1971-2.

Ezejiofor, G., 'Nigerian Judicial Structure and Distribution of Judicial Competence', *Nigeria Lawyers' Quarterly*, (6): 1, 1972.

Fabunmi, J. O., 'Mortgages in Nigeria', *Anglo-American Law Review*, 1: 240, 1972.

Fashokun, S. O., 'When Is a Sale a Trade', *Nigeria Lawyers Quarterly*, (6): 106, 1972.

Ijalaiye, D. A., 'Doing Justice in Nigerian Courts', *Nigeria Lawyers Quarterly*, (5): 59, 1972.

Kasunmu, A. B., 'The Matrimonial Causes Decree, 1970', *Nigeria Lawyers Quarterly*, (5): 1, 1972; 6: 41, 1972.

Land and Social Change in Nigeria, (T. O. Elias ed.), Ibadan 1972.

MacDonald, G. P., 'Recent Legislation in Nigeria and Ghana Affecting Foreign Private Direct Investment', *International Lawyer*, 6: 548, 1972.

Milner, A., *The Nigerian Penal System*, London 1972.

Muller, J. C., 'Ritual Marriage, Symbolic Fatherhood and Initiation Among the Rukuba', *Man*, 7: 283, 1972.

The Nigerian Magistrate and the Offender, Benin City 1972.

Nwabueze, B. O., *Nigerian Land Law*, Dobbs Ferry 1972.

Odubayo, W. O., 'The Process of Making and Executing Treaties in Nigeria (Aviation Agreements)', *Nigeria Lawyers' Quarterly*, (4): 78, 1972.

Ohonbamu, O., *Introduction to Nigerian Law of Mortgages*, Lagos 1972.

Ojo, A. O., 'Reforms in the Native and Customary Courts Systems', *Nigeria Lawyers Quarterly*, (4): 69, 1972.

Okonkwo, C. O., 'Bona Fide Claim of Right', *Nigeria Lawyers' Quarterly*, (6): 31, 1972.

Ola, C. S., *Income Tax in Nigeria*, London 1972.

Olawoye, C. O., 'The Acquisition of Lands by Aliens', *Nigerian Journal of Contemporary Law*, 3: 49, 1972.

Olawoyin, G. A., 'Statutory Protection of Minority Shareholders', *Nigeria Lawyers' Quarterly*, (6): 95, 1972.

Olofemi-Ekundare, R., 'The Economic Aspect of Customary Marriages in Nigeria', *Africa Quarterly*, 12: 109, 1972.

Oloyede, E. O., 'Juvenile Delinquency in Nigerian Law', *Nigeria Lawyers' Quarterly*, (5): 31, 1972.

Oloyede, E. O., 'Legitimacy in Nigerian Law', *Lagos Notes and Records*, 3 (2): 32, 1972.

Oloyede, E. O., 'A Review of the Hire Purchase Law in Nigeria', *Nigeria Lawyers' Quarterly*, (4): 42, 1972.

Oluyede, P. A., 'Search for Effective Registration in Nigeria', *Nigeria Lawyers' Quarterly*, (6): 11, 1972.

Omotola, J. A., 'Registration of Possessory Title', *Nigeria Lawyers Quarterly*, (6): 62, 1972.

Orojo, J. O., 'Companies Decree', *Nigeria Lawyers' Quarterly*, (4): 21, 1972.

Osidipe, W., 'Size and Nature of Estate and Interest in Land', *Nigeria Lawyers Quarterly*, (5): 48, 1972.

Park, A. E. W., *Sources of Nigerian Law*, (2nd ed.), London 1972.

Sangree, W. M., 'Secondary Marriage and Tribal Solidarity in Irigwe, Nigeria', *American Anthropologist*, 74: 1234, 1972.

Sasegbon, F., 'Contempt of Court', *Nigeria Lawyers' Quarterly*, 5: 78, 1972.

PORTUGUESE TERRITORIES — TERRITOIRES PORTUGAIS

Durieux, A., 'La révision de 1971 de la Constitution politique portugaise et les provinces d'Outre-mer', *Académie royale des sciences d'outre-mer, Bulletin des séances*, 18: 108, 1972.

Gomes, C. P., 'Casamento dos primitivos em Angola', *Scientia Iuridica*, 21: 70, 1972.

Sousa J. de A., 'Julgados municipais em Moçambique', *Scientia Iuridica*, 21: 28, 1972.

RHODESIA — RHODESIE

'Advertising and Unfair Trade Competition', *Rhodesian Law Journal*, 12: 4, 1972.

'Concursus Creditorum and Conflicting Interests', *Rhodesian Law Journal*, 12: 7, 1972.

Dewhurst, J. R., 'Tax Avoidance and Section 91', *Rhodesian Law Journal*, 12: 33, 1972.

Eisemann, P. M., *Les sanctions contre la Rhodésie*, Paris 1972.

Fleming, C. J. W., 'The Nature of African Customary Law in Central Africa', *NADA*, 10(4): 93, 1972.

'Foreign Exchange Control Regulations and the Conflict of Laws', *Rhodesian Law Journal*, 12: 24, 1972.

Le Roux, A. A., '"Illegal" Rhodesian Anti-Sanctions Legislation', *Rhodesian Law Journal*, 12: 62, 1972.

'Minority Shareholders and the Burden of Proof', *Rhodesian Law Journal*, 12: 28, 1972.

Rifkind, M. L., 'Land Aportionment in Perspective', *Rhodesian History*, 3: 53, 1972.

'Tax Avoidance and Double Taxation', *Rhodesian Law Journal*, 12: 15, 1972.

RWANDA

Daloze, A., 'La formation du personnel judiciaire au Rwanda. Le centre national de formation judiciaire', *Revue juridique et politique*, 26: 421, 1972.

Seyanga, J.-B., 'Le régime successoral dans la République rwandaise', *Revue juridique et politique*, 26: 775, 1972.

SENEGAL

Andre, G., 'La protection et les garanties de la personne soupçonnée ou poursuivie en droit sénégalais', *Revue sénégalaise de Droit*, 6: 3, 1972.

Bockel, A., 'La Cour suprême et l'exception de recours parallèle', *Annales africaines*, —: 165, 1971-2.

Boye, M. M., 'De la procédure de saisie-arrêt en droit sénégalais', *Revue sénégalaise de droit*, 6: 41, 1972.

'Le Centre de recherche d'Etude et de Documentation sur les Institutions africaines (CREDILA)', *Annales africaines*, —: 181, 1971-2.

Deschamps, M., 'Les frontières de la Sénégambie', *Revue française d'études politiques africaines*, (80): 44, 1972.

Diop, A., 'La dévolution successorale musulmane: détermination des héritiers dans le code sénégalais de la famille', *Revue juridique et politique*, 26: 799, 1972.

Diop, A. B., 'La tenure foncière en millieu rural wolof', *Congtès international des Africanistes*, 405.

Kane, M., 'Status of Married Women under Customary Law in Senegal', *American Journal of Comparative Law*, 20: 716, 1972.

Niang, M., 'La notion de parenté chez les Wolof au Sénégal', *Bulletin de l'IFAN (B)*, 34, 802, 1972.
'La réforme des études à la Faculté des Sciences juridiques et économiques de l'Université de Dakar', *Annales africaines*, —: 175, 1971-2.
Le Cour Grandmaison, C., 'Femmes dakaroises', *Annales de l'Université d'Abidjan, série F. Ethno sociologie*, (4): 1, 1972.

SIERRA LEONE

Donegan, C. E., 'Marriage and Divorce in Sierra Leone: A Microcosm of African Legal Problems', *Cornell International Law Journal*, 5: 43, 1972.
Fyfe, C., 'Documents Relating to the Sierra Leone in Tax Enquiry', *Africana Research Bulletin*, 2(4): 3, 1971-2.

SOMALIA — SOMALIE

Noor Muhammad, N. M. A., *The Legal System of the Somali Republic*, Charlottesville 1972.

SOUTH AFRICA — AFRIQUE DU SUD

Aden, M., 'Fault and Breakdown: A Comparative Survey of Modern Divorce Law', *Acta juridica*, —: 39, 1972.
Bamford, B. R., 'Conventional Penalties Act 1962', *South African Law Journal*, 89: 229, 1972.
Barrie, G., 'Oorgangstadium met die Verskuiwing van Wetgewende Gesag van Koning tot Parlement', *South African Law Journal*, 89: 84, 1972.
Belcher, C. I., *Norman's Purchase and Sale in South Africa*, Durban 1972.
Bester, D. H., 'Scope of an Agent's Power of Representation', *South African Law Journal*, 89: 49, 1972.
Boberg, P. Q. R., 'Liability for Omissions—The Case of the Defective Motor-Car', *South African Law Journal*, 89: 207, 1972.
Broomberg, E., 'Basis of Income Taxation in South Africa', *South African Law Journal*, 89: 179, 1972.
Broomberg, E. B., 'Taxation of Profits on Property Transactions', *South African Law Journal*, 89: 445, 1972.
Bührer, A., 'Zum Gesellschaftszweck im englischen und südafrikanischen Company Law und im schweizerischen Aktiengesellschaft', *Scheizerische Aktiengesellschaft*, 44: 205, 1972.
Burchell, E. M., Hunt, P. M. A. and Milton, J. R. L., *South African Criminal Law and Procedure, 1972 Supplement*, Cape Town 1972.
Burrel, T. D., *South African Patent Law and Practice*, Durban 1972.
Carey Miller, D. L., 'Some Aspects of Legal Aid in Criminal Proceedings', *South African Law Journal*, 89: 71, 1972.
Cilliers, A. C., *Law of Costs*, Durban 1972.
Cilliers, H. S., Benade, M. L. and Rossouw, S., *Financial Statements under the Draft Companies Bill*, Durban 1972.
Cilliers, H. S., Benade, M. L. en Rossouw, S., *Finansiële state ingevolge die konsepmaatskappywetsontwerp*, Durban 1972.
Coetzee, G. A., 'A Few Thoughts on Some of the Dilemmas of the Legal Profession', *South African Law Journal*, 89: 472, 1972.
Copeling, A. J. C., 'Copyright in Broadcasts in the Republic of South Africa', *Comparative and International Law, Journal of Southern Africa*, 5: 1, 1972.
Cowen, D. V., 'Expropriation and the Arbitration Process', *Tydskrif vir Hedendaagse Romeins-Hollandse Reg*, 35: 146, 1972.
Dean, W. H. B., 'Judging the Obscene', *Acta juridica* —: 61, 1972.
'Deliktuele eise tussen gades binne gemeenskap van goed getroud', *Tydskrif vir Hedendaagse Romains-Hollandse Reg*, 35: 175, 1972.
De Villiers, S. W. L., 'Payment to Directors for Loss of Office etc.—A Critical Glance at

s. 227 of the Draft Companies Bill', *Comparative and International Law, Journal of Southern Africa*, 5: 339, 1972.

De Villiers, S. W. L., 'Some Comments on No Bar Value Shares in Terms of the Draft Companies Bill, *Comparative and International Law, Journal of Southern Africa*, 5: 348, 1972.

'Does a Special Resolution upon Registration Operate with Retrospective Effect', *Tydskrif vir Hedendaagse Romeins-Hollandse Reg*, 35: 170, 1972.

Dutoit, D., 'Estoppel: The Decline and Fall of the Culpa Requirement', *Responsa Meridiana*, 2: 143, 1972.

Elliott, R. C., *Elliott se regsvorms*, Kaapstad 1972.

Elliott, R. C., *Elliott's Legal Forms*, Cape Town 1972.

'Exit aultra vires', *Tydskrif vir Hedendaagse Romeins-Hollanse Reg*, 35: 281, 1972.

Hahlo, H. R., 'Law of Concubinage', *South African Law Journal*, 89: 321, 1972.

Hall, C. G., *Maasdorp's Institutes of South African Law, Volume 4 (8th ed.)*, Cape Town 1972.

Hancock, D. J., 'South African Approach to the Defence of Superior Orders in International Criminal Law', *Responsa Meridiana*, 2: 188, 1972.

Harcourt, A. B., 'Crime and Punishment', *Tydskrif vir Hedendaagse Romeins-Hollandse Reg*, 35: 211, 1972.

Hiemstra, V. G., *Suid-Afrikaanse Strafproses*, Durban 1972.

Holloway, J. P., 'Transsexuals—Some Further Legal Considerations', *Comparative and International Law, Journal of Southern Africa*, 5: 71, 1972.

'The Internal Conflict between Bantu Law and Common Law', *Tydskrif vir Hedendaagse Romeins-Hollandse Reg*, 35: 290, 1972.

Khan, E., *The South African law of Domicile of Natural persons*, Cape Town 1972.

Kerr, A. J., 'Anticipatory Breach of Contract: Some Problems Discussed', *South African Law Journal*, 89: 465, 1972.

Kerr, A. J., *The Law of Agency*, Durban 1972.

Lighterness, T. J., 'Tax Consequences of Changes in Foreign Exchange Rates', *Cahiers de droit fiscal international*, 57B(II): 1, 1972.

Meskin, P. M., *The South African Encyclopaedia of Forms and Precedents, vol. 6 and 10, plus 1972 Cumulative Supplement*, Durban 1972.

Mostert, D. F., Joubert, D. J. en Viljoen, G., *Die Koopkontrak*, Durban 1972.

Naude, S., 'Toestemming deur 'n Maatskappy tot Mededinging deur 'n Direkteur', *South African Law Journal*, 89: 217, 1972.

O'Donovan, B., *Mackeurtan's Sale of Goods in South Africa (4th ed.)*, Cape Town 1972.

O'Regan, R. S., 'Pruning the English oak', *Comparative and International Law, Journal of Southern Africa*, 5: 81, 1972.

Rabie, M. A., 'Environmental protection', *Comparative and International Law, Journal of Southern Africa*, 5: 247, 1972.

Ramolefe, A. M. R. and Saunders, A. J. G. M., 'The structural pattern of African regionalism', *Comparative and International Law, Journal of Southern Africa*, 5: 30, 1972; 5: 171, 1972; 5: 299, 1972.

Randall, P., *Law, Justice and Society*, Johannesburg 1972.

Roeleveld, L., ''n Voorstel tot wetlike reëling van die ooreenkoms van persoonsversekering en van pensioen en pensioenfondse', *Acta juridica*, —: 169, 1972.

Rorke, R. F., *A Commentary on the Sectional Titles Act 1971*, Durban 1972.

Schmidt, C. W. H., *Die Bewysreg*, Durban 1972.

Shrand, D., *Shrand on the Sectional Titles Act*, Cape Town 1972.

Shrand, D. and Keeton, A. A. F., *The Registration, Management and Winding-up of Companies in South Africa—Supplement*, Cape Town 1972.

Silberberg, H., 'Probleme des deutschen "Zugewinnausgleichs" in England und Südafrika', *Rabel's Zeitschrift*, 36: 526, 1972.

Snyman, C. R., 'Die Beskermde Regsgoed by die Gemeenregtelike Misdaad Abduksie', *Tydskrif vir Hedendaagse Romeins-Hollandse Reg*, 35: 265, 1972.

Spirer, J. H., 'In re Johannesburg Operatic and Dramatic Society v. Music Theatre International', *Copyright Law Symposium*, (20): 140, 1972.

'Sovereignty—Not Again!', *Tydskrif vir Hedendaagse Romeinse-Hollandse Reg*, 35: 294, 1972.

Spiro, E., 'Artificial Insemination and the Law', *Acta juridica*, —: 213, 1972.

Spiro, E., 'Foreign Law', *Comparative and International Law, Journal of Southern Africa*, 5: 56, 1972.

Spiro, E., '1972 Income Tax Changes in South Africa', *Bulletin for International Fiscal Documentation*, 26: 318, 1972.

Steyn, J. H., 'Role of Punishment in the Maintenance of Law and Order', *South African Law Journal*, 89: 309, 1972.

Steyn, J. R., 'Common Knowledge as the Basis of Obviousness in Patent Law', *South African Law Journal*, 89: 333, 1972.

Suzman, A., 'Censorship and the Courts: The Suggested Abolition of the Right of Appeal to the Supreme Court from Decisions of the Publications Control Board', *South African Law Journal*, 89: 191, 1972.

Thomas, J. A. C., 'Minors and Contract: A Comparative Study', *Acta juridica*, —: 151, 1972.

'Tot and Tranquillizer', *Tydskrif vir Hedendaagse Romeins-Hollandse Reg*, 35: 283, 1972.

Unterhalter, B., 'Polaroid Experiment in South Africa', *Vanderbilt Journal of Transitional Law*, 6: 109, 1972.

'Van der Linden: 'n Kaapse eggo', *Tydskrif vir Hedendaagse Romeins-Hollandse Reg*, 35: 160, 1972.

Van der Vyver, J. D. en Van Zyl, F. J., *Inleiding tot die regswetenskap*, Durban 1972.

Van der Walt, J. C., 'Die deliktuele aanspreeklikheid van die vervaardiger vir skade berokken deur middel van sy defekte produk', *Tydskrif vir Hedendaagse Romeins-Hollandse Reg: 35, 224, 1972.*

Van Niekerk, A. F., 'Doel en motief van die belastingpligtige in die belastingreg', *Tydskrif vir Hedendaagse Romeins-Hollandse Reg*, 35: 105, 1972.

Van Rooyen, J. C. W., *Die kontrak in die Suid-Afrikaanse internasionale privaatreg*, Kaapstad 1972.

Van Wyk, A. H., 'Skenkings in fraudem uxoris', *Tydskrif vir Hedendaagse Romeins-Hollandse Reg*, 35: 252, 1972.

Verloren Van Themaat, R., 'Ontwikkeling in verband met die reg en regspleging van die Bantoe-Oorsig vir 1970', *Tydskrif vir Hedendaagse Romeins-Hollandse Reg*, 36: 38, 1972.

Visagie, G. G. 'The Effect of a Plea of Guilty', *Acta juridica*, —: 219, 1972.

Webster, G. C. and page, N. S., *Chowles and Webster's South African Law of Trade Marks, Company Names and Trading Styles*, Durban 1972.

Wiechers, M., 'South West Africa: the Background, Content and Significance of the Decision of the World Court of 21 June 1971', *Comparative and International Law, Journal of Southern Africa*, 5: 123, 1972.

Zeffertt, D., 'Payments "in Full Settlement"', *South African Law Journal*, 89: 35, 1972.

SOUTH WEST AFRICA/NAMIBIA — SUD OUEST AFRICAIN/NAMIBIE

Dillard, H. C., 'Status of South-West Africa: Namibia', *International Lawyer*, 6: 409, 1972.

Ducat, M., 'L'affaire de la Namibie', *Penant*, 82: 901, 1972.

Higgins, R., 'The Advisory Opinion on Namibia: Which UN Resolutions Are Binding under Article 25 of the Charter', *International and Comparative Law Quarterly*, 21: 270, 1972.

Jacque, J. P., 'L'avis de la Cour internationale de justice du 21 juin 1971, *Revue générale de droit international public*, 76: 1046, 1972.

Namibia: South Africa's Presence Found to Be Illegal', *New York University Journal of International Law and Politics*, 5: 117, 1972.

Obozuwa, A. U., *The Namibian Question: Legal and Political Aspects*, Benin City 1972.

Sachs, V., 'South West Africa, Final Phase?', *Kingston Law Review*, 3: 25, 1971-2.

Tunguru Huaraka, 'The 1971 Advisory Opinion on South-West Africa (Namibia), *Eastern Africa Law Review*, 5: 183, 1972.

Umozurike, U. O., The Namibia (South-West Africa) Cases 1950-71', *Africa Quarterly*, 12: 41, 1972; *Eastern Africa Law Review*, 5: 207, 1972.

SUDAN — SOUDAN

Aguda, A. and Aguda, O., 'Judicial Protection of Some Fundamental Rights in Nigeria and in the Sudan before and during Military Rule', *Journal of African Law*, 16: 130, 1972.

Aguda, O., 'Judicial Administration in the Sudan', *Eastern Africa Law Review*, 5: 245, 1972.

Moustapha, M. M., 'L'indemnisation de la victime de l'infraction pénale dans les législations des Pays Arabes', *Proche-Orient, Etudes Juridiques*, (75): 233, 1972.

SWAZILAND

Aguda, A., 'Discriminatory Statutory Provisions and Fundamantal Rights Provisions of the Constitutions of Botswana, Lesotho and Swaziland', *South African Law Journal*, 89: 299, 1972.

TANZANIA — TANZANIE

Carvalho, V. N., 'The Control of Managing Agents in Tanzania Parastatal Organizations, with Special Reference to the NDC', *Eastern Africa Law Review*, 5: 89, 1972.

Chirwa, O. E. C., 'The Prevention of Corruption by Legislation (The Tanzania Act of 1971)', *Eastern Africa Law Review*, 5: 225, 1972.

Frank, B., 'Tanzanian Permanent Commission of Enquiry—The Ombudsman', *Denver Journal of International Law and Policy*, 2: 255, 1972.

James, J. W. and Ligunya, S., 'Organizational Relationships and the Control of Parastatals in Tanzania', *Eastern Africa Law Review*, 5: 39, 1972.

Mowrojee, P., 'Public Entreprise and Co-operatives in Kenya and Tanzania: Some Comparative illustrations', *Eastern Africa Law Review*, 5: 141, 1972.

Read, J. S., 'A Milestone in the Integration of Personal Laws: The New Law of Marriage and Divorce in Tanzania', *Journal of African Law*, 16: 19, 1972.

Shivji, L. G., 'Introduction—From the Analysis of Forms to the Exposition of Substance. The Tasks of a Lawyer-Intellectual', *Eastern Africa Law Review*, 5: 1, 1972.

Temu, P. E., 'The Economic Implications of Management Agreements in Tanzania Parastatals', *Eastern Africa Law Review*, 5: 77, 1972.

Tunguru Huaraka, 'Cattle Trespass: A Tort under Customary Law?: A Note', *Eastern Africa Law Review*, 5: 261, 1972.

TCHAD — CHAD

Amandy, G., 'Aperçu sur le régime successoral chez les Moundangs du Tchad, *Revue juridique et politique*, 26: 819, 1972.

Seid, J. B., 'Coutumes successorales traditionnelles au Tchad islamisé', *Revue juridique et politique*, 26: 811, 1972.

TUNISIE

Ben Sedrine, A., 'Les testaments et la protection de la famille légitime contre les libéralités du défunt en droit tunisien', *Revue juridique et politique*, 26: 827, 1972.

Eldblom, L., 'Structure foncière d'une communauté musulmane', *Cahiers de Tunisie*, (79-80): 179, 1972.

Rowny, K., 'Independence and International Treaties Valid under Protectorate', *Africana Bulletin*, (17), 43, 1972.

Tibi, B., 'Das tunesische Genossenschafts-experiment', *Verfassung und Recht in Ubersee*, 5: 145, 1972.

UGANDA

Butagira, F. K., 'Graduated Tax Defaulters—A Proposal for Extra-Mural Employment', *Uganda Law Focus*, 1: 82, 1972.

Byamugisha, J. B., 'Uganda's Compulsory Third Party Liability Insurance of Motor Vehicles', *East African Law Journal*, 8: 25, 1972.

Carroll, D. W., 'Comments on Legal Education in Uganda', *Uganda Law Focus*, 1: 241, 1972.

Hodgin, R. W., 'The Need for Hire-Purchase Reform in Uganda', *Uganda Law Focus*, 1: 220, 1972.

Nanyenya, P., 'Consumer Protection in Uganda—Part I', *Uganda Law Focus*, 1: 251, 1972.

Obol-Ochola, J., 'The Pilot Scheme for the Registration of Titles in Kigezi', *Uganda Law Focus*, 1: 133, 1972; 1: 194, 1972.

Odoki, B. J., 'Recent Reforms in the Law Relating to Confessions', *Uganda Law Focus*, 1: 19, 1972.

Rowny, K., 'Independence and International Treaties Valid under Protectorate', *Africana Bulletin*, (17): 43, 1972.

Ssekandi, F. M., 'Kondoism in Uganda—A Study of the Methods Employed to Contain Kondo Violence', *Uganda Law Focus*, 1: 231, 1972.

Ssekandi, F. M., 'Self-defence in Uganda', *Uganda Law Focus*, 1: 6, 1972.

West, H. W., *Land Policy in Buganda*, Cambridge 1972.

Wilkinson, R. M., 'The Judgement in Criminal and Civil Cases', *Uganda Law Focus*, 1: 86, 1972.

Wilkinson, R. M., 'A Sliding Standard of Proof', *Uganda Law Focus*, 1: 146, 1972.

UNITED ARAB REPUBLIC — REPUBLIQUE ARABE UNIE

Accord commercial proférentiel entre le CEE et la République arabe égyptienne'. *Revue du Marché commun*, —: 775, 1972.

Afifi, H., 'The Egyptian Experience of Land Reform', *East African Journal of Rural Development*, 5: 193, 1972.

Cannon, B. D., 'A Reassessment of Judicial Reform in Egypt, 1876-1891', *African Historical Studies*, 5: 51, 1972.

Farag, A. B., 'Le Conseil d'Etat égyptien 25 ans après sa création', *Egypte contemporaine* (348): 43, 1972.

Feuerle, 'Economic Arbitration in Egypt: The Influence of a Societ Legal Institution', *Journal of International Law and Economics*, 7: 61, 1972.

Malache, M. K. A., 'Comparative Study of Marine Insurance in Egyptian, French and English Laws', *Egypte contemporaine*, (349): 101, 1972.

Mulack, G., 'Die neue ägyptische Verfassung', *Verfassung und Recht in Ubersee*, 5: 187, 1972.

O'Kane, J. P., 'Islam in the New Egyptian Constitution', *Middle East Journal*, 26: 137, 1972.

Tibi, B., 'Agrarreform und Genossenschaftswesen in einem Entwicklungsland: Agypten', *Verfassung und Recht in Ubersee*, 5: 57, 1972.

Tixier, G., 'L'Union des Républiques arabes et la constitution égyptienne du 11 septembre 1971', *Revue du droit public et de la science politique en France et à l'Étranger*, 88: 1129, 1972.

ZAMBIA — ZAMBIE

Aihe, D. O., 'The Issue of Closer Association with Southern Rhodesia in Zambia's Constitutional History', *ODU*, (8): 33, 1972.

Aihe, D. O., 'Neo-Nigerian Human Rights in Zambia. A Comparative Study with Some countries in Africa and West Indies', *Zambia Law Journal*, 3-4, 1971-2.

Church, L. W., 'The Power of the Courts to Call Witness: Chama *v.* the People', *Zambia Law Journal*, 3-4: 162, 1972.

Craig, J. T., 'The Privileges of Parliament and the Constitution: Ex parte Mundia (1971), Ex Parte Nkumbula (1970)', *Zambia Law Journal*, 3-4: 143, 1971-2.

Gluckmann, M., *The Ideas of Barotse Jurisprudence*, (reprint), Manchester 1972.

Kaunda, D., 'The Functions of the Lawyer in Zambia Today', *Zambia Law journal*, 3-4: 1, 1971-2.

Mubakom S. V., 'Jaffco Ltd *v.* Northern Motors Ltd', *Zambia Law Journal*, 3-4: 169, 1971-2.

Muna Ndulo, 'Abortion and the Law: The People *v.* Gulshan et al; Termination of Pregnancy Act, 1972', *Zambia Law Journal*, 3-4: 153, 1971-2.

Muna Ndulo, 'The Admissibility of Evidence of Character of the Accused: The People *v.* Mudenda', *Zambia Law Journal*, 3-4: 157, 1971-2.

Muna Ndulo, 'The Child as a Witness: Daka and Others *v.* The People', *Zambia Law Journal*, 3-4: 160, 1971-2.

Newton, E., *Zambian Income Tax,* Lusaka 1972.

ZAIRE

Balanda, G., *Le nouveau droit constitutionnel zaïrois*, Paris 1972.

Bile, M., 'Du rôle et des attributions du Ministère Public en matière de liberté provisoire', *Revue juridique du Zaïre*, 48: 105, 1972.

Bolela Wa Boende, 'Droits et devoirs du journaliste en République du Zaïre', *Zaïre-Afrique*, (63): 149, 1972.

Bulembu Nde-Bwawyi, 'La dation du nom en coutume lele', *Revue juridique du Zaïre*, 48: 244, 1972.

Coipel, M., 'Répertoire de droit international privé zaïrois (1890-1970)', *Revue juridique du Zaïre*, 48: 81, 1972.

Durieux, A., 'Quelques problèmes en matière de droit international privé zaïrois', *Penant*, 82: 473, 1972.

Durieux, A., 'Les institutions politiques de la République du Zaïre', *Revue juridique et politique*, 26: 389, 1972.

Kabange, C., 'L'ordre public et le droit traditionnel', *Revue juridique et politique*, 26: 271, 1972.

Kande, C., 'La responsabilité du banquier en matière de communication de renseignements en droit zaïrois et en droit comparé', *Revue juridique du Zaïre*, 48: 1, 1972.

Katanga, T., 'Le code des investissements de 1969 en République du Zaïre', *Zaïre-Afrique*, (65): 291, 1972.

Lamy E. et Lokwa, I., 'La dévolution successorale en République du Zaïre', *Revue juridique et politique*, 26: 517, 1972.

Lihau E. et Nimy, M., 'Droit successoral des sociétés traditionnelles du Zaïre', *Revue juridique et politique*, 26: 585, 1972.

Lunda-Bululu, V., 'La preuve en droit international privé zaïrois', *Revue juridique du Zaïre*, 48: 13, 1972.

Manzila Lutumba, 'Les successions en droit civil zaïrois', *Zaïre-Afrique*, (69): 517, 1972; *Revue juridique et politique*, 26: 507, 1972.

Mulumba Lukoji, 'Le code minier de la République du zaïre', *Zaïre-Afrique*, (63): 133, 1972.

Phanzu, L., 'L'équilibre des institutions contumières et les successions au Zaïre', *Revue juridique et politique*, 26: 605, 1972.

Verhaegen, J., 'L'incendie intentionnel et la mise en danger de la vie humaine spécialement en droit pénal congolais et belge, *Revue de droit pénal et de criminologie*, 52: 703, 1972.

Yabili Yalala Asani, 'Proposition d'une méthode de recherche en droit coutumier positif', *Revue juridique du Zaïre*, 48: 230, 1972.

GENERAL INDEX